On Moral Grounds

ON MORAL GROUNDS

The Search for Practical Morality

NORMA HAAN
ELIANE AERTS
BRUCE A. B. COOPER

NEW YORK UNIVERSITY PRESS
New York *and* London
1985

Library of Congress Cataloging in Publication Data

Haan, Norma.
On moral grounds.

Bibliography: p.
Includes index.
1. Ethics. I. Aerts, Eliane, 1943–   . II. Cooper,
Bruce A. B., 1947–   . III. Title.
BJ1012.H22 1985 170 85-4970
ISBN 0-8147-3426-X (alk. paper)

Kendall Bryant's collaboration on Chapter 7, "Friendship Groups and Situations"
and Martin Packer's, Paola Theodorou's, and Gary Yabrove's collaboration on
Chapter 14, "Moral Action of Four-Year-Olds,"
are gratefully acknowledged.

*Clothbound editions of New York University Press books are Smyth-sewn
and printed on permanent and durable acid-free paper.*

Contents

70
Hill

Figures

Tables

Acknowledgments

We want to thank many people for their interest and efforts. Norma Haan is most indebted to the following people who worked on the first study of adolescents: Abner Boles, Betty Lou Bradshaw, Phyllis Cohen, Harriet Curtis, Sandra Dobkin, Carol George, Louis Gomez, Bruce Hansen, Vicky Johnson, Linda Kastelowitz, Cynthia Marshall, Della Mosley, Connie Phillips, Lawrence Sullivan, Darlene Tong, Richard Weiss, Lani Wilson, and Michael Wynne. Janice Stroud trained people to do the scoring for the Kohlberg system.

We are all indebted to the following who worked on the second study of young adults: Suzanne Awalt, Rina Baker, Kathy Barry, Kendall Bryant, Albert Cotugno, Lynne English, Richard Ewy, Peter Lifton, Alberta Nassi, Shoshana Nevo, Andrew Phelps, Candy Reynolds, Trish Stoddard, Karin Wandrei, Jane Webber, Richard Weiss, Kathryn Willson, and Wendy Yang. Anne Colby trained people to do the scoring for the Kohlberg system.

The "kiddie" project—the study of four-year-olds—was shared with the following people: Christine Baker, Christine Baker (two different people), Caroline Cooke-Carney, Ellen Carlton, Elizabeth Keller, Beverly Lum, Martin Packer, Paola Theodorou, and Gary Yabrove. Their interest and care made our observations possible. We also thank Jane Hunt, coadministrator of the Child Study Center at the Institute of Human Development, and the two head teachers for the four-year-olds—Barbara Scales and Kay McElheney, who did far more than tolerate our presence.

Throughout, Norma Haan has benefited from critical, penetrating discussions and even arguments with many people, but she is especially appreciative for the cogent comments of Andrew Phelps, Peter Lifton, Richard Weiss, Vicky Johnson, David Shields, and Brenda

Bredemeier. A very special contribution to the clarity of this volume was made by Paola Theodorou, Sari Mendelsohn, and Michael Spinrad. They read various chapters and told us when we were not communicating. Paola Theodorou applied her intelligent analytic efforts to the entire book. Juliet Shaffer, William Meredith, and Roger Millsap provided invaluable statistical guidance. Kendall Bryant was an important contributor to our thinking in early stages of the young adult project, especially in regard to analyses of the group data. We appreciate his help. Martin Packer, Paola Theodorou, and Gary Yabrove provided insights gained from their work with the four-year-olds' morality and in preparing the chapter in this book that bears their names.

Several people helped organize and manage the details of these projects and the writing of this volume. We salute Sally Vrana, Candy Reynolds, Victoria Sanchez, Donna Ko, and Robert David Wong for the care, organizational talent and intelligence they brought to this work. Helen Cline's unflappable functioning and good sense under pressure was without match. Guyo Tajiri, lover of human communication, editor and journalist par excellence, reduced the academese of our writing.

The fine editorial work of Despina Papazoglou, Kitty Moore and Robert L. Bull, editors with New York University Press, has made this volume more interesting and readable than it would otherwise have been.

We gratefully acknowledge the permissions granted for a number of short citations:

Stuart Hampshire. Morality and pessimism. In Stuart Hampshire (Ed.), *Public and private morality.* Cambridge: Cambridge University Press, 1978.

For allowing the adaptation and abridgment of his table, "Six Stages of Moral Judgment":

Lawrence Kohlberg. *The philosophy of moral development.* New York: Harper & Row, 1981, pp. 409–412.

To Academic Press for allowing republication and adaptation of two tables, "Taxonomy and Examples of Ego Processes" and "Properties of Ego Processes":

Norma Haan. *Coping and defending: Processes of self-environment organization.* New York: Academic Press, 1977, pp. 36, 38–40.

With gratitude we finally acknowledge the institutions that provided funding: first, the Hazen Foundation of New Haven, Connecticut, for the study of adolescents; later the Spencer Foundation of Chicago, for the study of young adults; and finally, the National Institute of Mental Health (RO1 MM37290) for the study of four-year-olds. In addition, Norma Haan was supported by a Research Scientist Award (KO5 MH 00258) from the National Institute of Mental Health.

Norma Haan
Eliane Aerts
Bruce Cooper

Prologue

This volume is the outgrowth of some years of concern—and, admittedly, a degree of muddling—over how social science can properly go about investigating morality. Working out a possible solution to this question and its ramifications has taken some ten years. We assume that the only morality social scientists can properly seek is practical morality, that is, the morality people actually use—not the moralities they profess or even ratify when put forth by leaders. Whether all or only some aspects of human interaction are guided by a single or several moralities is not known. But in the past 20 years social scientists have joined the search for such a morality.

An underlying procedural question accompanies this search. Can scientific investigators maintain their commitments to objectivity and fair-mindedness as they search for morality? Or will they, in the end, only construct theories in the image of their own moral preferences? This issue must be squarely addressed or an eventual and discrediting war of ideologies among social scientists seems inevitable. Morality is a matter of emotional belief in everyone's own life, and it is too strong and pervasive a force in social scientific theories for the questions of objectivity and fair-mindedness to be cast aside.

The completion of this work comes at a time of controversy, even frustration and confusion, among social scientists about the direction, meaning, and importance of their investigations of morality. During the past several decades, many have confidently undertaken their search but avoided the underlying, knotty, and even professionally risky problem of identifying the value base of the morality they are investigating. We have had to take this risk here, too, and early chapters will provide the reasoning behind our decisions as to what morality is and how it must be investigated. Here we briefly mention several major conclusions about the ways social scientists should proceed and about the contributions they might make to our understanding the moral basis of life.

First, in any investigation of morality, social scientists will have already made—knowingly or unknowingly—a commitment to a core value; in other words, they will have chosen a ground. Following the scientific ethic—the special morality of science itself—this starting premise needs to be adopted, openly and explicitly, so it can be evaluated by colleagues and citizens and it needs to be fair—moral—to all people. It should be a working definition, open to correction, revision, or refutation and total abandonment.

Second, social scientists' special task and possible contribution is to discover the nature of everyday morality. Hopefully they will identify a common morality. But we have no certainty that there is a morality that is species-wide. Nevertheless, people and societies of widely different cultures seem to expect that the moral demands they make on one another will be understood, whether or not their claims are accepted and validated.

In any event, scholars have never seemed content to propose a theory for a small segment of humanity, and the scientific ethic does not allow social scientists to ally themselves with a parochial view and then claim that its meaning is "true" and general. The scientist's search for a common morality is radically different from the scholar's traditional procedure of developing hypothetical moral proposals from an armchair. The scientific exploration of moral life is a recent turn in history that could lead to fresh understandings, especially in four areas—moral motivation, action, development and moral functioning and default in sociopolitical contexts.

Third, we argue that understanding the conditions of practical moral action should have the highest research priority. What people think, or say they think, about morality is not of great interest, but we all care about what people do. We care because actions affect lives, so actions are surely the most authentic of moral activities. Furthermore the study of development is an uncertain enterprise unless we know *what develops*.

Fourth, as they study morality, social scientists cannot just content themselves with merely observing and recording moral actions that occur in the world, because humanity's cherished ideal morality has always marked and moved history. People are impelled by what *might be* as much as they are by *what is*. A morally accountable society—the dream of Martin Luther King, Jr.—would provide an enhancing place to live for all citizens.

Fifth, psychologists are now doing most of the research on morality, but they often ignore the sociopolitical implications of their conclusions. Their study is usually focused on individuals. Although moral choice ultimately is the act of each person, some social and political circumstances all but prevent adequate moral behavior by citizens; thus it is correct and necessary that we also understand the morality of societies as well as individuals. Indeed, in our view these two facets of morality have differences, but they are complementary so they should not contradict each other. Therefore psychologists who do research on morality need to broaden their purview.

To state it simply, psychologists need to become sociologists and sociologists need to become psychologists and all social scientists need to become philosophers. And citizens need to keep an eye on all of them.

Finally, our focus on practical morality has led to a working definition called "interactional morality." In this volume interactional morality is compared with another psychologist's proposal: Lawrence Kohlberg's theory of moral-cognitive development.

Of all moral proposals now set forth by psychologists, the interactional and Kohlberg's are in the clearest accord about two central points. First, the minds of people are involved in moral decision, action, and development; second, moral functioning is typified by various degrees of adequacy or effectiveness.

Nonetheless, comparison of the interactional and Kohlberg's theories is especially informative because they disagree in many ways. The Kohlberg theory follows the long tradition of a main and important branch of moral philosophy that has sought certainty and impartiality in logic and logical deduction. The interactional theory is inductive and contextual, so it accepts and attempts to describe and explain uncertainty in moral life. It does not particularly follow past philosophical theories or respect the boundaries between academic disciplines. This proposal is fueled, instead, by the conviction that the study of everyday life will yield new and different insights about the morality that we all seem to assume we understand—until we try to explain it.

This book will likely be controversial since it does not conform with much of what has long been assumed about morality nor with how ideas about morality should be studied.

It is irreverent toward moral philosophy in reasoning that fresh, clarifying insights may come out of attempts to understand the moral psychology of ordinary people.

It is irreverent toward research psychology by arguing that valuing cannot be denied so the cherished morality of people and researchers should be openly brought into account.

It is irreverent to the academy in general in contending that vested boundaries among the disciplines of social sciences and philosophy hinder our coming to understand the moral basis of life.

It warns citizens not to accept too easily psychologists' and sociologists' "scientifically based" claims about morality, as truth without dross.

It is irreverent toward old beliefs that the educationally, politically, and economically advantaged are morally superior and that the disadvantaged's complaints are merely envy and therefore without moral merit.

It is irreverent toward the theory and work of the pioneer psychologist, Lawrence Kohlberg, who stirred philosophy when he added the idea of development to classical moral theory, but who stopped short, in our view, of apprehending the promises and emendations that lie in practical inquiry.

All moral theories have a constituency. As Stuart Hampshire (1978) wrote, "Each moral philosophy singles out some ultimate ground or grounds for unconditional praise of persons" (p. 5). The constituency of most moral theories and certainly the cognitive theory has been the elite of humankind—the educated members of complex Western societies. In the cognitive theory the morally superior have also been frequently identified as male, but this is still in question given recent reviews of studies by Walker (1983) and Lifton (in press). That the elite were repetitively chosen over the centuries for "unconditional praise" is not surprising, since moral theories were almost always proposed by the elite.

But the interactional theory also has a constituency. In constructing this theory, we carefully tried to make provisions so that its constituency would be all humankind. In taking this course we followed the mandate of the scientific ethic that all evidence, irrespective of the prestige of its source, be given even-handed consideration. In this volume, however, the mainstream, traditional assumptions about who is morally superior needed to be countered. Thus, it may sometimes seem to readers that our advocacy is for particular groups—the disadvantaged, the powerless, the stressed, and even the very young. But this seeming advocacy was to correct an old error. We did not sentimentally commit the opposite error of arguing that the powerless are morally superior. In no sense do we think the meek will inherit the earth.

Instead, we gave reasons and evidence why *all* people can act badly when they find themselves powerless in personally debilitating circumstances and why people who continuously live in such circumstances may act badly more frequently. This is an entirely different explanation from saying that the powerless are morally weak in character and the powerful are morally superior. We argued and presented various evidence for our supposition that almost all people, whether four-year-olds or mature adults, have the same basic moral understandings and concerns; but how people act is a different matter.

The controversy that could follow our irreverencies can only be seen as good. Given scholars' disagreements and everyone's meager knowledge about the practical morality we cherish and try to use, debate will illuminate. This will be the gain whether or not the proposal of interactional morality withstands this scrutiny. Moral action is this theory's keystone and guide, so it begins and proceeds quite differently than other moral theories. This first assumption seems to bring the theory close to the practical morality of everyday life so it might improve our understandings of the moral basis of life. Whatever the case, it is new and different.

To introduce readers to the problems facing researchers of morality, we begin in Chapter 2 with two kinds of histories. We first very briefly relate philosophers' arguments from ancient Greece to contemporary times about the definition of morality and next give accounts of psychologists' and biologists' more recent formulations. In Chapter 3 we relate what we learned from past theorizing. We state our guidelines for investigating morality and the particular issues that psychological research can address.

In Chapter 4 the similarities and differences between Kohlberg's cognitive and Haan's interactional theories are set down, and the specific questions that our research tried to answer are stated. In Chapter 5 we describe two research projects concerned with moral action and development in adolescents and young adults. Beginning with Chapter 6 and continuing through Chapter 8, different influences relevant to these students' moral action and development are described including their morality in different situations, the character of friendship groups as social contexts, and finally the participants' personal methods of solving problems, represented by their characteristic ways of coping and defending, and how they actually coped or defended when they faced moral problems with their friends.

In chapters 9 through 13, we describe the effects on moral action and development when the influences of both situation and personal capability are considered together in an attempt to identify the critical conditions of moral action and development, as each is conceptualized in the two moral theories. In Chapter 14, we consider the early character of moral concern by describing a third study of four-year-olds' moral interactions and solutions in one of the same situations experienced by both adolescents and young adults. In Chapter 15, the influences of the students' family interaction on their moral functioning is discussed. In Chapter 16 the findings are integrated and their meanings are highlighted. In the final chapter we discuss the practical programs for society's use that follow from the interactional and cognitive theories and we suggest the implications that research about morality might have for educational and mental health policies. We have included a glossary of unavoidably technical terms at the end of the text.

Before readers begin this book, it is fair (in other words, moral) that they know the authors' general expectancies and commitments. Of course, we expected that the interactional formulation would more closely resemble the morality of everyday life—the measure of worth for the social sciences. Our expectancies with regard to the coordination of logical and moral reasoning are different from Kohlberg's, as are our suppositions about the relation of personality and morality and the relation between social context and morality. We undoubtedly place greater priority on understanding action than do Kohlberg and his followers. Despite these various commitments and professional disagreements, we have tried to write a reasonable, balanced account of each system and of the results that the research produced.*

---

*Technical reports providing all the statistical data will soon appear in professional journals (Haan, in press a; in press b).

PART I
BACKGROUND

Chapter 1

INTRODUCTION

To others, and particularly to many of the young in America and Europe, . . . it seems obvious that the large-scale computations in modern politics and social planning bring with them a coarseness and grossness of moral feeling, a blunting of sensibility, and a suppression of individual discrimination and gentleness (Stuart Hampshire, 1978, p. 7).

Background

THIS BOOK was written with professional social scientists in mind, but the primary concern is to address educators and parents. We thought they should be involved in the debate now going on among social scientists about their theories and investigations of morality. This debate should not be merely an academic exercise. Social scientists' definitions of morality permeate their theories, often skew research results, and color the recommendations that they make for public policies and moral curricula to educate the young. At the same time, social scientists would benefit from the reactions and criticisms of citizens.

This debate among social scientists follows on two increasingly evident developments. First, the theories of anthropology, economics, political science, psychology and sociology are now more generally understood to rest on moral suppositions, a circumstance that simply went unnoticed or was denied in the past. According to the ethic of their work, scientists must address, understand, and explain all important aspects of their theories, so examination of these covert value assumptions and their effects seems now to be well underway. (See, for example, various chapters in Haan, Bellah, Rabinow, and Sullivan, 1983; Bernstein, 1976; Habermas, 1975.) Second, many social scientists, but especially psychologists, are now investigating morality to try to determine how it develops and how it is enacted. This book focuses primarily on the two areas of moral action and development.

If social scientists are to know how moral ideas influence their theories and investigations, they have to have some notion of what morality is. This is the problem. For centuries it has been the central issue of scholarly debate among moral philosophers, and they have not reached agreement. Philosophers are usually clear about their definitions and assumptions, but psychologists frequently are not. In the next two chapters we briefly discuss the philosophical history and then in more detail, take up psychologists' current studies.

The morality of science is to treat evidence with fairness. Therefore social scientists must consider *all* pieces of evidence even-handedly and objectively; they must not favor moral values cherished by one group of people or one society. Undoubtedly there are particular local values held by specific peoples, but the pressing and more interesting question concerns those undoubtedly fewer, more basic values that are held in common. It is these moral definitions that may be "true" for all humankind that social scientists need to consider.

To be fair to the values of all people is not synonymous with being neutral, as social scientists often fancy themselves to be. Instead, it means openly proposing, even arguing that a particular moral value seems universal; that is, it is preferred or would be preferred by all people if they had freedom of choice. This is a bold venture for scientists to take; they stand to be corrected and, in the end, it may only turn out to be foolhardy. Nevertheless, there is little point in psychologists investigating morality if they do not intend discovering general truths. Otherwise they pursue only partisan choices or trivia.

Study of Two Theories

Two different moral definitions, proposed by two psychologists, Lawrence Kohlberg and Norma Haan, are thoroughly discussed, investigated, and evaluated in this book. The comparison of their theories will illustrate the problems and promises of study about morality. Among moral theories currently proposed by psychologists, these two seem to describe morality in ways that are most plausible to citizens. Grossly oversimplifying for now, we can say that Kohlberg believes that morality is based on the individual person's understanding of justice. For Haan, morality is a particular kind of social agreement that equalizes people's relations with one another.

To evaluate the theories of Kohlberg and Haan and understand their position in the present crisis in social science, readers need to know something about the evolution of moral philosophy and, in greater detail, the part that psychologists now play in it. As this history of a search for a satisfactory understanding of morality is related, readers are advised to rely on their own common-sense understanding of morality. People have little difficulty in understanding one another's practical moral meanings. It is these meanings that social scientists seek, but their problem is more complicated. Scientists are to uncover this thing that we call morality and then elucidate its meanings, its implications, and the conditions of its development and enactment.

Philosophers' controversies over the centuries make it clear that the true and universal morality—if such exists—is not easily discerned. Although a universally endorsed morality may never be identified, the hope that it might in itself justifies the search. Whatever the outcome, the new feature of this very old quest is that direct study of everyday practical moralities might illuminate the moral basis of human interchange.

Social Scientists' Special Contributions and Recent Interest

The social scientists' task is different from that of the philosophers. The latter have a more theoretical and analytic interest in proposing how life should be conducted. But empirical research may provide fresh understanding of moral life by taking into account the morality people actually practice and the cherished morality people think and believe should be enacted. Cherished and actual morality are by no means the same. Human fallibility produces the difference which is not necessarily due to moral weakness; it is also the result of the complexity and depersonalization of social conditions—to say nothing of bad luck. Social scientists are especially prepared to analyze the age-old tensions between what might or should be and what actually occurs.

Why have social scientists recently and energetically turned to studying morality? Two reasons may account for this. The first is that evidence of human interdependency can no longer be denied, and scientists are no more immune than citizens in general to social pressures, and more than pure intellectual curiosity drives their research. In the twentieth century, sociohistorical evolution has led to a massively dense world society pounded by electronic communication and threatened by nuclear disaster. Nations have become very dependent on one another. Citizens and scholars have come to know—if not understand—the fragility of moral interchange; they are aware of the dangers of human interchanges that are morally calloused and insensitive. Because morality lies at the heart of interchange among people and nations, everyone has a stake in how societies define their moral stance and in how they teach and encourage citizens, especially the young, to act morally. We know we are interdependent, but we do not understand how to make our interdependence morally functional so everyone's self-interest will be served by exchanges that are moral.

Recognition of the world's interdependence fuels hopes that social interchange could be guided by a universal morality while local differences would be tolerated. If a common basis for moral interchange between nations and persons could be articulated, the claims of one on another would be more meaningful and understood.

The Terrible Consequences of Admitting Interdependency. The consequences of admitting and accepting moral interdependency are not easily faced. Given present states of inequality and oppression, the logical step is to reallocate power. The powerful and advantaged always have much more to lose from moral improvement than the impoverished and oppressed. Thus the hope for a moral basis for human interchange is dismissed as sentimental, and to argue for it is considered a radical move. Of course it depends on what kind of moral system one proposes. Some systems are established to provide apologia and justification for extant distributions of power. They are used to justify the morally superior as being more deserving, although they must accept special obligation to contribute to charity. The complaints of the inferior are regarded as expressions of mere envy.

Recognizing the world's moral interdependency helps us see, as Francis Bacon argued centuries ago, that morality is the practical science of living. If it is, it is then not just a concern that should be handled by philosopher-kings, as Plato recommended. In fact, it is best if the elite are not entrusted with this job.

There is another consequence in our world society. As people come to know more about the strongly held a priori moral beliefs of others, like the beliefs which religions provide, they often become less certain about the unqualified rightness of their own a priori positions. The word of no single ideal legislator, however wise and humane, is endorsed by all humankind. We are thus thrown to our own devices. In this world context, the question then becomes: Is there a less-stringent but more-general moral ground that all humans depend on when they make moral agreements? Within this framework, the study of morality becomes empirical and practical, and this is the kind of study social scientists do well. Not surprisingly, moral philosophy has also become increasingly focused, within the contemporary sociohistorical milieu, on the morality that exists in the world.

The second reason for the recent interest in research on morality is probably more professional and self-interested. The understood task of social scientists is to describe and explain life. And morality is surely fundamental in human lives. But for some years social scientists ignored morality because they yearned to be scientists in the mold of the hard sciences, and this meant trying to be *more* than objective. It meant that their investigations of humans, who are evaluative creatures, became indifferent to value. When moral meanings are shunted aside, social-scientific theories and results become twisted and lack conviction. Furthermore, remaining value free while investigating morality is impossible, but being value fair is possible if the guidance of the scientific ethic is followed: We should try to weigh all evidence impartially.

Warnings to Citizens

All in all, we mean to caution consumers that claims of unqualified, factual truth cannot come from research about morality, nor does the entry of scientists into this field of research provide guarantee that moral "truth" will eventually be identified. Still, citizens are eager that their children become "moral." A Gallup Poll of several years ago indicated that 79 percent of a national sample of citizens favored school instruction about morals and moral behavior (*San Francisco*

Chronicle, April 19, 1976). But if morality can, in fact, be acquired by formal instruction, *which morality should be taught?*

American public educators have been cautious about undertaking instruction in morality because it has usually implied religion, and an historic mandate of this nation is the separation of church and state. Paradoxically, this is probably why the public has been attracted to recent psychological research. Because it is "scientific," it seems to suggest that neutral, fair ways of morally educating children are being identified—ways that transcend the different religions in this country. Logically this could be an eventual outcome of the empirical study of morality, but it is not now an actuality. Nevertheless, in 1976 a report in *Newsweek* magazine stated that more than 6000 school districts were using Kohlberg's curriculum materials for moral instruction (Woodward & Lord, 1976). This widespread use undoubtedly resulted from educators feeling that moral instruction was needed and the consequent publicity they gave the proposed curriculum. But citizens and educators need to know that when social scientists disagree with as much heat as they now do about morality, "truth" is yet to be identified. Citizens and educators need to know and evaluate what social scientists know about morality and how their knowledge is qualified.

Enthusiasm for research needs to be tempered. There are many kinds of knowledge, and research in social science produces only one generalized kind. In this early phase, descriptions of general moral trends are not necessarily accurate. Common sense is undoubtedly more informed about morality than researchers, although it is far from organized. However, it is one criterion for judging whether or not a moral theory reflects life. Relying on common sense will not invariably result in comprehensive or entirely correct outcomes, but for it to survive and eventually achieve the status of folk wisdom, it must represent some kind of truth. Common sense is one measuring stick that we will use to evaluate the two descriptions of morality tested in our research.

This volume is also meant to bring out the very real difficulties of doing research about morality. The following questions were asked:

   1. How do different social contexts affect people's moral actions?
   2. Do situations or people's moral capabilities or the interaction of both determine the quality of people's moral actions?

3. What is the relationship between the rational and the more personalized, emotional aspects of both moral thought and action?

4. What factors—personal and situational—make moral development possible?

5. What are the effects of earlier moral experiences on later moral thinking and action?

6. How is morality best measured by social scientists anyway?

7. What is the nature of moral interaction in its beginnings?

8. And, finally, what is the nature of practical morality?

Of all moral theories currently proposed by psychologists, the proponents of the two systems compared in this book most strongly adhere to the idea that people's thought is involved in moral decision making. Nevertheless, the theories are different in some important ways, and here we give one example. The Kohlberg system views people as developing through successively higher stages of mental ability. They are presumed at each stage to rediscover a set of ageold, but increasingly adequate moral rules and principles. When faced with moral problems, people are thought to make judgments—that is, decide on a "right" solution that accords with the guidelines of their developmental stage. This view of the person dealing with a moral problem follows philosophy's traditional approach of analyzing moral problems from the standpoint of the critic or the detached judge.

Haan maintains that out of the necessities of social interchange, people gradually develop from the very first year of life. Moral tension and disagreement are thought to be an inevitable and continuous feature of life, so people—even young children—act in terms of their experience. Thus in this view the moral agent is always an actor (one committing a positive act), who creates decisions in dialogues (real or imagined) with others.

At issue between the theories of Kohlberg and Haan, then, is whether practical morality's paramount feature is judgment based on logical conclusion, or whether it is the practical underpinning of social interaction.

Summary

The use of the term *practical morality* in the subtitle of this volume reflects several suppositions. We assume individual persons are responsible for their moral actions. They choose to act or not to act in moral situations. But we also assume that morality can only be understood within the context of different situations that facilitate or hamper the making of morally adequate actions. In other words, this book is concerned with the interactions of people and situations. Finally, we assume that morality as it is actually lived and implicitly cherished is the proper focus of social scientists' study, not public proclamations about how humankind should live. We further assume that this practical morality ultimately fuels the morality as well as the indignation of exchanges among nations.

Chapter 2

THE FORMAL STUDY
OF MORALITY

Developments in the . . . sheltered realm of moral philosophy have coincided with social and political trends in a way
that may be disconcerting to those for whom philosophy is
above and beyond the accidents of time and place and the
common cares of ordinary experience (Alexander Sesonske,
1957, p.1).

Differing Roles for Philosophy and Social Science

HISTORICALLY, the formal study of morality has been the exclusive work of theologians and philosophers. Social scientists
began the study only in recent years. Although many social scientists
are now attempting to understand the moral basis of life, psychologists
especially are trying to, probably because moral choice is usually regarded as the act of an individual person. In a simplistic sense this is
true since individual persons could, presumably, oppose any immoral
act their group might commit. But heroism is not usual, and it is
complex; there are always questions of timing, costs, strategy, and
efficacy. Therefore, contributions of the disciplines that focus on the
wider scope of human affairs—sociology, anthropology, economics,
and political science—are needed. Moral actors are never isolated.
They live, act, and interact within sociohistorical and immediate contexts. Plainly, a solitary person on a desert island has no pressing moral
problems since such questions arise from people's relations with one
another.

The fundamental problems of morality cannot be explained by the social sciences alone; philosophy is also needed. Still, philosophers increasingly see the futility of hypothetical attempts to formulate morality apart from its operation in everyday life. As a prominent British philosopher has said, "My first thesis . . . is that it is not profitable for us at present to do moral philosophy . . . it should be laid aside . . . until we have an adequate philosophy of psychology, in which we are conspicuously lacking" (Anscombe, 1969, p. 175).

Philosophers try to construct logically consistent systems of morality; their proposals are seldom checked against the morality of everyday life. At the same time, philosophers have freely considered and analyzed what morality *could* be if people would first accept certain basic premises concerning what morality *should* be. Philosophers' skills in logical analysis, examination of implicit premises, and their knowledge of the ways that moral questions have been resolved over the centuries are tools that very few social scientists possess. But Anscombe says moral philosophy seems to be at an impasse.

Psychological study is usually limited to what *is now*. Although this focus avoids what John Dewey (1934) called "vicious abstractionism," it also is a clear restriction, for it means that research cannot tell us what might be or what ought to be. We can observe widespread morally corrupt conditions, but these obscure our vision of what might be and what ideally could be.

The social scientist's point of departure is usually common sense, which is not always immediately helpful. Common sense notions are sometimes contradictory. Nor can one see common sense as a clearly designed system with ordered relationships. Psychologists always hope to avoid this confusion by identifying more general, integrative principles. Still, common sense is a good starting point for moral study; as Thomas Nagel (1970) observes, it is correct about most things. Nagel's description of how common sense becomes "true" is applicable to morality: ". . . for unless the apparatus [common sense] is useful . . . it will simply not be developed and refined in the endless dealings of countless ordinary individuals, it will not automatically become common property and a part of human life, and will not infiltrate our common language" (p. 33). Nevertheless, the psychologists' concentration on "what is" can become an occupational hazard. Their enthusiasm for careful, rigorous observation often results in their overlooking their implicit assumptions. Nor do they delve into questions beyond "what is," such as "what else is there" or "what else might eventually be."

Controversy surrounds the study of morality because most scholars do not agree on a definition of morality. But psychologists may make a new and potentially important contribution; their research may provide fresh understandings about every person's practical morality that philosophers may have missed because of their detachment from life. At this time in the history of moral discussion, psychologists especially need to turn to philosophers to learn what might be, and philosophers especially need psychologists to learn what is. Happily, the weaknesses of one field are cancelled by the strengths of the other.

A Brief History of Moral Philosophy

Many current arguments among researchers have precedent in philosophical disputes. Readers will thus be helped by brief histories of moral philosophy and moral study in psychology.

Early Moral Philosophy

The setting of moral philosophizing has varied through the centuries. For the great Greek philosophers, such as Socrates, Plato, and Aristotle, a virtuous man was one who lived as a good and thinking citizen in the city states. Morality, or as they said, virtue, was knowledge which was thought to be both natural and acquired. Natural virtues were identified as derived from reasoning, while acquired virtues resulted from character training in a "good" family and a "good" city state. The problem for ethical study was to discern which characteristics best represented the ultimate form of the Good, which Plato identified with living a moderate, temperate life. In this highly stratified society, only upper-class males were thought to develop these virtues. Neither duty nor guilt was known. Those who led loutish lives were simply disdained, and Aristotle doubted whether people of lowly station could be virtuous.

Later, Christian thought "democratized" morality since all people (now including women and slaves) were regarded as children of God and therefore intrinsically moral beings. Various philosopher-theologians, such as St. Augustine and Thomas Aquinas, attempted to reconcile the Grecian view of morality with the Christian ethic of obeying God's will. The problem was to reconcile human desire with the divine order. St. Augustine pointed out that people's freedom to sin in itself gave them the opportunity to act otherwise, so they could accrue credit by drawing good out of evil. Thomas Aquinas observed that although people are not responsible for their appetites, which are inherent to the human condition, they can decide to control their actions. Thus, their contemplativeness is the best of their moral powers.

After the Protestant Reformation, more responsibility was placed on the individual. As a result each person had to account directly to God without the intermediary help of a priest. The moral focus was shifted from good citizenship to personal salvation which was to be achieved by accepting one's duty to obey the laws of God. Consequently, individual guilt—symbolized by the original sin and the potential for sin in all actions—preoccupied moral philosophers. Guilt could only be alleviated by baptism and self-chosen actions of a Christian life. Philosophers were still theologians. Morality was embodied in God's commands.

Later Moral Philosophy

By the seventeenth century, many religious sects existed, and the adherents to each claimed privileged knowledge of moral truth. Uncertainty set in, for who was to say which truth was right? An additional trend was becoming evident: Questions showing scientific thought were being asked. Both these developments led directly to the notion that morality must have a worldly base, so philosophers began to construct moral systems based on the "natural" or realistic qualities that seemed to represent the human being's "essence." For example, in Thomas Hobbes' view, people were naturally pleasure loving, so they support the other's good only when their own pleasure would be jeopardized if they did otherwise.

Basing morality on human nature proved less unifying than either the perspective of the good citizen or that of the Christian moralist. Disagreements which continue to this day arose as to precisely what is "natural" about morality. David Hume countered early naturalists by arguing that reason reveals truth, but truth has no power to move the mind. Instead, he said morality is based on fundamental feelings and only feelings cause people to act. During this period, the two major ideas about morality were that it is either due to sentiment—

developed from people's living with others—or secondarily derived from people's wish for pleasure.

Hume's views were countered by Immanuel Kant in his analysis of rightness as the expression of universal justice, which, he argued, followed from certain categorical imperatives that can only be discerned by reason. People's feelings and interests are not relevant in their moral decisions, and duty directly follows on the reasoned recognition of rightness. His often quoted summarization is an example of reasoned duty: "Act only on such principle as you can will should be a universal law"—an echo of the Christian golden rule. In Kant's view, moral rightness was independent of any one human mind and its moral experience.

The British utilitarian philosophers also advanced theories derived from suppositions about humans' natural condition. Their basic idea, which was elaborated upon and refined by different scholars, was framed in terms of social context: The good is whatever provides the greatest good for the greatest numbers. Jeremy Bentham's specific version was called egoistic utilitarianism, because he contended that persons give priority to their own self-interests and commit themselves to other people's good only when they are threatened by negative sanctions from the laws of society or God. John Stuart Mill listed more such sanctions, but he added the important criterion that people internalize social feelings and thereby become "moral." Henry Sidgwick later refined the basic idea by arguing that an act is justified if it produces the greatest happiness for the persons who might be affected. Later, George Edward Moore elaborated upon the central idea of all classical utilitarians: States of social affairs, not individual persons, contribute to or detract from the greatest happiness of the greatest numbers. In other words, right actions are whatever bring about a state of affairs that produces the greatest amount of good. Persons themselves should be judged only secondarily according to the good or bad that they bring about.

Modern Moral Philosophy

In the early twentieth century, the strategy of deriving morality from humans' natural characteristics fell into disrepute because this procedure was based—or so it was argued—on a "naturalistic fallacy."

This famous argument was first presented by G. E. Moore, but it was later elaborated on by Harold Pritchard, David Ross, and others.

They pointed out that there is a clear and logical difference between "is" (a fact in the real world) and "ought" (the value underlying whatever is chosen as moral), and they argued that there is no way one can logically move from "is" to "ought." In other words, no amount of careful, pure logic can turn a fact into a value; a fact only becomes a value when someone *approves* of that fact. This argument implied that the naturalists' approach was wrongheaded because no natural facts about people could be the basis of a moral system. The argument led many to conclude that moral philosophy could not hope to be objective, empirical, and scientific, as the early naturalists had imagined. Alfred Ayer argued that moral elements were simply pseudo-concepts and moral philosophy was "merely" psychology, sociology, or one person exhorting and arguing with another. After this onslaught, moral philosophy fell into disarray.

Some scholars decided that the moral philosophers' solution was simply to admit a priori positions of value and accept people's sense of what is right as a given (David Ross). Others argued that morality was simply the everyday, pragmatic actions used to solve conflicts and that no absolute right and wrong existed. Morality lay in whatever practical actions solve conflicts (John Dewey). Some declared that morality was nothing more than an expression of emotional attitudes so morality was not a proper subject for objective study (the logical positivists). Consistent with this position was Charles Stevenson's study of how moral words are used. He concluded that moral language merely expresses feelings or attitudes of approval that a speaker uses to persuade listeners; for example, "I approve of such and such and you should, too" (Stevenson, 1960). The French existentialist philosophers also argued that morality was beyond reason and logical analysis. For them, the single goodness lay in each individual's making his or her own "authentic" and "sincere" choice.

Without a definition and identifiable grounds for morality, belief in the relativism of values and nihilism were encouraged. Morality was simply relative to each society and each person. It was either an expression of personally chosen moral beliefs or merely an unpredictable and individual expression of emotion. In either case, no basis existed for people to reach common moral understandings. During the same period, anthropologists observed and reported on the varying moral beliefs held by people in different societies. Early behavioral psychologists extended relativism to individual persons when they declared that minds were not amenable to scientific study and that, at root, all behavior was emotionally driven and conditioned. All these developments supported the idea that morality is relative to each society and to each person.

Nevertheless, the idea of a universal morality is compelling, so scholars and citizens have not stopped asking the basic question: *Do humans and societies have a common basis for coming to moral agreement?*

The Current State of Moral Philosophy

Three main grounds for morality have so far been discussed: 1. as arising from some other ethic—like being a good citizen of a Greek city state; 2. metaphysical beliefs—fulfilling God's vision of the Christian life, God being the Ideal Legislator; 3. natural states of humans, such as their striving for pleasure, their innate goodness or evil, or their state as social beings. Additional discussion concerned the idea that morality has no objective basis; it thus cannot be analyzed. Emotions chaotically drive us to defend our own positions only, and our so-called moral arguments are merely efforts to persuade others that they should feel and act as we do.

The four bases for the origin of morality are not equally tenable in the late twentieth century. Awareness of the world's heterogeneity makes it unreasonable to ground morality on an institutionalized ethic like being a good citizen of some homogeneous society. Not all societies have the same idea of good citizenship; each thinks its own is preferable. The same difficulty holds for humans' strong metaphysical beliefs, which vary from priest, shaman, Nietzsche, to tea leaf readers. Furthermore, the ethical commitment of philosophers and scientists to objective scholarship means that they cannot rely on metaphysical grounds, whatever their personal beliefs. Consequently, scholars are left with only two alternatives. They can conclude that morality is unanalyzable, or they can base their moral proposals on naturalistic aspects of people. The first choice is, of course, unthinkable for people who have career investments in the efficacy of scholarship. But the choice of naturalism is not an easy solution. The questions are: What naturalistic aspects? And what is "natural" about them?

The Naturalistic Fallacy

The "Ought" and the "Is."   Most contemporary philosophers try to construct moral theories based on some more convincing form of naturalism. This renewed interest has two implications: 1. Social science should be able to contribute to this effort because it studies the way life "naturally" *is*. 2. However, the naturalistic fallacy of how to derive "ought" from a naturalistic "is" is still not put to rest (Hudson, 1969). Can facts about people ever suggest what should be approved?

Earlier warnings about the naturalistic fallacy are now generally regarded as simplistic. For a secular morality, there can be *no other* basis than some form of naturalism, so choices have to be made, choices based on the best match with nature, if not the natural state of humans. This means the naturalistic fallacy might now be termed the "naturalistic necessity" because it seems that the fallacy must be committed. Accordingly, standards for evaluating moral theories have shifted. A proposal should be consistent within itself, cover most moral problems, be consistent with known facts, even though it cannot be based on facts, and be as morally convincing as possible about its a priori position of value. Above all, the theory should be open to further clarification and revision.

Accepting the Naturalistic Fallacy.   Acceptance of the inevitability of the naturalistic fallacy follows on a general shift in philosophy. To paraphrase the epistemologist Willard Quine (1966), philosophers now point out that the sum total of social-psychological knowledge is the sum total of people's beliefs. In other words, social knowledge is constructed by active efforts of imagination and has no material reality in the universe independent of humans' minds. In this light, we can see that *no* principles of justice or equality exist objectively in the world. Secular morality can only be constituted by humans making agreements and adjustments with one another. It can only be what people "naturally" make it.

The Elusive "Ought."   The question for researchers in social science then becomes clear: Are there common characteristics of humans and their social interactions that invariably result in common but tacit understandings about the nature and ground of morality? If such a moral ground—an Ought—exists as a universal agreement, the differing, practical instances of morality that can be observed—examples of the Ises—could be alternative manifestations of the same underlying Ought. The current search, then, is for an Ought common to humankind, but the hunt is fraught with hazard for the Ought scholars may "discover" their own and not the value that is approved by all humanity. Like all people, scholars construct the world in their own image. Their advantages are that their ethic requires impartiality, and their work will be routinely evaluated and criticized. Although we cannot escape being people, some aspects of being human may result in a universal ought, however implicit it is in our minds.

Recognition of these uncertainties is no reason to turn to nihilism and pessimism. As Quine (1966) counsels, we will continue, as humankind has for centuries, to free ourselves, bit by bit, from the preconceptualizations that we grew up with (p. 68). He adds that we can cunningly translate the meaning of our ideas into those of others as we scrutinize and criticize our own and the others' suppositions.

Most philosophers have abandoned earlier strategies of logically *proving* the truth of their moral proposals. Also grounds for morality are no longer explicitly sought in the innate morality or immorality of humankind (the noteworthy but nonphilosophical exception being the contention of different sociobiologists that humans are either innately selfish or generous). Instead, as Baier (1958) says, the most obvious vehicles for explaining the development of morality are reason and society. In other words, people's experiences with each other's reasoning and expectations bring them to a moral point of view. Only principles or general understandings form a moral position. Rules of thumb or emotional drives do not qualify. People, as Baier (1958) says, who are driven by forces outside their own processes of decision making cannot be said to be acting morally because they make no choice. Recognition that social knowledge is constructed by people raises hopes earlier for an important possibility: The value of morality might be discovered if the practical language of common sense and morality were analyzed. This alternative, followed by Richard Hare (1964, 1965) involves the analysis of the language that people use when they make moral statements and decisions. Another strategy is to analyze the meanings of humans' social interdependence, recognizing that moral concerns arise in social contexts (John Rawls, 1971; Kurt Baier, 1958; and Alexander Sesonske, 1957).

Characteristics of Moral Language

Close examinations of how moral agents actually think and speak have distinguished moral thought from other kinds of thought. It is *prescriptive* (the should); *reversible* (there but for the grace of God go I); *ideal* (the best possible reasons); *universal* (including all people in the same circumstances); *objective* (reasons, not whims, being the only kind of persuasion that others will accept); and *impersonal* (all people in the same circumstance including the self should act in the pre-scribed way). Compared to philosophers' past efforts, the strategies of analyzing moral language and social meaning are both empirical and practical.

Alexander Sesonske's Theory

We turn now to brief sketches of two philosophers' constructions of morality in terms of social understandings.

Alexander Sesonske (1957) explicitly rejects the early naturalists' and metaphysicians' suppositions that duty and obligation are embed-ded in the universe or in the "essential" nature of humans. Obligations still exist, he says, because they arise from the social requirements—interdependencies and expectancies—of community. The fulfillment of these obligations forms the bond between human groups. For Se-sonske, community means either an actual, immediate community or the ideal community of humankind. An actual community imposes obligations on its members; an ideal community does not. People can be urged to act as if the ideal community exists, but an ideal does not build expectancies that are fully obligating.

Obligations, as Sesonske sees them, arise from situations. They are established as persons make commitments: 1. as explicit promises or agreements with others, 2. as implicit commitments to fulfill the for-mal promise as best as they can ("I promised to help you with this problem and it goes without saying that this means that I will help you to the best of my ability"), and 3. as acceptance first and then continuation of their membership in the community. He also observes that a person who will not admit his or her obligation to the com-munity cannot be made to do so. All that can be done is to argue with the person that it would be good for him or her to become a community member.

The strong pull of community membership is the key to understanding Sesonske's position. His analysis underscores our roots in our community, our identification with social groups, and everyone's indebtedness to communities for the aid they receive. In short, communities help people become human by helping them to become moral. But the relation is reciprocal. Communities are fragile and cannot survive when members fail to honor their commitments.

Sesonske points out that individual rights have *no* meaning outside of community. When people assume they have a right they make themselves vulnerable to others, who hold sole power to prove the existence of that right by whether or not they recognize it. Furthermore, full reciprocity is implied in the understandings and language of all communities: When Person A takes his or her rights, he or she implicitly recognizes that B and all other community persons logically have the *same* rights.

Sesonske's analysis is made from the standpoint of the person who makes actual choices, rather than from the lofty, abstract view of the moral critic who judges. His analysis prepares the way for social scientists to discover more about the actual requirements of community life and how the young come to understand the obligations of community. His system is compatible with the interactional formulation taken up in this volume.

John Rawls' Theory

John Rawls (1971) is also concerned with social interactions. He builds his arguments, however, on what he thinks people would theoretically do *if* they faced a very special situation. To explain his theory, Rawls uses the device of the hypothetical "original position" wherein a group of people are imagined to be behind a "veil of ignorance." This situation can be understood by imagining a group of strangers, all shipwrecked on a desert island, who must agree how they will arrange their future lives and distribute the "goods" of their society. Society is defined as an association of persons who come to a common agreement about the rules that regulate the distributions of "supplies" (or advantages), which range from self-respect to economic goods. Since these people are strangers, they are all in the same position. That is, they are ignorant about what natural characteristics, like beauty or strength, might eventually lead to personal advantage. Consequently they *would* vote for equal distribution of the "goods" (not should vote, Rawls would point out; he essentially makes a psychological prediction). To support the likelihood that they would make this decision, Rawls argues for the rationality of people: It would be unthinkable (mad) for persons to agree to accept less than their equal share, and the community would not allow any one person to take more than his or her share.

Rawls later modified this principle of equality to permit those who do difficult or hazardous work to have greater supplies, but this could not be allowed unless their work would aid the least-advantaged members who would not otherwise accept this inequality. To sustain the basic contract of equality, wealth could not be inherited, occupations would have to be open to all, and some means of enforcement would be needed. The "freeloader" (the person who insincerely agrees to equality and enjoys its advantages but does not reciprocate) is a problem.

Rawls does not claim that the original position represents real life processes, whereas Sesonske proposes a formulation that he believes is based on practical morality. At the same time, Rawls chooses a moral ground, initially of equality which is later understood to be justice; Sesonske does not directly go into the question of a ground for morality; he seems to depend on the concept of community—invariably a human happening—as a moral ground. Rawls notes that equality is a "thin" assumption (meaning that the assumption is not a matter of strong metaphysical belief). He says that all persons have a natural interest in their own good and all persons must compete with others for goods; therefore people would logically come to the conclusion that equality is the best solution (if they did not know what their future advantages or disadvantages might be).

We turn now, with this brief philosophical account in hand, to a brief account of the moral theories proposed by psychologists.

A Brief History of Psychologists' Investigations

Philosophy is an ancient discipline, but psychology as an organized discipline is a phenomenon of the twentieth century. It is preoccupied with research and its understandings of morality are often based on facts gleaned from research. Some psychologists act as if the nature of morality is already known or self-evident. Consequently they move on to investigate secondary questions such as the differences between delinquents and nondelinquents, how parents help children develop morally, and the relationships between political position and morality.

The questions psychologists concern themselves with put the cart before the horse, for the issue remains: What is this morality that distinguishes between deviants and nondeviants and conservatives or liberals and causes parents such concern? Psychological research is too often conducted according to technological convenience. Easily tested and readily available formulations are often employed, such as, morality is whatever our society now says it is. So glib a definition can result in morality being seen as synonymous with conformity—clearly a misapprehension.

Five currently influential moral formulations are summarized here: the psychoanalytic, social learning, sociobiological, cognitive-moral, and the interactional systems. This list is not complete. Still other views exist. The two that are the focus of this book are included in this chapter so that readers can compare the different approaches taken by psychologists. More exhaustive comparisons between the interactional and cognitive formulations are taken up in the following chapters.

The Psychoanalytic View of Morality

In psychoanalytic theory, the word for morality is superego, indicating that morality is regarded as being in control of the ego. (The latter represents the person's more-conscious and deliberate thought and decisions.) Freud meant to imply this dominance. Since the theory assumes that humans are driven by instinctual desires, the superego, which is the internalization of society's control, is necessary for human socialization. Freud never formally took an a priori position about the nature of morality, but in his social psychology, the superego is represented as the control which is necessary if civilization is to survive.

Role of the Oedipal Complex.　A crucial experience originates the superego. It is the child's resolution of the Oedipal complex. According to this theory, children around age four develop erotic feelings for their parent of the opposite sex, yet identify, both positively and negatively, with both parents. Thrown into a quandary, they experience a mixture of love and hate for three reasons: Their erotic strivings are inevitable and universal; they are still helpless and dependent; and their parents must thwart childish self-interests.

Their only feasible resolution is identification with the parent of the same sex, and since their Oedipal attachments already make them guilty, they identify especially with that parent's prohibitions. In doing so, they conform to society's expectancies and maintain their family's harmony. This developmental event is regarded as inevitable and universal. Without Oedipal resolution, there could be no civility within the family or society. As Freud (1923) wrote, "When we were little children we knew these higher natures [parents] and we admired them and feared them; and later we took them into ourselves" (p. 26). The immediately post-Oedipal superego is still not a mature conscience. Subsequent learning integrates it with the culture's values, and other significant adults are models at later dates.

Because the superego is an internalization of authority, people do not really make independent, conscious moral choices to act. As Rieff wrote with respect to the theory, "Freedom of conscience is a contradiction in terms; there are only alternative submissions" (1959, p. 274). Still, two additional provisions of the theory relieve the superego's oppressiveness. The first is the ego ideal, that is, the thoughts people have about what they ideally should be. This is a troublesome concept for the theory since it is not easily reconciled with the basic concept of the instincts and the needs for their control. Attempting to preserve the primacy of the instincts, Hartmann, Kris, and Loewenstein (1964) argued that the ego ideal was a part of the superego. Prohibitions and ideals were said to be logically linked. People prohibit themselves to fulfill their ideals, and they fulfill their ideals when they prohibit themselves. This reasoning does little more than state the truism that abiding by one's prohibitions is ideal.

According to psychoanalytic theory, a person can alter the structure of the superego by undergoing psychoanalysis. In the process of exploring the self created in early life, their superego becomes more accurate, sophisticated, and "scrupulously self-centered." Still, "self-concern takes precedence over social concern and encourages an attitude of ironic insight on the part of the self toward all that is not self . . . psychoanalyzed man . . . is only outwardly reconciled, for he is no longer defined essentially by his social relations" (Rieff, 1959, p. 330). All in all the superego is an idea of unalloyed individualism.

The Social-learning Theorists' View of Morality

The social-learning theorists (as the neobehaviorists are now called) usually prefer the word "conscience" for morality. They expect that the specific ingredients of conscience are learned in different social situations, but these separate experiences are unified through generalization. Most social-learning theorists do not think that reason is an important factor; instead they focus on the description and explanation of moral behavior.

Learning to behave morally is in no way special; conscience is learned and performed for the same reasons as all other kinds of behaviors. Children learn to act morally in the same way they learn to speak or walk or ride their tricycle. The generalized laws of the child's learning and performance of socialized behavior apply. However, somewhat different mechanisms of learning are proposed by different theorists, ranging from operant conditioning (Aronfreed, 1968, and Goldiamond, 1967) to reinforcement (Mischel & Mischel, 1976) and to induction or parents' reasoning with children about moral problems (Hoffman, 1970).

Most learning theorists define morality as socialized behavior that accords with society's mandates. Leonard Berkowitz (1964) gives this definition of morality: "Moral values . . . are evaluations of actions generally believed by the members of a given society to be either 'right' or 'wrong'" (p. 44). In commenting on this view, Hoffman (1970) focused on moral behavior: "Learning theory defines morality in terms of specific acts and avoidances which are learned on the basis of rewards and punishments; the typical procedure is . . . to elicit behaviors in the laboratory which are 'good' in terms of some culturally shared standard of conduct" (p. 262).

The social-learning theorists' account of moral behavior is clearly drawn. Whether persons behave morally at any given time depends on 1. their unique history of reinforcement interacting with 2. the particular external cues in the immediate situation and their similarity to past learned cues, and 3. the incentives—both rewards and punishments—for them to behave morally. (In other words, the past influences the present. The consequences of past experiences shape one's actions later in similar situations along with the situation's possible rewards or punishment.) Learned generalizations occur as the external social aspects of previous situations are internalized (Mischel & Mischel, 1976). Aronfreed (1968) gives importance to internalizations that result from early conditioning since these readily attach emotions to moral behavior. He writes that "the powerful affective components of conscience are reflected in the sense of essentially unanalyzable rightness or impelling obligation that we sometimes perceive in its operation" (p. 13); later he states that these kinds of internalizations do not "require evaluative cognitions" (p. 8). Altogether then, we do not question our conscience since its rules are rooted in emotion and are therefore especially compelling.

These studies of learning need not be concerned with age differences since the course of development in one period of development is no different from another. Movement is toward greater internalization—greater ability to resist temptation, consideration of others, and ability to criticize one's self rather than depending on others for criticism.

Most early research was focused on prohibitions, but emphasis has been shifted to "prosocial behaviors." Aronfreed (1968) has shown that vicarious functioning in infants (they cry when others cry) can be conditioned and reinforced. He reasons that this is the basis for older people's empathy. Other recent additions to the theory include self-criticism (Aronfreed, 1968), again initially reinforced by parents' rewards but later internalized. The Mischels have added other influences that bring about socialization, especially delay of gratification.

The view that morality is embodied in the internalization of rules laid down by parents and society is more convenient for researchers than their attempting first to determine what practical, universal morality might be. Early social-learning theorists have followed the rule that they should only consider behaviors that can be precisely observed and recorded. Parents' overt acts of reinforcing and conditioning their children's behaviors are chosen for study, as are the children's resistance to the temptation to take forbidden objects, confessions after they have done wrong, and prosocial behavior, like generosity. By focusing on these kinds of behaviors, the learning theorists avoid dealing with the complex processes that go on inside of people, for example, the ego, id, superego, or the moral constructions and meanings that interest the cognitivists.

Conscience and Society in the Freudian and Social-learning Theories

When morality is seen as synonymous with society's dictates, morality is made culturally relative. The logical but absurd conclusion follows that persons are moral when they promote the causes of bad societies like Nazi Germany, which all sane persons regard as immoral. Still individual persons are also relieved of responsibility for their behavior in this view, since they act only as they have been taught.

The learning theorists' view of the relation between the individual person and society is like that of the Freudians. The older generation's—especially the parents'—conscience is transferred to the younger generation by the process of socialization, so consciences cannot change from one generation to another (Maccoby, 1968).

This view supposes that conscience represents the behaviors that societies secure for their survival, and it is accompanied by a more-implicit assumption that societies are both clear and morally right about desirable and undesirable behaviors. Therefore, more clarity and moral virtue are imparted to societies than to individual citizens, although some societies are thought not to socialize their young efficiently. For example, the Mischels observed that, in Trinidad, lower-class blacks do not efficiently delay gratification and commented that "they had participated in a culture in which immediate gratification was modeled and rewarded extensively" (1976, p. 99). Delay of immediate self-gratification is thought to be necessary if social regard is to take precedence over self-regard. The moral dissenter, as is also true in the Freudian view, becomes suspect. For the learning theorists, deviants are insufficiently or improperly socialized, whereas for the Freudians, deviants are persons who failed to resolve their Oedipal crisis and are therefore, likely to be neurotic.

Despite their intent of being neutral about values, neither the Freudian nor the learning theorists escape taking a moral position. Their grounds of morality arise from their view that the children's state of being is uncivilized and self-serving, and the young only become moral as they incorporate society's dictates.

The Sociobiologists' View

Recently a ground for, not so much a theory of, morality has been set forth and advocated by a group of scholars, mostly biologists, who call themselves sociobiologists. Their proposal has generated great controversy, and it is different from any other considered here since it does not directly deal with the sociopsychological activities of humans. Instead its main base is a hypothesis of evolutionary biology that survival of species depended on the gradual genetic selection of individual organisms who were "altruistic" in helping and protecting their own kin. This genetic program is assumed by analogy to apply to the human species. If this were true, an absolute, scientifically based ground for morality would exist in the natural world.

To support their case for the evolutionary "fitness" of altruism, sociobiologists cite numerous examples of "altruistic" behavior in lower animals such as the alarm calls that birds make as danger approaches, presumably for the purpose of warning relatives so that they too can escape and survive. This is the main thrust of sociobiologists' argument and we will not further describe it. Interested persons can read E. O. Wilson's (1975) *Sociobiology,* Richard Dawkins' *The Selfish Gene* (1976). Criticisms have also been published; perhaps the most comprehensive and careful evaluations are to be found in Stent's edited book, *Morality as a Biological Phenomenon* (1980).

If the sociobiologists' contention were true, it would profoundly affect sociopsychological and philosophical theories of morality. But the basic observation is questionable. Biologists who criticize this argument find as many instances of animal behavior that contradict the case for innate altruism as support it, such as the not uncommon and seemingly nonpurposeful infanticide that some animals practice.

Whether or not the sociobiologists' key observation is eventually verified, we find it irrelevant for several reasons:

1. The sociobiological case is built on an analogy between animal and human morality that is misleading, if not wholly incorrect, since at will, humans "mutate" their ways of sociopsychological living. Ways of living change, progressively and regressively, during the lives of people and history, so programmed genetic determination of their morality seems unlikely.
2. Genetic knowledge has not advanced—and probably never

will—to the point that complex, creative human behavior can be ascribed to genes. Although human thought would not be possible without organic structures, the existence of organic structures cannot explain the complex choices and creations of morality.

3. Two disparate levels of conceptualization are involved in thinking about humans' moral actions and the population trends that interest evolutionary biologists. Genes do not make choices.

4. Morality is not often immediately concerned with species survival. Instead, morality is almost always concerned with the enhancement of social living.

We regard sociobiology's contention as a dead-end road, taken in yet another quest for the security of an absolute and certain ground for why human beings act morally. Its disservice is that it turns attention away from our understanding how humans can deal with the necessities of their making moral agreements with one another.

The Cognitive View of Morality

Piaget's book, *The Moral Judgment of the Child* (1965), became the inspiration for studies of cognitive-moral development. In subsequent years a few studies were done of Piaget's ideas about the ethics of authority and mutual respect. More recent investigators have specifically tested his ideas that children first understand morality in concrete terms. Right and wrong are equated with the amount of good or bad that objectively results from actions. Later investigations have concerned Piaget's contention that children first base their judgments on the consequences of acts and later on the actors' intentions. This view that very small children are morally incapable seems not to be entirely correct (see for example, Anderson & Butzin, 1978; Darley, Klosson, & Zanna, 1978; Rheingold & Hay, 1980).

Piaget did not further consider morality. *The Moral Judgment of the Child* was his only incursion into moral psychology, but his work was later used by Lawrence Kohlberg to develop a philosophically oriented theory of cognitive-moral development. (A detailed description of Kohlberg's theory is given in Chapter 4, so the account here is brief.)

Kohlberg's theory approaches morality from the standpoint of the judge, one who reasons reflectively and logically about moral dilemmas to draw conclusions. Emotions are irrelevant and may actually disrupt this process. This view of morality as judgment is the system's most striking feature. Formal logic* is the kind of reasoning involved, and persons' moral development is restricted by their stage of logical development. Kohlberg (1976) notes that "since moral reasoning is reasoning, advanced moral reasoning depends on advanced logic reasoning. There is a parallelism between an individual's logical stage and his moral stage" (p. 32).

The moral rules or principles of each stage are said to be "structures," precisely defined to accord with Piaget's (1970) definition for logical structures, as organized, unitary understandings. Structures become transformed during development but retain basic continuity from one stage to another, much as musicians do when they shift the key for a piece of music. Still the identity of these moral structures is not entirely clear. On the one hand, it seems a number of structures are thought to be coherently organized to form the overall structure of each stage (Turiel, 1977). On the other hand, Kohlberg (1967) writes as if each stage represents a single structure that has been proposed in different moral philosophies over history.

The highest principled stages represent ideas of social contract and justice, which finally enable persons to make independent moral decisions. Consequently these stages best represent Kohlberg's definition of "true" morality. Self-chosen morality at these principled stages "is reached by a minority of adults and is usually reached only after the age of 20" (Kohlberg, 1976, p. 33). At earlier stages, persons are at first obedient, then self-serving, and then adhere to convention.

Reasoning as the Essence of Morality. The cognitive theorists are in accord with mainstream moral philosophers in making reasoning the essence of morality, but Kohlberg seems to be of two minds about the grounds of his theory. On the one hand, he asserts (1971) that he circumvented the naturalistic fallacy by empirically demonstrating the existence of the six stages he earlier proposed: "The claim we make is that anyone who interviewed children about moral dilemmas and who followed them longitudinally in time would come to our six stages and no others" (Kohlberg, 1976, p. 47). However, present controversies among scholars suggest that "moral maturity," as it is defined in

---

*"Formal logic is a system of logic that abstracts forms of thought from its content to establish criteria of consistency" (Gove, 1961).

Kohlberg's system, is not consensually accepted as the "true" morality. The question comes again: How are we to know that the way this system describes children's moral maturing represents, in fact, the true and fundamental moral value approved by humanity? On the other hand, Kohlberg draws away from this empirical claim of the truth of his system to take up an analytical stance. He asserts that the logically consistent structure of his theory makes at least one kind of empirical test unnecessary. He states, "Moral behavior is not a proper external criterion for 'validating' a moral judgment test" (1976, p. 46).

In contrast to the social-learning theorists who study behavior but minimize thought, the Kohlbergians have shown great interest in moral thought but not much interest in moral action until recently (but see Kohlberg, Levine, & Hewer, 1983). In the cognitive theory older, higher stage persons are expected to integrate their thoughts with actions because they can apply their more-developed moral structures to resolve complex situations better than those who have not attained a high stage. Most investigations of cognitive moral action have so far been based on the straightforward hypothesis that the stages of moral thought and action will be the same.

Although development follows an invariant stage sequence, progression is not inevitable since it results from interaction among humans' biological equipment, their understandings and expectancies, and the impingements of their world. In other words, children construct their understandings. Social interaction and the wish for more sufficient ways of resolving moral problems ensure development. Specifically, the cognitivists suggest development occurs because people become "disequilibrated," that is, they become dissatisfied with their understandings of lower stage, because these do not adequately resolve moral problems. But societies can discourage development in two ways: 1. by the simplicity of their sociopolitical structures, and 2. by the low level of logical development they require of citizens. Therefore, citizens of simple and harmonious agrarian societies are not expected to reach higher moral stages. Indeed, Kohlberg (1969) reports findings concerning social class and national differences that support this supposition; on comparison all results favor middle-class Western children.

Social class and national differences only roughly represent differences in social contexts. More-specific effects of social interaction have not been extensively investigated by the cognitivists. That they have

not is understandable; it follows on the view that the moral agent is a
judge whose developed moral capacity rises above the details of particular situations.

The Interactional View of Morality

The cognitive theory emphasizes the importance of reasoning, and
the social-learning theory the importance of society, while reason and
society are brought together in the interactional theory. (Again the
description here is brief; more detail is given in Chapter 4.)

In this formulation, morality is action. People with moral dilemmas
are actors involved in real or imagined dialogues and negotiate moral
claims so that balanced, equalized relations with others can be
achieved or reestablished. In other words, when people make moral
choices, they interact with others and within a given situation. This
can be seen even when they consider hypothetical dilemmas. For this
morality of dialogue and equality to work, people must be motivated
to negotiate, which may end up with less than they initially considered
fair. Thus a case must be made that moral motivation is strong, rather
than weak or nonexistent as most theorists have assumed. The selfishness of people has been seen as the central problem for most theorists.
For instance, Rawls' hypothetical "veil of ignorance" seems designed
to handle selfishness since it functions to prevent people from knowing
where their advantage lies.

Nevertheless, moral exchange arises by reason of humans' compelling interdependency. Invariably we all participate in this interdependency, whether in good or bad faith, and its pull helps us
compromise even our legitimate self-interests when other people confront us with their needs, claims, and contributions. Understanding
this reciprocity, parents go to the greatest lengths to insure their offspring's morality, placing this concern above all others that they have
for their children's lives.

The result of these reciprocal and unremitting demands is that all
persons, even the most hardened of criminals, cling to the view that
they are basically moral. Freud's theory of the ego defenses depends
on the single observation that humans will resort to all means of self-
deception to fortify their view of themselves as moral. Plato quoted
Protagoras as saying, "All men properly say they are righteous whether

or not they really are. Or else if they do not lay claim to righteousness they must be insane" (Havelock, 1957, p. 169). Altogether moral motivation is so compelling that people often act blindly and therefore without skill.

The interactional formulation leads to several conclusions that are somewhat unusual in moral theories:

1. Moral decisions are created and jointly achieved in actual or imagined dialogues instead of being drawn by single persons from principles or learned generalizations.

2. The reasoning involved is practical, not formally logical.

3. General self-interest is always a legitimate part of dialogue, although a particular self-interest may or may not be found legitimate in particular dialogues.

4. Moral decisions are not always expected to be perfect, absolute solutions; they are often compromises or choice between the lesser of two evils.

5. Young children are not seen as moral primitives; they engage in moral dialogues at a very early age and make self-chosen decisions.

6. Moral skill, but not moral concern, develops gradually rather than by stages.

7. All aspects of people's functioning, including thought, emotions, and motivations, are brought into play during the dialogue and influence eventual decisions.

8. The adequacy of moral actions can vary, depending on the contents or dilemmas and demands and stress of immediate social contexts.

The moral grounds of the conclusions listed above are given in the assumption that a person's view of what is good for him or her and the other's good *should* be served as equally as possible. When equality is achieved, it is the fruition of the cherished value because, in fact, in moral disputes equal opportunity to present one's case and equal consideration for one's interests in the outcome seems to be the moral ideal endorsed by all people. As one father participating in our study of four-year-olds commented, "When she is wrong she still has to feel her case was heard. She has to go away with her moral honor intact."

This choice starts with a weak or "thin" assumption, made, as Rawls (1971) does, to recruit people's affirmation and consensus, about the nature of people and their social living. (Rawls points out that strong assumptions, like those religions make, do not recruit wide support.) This assumption is that humans naturally have strong interest in having their morally relevant claims heard and considered by others— this is their means of self-validation. But given the interdependency of existence, their self-interest invariably becomes informed and qualified in contact with others' self-interest. So self-interest is not simply curbed. In fact, for dialogue to be moral, all participants must be ready and willing to express their self-interest. This practical interchange leads to the understanding that in both process or outcome, equality is the cherished moral value.

Dialogues with certain features are more likely to result in moral balances but all dialogues are conflictual and stressful. All participants must express their needs and positions. None should dominate, and all must be able to veto, as was suggested by both Rawls (1971) and Habermas (1975). If a full, accurate, and sincere exchange of views is not achieved, all become disgruntled, mute their claims, or refuse to cooperate. Equality is not then achieved. The result is a false moral balance which does not stabilize relations. Advantaged parties are uneasy and the disadvantaged pretend stupidity or resort to sabotage. Equality can only be guaranteed as a result of social interaction; it is not an ultimate guarantee outside human experience. It is unlikely that people in optimal social circumstances, which facilitate full and sincere exchange, would endorse any other ground.

In everyday life, literal equality, in amount and/or kind, is seldom the result of moral exchanges, given the differing circumstances, needs, and contributions of the negotiators. Nor does interactional morality require that literal equality be attained. Instead, the cherished value is that participants' claims must be balanced—*equalized*— after all participants' claims—interests in terms of facts, needs, and contributions—are considered, understood, and weighed. For example, people's different needs partly determine the "goods" that they are entitled to keep and those that they award to achieve or reestablish psychological equality with others. Some people are more needful than others, so they require more, in relevant ways, to be equal. Unequal contributions are also taken into account, so that allocations of "goods" are equalizing. When people do more, equality is established by their receiving more. If A contributed more than B to a mutual enterprise, their relationship becomes equalized when A receives more. Furthermore, moral discussants are mindful of their future life together. Thus, today's inequalities can and must be rectified tomorrow.

There are two more psychological reasons why equality has been adopted as a moral ground. Both may represent natural characteristics of human beings. Recent research instigated by Seligman (1975) has shown that people do not tolerate being helpless. Going beyond Seligman, we suggest that people cannot endure a state of helplessness because it is a moral outrage; it is direct evidence that their relations with others are not equalized. Helpless people do not necessarily become inherently "immoral." Instead, they become cagey and selective in their moral commitment, as juvenile delinquents do when they sabotage authority but maintain fidelity with their gang. To negotiate, people cannot feel helpless. They need hope that their self-interests will be heard, even if not entirely legitimized.

The second arises as an insight of modern psychiatry. People only honestly and freely give to others as they are given to. This being so, evaluative equality may be the preferred, ideal moral exchange. Hope is entailed in reciprocal giving. It is participants' anticipation that good faith is intended that initiates their dialogue and allows them to reach conclusion. If good faith is not anticipated, people and nations give up; dialogue stops or becomes a sham.

Summary

In this chapter we related brief histories of the formal study of morality in philosophy and psychology to try to understand an underlying question of this work: How can social scientists do philosophically acceptable research on morality (that is, be clear and analytical about the values embedded in formulations) and at the same time contribute important empirical knowledge about the moral basis of life? We also discussed the complaints of philosophers concerning their chronic failure to check their formulations with everyday life and noted their increasing interest in empirical analysis. Our account also included a brief discussion of complaints about psychologists for not being clear about the value assumptions they make. In the next chapter we will evaluate these complaints and propose guidelines for the moral psychologies.

Chapter 3

LEARNING FROM THE PAST

The important logical and methodological issue is whether
we can, in principle, through self-corrective inquiry, sort out
these [personal] biases even when we are initially unaware of
them (Richard Bernstein, 1976, p. 39).

Assumptions about Human Nature and Moral Grounds

PHILOSOPHERS' CONCEPTIONS of morality changed over the
centuries from the image of the virtuous citizen in the Greek city
states, to compliance with God as the Ideal Moral Legislator, to Kant's
ideas that pure reason identifies moral imperative, to the utilitarians'
focus on social context that morality must maximize the common
good. Modern moral philosophers became increasingly empirical, yet
no consensus was achieved.

Psychologists are in no better agreement concerning moral systems;
the proponents of each system discussed assume moral grounds that
resemble those in philosophical formulations. These similarities have
not usually resulted from the psychologists' deliberate decision to draw
on philosophy's conceptions of morality. Rather they suggest that despite the diversity, there are a limited number of ways to view the
relationship between self-regard and other-regard. Each view arises
from different preconceptions about human nature.

If humans are innately selfish, morality becomes society's method
of control to insure survival. If humans are innately altruistic, then
interest in self is evidence that societies invariably corrupt, since they
would thwart citizens' natural propensity.

Both positions violate the notion that individuals are responsible for their moral choices, for both assume that without society, people would simply live out their biological destiny. Although the abstraction of "species survival" is the central concern of evolutionary theory, it is rarely relevant in individual lives. Everyday practical morality, which is the only kind that social scientists can investigate, is more concerned with harmonious social living than with the cataclysm of the demise of the species. A biologically based moral ground is simplistic and illogical.

Clearly, biology *is* important in human lives, but the plasticity of human minds and social interchange indicates biology explains little about the complex moral systems of human beings. The more decisive counterargument *is*, however, that the premise of innate selfishness or altruism *already* is a moral judgment of humanity. Scientists should investigate morality and not merely reflect moral judgments of the prevailing social order.

If we assume that morality is dictated by society, then we conclude societies are always just. Plainly this is not the case. For one, moral strength is often defined by the ability to counter conventionalized immorality. Furthermore, this moral ground leads to a relativism that rules out all common concern. Neither person nor society has moral responsibility; both are defined by external societal circumstance. Accordingly, Nazi Germany cannot then be condemned. No more can be expected from human interchange than a nihilistic war of society against society. Still, relativists are seldom wholly relativistic. They often implicitly hold that there should not be a universal "ought" because human differences *should* be respected. But this ground does not exclusively belong to this formulation. Respect for human differences is part of most moral formulations.

Of all psychologists, Lawrence Kohlberg (1970) has most pointedly discussed the issue of a moral ground. On the one hand, he believes, as do others, that the naturalistic fallacy must be committed, so he openly chooses the moral ground of justice. On the other hand, he suggests that empirical evidence for the "existence" of his proposed six stages allows him "to get away" with violating the naturalistic fallacy. Investigators are not all convinced by Kohlberg's facts nor convinced that the naturalistic fallacy can be sidestepped. (See Levine (1976), Locke (1979), Phillips and Nicolayev (1978), Trainer (1977).) Kohlberg's empirical claims are not altogether clear with regard to the meaning of "justice." Clearly he does not assume that justice is innate; he seems to think it is the inevitable result of social interchange and he endorses the idea of social evolution (Kohlberg, 1976); in other words, humans have progressed over the centuries in achieving more mature moral judgments.

Equalization of relationships, the moral ground of the interactional theory, is also assumed to be the inevitable value that people come to endorse as a result of the reciprocity of social interchanges. This is further specified in two psychological characteristics that are assumed to be basic in human nature: People cannot tolerate being helpless and they intelligently give only as they are given to. More is said about this moral ground in the next section.

As we know from Lerner's (1980) extensive studies, people want to believe that the world is just. So justice as well as all moral words are charismatic. Thus social scientists take risks in proposing a moral ground and they cannot avoid basing their choice on values they already hold. Of course, science has built-in safeguards against wanton bias. Happily, there are special methods for diminishing personal bias. Social scientists routinely decide whether social-psychological phenomena "exist" and interpretations have "truth" by checking their observations and interpretations with others.

Validation by consensus is an important criterion. Demonstrating that observations are reliable and valid in the real world is not done just to comply with scientific standards. These procedures are formalized extensions of the ways all humans come to know social-psychological reality. More importantly, they are moral regulations, methods scientists devised to protect their work from human fallibility. The underlying moral purpose is clear: Scientists know that their work is susceptible to bias, and they strive for fairness in their procedures and conclusions. But in the end, consensus is the *only* basis for "knowing" whether social scientific knowledge is "true."

General Guidelines for Research

Given all these considerations, we propose certain guidelines for investigating morality. *First, the naturalistic fallacy must be committed, and a tentative, working formulation of moral grounds that is forever open to revision, refinement, or abandonment must be chosen. Second, we assume that the social scientists' special task is to discover, describe, and explain the practical morality that people and societies actually idealize. Third, we assume that social scientists' effort will be more fruitful and society will be better served if a universal morality—if such exists—is the target of their work.* These guidelines are stated simply and brashly, but each is complex and demanding as well as promising, so each is further discussed below.

Committing the Naturalistic Fallacy

Since Moore (1903) brought attention to the naturalistic fallacy, more is known and understood about the "naturalistic" characteristics of humans. Although empirical facts can never generate a moral ground, they may allow, by inference, a closer approximation to the values that all humans *would* approve—by their very nature. All that social scientists can assume about infants at birth is that they are inexperienced but social interchange promptly brings them to some understanding of reciprocity. Nevertheless, there may also be natural universal psychological characteristics. For instance, in the previous chapter it was suggested that humans cannot tolerate helplessness and that being rendered helpless is a moral outrage. We meant that humans are just naturally that way. Also, humans do not naturally give to others unless they are given to. (Obvious exceptions to these statements exist. Some people—like masochists—may enjoy some kinds of helplessness, but these and other exceptions can be explained on other bases.) These ideas about natural characteristics led us to assume the moral ground for the interactional theory of equalization of relationships which avoids helplessness and promotes mutual giving. This working definition is simple in form so it can have general applicability to all societies and all people of all ages in all times and places.

Choosing this moral ground was aided by Rawls' (1971) recent suggestion that "thin" grounds, that is, those that seem usual, commonly accepted, and simple, are more likely to be accepted than a moral ground based on strong grounds. The latter are likely to mobilize intransigent spiritual beliefs or all manner of firmly held objections. Both reactions would signal that strong grounds may not represent the kind of common working "truth" that researchers need to proceed. At the same time, a thin ground will likely not characterize *all* moral activity. The hope remains that some moral forms are common.

Discovering Practical Morality

The second moral guideline, concerning social scientists' task of investigating and describing practical morality, follows from their skills, and the special needs of societies to understand moral activity as it actually occurs. Little more needs to be said.

Is There a Universal Morality?

As we turn to the third guideline concerned with the search for a universal morality, attention needs to be drawn to the different ways that philosophers and psychologists use the term "universal morality." Philosophers refer to individual speakers who mean that their moral judgments *ought* to be universally applied, without revision, by all persons in the same circumstances. Psychologists usually refer to the empirical status of a morality, whether or not the morality *is in fact* universally used and endorsed. The latter is strictly a question for investigation that cannot be answered by assertion or logic alone. Despite this distinction, both philosophers and psychologists respond to a common feeling about morality: People often feel that the morality which they espouse is so compellingly correct that it should be universally accepted and enacted. Thus they hope it is in fact universal.

The idea of universality is rejected by relativists. Yet most relativists would have to agree on the universal notion that differences among people should be respected. Limits to the relativists' tolerance for moral differences can usually be easily demonstrated. For example, no reasonable person tolerated Nazi Germany's genocidal policies. As Ladd (1957) notes, the arguments around ethical relativism have almost always been oversimplified. Tolerating people's differences does not demonstrate a lack of moral standards.

The possibility that a universal morality exists is based on the assumption that the problems of social living, across time and place, are sufficiently common to elicit the same moral forms. Certain characteristics of all human groups generate this expectation. For example, all societies, as well as families, must maintain a degree of common understanding to conduct business, insure survival and enhance living. All societies have legal, religious, and moral stipulations about personal violence, property rights and mutual help. Informal, smaller groups are characterized by similar fundamental concerns.

Nevertheless, variation among cultures in the immediate contents and details of their moral demands is plainly evident. If these contents and details are regarded as critical moral elements, universal moralization clearly does not exist. Ladd (1973) suggested that more-abstract theories of morality were needed to rise above concrete, local details. The solution may lie, instead, in deepening and enriching moral accounts with more psychological and sociological information. Nonetheless, superficially different moral features may actually be morally identical in meaning. For example, some people are certain that the Eskimos' custom of leaving aged persons to die when the band moves on to a new location is immoral. But this is a time- and group-honored moral decision that aged and dying Eskimos make for themselves to insure their families' survival in bitter Arctic winters. At any rate, the possibility that social union has similar, basic meanings to all peoples produces the hope that moral commonality may exist in some degree or way.

Difficulties of Investigating Morality

Psychologists have intended to describe morality in a practical sense, yet certain difficulties stand in their way. At this early phase of inquiry, we need many separate searches, guided by different working definitions of morality. In the end, social science is nothing more than an organized inquiry into the nature and meaning of life with all the pitfalls we have enumerated. Although empirically based research about the everyday meanings of morality might settle some of the philosophers' arguments, social scientists face a special set of problems if their research is to be effective:

First, morality is understood to mean "value" in the language of all societies, and a fact only becomes a value when someone *approves* of that fact. Thus the question for researchers is, Which value *should* they approve by choosing it as the target of their investigations? Plainly, scientists *ought* to choose a value that could conceivably be endorsed by all humankind if they follow the scientific ethic of impartially accepting all relevant evidence. They need to justify their choices and, given their special relationship to society, show that it does not violate common-sense convictions about moral rightness. Theologians and politicians do not need to justify their choices since they do not give the public the impression that they are impartial as social scientists assuredly do.

Second, there is an occupational hazard in the social scientists' preoccupation with the observable aspects of life. They are tempted to believe that what they see is the whole of truth, a mistake called the "empirical fallacy" by R. S. Rudner (1966). But humankind has always cherished ideal forms of morality, so moral observables cannot be the whole truth about moral meaning. Cherished moral ideas have the power to move history, so it is clear that social scientists need to take more than observable morality into their accounts. A morally functional society is a powerful human aspiration, for it would be an enhancing and harmonious place to live.

Third, people's unremitting need to present themselves as "morally desirable" makes trouble for researchers. Even to give the appearance of rejecting moral commitment is tantamount to casting oneself out of community. Consequently people sometimes feign moral concern. The impetus for Freud's theory of the ego defenses was his understanding that people engage in all manner of self and social deception to avoid feeling immoral. Convicts on death row do the same: They either argue for their essential moral innocence or demonstrate their transcendent morality by pleading for punishment. For this reason, social scientists cannot naively accept public declarations of morality (like resolutions to hypothetical moral dilemmas) as pure and true indications of morality.

Finally, there is often great difference between people's "knowing" morality and their acting morally, since the store of information, skills in social manipulation, and logical reasoning of well-educated people enable them to appear moral even when they might not be. Action is the commonly used criterion for judging the authentic moral worth of others. As a result, action is probably the best, first focus of investigation.

The Knotty Problem of Self-interest

Since theorists have assumed that morality is achieved when self-interest is replaced by interest in others and in society, self-interest has not had legitimacy. Since psychologists customarily focus on individual welfare (often to the exclusion of the general welfare), their move to investigate morality may cast a different light on the role of self-interest in morality.

Self-interest has usually been represented by either personal "rights" or "goods." A first issue, roughly, involves whether or not priority should be always granted to the common interest over self-interest. They conflict when benevolent societies decide the good for individual citizens in ways that violate individual citizens' rights. For example, East German leaders may argue that maximization of industrial development and production is for the good of all and future generations; however, uncontrolled pollution violates present workers' rights to health and safety.

The "good" is a slippery idea; its very meaning varies according to the preferences of persons, social circumstances, and societies. It has been defined by various scholars as intrinsic, as obvious and self-evident, as the fullest development of a person's faculties, as the greatest happiness for all, and as simple pleasure. Conflict between two persons' good is brought out by questioning whether morality requires that one promote another's good when one's own circumstances are extremely difficult and the expense to one's self is great. Consider the following example: Jane sees someone drowning in the middle of a deep, swift river, but she is a poor swimmer, and there is no other means of rescue. If she does not attempt to rescue the person, surely no one would condemn her, although surely she would feel remorse. According to common sense, others' goods are not always their right to have fulfilled nor the other person's obligation to fulfill.

A requirement that good be constantly produced, irrespective of cost to the self, also leads to a logical absurdity: Relaxation is immoral (Baier, 1958). During the 1960s, some student activists worked day and night to secure civil rights for minorities and to end the Vietnam war. They eventually became physically and emotionally exhausted and so they were lost to their own cause and others had to care for them.

The idea of quantity is also embedded in the good, as was foreshadowed by the early utilitarian's principle of the greatest good for the greatest numbers. This moral ground has led researchers to apply cost-benefit analysis (which is now the basis of many decisions made by governments and business). For example, is the larger amount of good (benefit) that might come from installation of nuclear power plants greater than the costs might be to neighboring people if there were an accident? Thus many objections are raised by the concept of the good: How much common good overrides an individual's diminished good? How much good is any one person entitled to have? Do people have certain irreducible rights that *should* override whatever good might be produced for others and society?

The second related issue is whether individual rights take priority over the common good. In contrast to goods, rights are certain and categorical (or absolute), not quantitative, in the sense that people have rights that are not subject to calculation of costs and benefits. In this view rights are naturally given, a classical definition that is endorsed by Kohlberg. But questions concerning the source of rights arise if they are not God given or "sacred" but merely proposed as "natural" rights of personhood.

Psychologists are likely to think very practically about this complex of issues that bears on self-interests; the interactional formulation is an example. It avoids the convoluted problems of attempting to find the universalized good and its acceptable exceptions; it also avoids the a priori assumption that some rights naturally arise from personhood and its attendant problems of determining which rights are natural. This more psychological approach leads to the proposal that all people have the right at least to pursue their own good whatever they perceive that to be. And this right is granted to them by dint of all other people's right to pursue their own goods whatever they perceive them to be. By this reasoning, problems of defining the good disappear; the good is whatever individual people think is in their self-interest and rights lose their special aura of being given and absolute.

But in the interactional theory, rights only acquire meaning in context since they are thought to be mutual recognitions and expectancies that arise among people. They are sometimes modified or held in abeyance unless the right is the ultimate pressing question of a person's life. Then, however, it is not the person's life per se but the fact that if it is concluded, the person is deprived of all later rights to participate in dialogue. For this reason, the wishes of dying persons are especially honored. As Hampshire (1978) observes, "The idea that human life has a unique value has to be recognized as a human invention" (p. 19).

Whether rights can be modified or not depends on the right in question and the nature of the other parties' rights. Persons are not continuously required to fulfill others' rights, nor can they expect others to do likewise. But when people give up their right to achieve their own good, their choice is regarded as shortsighted and they are thought to be "prostituted." Sesonske (1957) wrote that to insist on one's own rights is understood to be a promise to recognize the other person's rights.

From this view, the essence of moral problems lies in the conflict among people who understandably and legitimately pursue their self-interest within actual or imagined dialogues. The dialogue winnows self-interests to decide on the legitimacy or illegitimacy of each participant's claims. In everyday life we can see that dialogue does not always produce legitimate solutions. Still a standard is offered; the good is recognized, and rights are defined. It follows that the common good is served, though not always perfectly, when all persons have equal rights to pursue their own self interests and have them seriously considered by institutions and all concerned. If the moral claims of dissidents are heard, then right should generally prevail when their arguments have merit.

The more-psychological argument described above is separated from the usually more-sweeping philosophical arguments if we allow for people's legitimate self-interest in their personal good, which is still not evidence of their selfishness. Life gives no guarantee to anyone that his or her rights should *always* take priority over those of others; such a decision depends on the context.

Chapter 4

THE COGNITIVE AND INTERACTIONAL PROPOSALS

Each moral philosophy singles out some ultimate ground or grounds for unconditional praise of persons, and prescribes the ultimate grounds for preferring one way of life to another (Stuart Hampshire, 1978, p. 5).

Different Approaches

BEFORE WE DESCRIBE the research comparing the cognitive and interactional theories, readers need more specific detail about them. In this chapter we first note their similarities and then their contrasting conceptualizations of how a person deals with a moral problem. We then present the theories' different views of moral action and development and the family's role in moral development; all are the main issues of this volume. Finally their contrasting explanations for moral differences among people of the same age and among all adult people in the same societies are discussed.

We stated in the Prologue that we thought, not surprisingly, that the interactional formulation was the better match to the morality that we actually use and cherish. At this point readers need a more complete understanding about our views of the Kohlberg theory. Lawrence Kohlberg has, almost single-handedly, led the way for psychologists to do research about morality. In offering ways to think about morality, his own formulation and investigations were rich and meaningful and his proposal for the moral education of children immediately captured the attention and commitment of educators, religious educators, parents, and even law-enforcement officers. But the fact that his proposal was applied to the moral education of children makes evaluation by his colleagues mandatory.

Kohlberg has drawn heavily on the works of moral philosophers, past and present, as well as the work of Piaget on children's development of logic. He has applied his ideas primarily to the field of child development. These two strategies of relying on philosophy and giving top priority to development give the Kohlberg theory a particular character. Our difference with Kohlberg lies in our judgment that these are not the best starting points for social scientists. If moral philosophy is at an impasse, as Anscombe (1969) and others declare, then it seems that the scientific study of morality should begin anew. We should take the fresh look at practical morality that research might allow. The interactional theory is based on such a search. A serious attempt must be made to avoid historic, possibly biasing assumptions if different understandings are to be gained.

Also it seems to us that development is the second question for researchers to consider, not the first. Surely action is nearer to being the litmus test for bona fide morality, and we need to be reasonably clear about *what* develops before we can say *how* it develops. Whatever question and criticisms are leveled at Kohlbergian theory, and there are now a number of critics including Gilligan (1982), Holstein (1976), Locke (1979, 1980), Phillips & Nicolayev (1978), Trainer (1977), there can be no doubt but that this theory represents some kind of developmental dimension, whether or not it is the development of practical morality that we argue social scientists should study. The formulation does less well with action, but here Kohlberg and his colleagues have recently made proposals that they think will improve the theory's ability to predict moral action (see Candee & Kohlberg, 1982; Kohlberg, Levine, & Hewer, 1983).

We did not conduct our studies simply to disprove Kohlberg's position, although we admittedly thought it would not stand up as well as the interactional theory. We had genuine curiosity about the kind of morality people use to solve actual moral problems with their fellows. We also wondered what kind of people rely on morality as Kohlberg conceived of it because it surely exists as a way of thinking. Also, we wanted to find out what kind of people rely on interactional styles.

Similarities between the Two Formulations

Both the cognitive and interactional formulations are "constructivist." In other words, an assumption is included in both theories that morality is constituted, considered, and decided in the minds of people. This constructivist position has two ramifications: If morality is based on reason, it cannot then be an entirely emotional apprehension of rightness or wrongness. If people are thought to construct moral ideas through interaction with experience, then people's morality cannot be wholly shaped by external influences.

Moral growth is expected to occur in both theories. Following the present fashion in the social sciences, these organized, coherent moral understandings are called "structures" in both theories. Both are endorsements of the idea that humans' minds become more skilled in interaction with experience, but they part company with regard to what develops, the nature of the developmental experience, and how people process this experience. In conceptualizing development as an interaction, they reject the view that morality is the accumulation of discrete, reinforced behaviors or that it is initiated by a single dramatic event, like the resolution of the Oedipal complex.

Differences between the Two Formulations

Views of the Moral Agent

The two theories differ in their vision of the person dealing with a moral problem. The moral thought of the person who judges and acts alone is the focus of the cognitive theory. Following this theory, people consider the logical, moral elements of issues and determine what is right by referring to generalized rules and principles. Moral judgments are thought to be best when they are impersonal, ideal, universal, and objective. Good moral thinking requires that the immediate moral dilemma be impersonally and objectively judged; thus judgment must transcend or rise above immediate circumstances; all similar situations must be solved in the same way. This allegiance to good logical reasoning gives the theory a Kantian flavor, a kinship often noted by Kohlberg (1967b, 1981). Kohlberg (1969, p. 397) stated that its main force was the "cognitive definition of the situation rather than because strong attitudinal or affective expression of moral values activate behavior."

In contrast, the moral agent in the interactional theory is envisioned as an actor in a social setting, engaged in a real or imagined dialogue with others or "society." By necessity, the actor takes into account all sociopsychological aspects of participants and extenuating circumstances, including moral understandings, emotions, motivations, and cognitions, as well as the social meanings and the outward characteristics of the situation. The moral person need not be educationally sophisticated nor necessarily chronologically mature. Instead he or she skillfully deals with conflict, and tolerates tension to achieve and sustain mutually sensitive moral balances that equalize relationships. Reasoning is applied and practical; it deals with the immediacies of the conflict. It may not always be strictly logical, and participants' emotions are always critical communications. *Resolutions should fit the particular situation, not rise above it.*

Moral problems seem so affectively compelling that people are always acting in some degree from the position of the "first person (I or we)." Even when presented with a hypothetical dilemma, they become directly involved and want to convince themselves and others that they are, indeed, moral. Instead of merely thinking about morality, people seem almost always to *do* morality. The separation of thought and behavior does not then seem to be a fruitful distinction. This view of the moral agent as actor (that is, as one who acts rather than talks *about* morality) has no precise precedent in philosophical theory. It is similar to Sesonske's ideas, which were discussed earlier.

As cognitive theory focuses on the individual, it is consistent with mainstream psychology's concern with the individual person without reference to his or her place in a social group. The interactional theory has a more sociological orientation in envisioning the agent within a social context. In emphasizing the capacity of persons to think morally, the cognitive theory is one of fixed abilities, whereas the interactional theory is one of adaptation to life.

As a result of the differences stated above, researchers have taken different tacks. The cognitivists more often use responses to hypothetical dilemmas to test the development of people's capacities to think morally and action is thought to proceed from capacity. The interactional theory leads to testing people's moral skill in action situations and moral solutions are thought to be particularly created for each situation.

Different Views of Moral Development

The Cognitive View.   The cognitive theorists view moral development as occurring according to an invariant sequence of stages, each being a unified way of thinking. Higher stages evolve out of lower stages as moral structures are transformed. Kohlberg expressed his certainty about this sequence when he wrote, "We know that individuals pass through the moral stages one step at a time as they progress from the bottom (Step 1) toward the top (Stage 6)" (1976, p. 31).

Further research may identify the structures of each stage and reveal how they become transformed between one stage and the next. But a general reason for development is offered. Persons become dissatisfied with the moral ideas of their own stage when these seem inadequate or insufficient compared with other people's reasoning at a higher stage. Turiel (1966) and Rest, Turiel, and Kohlberg (1969) offered experimental support for this view of development. They presented children with arguments one or two stages higher than their own or one stage lower. The children preferred higher-stage over lower-stage arguments, but they could only reconstruct arguments from memory that were one stage above their own. This pattern of preference and comprehension was regarded as evidence of a developmental impulse that proceeds to higher stage reasoning.

An alternative explanation may be that the language of higher stages is more morally desirable, and wanting to *appear* morally desirable might be a sufficient and universal motivation for higher moral statements. For instance, in an analysis (Haan, 1974, unpublished) of the ranks that 145 middle-aged adults made of six moral arguments that they would use if their adolescent offspring had done wrong (each represented one of the six Kohlberg stages), 73 percent gave the highest or next highest rank to Stage 6 and 79 percent gave the lowest or next lowest rank to Stage 1. According to their own moral stage on the Kohlberg scoring system only two of these persons were themselves assigned to Stage 5 and none were Stage 6. Whatever stage these people were in, they apparently "liked" the reasoning of the higher principled stages.

Table 4.1.

Six Stages of Moral Judgment[a]

Level A. Preconventional Level

Stage 1. The Stage of Punishment and Obedience
<u>Content</u>
Right is literal obedience to rules and authority, avoiding punishment, and not doing physical harm.
<u>Social Perspective</u>
This stage takes an egocentric point of view. A person at this stage doesn't consider the interests of others or recognize they differ from actor's, and doesn't relate two points of view. Actions are judged in terms of physical consequences rather than in terms of psychological interests of others. Authority's perspective is confused with one's own.

Stage 2. The Stage of Individual Instrumental Purpose and Exchange
<u>Content</u>
Right is serving one's own or other's needs and making fair deals in terms of concrete exchange.
<u>Social Perspective</u>
This stage takes a concrete individualistic perspective. A person at this stage separates own interests and points of view from those of authorities and others. He or she is aware everybody has individual interests to pursue and these conflict, so that right is relative (in the concrete individualistic sense). The person integrates or relates conflicting individual interests to one another through instrumental exchange of services, through instrumental need for the other and the other's good will, or through fairness giving each person the same amount.

Level B. Conventional Level

Stage 3. The Stage of Mutual Interpersonal Expectations, Relationships and Conformity
<u>Content</u>
The right is playing a good (nice) role, being concerned about the other people and their feelings, keeping loyalty and trust with partners, and being motivated to follow rules and expectations.
<u>Social Perspective</u>
This stage takes the perspective of the individual in relationship to other individuals. A person at this stage is aware of shared feelings, agreements, and expectations, which take primacy over individual interests. The person relates points of view through the "concrete Golden Rule," putting oneself in the other person's shoes. He or she does not consider generalized "system" perspective.

Stage 4. The Stage of Social System and Conscience Maintenance
<u>Content</u>
The right is doing one's duty in society, upholding the social order, and maintaining the welfare of society or the group.
<u>Social Perspective</u>
This stage differentiates societal point of view from interpersonal agreement or motives. A person at this stage takes the viewpoint of the system, which defines roles and rules. He or she considers individual relations in terms of place in the system.

Level C. Postconventional and Principled Level

Moral decisions are generated from rights, values, or principles that are (or could be) agreeable to all individuals composing or creating a society designed to have fair and beneficial practices.

Stage 5. The Stage of Prior Rights and Social Contract or Utility
<u>Content</u>

Table 4.1 (cont.)

The right is upholding the basic rights, values, and legal contracts of a society, even when they conflict with the concrete rules and laws of the group.

Social Perspective

This stage takes a prior-to-society perspective--that of a rational individual aware of values and rights prior to social attachments and contracts. The person integrates perspectives by formal mechanisms of agreement, contract, objective impartiality, and due process. He or she considers the moral point of view and the legal point of view, recognizes they conflict, and finds it difficult to integrate them.

Stage 6. The Stage of Universal Ethical Principles

Content

This stage assumes guidance by universal ethical principles that all humanity should follow.

Social Perspective

This stage takes the perspective of a moral point of view from which social arrangements derive or on which they are grounded. The perspective is that of any rational individual recognizing the nature of morality or the basic moral premise of respect for other persons as ends, not means.

---

[a]Abridged and adapted from pp. 409-412 of The Philosophy of Moral Development by Lawrence Kohlberg. Copyright © 1981 by Lawrence Kohlberg. Reprinted by permission of Harper & Row Publishers, Inc.

Descriptions of the cognitive moral stages are contained in Table 4.1. There are three different levels: the preconventional, conventional, and postconventional or principled; each contains two stages. As persons move through stages, their thinking becomes qualitatively different, as can be seen from the descriptions. Very few people—Kohlberg (1976) says only about 5 percent—attain Stage 5. Stage 6 is attained so seldom that provisions for scoring this stage have been dropped in the most recent scoring manual (Colby, Kohlberg, Gibbs, Speicher-Dubin, & Candee, in press). Kohlberg, Levine, and Hewer (1983) state, however, that they will "continue to hypothesize and look for a sixth moral stage" (p. 60). Children up to age 9 are generally expected to be at the first two stages; almost all other people are at Stages 3 and 4.

Although the cognitive theory describes development as constructed, it seems not entirely constructivist in the sense of creating new solutions. Instead children successively "rediscover" sets of age-old rules or principles as they move to a new stage. Kohlberg (1967b) writes that these six sets of rules represent different philosophical systems that were proposed much earlier in history. Therefore, traditional moralities are "rerevealed" to the young instead of constructed by them. The theory seems to be based then on an assumption that humankind evolved, socially and morally, over history. Thus, each child's individual development recapitulates history.

Evidence from research by the cognitivists consistently shows that moral development is retarded in preindustrial, presumably less-evolved societies. Also, citizens of preindustrial societies are thought to be retarded in formal logic (Teague-Ashton, 1978). This observation is consistent with another feature of the theorists' developmental view: Logical development is hypothesized to be the necessary condition of moral development; that is, children cannot move to a higher moral stage before they have achieved the particular logical stage that underlies each moral stage. This stipulation not only ties cognitive morality to logical development, but it also means that the quality of moral actions is also restricted by the actor's stage of logical development. Since Western cultures place great weight on logic, some critics, such as Simpson (1974) and Haan, Weiss, and Johnson (1982), suggest that the theory favors Western industrial cultures. Indeed, Kohlberg (1979) himself seems to support this view when he states that "the liberal interest in moral education is a rediscovery of the principles of justice behind the founding of our nation" (p. xv).

Kohlberg and his colleagues devised a model intervention for education designed to ensure and possibly accelerate moral development. In this model, a "training session" takes place wherein children discuss hypothetical moral dilemmas (Blatt & Kohlberg, 1975). These discussion groups should include children of different moral stages so that the morally less-mature children can hear higher stage reasoning and thereby become dissatisfied with their own reasoning, or "disequilibrated," and thereby develop.

Discussion of hypothetical dilemmas is properly regarded as a good and sufficient learning experience in this theory since its essence is logical cognitive development. Real contexts, where greater emotion is involved, could disrupt carefully logical moral reasoning. Kohlberg later worked with "just communities," that is, prisons and schools. Reports of recent studies (Kohlberg, Levine, & Hewer, 1983) mention that there are phases or stages whereby higher group norms develop. However, the developmental interaction between the individual person's stage and these group norms is not taken up. No basic revision of theory seems to have resulted from the study of prisons and schools despite the strong social-emotional impact of these institutions.

The Interactional View. Development is wholly constructivist in this system since the actor as a growing person creates particular solutions for particular moral dilemmas. Nevertheless, there is some similarity between historical views of morality and a person's formulations for three reasons. First, all people—children and adults—face similar moral problems across time and space. Second, social interaction itself can occur only in a limited number of ways across time and space. Third, children and adults use but do not copy learned moral tradition in their dialogues. Traditional moral solutions are only one kind of knowledge that people possess and they remake it according to their own understandings. Far more influential is their understanding of the other person's position and the existing objective options for resolution within their immediate situation.

Development is thought to occur as children improve their grasp of the subtle meanings in moral interchange and come to tolerate conflict. Recent research by others (which is described in Chapter 14 along with our own study of four-year-olds) suggests that whatever develops, it is not moral concern or even understanding of the fundamental conflict between self and other interest. Instead it seems that it is increasing skill in resolving moral conflict. If this is true, gradual development—not stage development—must occur. This point of view is in marked disagreement with the cognitive description that development occurs by stages and that children do not have moral concern or understanding. In fact, it is not clear that self-chosen moral understanding characterizes the cognitive conventional stages, most often occupied by adults, since conformity to convention guides their judgments. In Chapter 14, the issue of what develops is analyzed in detail.

The issue as to whether moral development occurs gradually or by stages is critical. Piaget's influential conceptualization that logical development occurs in stages seems reasonable since children experience regularities in the physical-mathematical world that are never contradicted. Consequently, when small children discover important mistakes in their logical understandings, their corrections could cause them to shift to new methods of thinking. This change fits the idea that development occurs by stages. But children do not experience such certainty in moral exchange. In contrast to logical conclusions, everyday moral conclusions are seldom wholly true or wholly false; small violations are accepted. Furthermore, moral irregularity is frequent, and small sensitive differences in mood can lead to different solutions.

The conclusions of classic formal logic are most certain when they concern the present rather than the future; so again the analogy between logic and morality fits badly. Moral actors are not only future oriented, but they can never know for certain what the consequences of their decisions might be. Moral decisions are also sometimes wisely "illogical" in yielding to strongly felt but objectively erroneous claims. Gilligan (1978) recalls the woman who came before Solomon and lied about her maternity to save her child's life to illustrate the point that emotional need sometimes intelligently overrides truth and logic. As Gilligan comments, "The blind willingness to sacrifice people to truth . . . has always been the danger of an ethic abstracted from life" (p. 86).

From the interactional view, moral skill is thought to be gradually acquired, but research requires numbers. Therefore, the levels shown in Table 4.2 were arbitrarily drawn as divisions of a continuous dimension which is more of quality than development. But children seem increasingly to organize their understandings of *how* to conduct moral dialogue and *how* to achieve solutions. Within optimal conditions, they may achieve high levels. The organized understandings or structures are also shown in Table 4.2.: 1. The primary structure of the interchange is necessarily a joint search for moral balance. 2. The more personal secondary structures of regard for the self as a moral object and others as moral beings, taking chances on the good faith of others, and righting wrongs the self commits. These structures are commonplace, and they seem to represent what people commonly think should take place in moral dialogues.

Development of moral skill occurs as forms of dialogues and solutions achieved earlier are reused, but most often revised, modified, or elaborated in new dialogues. This "creative," inductive, particularized quality of moral discussion and solution makes it highly unlikely that the development of moral skill is accurately characterized by successive structurally homogeneous stages.

The levels shown in Table 4.2 represent progressively more demanding criteria for identifying the quality of people's moral activity. Small children can be moral in a comfortable, supportive situation, and the problem is not cognitively complex. Given deleterious situational supports, adults can produce less acceptable morality. The definitions of several levels are in some ways indebted to Kohlberg's descriptions of his proposed stages; however, readers will note that the levels are always described in interactional terms.

The feature of interactional development, which most sharply sep-

Table 4.2.

Levels of Interactional Morality

	Level 1	Level 2	Level 3	Level 4	Level 5
Forms of Moral Balances					
	Assimilation > Accommodation (Self-interest > Other-interest)	Assimilation > Accommodation (Self-interest > Other Interest)	Accommodation > Assimilation (Group) > Self or Other-interest)	Accommodation > Assimilation (Group) Self or Other-interests)	Assimilation = Accommodation (equilibration of Self, Other, Mutual-interests)
	Assimilation of experiences to self's interest. No sustained view of other's interest; no view of mutual interest.	Accommodation to other's interests when forced. Differentiates other's interests from self but no view of mutual interests.	Assimilation of self interests to others' interests as the common interest. Differentiates others' interests from self but mutuality is harmony.	Accommodation of self interests to common interests. Assimilation of common interest to self interest (self is object among objects).	Assimilation of self, other and mutual interests. Self, other, and mutual interests differentiated and coordinated.
Primary Structure: The Moral Balance					
	Vacillates between compliance with others/ thwarting others. Balance occurs when self is indifferent to situations, unequal exchanges of good and bad; momentary compromises.	Trade to get what self wants; sometimes others must get what they want. Balances of coexistence (equal exchange of good and bad in kind and amount).	Emphasis on exchanges is based on sustaining good faith (and excluding bad). Self-interest thought to be identical with others' interests).	Systematized, structured exchanges based on understanding that all persons can fall from grace. Thus balances are conscious compromises made by all people including the self (common interests protect the self's interest).	Integration of self interests with others and mutual interests to achieve mutual, personally and situationally specific balances. (Balances are preferably based on mutual interests or if necessary, compromises or the lesser of two evils.)
	A versus B	Prudential compromises by both A and B.	A compromises to "good" Bs; bad Bs rejected.	A and B = AB common	A = B

Table 4.2 (cont.)

Secondary Structure: Self as a Moral Being and Object

I have unqualified rights to secure my own good.	I have a right to secure my own good as others do.	I am a moral being and demonstrate that by my goodness. Thus I have a right to good treatment as do other people.	All persons fall from grace. Thus I subscribe to the common regulation to promote my own interests as well as others'. (Some private self-interests are not subject to negotiation.)	I have human vulnerability, weaknesses and strengths as a moral agent but I have responsibility to myself, others, and our mutual interest to require that others treat me as a moral object. If I don't, the moral balance will be upset.

Secondary Structure: Others as Moral Beings and Objects

Others are objects who compel or thwart self or who can be compelled by self.	Others are subjects who want their own "good" as I want my own "good."	Most others are morally good; those who act badly to me are exceptions or are "strange," incomprehensible or outside my moral obligation.	Others (and myself) can be culpable. Thus, we must all agree to common regulation to protect our interests. Does not see that the common interest is not synonymous with the mutual interest.	Others also have strengths and weaknesses as moral agents that are variously manifest. I must require others to collaborate in achieving and sustaining moral balances. I need sometimes to forgive others for their impositions, given the complexity of situations and the individuality of others and myself.

Secondary Structure: Taking Chances on Others' Good Faith

Self waits momentarily for others to demonstrate their good faith.	Takes blind chances on others' good faith; can't understand others' defaults as connected with own defaults.	Most people have or should have good faith; negotiates with those of good faith; shuns persons of bad faith as outside one's purview.	To gamble that others negotiate in good faith is foolhardy; the common practice protects all from bad faith and determines the limits of the chances that must be taken for moral balance to be achieved.	Gambles on good faith; instances of bad faith need to be handled in terms of one's moral consideration for one's self, other's individuality, the circumstances, and the self's own occasional transgressions.

Table 4.2 (cont.)

Secondary Structure: Righting Wrongs Self Commits (Guilt)

No idea self can do wrong; others cause self's wrongs.	Self can make a mistake (in the sense of taking more than others will allow).	Self can commit wrongs, irrespective of intent. Self confesses and must "pay for" wrongs before one can be readmitted to the moral exchange.	Given the complexity of life, self can commit wrongs; reparations re-establish moral balance.
Redress: blame projected.	Redress: avoid further difficulty with other.	Redress: debt must be cancelled by repayment.	Redress: wrong cannot be undone but can be repaired, forgiven, or explained.

Overall Justification for Balance at Each Level

Others force me/I force them.	Others get what they want so I deserve to get what I want.	I commit myself to the common structured exchange, so I deserve the same considerations and privileges as others receive from common practices.	I am a moral agent among other moral agents; thus I am responsible to others, myself, and to our mutual interests; we are a part of each other's existences.

Reason for Transitions between Levels

Increased capability of person to fend for self and awareness that others' desires and interpersonal exchange exists; negotiation is possible and necessary.	Growing awareness of the self's isolation from others if others' interests are not taken into account.	Basic assumption of self and other's goodness becomes insupportable in the face of countering evidence that others act with bad faith on occasion.	Admission of self's culpability; recognition of the insufficiency of common practice to resolve moral dilemmas in sufficient depth for self's and others' needs and rights.

arates it from cognitive development, is that real, that is, self-conducted, moral construction within social negotiation is thought to begin even during the first year of life and to continue throughout life. The interaction between baby and caretaker becomes a moral situation since the baby's self-interests are not always immediately served. The usual and the cognitive supposition that young children are morally deficient and always self-serving seems simplistic and possibly not correct. However, young children are especially vulnerable to stress, so they need optimal conditions to give evidence of their moral understanding. Their moral failures may be due to limited resources rather than incapacity. The point is that from the early months of infancy, social life requires and fosters interchange that rapidly becomes morally bilateral and reciprocal, and infants are not without moral power in these circumstances. In fact, they can be intransigent if their needs are not met, but their parents' own self-interest immediately necessitates some accommodation from infants. More detail and evidence about the morality of the very young are provided in Chapter 14.

Because the agent is always viewed as an actor, he or she can only develop as a result of actual social-moral experiences. The motivations for development are 1. practical social experience that helps people realize that all benefit when interactions are moral, and 2. the social-psychological need of all persons to regard themselves as moral. To elaborate on Sesonske (1957), pressing the legitimacy of one's own claims is soon understood by the very young to be an admission, in itself, that others also have legitimate claims.

The educational intervention that logically flows from the interactional formulation is moral conflict itself. It is a full-bodied confrontation with one's own and the others' ideas, emotions, and interests within the context of real situations. Because practical reasoning, not classical logical deduction, is involved in real moral dilemmas, development does not depend on learned sophistication. Instead, opportunities to participate in social interchange, which more likely occur in open than in closed societies, are necessary. The complexity of a society is not relevant; the complexity of all human interchange in itself is sufficient to produce development.

The two systems agree that people must be disequilibrated in order to develop (no one need cope when there are no problems to face). But they differ as to the kind of conflict that is necessary. In the cognitive view the conflict is cognitive in nature; in the interactional theory, threat or the actual experience of miscarried or failed relations with others (the self's reactions to the self and the other, the other's reactions to the self, and the other's reactions to him or herself) constantly provide social disequilibrium. There are limits, of course. Persistent, drastic experiences that are never mutually resolved can be harmful. Children then lose expectancy that good faith in dialogues is possible, that is, confidence that their self-interests will be recognized and considered, if not necessarily fulfilled.

Comparison of the views of moral development presented in the two systems was a main task of the research which is described in later chapters. Here the readers may find a summary of the two views of development helpful (see Table 4.3).

Different Views of Moral Action

The Cognitive View.   The study of action has been of secondary interest for the cognitivists, primarily focused as they were on development. Also the study of thought probably seemed sufficient, given their earlier general view that people's action judgments must accord fairly well their stage of development. Kohlberg (1969) had early written that action is a function of individual differences and situational specificities and that neither of these considerations was necessary for the advancement of his theory. This thought follows the cognitive view that those who make moral decisions are expected to rise above the specific aspects of situations. And individual differences, in themselves, are not generally interesting to science (only being so if they characterize a subgroup whose nature might modify or elaborate a theory). Kohlberg (1976) later also argued, as previously noted, that "moral behavior is not a proper external criterion for 'validating' a moral judgment test" (p. 46). The logical consistency of the theory itself and its developmental findings, he seemed to be saying, was sufficient validation. The conclusion readily follows that the people act according to the stage of their attainment.

Still, some early stipulations about moral action were set forth. Turiel and Rothman (1972) suggested that the levels of action and reasoning of those who had reached a higher stage should more often be the same because their more developed structures of thought would more adequately deal with real-life problems. Kohlberg (1976) also wrote, "To act in a morally high way requires a high stage of moral

Table 4.3.

Comparison of the Formulations of Development According

to the Cognitive and Interactional Theories

Aspects of Development	Cognitive Theory	Interactional Theory
Starting status of the young	Blindly obedient, then egoistically self-serving	Morally naive but immediately induced to participate reciprocally
General description of movement	Invariant stage sequence recapitulates the history of moral philosophy	Gradual progression toward more complex, discriminating dialogical skills
Necessary condition	Logical development	Social-emotional experience
Motivation for development	Comparison with others' higher stage thinking and preference for more differentiated moral thought	Practical realization that more differentiated exchanges and solutions work better. The need to regard oneself as moral.
Vehicle of change	Cognitive-moral disequilibrium	Social/intersubjective disequilibrium
Use of moral tradition	Rediscovers historical moral principles; deductively using these to make decisions	Uses historic moral principles in own constructions; reinterpreted, creative use of tradition
Social interchange	A sufficient but not necessary element of development and action	The necessary but not sufficient element of development and action
Limiting condition	Lack of exposure to organizationally complex societies	Human interchanges that prevent participation whether in simple or complex societies
Recommended educational intervention	Exposure to higher stage moral thought which produces cognitive disequilibrium	Opportunity to participate in actual and important moral experience

reasoning. One cannot follow moral principles (Stages 5 and 6) if one does not understand or believe in them" (p. 32). Presumably then, behavior and thought of persons of lower stages match only when representatives of convention or authority are present and vigilant. This difference between principled and conventional reasoners brings out an assusmption of the stage theory which Locke (1980) pointed out: Autonomous or self-chosen morality (as common sense thinks all morality is) typifies only persons at the principled level. Of course they are rare.

More recently Candee and Kohlberg (1982) observed that "low level correlations are repeatedly found between moral knowledge (thought assessed in interviews) and performance." To deal with this problem, Kohlberg, Levine, and Hewer (1983) recently proposed several elaborations of stage theory. People are thought first to make a moral judgment by reasoning (a deontic choice) and then a second judgment as to whether they are responsible, "either by virtue of their Stage 5 reasoning or by virtue of their B-substage intuitions" (p. 51), and third, they may act. B-substage reasoning, which is newly proposed, is thought to occur at lower and higher stages although it is said to have prescriptive and "universalistic" qualities. No predictions are given for the action of persons at substages other than B or stages lower than Stage 5, nor are relationships among actions in different situations considered. Measurement of relationships between capacity and behavior are also expected to be improved in future research as the more standardized methods of scoring are used, which are described in the recent manual by Colby, Kohlberg, Gibbs, Speicher-Dubin, and Candee (1983).

Whatever the eventual empirical status of the recent additions, they do not revise stage theory. Action follows stage-specific cognition, and emotion and differences among situations are not considered. Thus the cognitive system seems to take clear positions on two current controversies among psychologists: the primacy of emotion or cognition [see Zajonc (1984) and Lazarus (1982)], and the consistency or inconsistency of personal functioning. The Kohlbergian theory gives primacy to cognition and the thought and performance of people at B substage and Stage 5 are thought to be consistent.

The Interactional View.   Dialogue is the form of all moral activity, and dialogue is action. Thus, the very core of the interactional formulation is action. People use their own and others' emotions about dilemmas as important signals. Emotions are almost always part of dialogue, even when the dilemma is hypothetical. While emotion surely does not describe all there is to moral activity, close attention to practical morality indicates that emotion is one of its persistent features. Communication of emotions, say, moral indignation, may occur precognitively (Zajonc, 1984) and signal a moral evaluation that is not verbalized or not yet entirely known even to the self. At first emotions put people out of motion. They are overcome with emotion, we say. However, when the feeling is negative, people do not tolerate this state for long. They develop motivations that give some direction to their emotions. In moral conflict, first motivations are often heated attempts to defend the rightness of individual moral claims, as Packer (in press) has demonstrated in a detailed analysis of a game situation used in a research project described in this volume.

People want to feel moral, so they work to maintain consistency between their actions and self-views and between moral agreements and subsequent actions. Guilt follows on discrepancies between what people see themselves doing and their idealized view of what they feel they should do.

From the interactional view, two well-known characteristics of practical morality are inconsistency in the quality of the same people's moral actions in different situations and the emotions moral issues generate, both moral indignation and the glow of the good conscience. Thus practical morality cannot be understood unless this inconsistency and the role of emotions are explained. Study of people's strategies of coping and defending when they face moral conflict should elucidate both these phenomena. People will not see an issue if they defensively deny its morally troubling elements or its implications that they may be at fault. Or they may see the moral issue but defensively distort both its objective and emotional meaning in the manner of Marie Antoinette's recommendation "Let them eat cake." In these and like instances, levels of moral action fall below aspired levels as well as levels of capability.

In other instances, people may do far better than they usually do if they succeed in coping with the moral costs and emotional elements of a situation. Moral courage is said to be displayed when persons, energized by need and outrage, take action at great cost to themselves. Altogether stress is a part of all moral situations that are at all problematic, and stress can work either to raise or lower the quality of moral action, depending on the context and the person's personal resources. For these reasons, as explained in Chapter 8, we bring ego strategies of coping and defense into the study of morality.

In moral dialogues, mutual expectancies and final agreements motivate people to carry out their side of agreements. The fact that these agreements are "public" contrasts with the cognitive theorists' view of the individual acting alone. The person who makes decisions alone easily reverses judgment in the privacy of his or her mind. For this reason, promises stated in writing give people comfort.

In the interactional theory moral action is thought to be a two step process of identifying the pertinent moral, personal, and objective

elements of particular situations and then separating the wheat from
the chaff; consequently final actions are likely to be found that "fit"
the actors and the situation. When this process is shared among participants, they are more likely to achieve moral balances and enact
them. However, all situations are new, so in some degree moral solutions are always created. Because young children lack experience, they
more often need to create solutions; therefore, for them, moral activity
is harder work.

This view of human social interchange leads to the idea that many
acceptable moral solutions are still not "perfect"—the aspirations of
some philosophical theories as well as the cognitivists' idea—or that
higher-stage reasoning leads to comfortable coordination between
structures and experience (Turiel, 1977). Psychologizing morality, as
we do, necessarily relaxes requirements that morality should always
be pure or certain. Of course, this troubles people who hoped for
clarity, but everyday life leads to compromises, temporary injustices
that are rectified later, and choices between the lesser of evils. From
this reasoning, the interactional system implies more awareness and
forgiveness of human fallibilities and complexities than most formulations. Even the possibility that feeling *should* on occasion override
fact is not ruled out. (The essential differences in the two theories'
view of moral action are summarized in Table 4.4.)

Other Differences between the Theories

Most major differences between the two theories are evident in their
formulations of moral development and action. However two additional disagreements need to be mentioned: first, contrasting explanations of individual moral differences among persons of the same
age and among citizens within the same society, and, second, the role
of families in children's moral development.

In the cognitive theory individual differences arise from people's
different stages of development. Morally deviant persons have simply
not developed the same capacity as their contemporaries. Kohlberg
and others suggest criminals and juvenile delinquents are at the preconventional level (Hudgins & Prentice, 1973). Since people's logical
development is the precondition of their moral development, simple
environments, such as simple tribal societies, may not require or nour-
ish the development of formal logic. Simple environments put a ceiling

Table 4.4.

Difference in the Views of Action in the Two Theories

Conditions of Action	Cognitive Theory	Interactional Theory
Context	Cognitive choices of separate persons drawn from the general rules or principles of their attained stages of development	Dialogue between persons that considers the particularities of the situation
Process	Deduction of proper action from previously acquired generalized rules or principles	Participants' inductive clarification of everyone's self-interests and claims through full and free participation in dialogues
Critical determinant of action choice	Determination of which general class of rules or principles apply to specific situation	Determination of the particular agreement that restores or maintains moral balance between participants
Effects of nonmoral concerns, e.g., emotions or peculiar	Irrelevant but often distorting of proper moral action and choice of the right	Essential conditions that facilitate or deter equalizing moral action
Capacity for enactment	Persons' achievement of the principled stages or B-substage thinking, or judgment that self is responsible	Persons' level of moral skill, the public nature of dialogues, participants' mutual expectancies, the inductive discovery of solutions that match situations and ought therefore "to work"
Deterrents to action	Development only to lower stage	Persons' experience of stress and the situation's potential for moral oppressiveness
Reasons (motives) for acting	Judgment that self is responsible	To maintain a view of self as moral along with maintaining enhancing relations with others
Social stipulations that ensure citizens' moral action	Promote higher stage development in individual persons	Provide opportunities for full participation

on moral development. Diminished opportunities for role taking, which are regarded as sufficient but not necessary conditions for moral development, are also expected to account for variation among people. So far, role taking has not received detailed attention in the cognitivists' research.

Individual differences are explained in the interactional theory in three ways. First, powerless people with limited socioeconomic resources or children with undeveloped moral skill more frequently fail morally simply because they have fewer ways to deal with stress. Second, when environments consistently thwart people's expectancies of good faith, they will constantly be stressed and may then persistently default morally. Nonetheless, honor among thieves and the moral commitments of juvenile delinquents to their fellow gang members suggest that few people are totally unselective about their deviances. Third, even persons of great resources and moral skill may default when they are especially stressed.

The interactional treatment of moral deviance thereby includes the notion of moral default to account for the failure of persons who have skills and resources to act morally but who do not. The cognitive theorists' commitment to a structural logical progression makes it difficult to account for these kinds of temporary "regressions," since structural achievement is thought to be irreversible (see Kohlberg, 1969; Turiel, 1974). Likewise marked and sudden accelerations—instances of moral courage—are explained in the interactional theory as the result of strong motivation and emotional courage. But they, too, give the cognitive theorists difficulty because their strict structural view of development means people cannot act at a stage higher than their development.

Detailed discussion of the differences between the views of the family's role in the offspring's moral development is presented in Chapter 15. Kohlberg (1969) wrote that families are no more important than other social institutions in helping children develop morally. Instead, he favored interaction with peers as a more potent support for children's moral development. According to Kohlberg, moral development is entirely the child's accomplishment. Peers will often be at nearly the same moral stages; thus peer arguments are more likely to be disequilibrating. Children are less likely to comprehend adults' argument, so development cannot usually be expected from these interactions. Consequently, the family is not especially important.

In contrast, the interactional theory expects both families and peers to play important roles in children's moral development because both provide important and persisting social contexts for children to participate in dialogues, achieve balances, and develop a set of expectancies about others' good or bad faith.

Tests of the Theories' "Correctness"

The theoretical background of the two research studies described in the remainder of this book is now set down and following chapters describe how the research work was done. Here we suggest criteria for testing adequacy of psychological moral theories that readers might want to have in mind.

1. How closely does the theory describe the morality of everyday life?

2. Does the theory contain provisions that satisfactorily resolve ordinary moral problems as well as difficult dramatic moral puzzles that sometimes occur?

3. Do the various propositions within a theory seem internally and logically consistent?

4. Can the theory predict the course of moral development and moral actions?

Summary

After bringing out the considerable differences between the two theories, we again want to emphasize their critical similarities. In being constructivist, both theories depend on the power, complexity, and inventiveness of the human mind; they only disagree about which ingredients of mind are relevant to moral activity. Neither avoids the naturalistic fallacy; both are based on an ultimate ground that singles out one preferred morality instead of others. By choosing grounds, both theories are liberated from the scientific stance of remaining neutral about values, so they are able to deal with moralities that vary in quality. Each in its own way distinguishes between good and poor morality. Both agree that the study of moral development is a task especially for psychologists and that an efficient way, but not the only way, to understand any phenomenon is to learn how it comes into being; they disagree, however, about priorities: Is it strategic to focus first on action or on development? As we later move to relating the research results, we will be as interested in these theories' similarities as in their differences.

Briefly reiterated, their different views of development and action essentially spring from Kohlberg's model of the moral agent's single-handed moral reflection and Haan's view of the moral agent's immersion in real and imagined social interchange and conflict. Oversimplifying in a way that slights both theories, we can say the cognitive model is that of rational being, the interaction model is that of social being.

PART II

DESCRIPTIONS OF
TWO INVESTIGATIONS

Chapter 5

YOUNG ADULTS' AND ADOLESCENTS' MORALITY

Psychology has to focus its descriptions on what organisms have become focused on. . . . Otherwise there would remain a white spot on the landmap of possible scientific knowledge (Egon Brunswik, 1939, p. 40).

The crucial point is that while God may not gamble, animals and humans do, and that they cannot help but to gamble in an ecology that is of essence only partly accessible to their foresight (Egon Brunswik, 1955, p. 236).

FROM TIME TO TIME we have suggested that the social scientific study of morality might provide fresh understandings of the practical moral basis of life. This hope is fueled by two thoughts. First, the efforts of philosophers have not resulted in clarity or consensus about the nature of morality and a number of them look to empirical study for new information (for instance, Anscombe, 1969; Locke, 1979 & 1980). Second, moral exchange among all people is as common as the air we share and breathe; therefore it seems that direct investigation should be able to describe practical morality. In any event, we now describe two complex research projects that were designed to learn about morality as it occurs in situations that are close to life. The cognitive and interactional systems provided two different measuring sticks of the students' morality.

Schedule of Contacts with the Participants

For these studies we recruited groups of young people who were friends. For the adolescent study we found six friendship groups from churches and youth centers, each consisting of approximately five boys and five girls; for the young adult study, 15 friendship groups of four men and four women were recruited from the dormitories at the University of California, Berkeley.

The adolescent friendship groups were different; the members of each group were either all white or black or all junior-high or senior-high students or all from families of lower or middle socioeconomic status. Two groups were from churches in Berkeley, but the other four were contacted in churches and youth centers in communities where residents were predominantly of lower or upper middle socioeconomic status. The university groups were quite varied in background, although all members were first year students and accomplished academically. A typical university group included three students from Los Angeles, two from Marin County, two from small Bay Area communities, and one from Sacramento. Fathers' occupations ranged from fork-lift operators and auto wreckers to architects and aerospace engineers; families ranged in size from one child to 12 children. The young people's ambitions varied; they range from three who thought they would go to graduate school or law school to two who were undecided. The students were majoring in business, history, economics, psychology, and biology; two had not yet chosen a major.

After contracts for all members of a group were signed, the participants were individually interviewed to get their reactions to several hypothetical moral dilemmas and descriptions of themselves and their friends. Later they participated as friendship groups once a week in a series of five group experiences. Most groups played "moral games" that threw them into direct conflict with each other. These games are described below.

"Comparison" groups were needed to highlight the effects of the moral games, so five of the 15 groups in the young adult study discussed hypothetical moral dilemmas for five sessions. In the adolescent study, a different kind of comparison group was used. Two or three friends, known to each group, were recruited, but they were only interviewed and did not participate in the group experiences. When the group sessions were completed, all participants were again individually interviewed to see how they handled hypothetical moral dilemmas, and the young adults again described their friends. Three to four months later, we interviewed the participants for the third and last time with regard to hypothetical problems.

Why We Chose This Research Design

By observing the group sessions, we expected to learn how moral action occurs in different situations. We also expected to learn more about moral development. The intervening group sessions were expected to facilitate development and comparison between moral scores from the first interview with those obtained in the later interviews would allow us to assess whether development had occurred. The group experiences, which involved either discussion of hypothetical dilemmas or direct moral conflict in games, were meant to produce "cognitive disequilibrium" as well as "social disequilibrium"—the two different vehicles of development for the cognitive and interactional theories.

Group discussion of hypothetical dilemmas is the curricular intervention the Kohlbergians recommend for the facilitation of development. From the standpoint of the interactional theory, discussion of hypothetical dilemmas is an intellectual exercise that only weakly disequilibrates; fuller socioemotional experience is required to bring about social disequilibrium. The game groups were designed to provide this experience so the game students were expected to show greater moral gains than the discussion students, especially in their interactional moral scores.

We were not entirely certain that the first-interview scores would give an accurate prediction of the scores from the group sessions, despite the usual supposition of psychologists that reasoning about hypothetical dilemmas is a good and stable test of moral capacity. From the interactional perspective, there are variations in levels of moral reasoning along with important variations in situations, like the degree of stress. Therefore, other factors, like the students' ways of handling stress, the objective character of the games, and the tendencies of the friendship group to become supportive or destructive of its members in reaction to stress, were expected to account for variations in moral scores. In other words, from the standpoint of the interactional theory, context is a critical influence on moral action, but not the only one. People still try to make sense out of what life tries to make out of them.

Several other considerations led us to adopt the research model we did. Morality is most truly witnessed when it occurs naturally as action in a real-life situation, but naturalistic investigation is difficult. A real moral situation that involves the number of persons that researchers need is not easy to come across. Even when such a situation presents itself, it still does not provide all the information that a researcher needs.

For instance, Haan (1975) studied a single natural situation that involved many persons—the 1964 sit-in of University of California students in response to the administration's withdrawal of their rights to free speech. After three months of public argument, which was often couched in moral although civilly disobedient terms, some 800 students held a sit-in at the administration building and were arrested. Haan set out to test the hypothesis that students who acted in accordance with their own moral arguments—sitting or not sitting in—were more "morally mature," according to Kohlberg's system, than those whose actions and arguments did not accord. Although the results supported that expectancy, this naturalistic study had two important limitations. Haan knew nothing about the individual students *before* the sit-in or about special pressures that undoubtedly influenced individual students' actions. For example, some students probably sat-in because their friends did. But one student was much annoyed that the research did not count him as having been arrested, although he had wanted to be. He had been working late at the computer center and did not know the police had arrived at the administration building. When he knew, he rushed there but the police would not let him in, so he was not successful in his attempt to be arrested.

Wanting to control influences on moral behavior, psychologists have devised moral problems to be solved in laboratories. However, the setting is artificial, the moral problems are often trivial, and participants confuse results by their wish to appear morally desirable. An exception to these criticisms is Milgram's (1974) well-known study. His subjects were expected to administer "electric shocks" to a slow learner (actually, the electric shock was not applied). Although Milgram apparently did not intend to study morality, consensus among psychologists was immediate. Subjects who disobeyed Milgram had taken a moral action. The demands of this research surprised and stressed subjects and presumably that is why they did not disobey in great numbers. Many became very upset about exposing their "immorality." This work was widely criticized by psychologists and others for its violation of the subjects' well-being. So it seems laboratory study of morality is caught between two poles: If it is ethically conducted, the moral problems are likely to be bland and artificial; if the problems are vivid and real, the experimenter is likely to be unethical.

The solution adopted for our studies lies between naturalistic and laboratory study. Although the moral games and discussions in our studies were conducted in a "laboratory," they were not laboratory situations but rather "occasions" for instigating moral activity at a particular time and place, so researchers could observe the nature of each person's participation, the objective nature of the situation, and each group's functioning.

We chose to work with friendship groups for two reasons—to secure a naturalistic setting and ethical protection for the participants. Under moral stress, friends in a group provide support and protection to the group and individual members. Cohesive groups can disengage themselves from the research and turn their anger on the researcher. As for the naturalistic setting, the friendship group is the natural social context in which adolescents and young adults make many moral decisions.

We had two similar purposes in using moral games. First, in a stressful game, participants can easily disengage themselves with the minimizing defense that the situation is "just a game." At the same time, people's usual involvement in games indicates that games are "serious." Second, games cause participants to react to one another. This kind of opportunity for action may be as close to real life as research can practically and ethically come.

The Student Participants

First-year University Students

The young adults learned from posters that advertised that friendship groups of first-year students of four women and four men in each group were sought for a research project about morality. They would be paid $3.00 an hour for about 18 hours' work. Fifteen groups were recruited in the order of their application and resulted in a total of 120 individual participants. To avoid biases, we tossed a coin to decide whether the first group that completed contractual arrangements would take part in the discussions or the games. Thereafter groups were alternately assigned to games or discussions until five discussion groups and five games were secured. Five more groups were assigned to games, making ten in all. Only one person, who developed a scheduling conflict, dropped out after attending one group session. The effective sample then became 119 persons.

We secured various background information from the students and asked permission to secure their first-year grade point average (G.P.A.) and their entering Scholastic Aptitude Test (S.A.T.) from the registrar's office. The 119 people did not differ markedly in objective background from their classmates who entered the university in the fall of 1979 (we call differences only those that were greater than 20 percent or separated by one standard deviation). They were much alike in terms of G.P.A. and S.A.T. Verbal scores. Blacks and Hispanics in our sample matched the campus incidence of 3 percent; whites were over-represented and Asians somewhat under-represented. Approximately 28 percent of the first-year students lived in the dormitories in the fall of 1979 whereas 98 percent of our sample did. Some participants probably received financial aid, but unfortunately we did not ask for this information. Fewer of the sample's fathers had received professional training than was the case for their classmates, but more fathers of our sample were college graduates. During the following fall quarter, we checked our sample's rate of return for a second year at the university. All but two students returned (the two had transferred to other universities). Some staff members like to think that the high rate of return was in part due to the experience of participating in this project, which gave these 199 first-year students (in a class of about 3300), what they termed, by their own report, an intensely personal and meaningful experience with their friends.

Adolescents

The scope of the adolescent project was more modest. Because it was conducted first, it was more exploratory. Also, its funding was more limited. For these reasons, more interesting questions were addressed with the young adults. The 58 teenager-participants ranged in age from 13 to 17 years. As has been said above, each group of approximately ten members was either all white or all black, all primarily of lower or middle socioeconomic status, relatively the same age in junior or senior high school, and approximately evenly divided between the sexes. Two white and two black groups were from middle-status families and one white and one black group were of lower socio-economic status. All participants were paid $2.00 an hour.

Two groups were from Berkeley, but the other four were from nearby towns, which meant some traveled as much as 20 miles. Understandably, their absentee rate of 6.5 percent for the group sessions was somewhat higher than for the university students (2.2 percent), who only had to walk across campus to attend the sessions. However no teenager dropped out of the project until the third interview, when two were lost. Despite our efforts to secure blacks and whites of comparable socioeconomic backgrounds, the white teenagers were more often from advantaged homes. The teenagers were not asked for their grades or intelligence scores because we were concerned about the sensitivities of the two lower-class groups.

Because the moral scores of the two contrast subsamples, consisting of the discussion groups from the university and the 17 friends of the adolescents, were to be compared with the game groups, we hoped there would be no differences in their background. They were compared on socioeconomic level of their families, family size, birth order, size of hometown and additionally, for the young adults, grade-point average for their first year of university study and Scholastic Aptitude Test scores. No significant differences were found.

The Staff's Interaction with the Participants

Since we wanted to study a relatively vivid form of moral action but not ethically violate, we wanted the students to be able to cope with the stress they would experience. We wanted the participants to relate to us as partners—which is not entirely possible—and not as "subjects." To achieve these objectives we were always candid with regard to the purposes and operations of the project. The participants were told that the purpose of the project was to study the way young people go about solving social-moral problems as they work together as groups. The formal contract also stated the purpose of the project, the measures taken to protect privacy, the right to withdraw, among other provisions.

When the participants came for the first group session, they were shown the observation room, which was behind a one-way screen; they were introduced to the observers and shown the video equipment that would record their activities. The game groups were warned that, understandably, they might become angry with one another at some points, but that they should try not to carry their feelings outside of the session. We could not prevent their doing so, but our advice seemed to be taken for the most part since later on members reminded one another of it.

The group sessions usually lasted from two and one-half to three hours. Then, the staff leader led a discussion and evaluation of the session's events. These evaluation sessions allowed the students to expend their anger and readjust their relationships. Of course, it also encouraged them to evaluate themselves.

In the last minutes of the fifth group session, the students were asked to evaluate the group experiences. We wanted the students to have the opportunity to "talk back" to us after their some 15 hours— "in a fish bowl," some said. We also wanted to know how seriously the different groups had related to the experiences. After a group completed the sessions, a special time was set for the members to watch themselves on video playback. The parents of the teenagers were invited to these sessions. When results later became available, a brief summary was sent to all participants.

The Participants' Experiences

The following descriptions are given from the standpoint of the participants' experience. Detailed description of the observations and measures is given in subsequent chapters.

The First Interview

After all members of a group had signed the contract forms, appointments were made with each individual student for the first interview, which took two to three hours. (Staff persons never saw the same participant twice, either for interviews or for observation in the group sessions.) The participants' moral reasoning and resolutions for four moral dilemmas were secured in a "clinical" fashion. In other words, they were asked to reason about each dilemma and encouraged to elaborate and justify their thoughts and solutions.

Two dilemmas were Kohlberg's and two posed interactional moral problems. All dilemmas used in these projects are in Appendix A. We give examples here. The first is Kohlberg's story about Heinz, whose wife is dying of cancer. A druggist has a miracle cure which Heinz cannot afford to buy. The question is whether or not Heinz should steal the drug. The major moral issue is, of course, whether life is more valuable than property. Additional conditions that were proposed concern Heinz's obligation if he does not love his wife, if the dying person is a stranger or a pet animal, whether Heinz should break the law, and whether laws in general should be obeyed. An example of an interactional story is that of two friends, John and Charles. John has no driver's license, but he "borrows" his father's car one night and accidentally hits a motorcyclist who falls but does not appear to be badly hurt. The question is whether John should stop or not, how these alternatives can be reconciled and balanced, what Charles should do if John does not stop, and whether their friendship is more important than caring for the possibly injured cyclist.

During the first interview, the young adults also rated all members of their group on a number of qualities, for example, makes penetrating arguments, dominates, is fair, is straightforward, and so forth. They also provided information about their background. The young adults were also handed the California Psychological Inventory (CPI) to take back to their dormitories and complete by the first group session. The CPI is a standard test of personality of 480 statements which are answered "true" or "false." Further description and reasons for collecting these measures are included in later chapters.

The Moral Games

Of the five games, three were the same for both projects. Two games used with the adolescents were too simple for university students, so alternatives were chosen. In both projects, games were ordered according to the same rationale: The first game was relatively easy to handle, the second was intended to be stressful, the third less stressful, the fourth stressful, and the fifth relatively easy. This order was established to protect the participants' well-being and rapport with the project.

A staff leader explained the game but let the groups control the course of the games. At the conclusion of each game, the leader conducted an evaluative discussion about the interactions that had occurred. When anger was voiced toward a member for his or her action, the leader came to that person's defense, suggesting that he or she had been surprised and that this could happen to anyone. Descriptions of the games follow.

Humanus. This simulation was directed by "Humanus," an authoritative male voice on a tape recorder that announces he is a "computer's voice printout." Humanus informs the group that they are the last surviving people on earth after a disaster. He gives the group choices that require group discussion and decision concerning what ten objects they want in their "cell," what kind of group regulation they will use, whether to let a possibly contaminated survivor join their group, whether to help a person who wants to commit suicide, and so on. The moral problems posed are issues of group regulation, preservation of life, and caring for others.

NeoPd (NeoPrisoners' Dilemma). Two subgroups of four persons were randomly selected to play a game similar to the one that psychologists call Prisoners' Dilemma. The game was played for a penny a point, and each subgroup's final earnings were to be divided among its members. Each person had a card that was blue on one side and white on the other. In addition each person had a matrix that indicated the number of pennies each subgroup would receive on each play. The matrix showed that pennies awarded depended on the coordination between the number of blues both subgroups turned up. Cooperation would give both groups moderate benefits while attempts of one subgroup to score heavily would penalize the other. If both groups tried to score heavily, the result was a stalemate with no payoff for either. The intent of one group to gain at the other's expense invariably led to the other group retaliating at the next opportunity. After five plays, the leader suggested that representatives of the two subgroups might want to negotiate with each other; they almost always did and they continued to do so freely after each block of five plays. Group interchange was almost always typified by oscillations between respecting and breaking agreements. Although the principle of the game was readily grasped, the morality of agreements was delicate, and when agreements were broken, moral relations were disrupted. This game was clearly stressful for all groups.

Ghetto. The staff leader first assigned two members to take the roles of police officer and judge. A woman staff person played the role of the "System." All other members were residents of the ghetto. The System tried to co-opt the police officer and, occasionally, the judge. The System also attempted to separate ghetto members from one another by offering some of them small payoffs, suggesting that they could buy their way out of the ghetto. Play involved shooting marbles at other marbles representing jobs; or members could attack the System's "power structure" (a tower of blocks). This continued until the ghetto members understood the immorality of the System and then organized or rebelled against it, a strategy that was evident from the beginning. The moral conflict between personal gain and the common interest was clear. However, other moral problems arose from broken social contracts, using people as means, and so forth.

Starpower. Players were randomly divided into three initial subgroups, identified as the Circles, Triangles, and Squares. They individually traded chips of different colors and values to achieve series of chips that were worth varying numbers of points. Players with more points moved to the "highest" of the three subgroups, the Squares. After several trading sessions, the leader passed control of the game over to the Squares, who then invariably imposed new oppressive rules. As a result, they unthinkingly constructed, to their own advantage, a three-tiered society where possibilities for "socioeconomic" mobility soon vanished. Play usually ended with the lower groups rebelling and refusing to play. The essential moral issue was the conflict between the self-serving stance of the Squares as opposed to the plight of the lower groups, the Triangles and Circles.

Three Countries. Three subgroups were formed to represent three different countries. Each country was given a supply of red, yellow, and green balloons that respectively represented people, food, or money. The game leader passed out "event" cards that brought either good fortune or natural disasters and affected each country's ability to feed its people. Countries could risk their food resources on the "world market" to gain more. Risking a food balloon meant giving it to the game leader, who tried to puncture it with a dart. If a country had insufficient food to feed its people at the end of a bargaining session, the leader "killed" the red people (balloons) by puncturing them with a dart. This simulation of life and death was not stressful for university students; almost all groups easily found the solution: When the three countries pooled or temporarily exchanged their resources, life could be maintained and few people-balloons had to be sacrificed.

BaFa. Two games of a different kind were presented first and last to the adolescent friendship groups. The first game was BaFa. Two "cultures" were formed. Each culture was allowed to practice its designated mode of communication and the expression of its particular values privately. One culture was instructed to be egalitarian and fair but highly competitive, whereas the other was to be authoritarian, sexist, and noncompetitive. Each culture first observed the other in operation; subsequently, single players visited and attempted to participate in the opposite culture. Their hosts accepted them to varying degrees. When all members had visited, play terminated. The mild moral problems were merely over whether or not the hosts would help an "outsider" and whether the visitor could adapt to cultural differences.

Role Playing. The last game for the teenagers was Role Playing. Three situations were involved, including a teachers' strike concerning the government's failure to keep its commitment for food and medical care for poverty-level children; a husband returning home from war after he had been declared dead and finding that his wife had remarried; and a mother's necessity of choosing which of her two daughters would get to participate in a track meet which either one was bound to win. Although these hypothetical dilemmas involved serious moral questions, their theoretical nature did not provide a stressful experience.

The Moral Discussions

From a "library" of hypothetical moral dilemmas accumulated over some years, 15 dilemmas were chosen as appropriate for university students. Three dilemmas were selected. One was intense and two were mild for each of the five sessions. They were presented in fixed order, as had been done with the game sessions. For example, the three moral dilemmas used in the first discussion session were the following:

1. At the end of routine questioning by an FBI agent about a security clearance for a former roommate, Bill is asked whether his roommate had ever been involved with illegal drugs. Bill recalls that one time—and one time only—his roommate came in late, very excited because he had just earned $500 for delivering heroin from one address to another. Should Bill tell the FBI agent?

2. For some years Andrew had been eagerly waiting to join the Peace Corps. At the completion of his training, his widowed mother develops a severe chronic illness. He is her only child. Should he go on to the Peace Corps?

3. The teaching assistant for Gary's science class announces that he will tear up the exam paper of anyone he sees talking. A girl asks Gary for help; he answers he cannot help, but the teaching assistant only sees Gary as he answers. The girl insists she was at fault and tears up her paper, but the assistant will not change his decision concerning Gary. What should Gary, the girl, and their classmates do?

The leader's conduct during the discussions of the dilemmas listed above was determined beforehand. We wanted this person to follow the Kohlbergian recommendations for the conduct of discussions that accelerate moral development. We talked with several associates of Kohlberg's and selected a leader who fit their recommendations: The person we chose had had five years of college teaching experience; she learned the cognitive scoring system by taking part in a four-day workshop conducted by a co-author of the most recent scoring manual (Colby, Kohlberg, Gibbs, Speicher-Dubin, and Candee, in press); she read *Promoting Moral Growth* (Hersh, Paolitto, & Reimer, 1979) and discussed its recommendations for teachers with several staff members who were very familiar with the cognitive system. The following guidelines selected from *Promoting Moral Growth* were established for the leader's behavior. Discussion should first be centered on disagreements over the hypothetical dilemma. The participants should be asked to put their moral reasons in an order of priority, clarify their thinking, and specify the meanings of the abstract words they used. Participants should be urged to take the perspective of each story character. Discussion should be "heated up" by focusing on disagreements among the story characters and among the participants. Each participant should be asked to state his or her thinking and choices. Abstract or general questions like, Why are laws made? should be asked. Interchange between participants should be fostered. Participants should be asked to restate moral problems in their own words and reidentify the main reason for their moral judgment. The leader should complicate the circumstances of the dilemmas in terms of universal consequences, such as, What if everyone decided to steal? The leader particularly should highlight arguments that represent adjacent moral stages, but she herself should remain neutral.

The Second Interview

The participants were again seen individually within two weeks after the group sessions. Four more hypothetical dilemmas—two each based on the cognitive and interactional theories—were discussed. In addition, the young adults rated themselves and the members of their groups again with the same sociometric variables used in the first interview. They also answered a questionnaire concerning aspects of their families' interpersonal relations. This questionnaire is analyzed in Chapter 15.

The Third Interview

Three to four months later the participants were again seen individually. Four hypothetical dilemmas, two based on each moral theory, were presented for their resolution.

Difficulties with the Research

Compared to other studies of moral action, these projects required substantial funding and a considerable amount of time from the participants. Perhaps more important, we had to be concerned that students not become overstressed, so Haan attended all group sessions. In only one instance did she intervene—in the case of a lower socio-economic group of white teenagers. Their argument had veered away from the issue of the game and focused on the girls' anger toward fathers who do not care for their offspring. (Many of these youngsters were reared by their mothers alone.)

Although the games were constructed as occasions for evoking moral activity that we could observe, the students' interests in the experiences carried outside the project. Most groups mentioned that they had discussed their experiences in the dormitory or at their church and youth center—sometimes with anger. Consequently our intention of knowing *all* relevant factors that might bear on moral action was not accomplished. We have no way of knowing how these outside discussions affected our measures. A few participants later told us that they had reconsidered their actions of an earlier session and wanted us to know they had changed their mind. But of course we could not change their scores.

Chapter 6

ASSESSING MORALITY

> The computational morality, on which optimists rely, dismisses the non-propositional and unprogrammed elements in morality altogether, falsely confident that these elements can all be ticketed and brought into the computations (Stuart Hampshire, 1978, p.18).

Background

THIS CHAPTER concerns the technology of assessing morality. Even to begin work, investigators must invent some means of measuring the morality they have in mind. Previous chapters concerned various conceptualizations and assumptions about the nature of morality. Here we turn to the mechanics of its investigation.

Using Numbers to Represent Morality

In psychological jargon, "assessing" means assigning a number, in this case to represent the person's complex processes of morally asserting, reasoning, interacting, negotiating, compromising, deciding, and acting. Plainly, a number cannot adequately represent this complex chain of actions. Furthermore, the research context in which numbers are assigned sets up, in itself, an extraneous moral interaction between researcher and subject since this interaction is quite out of balance. "Subjects" are always objects of researchers' observation, and therefore not persons who expect to interact with researchers in an entirely open and free moral exchange.

The Equitable Imbalance between Researcher and Subject

People who agree to become subjects usually accept the inequality between them and the researcher as legitimate for the following reasons. They are usually compensated—though inadequately—in money or course credits; they hope that they are making a contribution to science; they are curious; and they know that the inequality is short-term. Investigators reason that the inequality is morally legitimate because research is a special case of human interaction that is made "right" by the subjects' willingness to enter the situation and researchers' own conviction that their project serves the "higher" purpose of enriching human knowledge. Clearly no investigator would design nor would any subject willingly participate in a research project if they thought it was worthless. Nonetheless, the worth of any single piece of research is seldom established with certainty. The subjects' contributions are often altruistic because the interaction between researcher and subject cannot be fully equalized. The straightforward moral claims that people ordinarily make on one another are temporarily suspended. This lopsidedness marks the interchange and, undoubtedly, affects the data secured.

For the sake of objectivity, investigators try to assume a third person's attitude of neutrality. But observing, rather than participating in, the interaction, gives investigators an advantage over the subject, especially when the research is about morality. The researchers seem to be morally superior since they judge their subjects' moral worth. But who is to say whether the guidelines proposed by any one scientist are correct? Still, researchers have no other choice; they can only, with embarrassment, become a temporary Godhead.

Altogether, then, the mechanics of assigning moral scores has the following implications. The first is that the researcher knows what morality is and how it is manifested in everyday life. The second is that the complexity of a person's processes (of deciding, concluding, and acting) is reasonably reflected in a single "score." The third is that researcher-subject interaction is in itself a morally imbalanced relationship that can be justified only in the short run. These implications unavoidably limit the worth of research. Moral scores are technical conveniences, not reality in themselves.

Scientific formulations are always metaphors for what might really exist. Albert Einstein made just such a delightful distinction between science and life (Quine, 1966) when he commented that describing the taste of chicken soup is not the same as tasting it. When the science is social science, its descriptions are of life, and to be informative, these need to model life. But they are not life. By extracting generalities, social scientists violate life, even when their only error is to oversimplify it.

Rationale and Procedures for Scoring Morality

Social scientists need to specify just how moral processes can be recognized in actual human interaction. In research, the nature of systems—here the similarities and differences between the two moral theories—ultimately rest on their scoring methods. Manuals for both moral theories set down technical procedures for assigning moral scores. For the remainder of this volume, we report generalizations that were extracted after the manuals for the cognitive and interactional theories were used to assign moral scores to the students.

Each new edition of the scoring manual for the cognitive system has been made more specific in identifying the statements typifying each of the six stages in the system's developmental sequence. The manual used in the adolescent study was not the same as the one used in the young adult study. For the second study, an expanded *Measurement of Moral Judgment: Standard Issue Manual* (Colby, et al., in press) became available.

Using two different manuals could mean that our two studies are not comparable. But we think they are for several reasons. Essentially the same results for both cognitive and interactional morality were found in both studies, as we shall relate in subsequent chapters. Furthermore, no important revision in the cognitive theory—the source for developing the manuals—was made in the interim. An unimportant difference between the two manuals on cognitive theory is that the authors do not include guidelines in the second manual for scoring Stage 6, the highest stage, since it was rarely found. Such a difference could not affect present results anyway because no adolescents had reached Stage 6 and very likely none would have been found among the young adults.

Both manuals for the cognitive and interactional theories focus on the thoughts and actions of people, but they differ in the general mind-set and approach each scorer is instructed to take. Perhaps responding to criticisms from some psychologists who are oriented toward constructing paper-and-pencil tests, such as Kurtines and Grief (1974), the cognitivists' last manual sets down concrete and detailed procedures. Scorers are to focus on two predetermined issues (like preservation of life versus property rights) for each of the six hypothetical dilemmas. They decide—usually from the respondent's first statements—which issue is the person's "chosen issue." Each issue is then broken down into "norms or elements" (like punishment or preserving human dignity). Scorers then determine the proper score by matching the person's responses to the stage-exemplary sentences included in the manual.

We had two concerns about this new manual. The students were not only frequently concerned with issues that were not included in the manual, but also their first statements seldom seemed to represent their true position. At first they seemed to respond "off the top of their head." Because moral decision seems to be a creative process that involves all manner of concerns, we were perturbed by the guideline that a specific "match" to a student's response must be found in the manual. Although we followed these new guidelines, they worried us. They seemed to bend the morality of everyday life too far.

However, we concur with the cognitivists that use of their new manual produces good reliability—that is, agreement between different scorers judging the same responses. However, a limitation is the difficulty of applying this manual to moral problems other than the six hypothetical dilemmas. Nevertheless, the overall conceptual scheme of the cognitive theory is still represented in the manual, and we applied its stage descriptions to the students' responses in the games and group discussions and finally achieved good agreement between scorers.

The procedures for scoring interactional morality, as described in its manual, involve a different approach to scoring. Because interactional moral performance is thought to be creative, the manual does not predetermine the formulations that will be scored. Rather than following highly specific procedures, beginning scorers are first asked to grasp the overall conceptual frame of the scoring system—its structures, the moral balances that are endorsed at each level, and the logic of the transitions between levels. (This overall framework is shown in Table 4.2 following page 61.) A scorer first tries to understand the respondent's overall construction of the moral dialogue in a real dilemma or one imagined by an interviewed respondent. Scorers then identify the conditions of the moral balance that the respondent finally endorses. Having achieved this general understanding, scorers then turn back to separate the responses into units of actions and/or thoughts and assign a score showing the level of each one. From this array of scores the respondent's pivotal statements and/or actions are determined. Initial responses are hardly ever determinative since they are often crude, ill-considered, and badly formulated. Since confronting a moral dilemma is always stressful in some degree, people inch their way through. The final score is based on one of two considerations. Either it is given on the most frequent score assigned to the separate statements *or* on the respondents' final switch to a different level of thought and action as they face countering arguments and accommodate to new or developed evidence. These procedures were designed to put the scorer, as much as is ever possible, into the mind of the actor.

The cognitive theorist depends on the idea that morality is represented by cognitive-logical competencies. If morality is a function of the person's moral-logical operations, then the cognitivists' scoring system is the correct one to use, since the character and threads of people's logical steps can usually be traced. However, the interactional system is based on the assumption that all circumstances of the negotiable, objective situation and all reactions of the discussants are critical. If morality is a process of interacting with particularized circumstances and if participants' emotions, motivations, and practical reasons are totally engaged, then the interactional scoring system is the correct one.

The two approaches point up an old and sometimes bitter controversy among psychologists about the best way to assign scores: Can understanding of people's meanings be truthfully (and therefore better) achieved by scoring their specific and concrete responses—a procedure of relatively great precision—or must "true" understanding of their meaning be obtained by scorers' reconstructing organized meanings, a procedure of greater approximation but perhaps greater validity?

Preparations for Scoring

Two series of training sessions were held before the research was begun to prepare approximately ten graduate students in psychology or educational psychology to become observers, interviewers, and scorers of the two moralities. To ensure that we would assign proper cognitive scores, two different sets of expert scorers in the cognitive and in the interactional systems each gave week-long workshops.

We assigned moral scores for interactional and cognitive morality in a variety of contexts. Also, one goal was to determine whether levels of moral functioning remain consistent or change in different situations. Consequently, as previously described, both projects were conducted in two main contexts—three individual interviews and five group sessions—so each student received eight moral scores. In the young adult project the group sessions were further subdivided. Five groups discussed hypothetical dilemmas and ten groups played moral games. All adolescents played games except for 17 friends of the game participants who were only interviewed. Each moral game posed a different problem. Although the hypothetical dilemmas presented to the discussion groups were different for each session, the general social situation remained the same.

The material for scoring individuals' moral reasons and actions was obtained in the same way for both interviews and games. Interviewers recorded each student's responses to the hypothetical dilemmas; observers recorded the moral responses and actions during each group session, with one observer for every two students. Recordings were always scored later and then another staff person also scored the responses at least once so we could assess the agreement among scorers and take average evaluations to obtain a final score.

Because students were seen on eight occasions, we wanted to make sure that evaluations would not be influenced by staff members' prior knowledge of a student's performance; interviewers of a friendship group *never* observed that same group again; interviewers *never* reinterviewed the same student; and observers watched the same student *no more* than twice. All information that might identify a student was removed from the records for second or third scorings; while staff persons might score a record for a student they observed, they would not know they were doing so. To prevent the staff's contaminating their scores for one system with the other, they scored one system, and then they waited a week before scoring the other.

The scores assigned could be either for one stage or level only, or they could be a combination of two, like 2/3, meaning that the student used mostly Level or Stage 2, but also some Level or Stage 3 reasoning or action. Two scores were considered reliable. That is, agreement between two judges as to level or stage was "good" if the scores assigned by two judges were within three-quarters of a stage or level of one another. If the two scorers' evaluations were farther apart, additional staff persons scored the record. Because we made the unusually strenuous effort of scoring all records at least twice, the final agreements were very good, judged by standards accepted by most psychologists. The final scores used were always the average of the scores given by two judges.

Preliminary Description of the Moral Scores

Our purpose is to present findings in a clear, straightforward manner with a minimum of psychological and statistical jargon. Professional readers may want to check the statistical details, so we refer them to two technical reports (Haan, in press a & in press b). We will explain statistical procedures in straightforward language but nonstatistical readers may sometimes want to check the Glossary. We will need to refer to the probability levels of findings; almost without exception we will only report findings that reach at least the .05 level (two tails of the normal curve) meaning that the result has a 5 percent chance of being false but a 95 percent chance of being "true"; findings at the .01 level mean that they have a 1 percent chance of being false, but a 99 percent chance of being true, and so on.

In this section the associations between the two sets of moral scores and the students' background characteristics including their age, socioeconomic status, and sex are first reported. Then the relationship between the cognitive and interactional scores are considered, disregarding for the time being other influences like the effects of playing games or participating in discussions.

Associations between the Moral Scores and the Students' Objective Characteristics

The young adults were all approximately 19 years old. To have been accepted as students at the University of California, they had to have been in the top 10 percent of their high-school graduating class. Likely as a consequence, their age, their scores on the verbal portion of the

Scholastic Aptitude Tests (S.A.T.), and their first-year grade point averages (G.P.A.) were not related to their eight moral scores, but with one exception, G.P.A.s were positively related to both sets of moral scores for the pretest interviews. Possibly those students who were especially grade oriented tried harder to produce "sophisticated" moral reasoning in the very first interview, but this intention would be less functional when they later faced the more emotional group experiences. Socioeconomic status, family size, birth order, and the size of their hometown did not affect either set of moral scores. No differences between the sexes occurred for the interactional and the cognitive scores produced in the group sessions. However males achieved higher cognitive scores during the first and third interviews.

The adolescents varied in age from 13 to 17 years and were white or black and from middle- or lower-class families. We did not collect any measures of IQ, G.P.A., family size, or birth order. Their age was somewhat modestly but consistently related to both sets of moral scores (correlations of about .35); their socioeconomic level related positively to their moral scores for the second interview and for the highly verbal game Humanus. The number and level of significant associations with sex and race were no greater than could have occurred by chance. Altogether, the objective characteristics of these adolescents and young adults did not account for any strong or consistent differences in the level of their moral scores for either system.

Our Interest in Sex Differences in the Moral Scores

Despite the lack of consistent differences between the sexes, we retained an interest in this matter for several reasons. In a number of studies, sex differences for the cognitive system have been in favor of males. For contrary conclusions, see Walker (1984) and Lifton (in press). For supportive conclusions see Holstein (1976), Gilligan (1979), and Murphy and Gilligan (1980). However, the sexes can differ in ways other than the absolute levels of their moral scores. For instance, the variability for both the cognitive and interactional scores was consistently greater for the young adult males than females. In other words, the males' moral activity was more mercurial than that of the females. Averaging males' performance would then make it appear that there were no sex differences. Knowledge of this sex-linked variation and the longstanding controversy over the possible sex bias in the cognitive scores caused us to take the students' sex into account in all later analyses. Sex bias is not just a feminists' issue (Gilligan, 1982); if a theory is to characterize the morality of all humankind, it should apply irrespective of sex.

Relations between the Cognitive and Interactional Scores

The shapes of the distributions of moral scores for the two systems were different in both the adolescent and university samples. The interactional scores were higher for the third interview and for *all* five group sessions, while the cognitive scores were higher only for the first and second interviews. In addition, the interactional scores had a greater range than the cognitive scores in seven out of the eight situations. These two differences are depicted in Figures 6.1 and 6.2, which show the arrays for pairs of the interactional and cognitive scores for each young adult. In Figure 6.1 are shown 350 pairs of scores obtained from the three interviews and in Figure 6.2 the 558 pairs of scores obtained from the group sessions.

Comparison of the arrays shown in the figures indicates that the differences are especially striking for higher moral levels; applying the interactional system results in many higher scores. The two systems do agree rather well over the assignment of scores in the lowest range of Stage and Level 2, although the number of pairs here is small. Cross classification of the adolescents' scores produced these same patterns. In other words, the two scoring systems result in an agreement about low-level morality, produce substantial disagreement for high-level morality, and moderate agreement for middle-level morality. Also the two figures show the greater variability of interactional scores. These major differences occurred despite the sizeable statistical associations between the two systems, which for the young adults was .51 for the interview scores and .66 for the session scores. Somewhat lower levels, ranging from .19 to .68, were obtained for the adolescents.

Comparison of Figures 6.1 and 6.2 also indicates that interview scores for both interactional and cognitive morality are more tightly clustered than are the session scores. This difference brings out a main

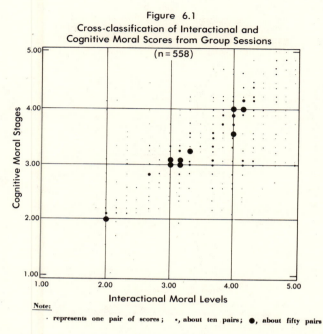

Figure 6.1
Cross-classification of Interactional and
Cognitive Moral Scores from Group Sessions

Note:

· represents one pair of scores ; •, about ten pairs; ●, about fifty pairs

reason why we undertook these two studies: We suspected that the level of moral performance varies from one situation to another, and that doing morality produces more variability than talking *about* morality. Most moral research, done by the cognitivists as well as other developmentalists, relies on scores obtained in interviews. The present results strongly suggest, moreover, that moral performance in interview situations is highly constrained. In fact, every measure of variability in both systems (*the standard deviation*) is higher for the group sessions than for the scores from interviews. But action in these group sessions is closer (but still not identical) with action in everyday life while successful performance in an interview situation is more likely to be an intellectual exercise. This finding, based on these large arrays of scores, indicates that studies of moral interviews are no substitute for studies of moral action. Comparison of Figures 6.1 and 6.2 also suggests that requirements for action have a two-pronged effect: More lower as well as higher scores occurred in the group sessions. Later we will be able to show that when the students were stressed, they either morally defaulted or rose above the situation.

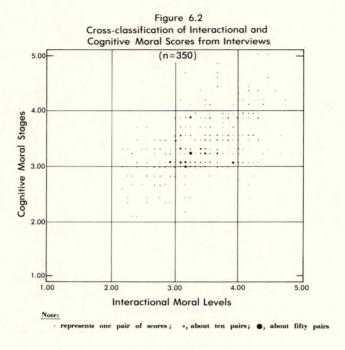

Figure 6.2
Cross-classification of Interactional and
Cognitive Moral Scores from Interviews

Note:

· represents one pair of scores ; •, about ten pairs; ●, about fifty pairs

Summary

The limitations of attempting to assess complex phenomena like morality, the implicit moral imbalance between investigator and subject, and the hubris of investigators who would research morality were discussed. Readers were also reminded that science is merely a metaphor for what may exist in the real world; it is not the real world. We argued that the fundamental test and meaning of cognitive and interactional morality ultimately and entirely depend on their scoring systems as described in their manuals. The different scoring strategies recommended in the manuals for the two systems and our training procedures were described.

Preliminary and general descriptions were then made of the scores attained by the students. The procedures for obtaining reliable measures of cognitive and interactional morality were described. Neither set of moral scores were related to the students' background characteristics of age, socioeconomic status, and so forth, with the exceptions that the young adult males tended to have cognitive scores for interviews and they were more consistently variable in both moral systems than the females. Comparison between the two sets of scores showed that the interactional scoring system produced not only higher scores but also a greater range than did the cognitive scoring system. Most important, the group sessions produced more variation in both cognitive and interactional action scores than the interviews. This last finding, we argued, means that researchers on morality cannot substitute interview scores for action scores as authentic measures of people's morality.

Chapter 7
FRIENDSHIP GROUPS
AND SITUATIONS

Norma Haan, Eliane Aerts,
and Kendall Bryant

Social anthropologists may record fairly wide variations in
the range of the morally impossible and also, I believe, some
barriers that are very general, for example . . . there are also
types of disloyalty . . . particularly disloyalty to friends, which
are very generally, almost universally forbidden and forbidden
absolutely (Stuart Hampshire, 1978, p. 9).

MORAL DECISION and action, and also moral development,
take place within contexts. In this chapter we analyze two contexts for the implications they have for moral activity: first, the meaning and importance of friendship groups, and second, how different
situations affect moral activity. The analysis will show why we worked
with friendship groups and with a variety of situations. We describe
how these two contextual effects were measured and how the measures
worked within the research. We do not yet report how these contexts
affected the students' moral performance and development. These
results are described in later chapters.

Background Considerations

Moral Activity in Groups

To describe the moral activity in group situations, we draw on the
analysis of games as social episodes by Harré and Secord (1973) and

on analyses of Garfinkel (1967). Consistent with the inclinations of mainstream social scientists, neither discussion took morality into account. But we extend these analyses to suggest that people's moral commitment leads to the expectation that others share the same moral commitments. Networks of moral expectancy are especially clear among friends. *In fact, unalloyed moral commitment only makes sense if one's companions are also morally committed.* If they are not, prudent self-protection is needed. Nevertheless, when people—even friends—first face a moral problem, they have conflicting views about the legitimacy of one another's claims. The function of their dialogue is to winnow everyone's self-interests to determine which interests are legitimate and to what extent.

Moral episodes and games are similar in that both have rules of fair operation. The common but not always explicit rules of practical moral dialogues seem to be that all may speak, none may dominate, and all participants can veto if they think a proposed resolution violates their own or any other participant's legitimate self-interest. Needless to say, these rules are violated, but when they are, "public opinion" exerts a countering force. The culprit is penalized not only by the victim but also by outside observers if only by a passing coldness that signals temporary distancing. Unlike games, moral interchanges seldom end in a clear victory for one party over another. Instead, the expected moral outcome is the restoration of balance and harmony within the group.

Moral episodes also have some similarity to the liturgical model of social episodes, described by Harré and Secord (1973). In everyday life, morality has a flavor of "sacredness," that is, inviolability in human affairs. It tests the quality of social life; without morality there could be no peace or enhancement among humans, nor could others' actions be reasonably predicted. This necessity of human sociability is implicitly but seemingly universally understood. The absence of moral concern distorts and destroys humans and their affairs; therefore people protect and are moved by its practice, almost as if it were a sacred ritual. If people do not at least profess moral commitment, they are excluded from community membership and are regarded as not quite human.

A potent, but concealed, force is the moral concern that the very formation of a group brings into play. The group, as a group, becomes committed to its survival and is even hopeful that it can enhance its self-esteem. But if the group's exchange is not marked by moral sensitivity, both its survival and its self-esteem are jeopardized and members will defect. People experience the moral meaning of situations only in relation to others.

Directly faced with moral problems individual members start tentative actions from their initial reactions but make adjustments as their and their fellows' assessments of the situation are formed and become clear. This interactive basis of morality means that no definite demarcations occur between thought, spoken thought, emotion, and action. To speak of one's thoughts and emotions during moral conflict is already an *action,* even if it is only an attempt to persuade another. Discrepancies between moral thought and act occur only when people engage in deliberate falsification of their positions.

Emotion: The Constant Companion

Underlying our work is the idea that the emotion of moral stress is a constant accompaniment of all moral problems. If a moral problem is not stressful, it is not a problem; its resolution is automatic. Moral problems cause people stress because their view of themselves as moral beings and their group as morally functional and sensible is challenged. To think of oneself as immoral and recognize that others also view you as immoral unbearably threatens one's membership. To continue voluntary membership in a group that one considers morally insensible is to consider oneself a fool.

The reasoning above leads to a practical research plan, revised from ideas of Garfinkel (1967). If moral exchange is to be understood, then the group's moral functioning must be put under pressure. The resulting stress will expose the basic rules that govern the moral exchange of the group and its members.

Stress is a tricky concept, however. Ultimately, stress is in the "eye of the beholder." Two people can evaluate the stressfulness of the same situation in different ways. They may disagree because they have different positions in relation to the problem, whether they are the victim or victimizer for instance; they may have different histories in dealing with just this kind of stress; they may be in different states of vulnerability at the onset of the problem. Therefore stress is not a matter of objective reality. Despite people's discrepant evaluations, the general meanings of stress are shared and well understood by people in their everyday lives because we all participate in common human experience. We know when we are under stress and recognize when others are. Still, situations can only be identified as stressful because they cause stress—an entirely circular line of reasoning. But we do reasonably well in predicting what circumstances cause stress. The most general, simple, and direct definition is that a situation is stressful because the people acting within it believe it is bad for them.

Despite the complexities of defining stress, we identified two kinds of friendship groups—those led by a single member who was considered fair by other members and those dominated by a single member—and certain situations that we thought would be stressful. (These choices of terms are explained later.) Relying on the interactional theory, we thought dominated groups would likely stress their members since they violate the rules of fair moral exchange, so moral outrage and indignation would follow. In contrast, we thought led groups would alleviate their members' stress. Relying on our common sense, we chose two games, NeoPD and Starpower, that seemed stressful because they would put friends in moral conflict with one another. (We eventually learned that the game Ghetto also caused stress because the groups playing it were clearly distressed.) The factual observations that support these two suppositions will be presented below.

The effects of stress are sometimes misunderstood. Stress does not invariably lead to personal deterioration. Indeed the opposite also occurs. Stress may bring out the best in people so they act far better than they ever have before. They may become more humanized—humble, sensitive, tender—but hardy (Kobasa, 1979). Otherwise, stress may cause some people's moral action to deteriorate. But their outrage may lead to moral improvement in their immediate action and more enduringly in their growth.

Friendship Groups

Friendship groups were recruited because they are a natural context wherein young people make moral decisions and take actions. Even the daily interaction within a friendship group generates moral issues, and members have a stake in maintaining their future relations with one another.

In their intimacy, friendship groups are not unlike family groups, as is discussed in Chapter 15, although friends are not as tightly bound to one another as family members. Being based on voluntary membership, friendship groups have shorter lives, even though the members of the group often strive to perpetuate it. Nevertheless, youth are attempting to build independent lives, so they have special interest in intimate, nonfamilial groups, as can be seen from the number of clubs and fraternal organizations that they join.

Cohesive groups are more than the sum of their members' individual characteristics. They have lives and characters of their own. Individual members play different roles and perform different tasks that the group needs for its survival and well-being. Some members need to be leaders; others peacemakers, facilitators, and humorists. In many ways, friendship groups are microcosms of society.

Like family members, friends know one another's history, so they expect each other to act in certain ways. When expectations are betrayed by moral manipulations and falsifications, the members of intimate groups become troubled. However, when strangers are brought together as they are in many social-psychological experiments, they cannot know one another's history. Thus, their expectations of one another and falsifications can go unnoticed or, at any rate, are often considered not worth correcting (Harré & Secord, 1973). Also, groups of strangers have neither a cohesive moral structure nor a mutual moral future except in a most attenuated way. For these reasons, a friendship group should offer the possibility of revealing a more authentic moral picture of its members. At the same time, the friendship group is more resistant to the intrusion of researchers; its very cohesiveness protects it.

Friendship groups differ from one another mainly in two ways. They are set apart by the characteristics of the members, that is, by their age, sex, race, and so forth, and by the ways they function. As we mentioned before, the adolescent friendship groups we studied varied on several characteristics—age, race, and socioeconomic background. Conversely, the young adults' friendship groups were much more alike. But by the time of the young adult project we were acutely aware that friendship groups do not function alike. Consequently, we secured descriptions of the groups' structures as led or dominated and ways of functioning before, during, and after the group sessions. We describe these characteristics later in this chapter.

Objective Nature of Situations

During the first session, the game groups discovered a fact about their situation that we maintained throughout the five sessions. That is, the staff leader would not act to repair the group's functioning if it began to disintegrate (although he would have if interaction had become extremely chaotic). The staff leader only explained the rules of the game, divided members into subgroups, called the rounds of plays, and tallied points. In contrast and following the cognitivists' recommendation, the staff leader for the discussion groups was directive. She held control and monitored disagreements. When discussion became too emotional, she encouraged members to look at the problem more objectively. In other words, she drew the reserved into the discussion and prevented the outspoken from becoming overly hostile. As a result, members' affective reactions were limited. By acting morally on behalf of the groups, she protected them from stress so they probably did not confront the moral issues fully or deeply. The discussion groups were also deprived from experiencing the satisfaction of mutually solving a moral problem. This seemed to create frustration and apathy which deepened in later sessions.

The difficulties of studying natural moral action which arise, for example, if investigators are not present when action occurs, the ethical problems of interfering by collecting data from people while they are dealing with an actual moral problem, and so forth have usually been solved by having subjects take the role of a hypothetical other person within a hypothetical situation. Our game situations did not entirely avoid this dependency on hypothetical morality, particularly not in the simulations of Humanus and Three Countries.

In thinking about hypothetical dilemmas, the roles of the self as a first and third person are quite separate, so discussants can speak from the third person position; they can easily falsify their private thoughts and hide their real feelings. More convergence between the self acting as a first and third person occurs in group discussions of hypothetical dilemmas because people must take public stances. Even more convergence occurs in group simulations since people's imagination enlivens self-involvement. But the purest expressions of self-morality occur when the moral problems arise from people's own actions. In three games—NeoPd, Starpower and Ghetto—selves were directly involved. These games presented simple, innocuous problems that any participant could easily have solved as hypothetical issues. Conflict arose because of the participants' own actions.

Most of the time discussion students took the position of third person. Since they essentially experienced the same situation for all five sessions, they could predict their experiences and therefore were not threatened. But their boredom by the end of the five sessions was palpable.

The Moral Tasks in the Games

Here we briefly highlight the moral tasks of the games to show why the students' solutions for one game did not necessarily work for the next. In Humanus, classical moral issues of philosophy were involved—life versus death, property, and so forth. The problems were not generated by the participants but they were concerned, as people always are, that they and their group appear morally adequate. All members started with the same opportunity, and discussion involved all members.

In NeoPd, one-half of the friendship group was pitted against the other half, a situation contrary to friends' principles of intimate cooperation and equality. The staff leader offered the subgroups opportunities to negotiate, but promises were often broken, which, of course, exacerbated members' distress. When the subgroups honored negotiations for equal benefits, the moral issue was solved. This game was the most stressful for a majority of the groups.

In Ghetto, two members were selected beforehand to be the judge and police officer, and the System's immoral co-opting of these two members placed them outside their friendship group's community. Most moral violations were committed by the System and when divisiveness arose among ghetto citizens, it was quickly exploited by the System. The solution was for the citizens to organize and defeat the System.

In Starpower, the Squares had the most points and the power to run the game which they often did by oppressing their friends, so the moral issues were wholly generated by the participants themselves. The conflict was resolved readily when the Squares allowed each member a vote, a move most groups took after two hours or more of play.

In the last game, Three Countries, three subgroups were pitted against one another, but luck in drawing the "fate" card was crucial. Tensions were often released by teasing the staff leader about his lack of skill in throwing darts at balloons. Also stress was perhaps avoided because they had learned how to operate as groups, because they could turn on the staff leader, and because luck, not deliberate choice, determined a subgroup's situation.

The adolescents played two other games—BaFa and Role Play. BaFa involved almost no conflict among friends, who were divided into two cultures that had different values and modes of communication. The only issue was whether the adolescents could take the role of the foreign visitor. Role Play was lively and playfully conflictual, but the adolescents were playing imagined roles, so it was not stressful.

How Groups and Situations Were Assessed

Friendship groups and the situations they deal with can be characterized by superficial and profound features. Groups can be described by more obvious features, such as the members' ages, sex, race. But they can also be characterized by more subtle features of how they function and come to decisions. Situations can also be described by the demands of the tasks and decisions involved, for example, either simple discussion or actual resolution of issues. But situations can also be characterized by the more profound features of the moral considerations they evoked and the options available for resolution, for example, whether participants start with equal resources.

Assessment of Groups' Natural Functioning

The background of the adolescent groups was not assessed beyond the objective features of members' socioeconomic status, race, and age. However, the natural structures of the friendship groups were also determined. Consequently, during the first individual interview each university student was asked to rate every other member of their group on 11 characteristics. (They also rated themselves, but here we are not concerned with self-reported personality.) The evaluations included how well they knew and liked the person; whether they saw the person as dominating, straightforward, or as a leader; whether they believed the person was fair, knew right from wrong, could understand the other's point of view, could change his or her own point of view, and could make clear arguments; and finally, how well the person handled conflict. After the five sessions the students repeated these same ratings. This allowed us to assess the experiential impact of the sessions. Each person's score on these 11 characteristics was the average of the evaluations made by seven friends. One general indication of the stability or change in the friends' views is the correlations between the ratings made before and after the sessions, which averaged .55, but ranged from .36 to .72 across the 11 characteristics.

Led and Dominated Groups. We reasoned that when friends of the same age and status are faced with stressful moral problems, their reactions would be differentially affected by belonging to a group that was either dominated or led by one of its members. Dominated groups would have difficulty following the rules of interactional moral dialogue whereby all may speak, none should dominate, and anyone may veto. By its very organization, a dominated group violates a stipulation of the interactional theory that conclusions are moral only when achieved through moral processing. Creative solutions were expected to occur more often in led groups. Moral ends are only accidentally achieved by immoral means.

Three ratings done by the students of their friends before the sessions were used to identify each group as being dominated or led. A group was designated as dominated if a single member had a score of four or more—averaged from seven friends' evaluations—on "dominant" (five was highest). A group was designated as led if a single member had a score of four or more on "leader" *and* an above average score on "fair."

Nine groups qualified as dominated and six as led. Of the five discussion groups three were dominated and two led; of the ten game groups, six were dominated and four led. In other words, the proportion of dominated and led groups was the same as the proportion of game and discussion groups. These identifications were made after the data collection and all scoring were completed, so a group's "label" could not have biased results. Seven of the nine dominated groups were dominated by males and four of the six led groups were led by males, a finding not unexpected for this age group and culture.

Assessment of Groups' Behavior in Different Contexts

By now readers are familiar with the distinctions between the staff-dominated discussion groups and the student-controlled games, and between the student dominated and led groups, and with the distinctions among the five game sessions. We now consider how these differences affected the groups' and individual members' behavior.

Group Functioning as Entities

Because the effects of a situation as moral context may be inferred from the way a group behaves, a Q sort of group processes of 73 items for the adolescent project and a condensed version of 49 items for the young adult project were designed. (For example, "Members distrust one another or trust prevails among all." Other examples are shown in Table 7.1.) This Q-sorting procedure involved dividing the items into steps 1 through 9. A predetermined number of items is placed in each step. The pile for Step 9 includes only those items that are *most characteristic* of the situation (or the person, as is described in the next chapter); Steps 8 through 6 are also most characteristic but in lesser degrees; Step 5 includes items that are intermediate in importance, and the range from Step 5 to Step 1 includes items that are *most uncharacteristic*.

After observing each session, a sociologist and a social psychologist used these Q sorts of group processes to describe each group's functioning. From this, 30 descriptions of the adolescent groups' functioning (5 sessions multiplied by 6 groups) and 75 descriptions for young adult groups (5 sessions × 15 groups) were generated.

The two observers did their sorts without consulting each other; whenever their agreement proved divergent, a third observer made another sort. If sufficient agreement was still not achieved, the observers met, reexamined tapes, discussed the highly discrepant items, and then reconciled their differences. Finally the scores for each item were added and averaged to obtain scores for the five sessions for each group. Later on, 16 items were dropped from the young adults' sorts because some were unreliable, and others were so highly correlated with other items that they provided little additional information. The average agreement between two judges among the remaining 33 items

Table 7.1.

Five Groups of Items That Describe Group Processes[a]

Positive Items	Weights	Negative Items	Weights
Disintegrative versus Integrative Processes			
Members stonewall in conflict situations versus compromising, negotiation	.83	Negotiators play important roles versus conflict is free for all	-.67
Members distrust one another versus trust prevails among all	.82	Groups work together as a whole more than required by game or discussion structure versus group is in disarray	-.61
Members are angry versus members are never angry, but amicable and friendly	.58	Members try to convince each other by reasoning versus use power to win points or don't try to solve problems	-.59
Members are depressed versus members are lively and cheerful	.54		
Hierarchical versus Communal Functioning			
Members have different amounts of status in decision-making versus members are treated equally	.77	Group's organization is communal versus no organization or centrally organized	-.73
Members are excited	.54	Group pressures members to be actively involved versus ignore nonpartici-pants, each operates for self	-.69
		Leaders are oriented toward helping the group complete its task versus leaders are oriented toward maintaining their own status	-.57
Easy versus Cautious Disagreement			
Members overtly disagree with each other versus do not disagree either overtly or in actuality	.79	Members careful and cautious with each other in disagreements versus members are direct with each other whether frank or hostile	-.90
Members work to sharpen differences	.73	Group optimizes its own solidarity at the expense of task completion versus completion of task is priority irre-spective of expense to group or persons	-.62
Active versus Depressed			
Members are active versus members are calm	.88	Members are depressed versus mem-bers are lively and cheerful	-.50
Members attempt to get group's atten-tion by showing off versus no one's actions are more than situationally needed	.75	Members are oriented toward activity leader versus activity leader is ig-nored and rejected	-.47
Resistance versus Dependency on Staff Leader			
Members reject or rebel against the rules or situation versus complete conformance	.83	Members are oriented toward activity leader versus activity leader is ig-nored or rejected.	-.54
Group optimizes its own solidarity at the expense of task completion versus completion of task is priority irre-spective of expense to group or persons	.40		

[a]These item groups were derived from a factor analysis. Weights can vary from 1.00 to -1.00.

was .68 with a range from .53 to .82. These 33 items were reduced to a manageable number by factor analysis (a statistical technique), which located five subgroups of closely associated items. Table 7.1 shows the names we gave these five factors, the particular items that were involved in each group, and their weighing on each factor, which can vary, positively or negatively, from − 1.00 to + 1.00.

The first scale, disintegrative versus integrative processes, represents how groups acted when they are under stress. Members refused to compromise; they were angry and depressed and used power, rather than persuasion, to win points; the group's attempts to accomplish the tasks led to disarray. This scale seemed to represent "social disequilibrium," which leads to moral development according to the interactional theory.

The second scale, hierarchical versus communal functioning, reflects the structural organization of the groups. It indicates whether or not their decisions are made under the influence of persons of high status or whether their processes were communal, which equalizes members' roles and influence.

The third scale, easy versus cautious disagreement, represents the extent of intellectually detached, reflective consideration of the cognitive aspects of issues made by the members as against their caution in disagreement. This scale seems to represent "cognitive disequilibrium," which leads to moral development according to the cognitive theory.

The fourth scale, active versus depressed, reflects the groups' contrasting motivations and emotional tone: It showed whether they expressed active, personalized involvement or apathy.

The fifth scale, resistance versus dependence on the staff leader, reflects the cohesiveness of some friendship groups in opposing the staff leader as contrasted with other groups' compliance with the staff leader's direction.

Descriptions of Individual Students' Behavior in Groups

These descriptions of the groups' functioning were supplemented by observations of individual students' commitment to the group sessions. After each session, both group observers also rated individual students on their involvement and ability to "suspend disbelief" (will-

ingness to commit themselves to the moral tasks even though this was
a research situation). Game members were also rated on their analytic
attitude toward their group's processes. Agreements on these three
variables ranged from .52 to .77 across all sessions with a midpoint
of .72.

Roles the Students Played

At the end of each session, the group observers checked whether
or not each group member had assumed the role of task leader, social-
emotional leader, negotiator, conformist, isolate and antagonist. Scores
for roles were used only when both observers agreed. As it turned
out, the observers' evaluations corroborated the evaluations students
had made of their friends. Those regarded as task leaders by the two
observers (summed across sessions) were given high ratings by their
friends for leadership ($p \leq .001$), making clear arguments ($p \leq .001$),
and being dominant ($p \leq .001$). Those students who were observed
as failing to participate were given low ratings by their friends in
categories of making clear arguments, dominance, and leadership ($p
\leq .01$, $p \leq .001$, and $p \leq .001$, respectively). Students who were ob-
served as antagonists were given low ratings by their friends in
straightforwardness ($p \leq .001$), likability ($r = -.27$, $p \leq .001$), and
leadership ($p \leq .001$).

Preliminary Descriptions of Situations
and Friendship Groups

In the remainder of this chapter we focus on whether groups' and
individual students' behaviors are determined by the experiences of
gaming or discussing or by the nature of their groups' natural organization of being led or dominated.

Friends' Evaluations of One Another:
The Presession Sociometric Ratings

Comparisons of the friends' initial evaluations of one another are
shown in Figure 7.1 for the dominated versus led and the game versus

the discussion groups. However, apart from these comparisons, we can see from Figure 7.1 that all students thought their friends were likable, fair, and knew right from wrong. Most did not think their friends were dominating, leaders, and able to change their minds. They struck a middle ground in judging that their friends were straightforward and that they knew them well (average scores about 3.0, the midpoint of the scales).

When compared to the members of dominated groups, the members of led groups charitably gave their friends significantly higher marks for three qualities: knowing right from wrong, understanding others' points of view, and being able to handle themselves in a conflict. Evidently, these students' experience with one another *before* they entered the project left them better prepared to deal in good faith with the conflicts they would face.

Since the game and discussion groups had been randomly assigned to gaming or discussing, we hoped that they would initially be alike. Nevertheless, the game groups gave their friends higher marks for two qualities: knowing right from wrong and understanding others' points of view.

Students' Engagement with the Moral Tasks

The results for comparing the three kinds of commitment of involvement, willingness to suspend disbelief, and analytic attitude are shown in Figure 7.2. Significant differences between the led and dominated groups were found in the extent of the commitment to suspension of disbelief and the analytic attitude toward group processes. In all five sessions students in led groups were consistently more analytic and more capable of suspending disbelief than were students in dominated groups. Conversely, dominated groups did not freely enter the moral experiences, nor did they try to analyze their group's functioning, perhaps because they were too preoccupied with their own emotional reactions.

Students in game and discussion groups were not significantly different in their commitment. Consequently, even though the discussion sessions were less vivid and dramatic than game sessions, both kinds of experiences were equally involving. However, there were differences on the levels of suspension and disbelief. It dropped markedly

Figure 7.1

Presession Ratings by Group Members of Their Friends   (comparisons of average scores)

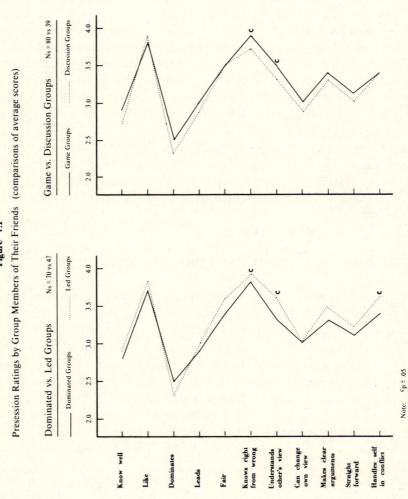

Note: $^c p \leq .05$

and significantly during the games NeoPd and Starpower. The discussion groups generally increased their suspension of disbelief from sessions 1 through 5 (only game students were rated on analytic attitudes). In sum, the game and discussion students were equally involved, but the game students were less able to suspend their disbelief in the more stressful sessions.

The Groups' Functions and Operations during the Five Sessions*

Young Adults' Group Behavior. Comparisons of the groups' ways of acting are shown in Figure 7.3; the adolescent groups are shown as well, but we first consider the university students. The led and dominated groups adapted to the five sessions in distinctively different ways. The dominated groups were consistently more disintegrated, more hierarchical in their operation—significantly in both respects for sessions 1, 3, and 5—and consistently resisted rather than depended on the staff leader. But both groups handled disagreement in a similar manner and displayed the same level of activity. We may conclude then that led and dominated groups differ more in structural ways—their intactness, the thrust of their organization, and their relationship to the staff leader.

The main differences between discussion and game groups lay in the fact that the discussion groups were consistently more relaxed in disagreeing with one another because, we suggest, the conflicts meant much less to them. But they also grew increasingly dependent on the staff leader, because, we think, she was an authority figure, despite her pleasant manner. Other isolated differences were observed. Game groups were less integrated when they faced the stressful Starpower; they were more communal and more active when they organized against the System in Ghetto.

All in all, the hypothesized distinction between led and dominated groups seems verified by the ways these groups operated during the

*Because the statistics in this section are based on small numbers, that is, the number of groups instead of people, some differences in Figure 7.3 are for *p* ≤ .10; that is, they could occur ten times out of 100 by chance. This change relaxes the standards of reporting, so readers should regard these results with caution.

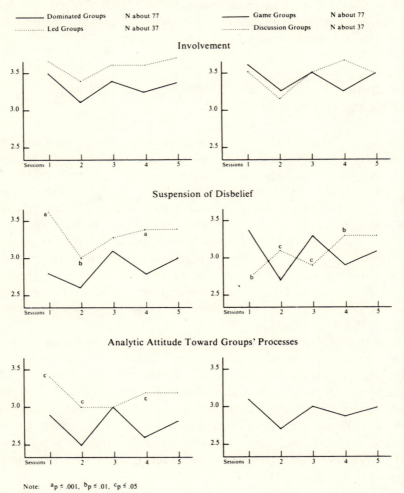

Figure 7.2

Observers' Ratings of Students' Commitments to Group Tasks
(comparisons of averages)

——— Dominated Groups   N about 77   ——— Game Groups   N about 77
·········· Led Groups   N about 37   ·········· Discussion Groups   N about 37

Involvement

Suspension of Disbelief

Analytic Attitude Toward Groups' Processes

Note: ^{a}p ≤ .001, ^{b}p ≤ .01, ^{c}p ≤ .05

sessions. The experiences of discussing (and the groups' different relationships to the staff leader) seemed to prevent disagreement, but
at the same time it seemed to encourage the students to throw moral
responsibility for their operation and direction to the older adult.

Adolescents' Group Behavior.   The profiles for the adolescent groups, all of whom played games, are also shown in Figure 7.3. The Q sort items that became part of these scales were identical for the adolescents except for two items. In this study, led and dominated groups could not be determined and discussion groups were not included, so the adolescent groups could only be compared to the young adult game groups. They have similarities and interesting differences. Their stress profiles are much alike with high levels of disintegrative processes and hierarchical functioning being observed when both played NeoPd and Starpower. But the teenagers' style of disagreement was quite different. When they first entered the project, they cautiously disagreed, but when they confronted NeoPd, they strongly and openly disagreed. Thereafter, they became wary of one another's opinions. The adolescent and young adult groups also had similar patterns of activity during the last two sessions, which were especially marked by their depression during Starpower, and by greater activity in dealing with the easy tasks of the final session. The two age groups markedly differed in their relationships to staff leaders. The university students were resistive, whereas the adolescents depended on their staff leader.

Altogether, the adolescents acted much like the young adults, especially when working with NeoPd and Starpower. However, the adolescents were more mercurial in their manner of disagreement and consistently more dependent on their staff leaders, perhaps because they were younger and more gullible about research.

Roles Students Played

Various roles taken by individual students during each session were summed up for all five sessions, and these scores were compared for members of game and discussion as well as dominated and led groups. Proportionately more conformists and fewer social-emotional leaders were found in dominated than led groups ($ps \leq .03$ and $.04$); nearly as significant was the finding that more members of dominated groups were antagonists and isolates. The discussion groups contained fewer conformists ($p \leq .07$) and fewer social negotiators ($p \leq .10$).

Altogether, then, the groups' natural structure, more than their actual experiences of gaming or discussing, determined the roles members played. Discussion groups probably had little need of social negotiators because the staff leader handled disagreements. She also

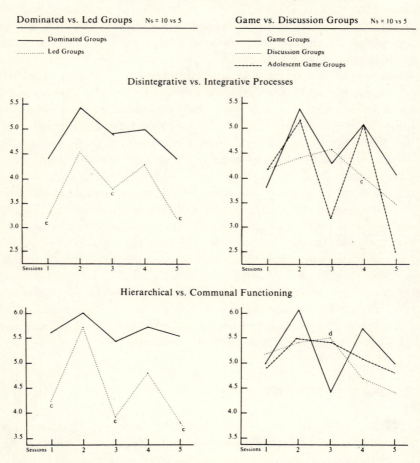

Figure 7.3

Descriptions of Groups' Behavior During Five Sessions

Dominated vs. Led Groups   Ns = 10 vs 5   Game vs. Discussion Groups   Ns = 10 vs 5

——— Dominated Groups   ——— Game Groups
.... Led Groups   .... Discussion Groups
                                                       -------- Adolescent Game Groups

Disintegrative vs. Integrative Processes

Hierarchical vs. Communal Functioning

urged each student to express his or her own opinion; consequently, fewer discussion students probably needed the refuge of conformity.

Friends' Evaluations of Friends after the Fifth Session

After experiencing moral conflicts, the students gave their friends higher marks, compared to their initial evaluations, for being "straightforward" ($ps \leq .001$), and they increased their ratings for

Figure 7.3 (cont.)

Easy vs. Cautious Disagreement

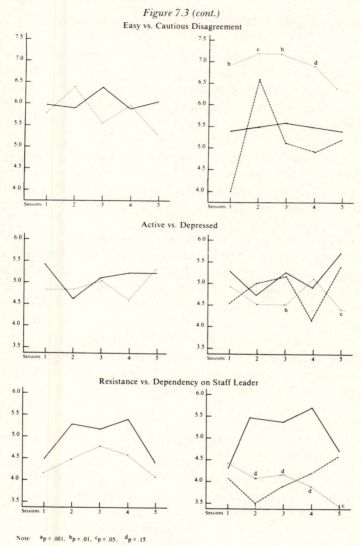

Active vs. Depressed

Resistance vs. Dependency on Staff Leader

Note: ^{a}p = .001, ^{b}p = .01, ^{c}p = .05, ^{d}p = .15

"well known" (*p*s range from .05 to .01). Members of all groups but the discussion students rated each other higher on being "dominating." The discussion group members actually lowered their ratings for "likability" ($p \leq .05$) which we suggest is due to the structure of the discussion situation. Because the Kohlbergian curriculum recommends that all discussants' opinion is to be respected, the students were deprived of the satisfaction of mutually resolving the dilemmas.

Students' Evaluations after the Group Experiences

The students evaluated the group sessions immediately after the fifth session was concluded. Most evaluation sessions lasted about 30 minutes. They were conducted in an open-ended way and video recorded with the students' knowledge. Typed transcripts were made. Two persons not associated with the project studied the transcripts to rate whether the groups seriously discussed the experience or avoided it, usually by cynical joking, and whether group members said that the experiences had affected them. In addition, separate counts were made of the number of typed lines required to reproduce first the students' comments and then the staff's. Ratios of staff to student comments were computed.

Comparisons between the led and dominated groups were significant on all three ratings. The led groups soberly discussed their experiences without cynicism ($p \leq .03$) and reported that they had personally learned from and were affected by these experiences ($p \leq .04$). They, rather than the staff, carried the weight of the discussion in evaluating their experiences ($p \leq .05$). Altogether, the led groups were satisfied with their experience, whereas the dominated groups seemed disgruntled. If individual members benefited, they did not say so in front of their friends. None of the comparisons between the game and discussion groups was significant.

Summary

Descriptions were given of the friendship groups and their particular experiences that we expected might affect moral actions and development. The underlying theme was evaluation of the stress that invariably accompanies moral situations and affects the protagonists' moral activity.

We have established the following two points:

1. Before the group sessions, students in the game and discussion groups and in led and dominated groups described one another quite similarly. Friends were thought to be likable and fair and to know right from wrong. Thus the friendship groups who were to have the experiences of gaming or discussing were rea-

sonably alike and whatever moral differences that might appear could be due to the ways groups and individual students interacted with the different experiences.

2. The classification of friendship groups according to whether they were led or dominated (with balanced representation of game and discussion groups in each classification) was based on the idea that the natural structure of groups themselves is a critical influence on moral action and development. As it turned out, this simple distinction gave distinctively different pictures of the operations of the friendship groups.

Although both kinds of groups were equally involved in the project, led groups were more able to suspend disbelief and take an analytic attitude toward their own group's processes; they were generally less distressed, more communal in their functioning, and less resistant to the staff leader. More of their members took roles of social-emotional leader and less often took the roles of conformist, isolate, and antagonist. At the conclusion of the group sessions, led groups thoughtfully evaluated their experiences. More often they stated that they had been personally affected by the group experiences, and they talked more than the staff.

In comparison, the dominated groups, although observed to be equally involved in the group sessions, were less able to suspend disbelief and take an analytic attitude toward their group's processes; they were more stressed, hierarchical in their functioning, and resistant to the staff leader. Members more often took roles of conformists, isolates, and antagonists, and less often took roles of social-emotional leaders. Dominated students gave higher marks to their friends at the sessions' end for being able to handle themselves well in conflict. Their evaluations of the experience were handled with some cynicism; they denied having been personally affected, and the staff had to talk more during the evaluation to keep the discussion moving.

Although game and discussion groups were equally involved, according to the observers, game groups were more able to suspend disbelief—except during the two stressful sessions of NeoPd and Starpower. They were more active and resistant to the staff leader but more cautious in their disagreement with one another. More game students took roles of conformists and social negotiators and the groups gave their members higher marks at the conclusion of the group experiences for being able to handle themselves well in conflict. Discussion groups did not generally suspend disbelief. They were less active and more dependent on the staff leader who encouraged members to disagree, so there were few conformists and fewer social ne-gotiators. In the end, however, they liked one another less than they had before the group experiences began. The intellectual exercise of discussing hypothetical dilemmas in a group seems to have been a wearing but pallid experience that eventually generated some es-trangement among friends.

Altogether then, the natural structure of friendship groups had expected effects. Led groups operated smoothly and consistently in an egalitarian fashion, and members took this experience very seri-ously. Dominated groups were perturbed, disjointed, and inconsistent; members clearly did not pull together and some were forced into becoming conformists, isolates, or antagonists. Gaming had the ex-pected effects of encouraging fantasy, activity, and self-determination. As groups, the participants behaved differently as they moved from one kind of a situation to another. Discussion groups were well reg-ulated by the staff leader, and they counted on her to modulate their disagreements. The similarity of their situations produced consistency in their behavior, but in the end they liked each other less.

We have identified and elaborated upon the two main aspects of context: the natural structure of friendship groups and their different types of experience. Despite their importance, these two influences did not fully account for the variation observed in either moral action or development as later chapters will show. By their own invention and strategies for problem solving, people make their own contributions to moral resolution, sometimes irrespective of the immediate situation and their group's propensities and organization. This is a question of people's ego strategies—how they cope or defend themselves against the moral problems they face.

Chapter 8

COPING AND DEFENDING
WITH MORAL CONFLICT

> The person will cope if he can, defend if he must and frag-
> ment if he is forced to do so. . . . Coping does not insure
> success, nor do defending and fragmenting entail failure,
> since outcomes depend on matches between situations and
> resources (Norma Haan, 1977, p. 79).

The Connection between Ego Strategies and Moral Conflict

WHEN PEOPLE confront moral issues, they experience a degree of stress. They then undertake a complex sequence of considerations and strategies. At first, each person understandably believes that his or her own self-interest should legitimately take priority. Yet, faced with others' self-interest, all feel pressured to adjust their self-interest to those of the others, but they still need to maintain a sense of their own moral honor.

Stress is not always a detriment to the resolution of moral disputes. It may heighten people's awareness and involvement and increase their efforts to cope, thereby improving the quality of their deliberations. But more often, stress reduces people's effectiveness. When "overloaded" with threat, they often become defensive and consider only some aspects of their situation or warp the meanings they do recognize.

In our studies, stress arose from the nature of the tasks, but also from conflict generated in the friendship groups themselves. Nevertheless, some students were not stressed in stressful sessions or were stressed in nonstressful ones. Ultimately, of course, stress is in the eye of the beholder, a consequence of a person's view of a situation. In this chapter we are concerned with the strategies that individual students used to handle moral stress—in other words, how they coped and defended.

When we say people cope with stress, we mean that their considerations and choices of actions are likely to be more apt, differentiated, and sensitive. When persons defend themselves, their considerations and actions are likely to be distorted, diffused, rigid, and obtuse. This reasoning is behind a major hypothesis of this work: Students' moral levels will be higher when they cope and lower when they defend. From the interactional perspective, effective moral dialogue requires that parties fully and accurately exchange views about the legitimacy of each other's claim. This is the essence of social coping. Dialogue is surely of no use when one or all parties defensively distort or negate critical aspects of their mutual moral problem. Dialogue is enhanced when parties deal accurately with the issue that confronts them. All social discourse is based on the assumption that in general we can depend on what people say.

Describing Coping and Defending

The words "coping" and "defending" are used in their ordinary sense to describe the actions that people characteristically or immediately take to try to solve problems. The model of ego processes we used was proposed by Haan (1963; 1977) and Kroeber (1963) and is intended—however approximately—to include all the problem-solving strategies that people use. It is composed of ten defenses and ten coping processes. Each coping process is paired with a defensive counterpart. For instance, coping empathy is paired with defensive projection while both are subsumed under the generic process of sensitivity. (In Table 8.1 each process is defined.) Examples for each coping and defending pair of processes show how a problem can be dealt with by either coping or defending. Readers may find further examples in Appendix B helpful. Table 8.1 also shows that three sets of processes are cognitive in nature; three are self-reflexive (whereby people interact with their own thoughts and feelings); one is for focusing attention; and finally, three regulate emotions and feelings. In

Table 8.2 the contrasting properties of coping and defending are summarized.

Table 8.1.

Taxonomy and Examples of Ego Processes[a]

	Modes	
Generic Processes	**Coping**	**Defending**
	Cognitive Processes	
Discrimination: Separates idea from feeling, idea from idea, feeling from idea	**Objectivity:** "I am of two minds about this problem."	**Isolation:** "There is no forest, only trees."
Detachment: Lets mind roam freely and irreverently, speculates, analyzes	**Intellectuality:** "My past economic insecurities have led me to a degree of petty stinginess."	**Intellectualizing:** "My stinginess can be explained by my upbringing."
Means–end symbolization: Analyzes causal texture of experiences and problems	**Logical analysis:** "Let's start at the beginning and figure out what happened."	**Rationalization:** "I was trying at first, but one thing after another happened."
	Reflexive-intraceptive Processes	
Delayed response: Holds up decisions in complex, uncertain situations	**Tolerance of ambiguity:** "There are some matters that can't be resolved when you want them to be."	**Doubt:** "It's the decisions that get me; I don't know what will happen if I choose to do it."
Sensitivity: Apprehends others' reactions and feelings	**Empathy:** "I think I know how you feel" (second person agrees that first speaker does).	**Projection:** "Don't think I don't know what you have in mind" (second person surprised and mildly guilty).
Time reversion: Recaptures and replays past experiences—cognitive, affective, social	**Regression—ego:** "Let's brainstorm this for a while."	**Regression:** "I just can't deal with this; I'll just give up."
	Attention-focusing Processes	
Selective awareness: focuses attention selectively	**Concentration:** "I intend to work on this job now, and I'll worry about that later."	**Denial:** "Every cloud has a silver lining, so there's no reason to be concerned."
	Affective-impulse Regulating Processes	
Diversion: Emotions expressed	**Sublimation:** Person expresses emotions, both positive and negative, toward objects, people, and activities in relevant and understood ways	**Displacement:** Person displaces emotions from the instigating situation to express them in another situation of greater safety

Table 8.1 (cont.)

Transformation: Primitive	Substitution: Person appears to have thoroughly and comfortably transformed uncivil feelings into their socialized forms	Reaction formation: Persons reactions are so socialized that they seem strained, excessive and brittle
Restraint: Emotions restrained	Suppression: Person restrains emotions when their expression would be dysfunctional, but knows what she or he feels and what she or he is doing	Repression: Person curtails cognitive knowledge and reactions, irrespective of her or his condition and the situation, but emotions are free-floating

[a]Adapted from N. Haan, <u>Coping and Defending</u>. New York: Academic Press, 1977, with permission.

The defensive process, as it was first described by Freud (1923), elaborated by Anna Freud (1937), and as it is understood by clinicians, helps to fortify the self's well-being. Yet this security is often achieved at a cost to the self's long-term interests and the person's ability to engage in social interchange. The Freudians were preoccupied with the fate of the individual person, so they did not take social costs into account. But in studying morality, we are specifically concerned with the social-moral cost. People do not put up with one another's distortions and negations of responsibility, especially when they are faced with conflicts. Of course, people are not defensive without cause. They usually react in light of their past experience which they apply blindly to present problems. But even if a person characteristically copes, any person can revert to defensiveness when his or her welfare seems to be at stake and there seems to be no way out.

All in all, as we can see from Table 8.2, defensiveness causes people to forfeit choice and prevents them from exercising whatever options exist within a situation. It is defined by past expectancies, and distorts views of situations and people, so defensive constructions are undifferentiated and perceptions are exaggerated. Magic is evoked to shed unpleasantness, but satisfaction is often secret and second rate.

The coping process, as described by Haan (1977), is far more attuned to the immediate options within situations and their future ramifications. Thinking is differentiated; feeling is understood rather than blindly experienced. Negative feelings are endured and positive feelings and enjoyed.

Defensiveness is not a weak maneuver nor coping always a strong one. Even when defensiveness may superficially appear to be passive and regressive, it is an active move to protect the self. The coping process may consist of sheer endurance and it can also be a matter of

Table 8.2.

Properties of Ego Processes[a]

Coping Processes	Defending Processes
1. Involve choice and are therefore flexible, purposive behaviors.	1. Turn away from choice and are therefore rigid and channeled.
2. Are pulled toward the future and take account of the needs of the present.	2. Are pushed from the past.
3. Are oriented to the requirements of present situation.	3. Distort aspects of present requirements.
4. Involve differentiated process thinking that integrates conscious and pre-conscious elements.	4. Involve undifferentiated thinking and include elements that do not seem part of the situation.
5. Operate with the organism's necessity of "metering" the experiencing of disturbing affects.	5. Operate with assumption that it is possible to magically remove disturbing feelings.
6. Allow various forms of affective satisfaction in open, ordered, and tempered ways.	6. Allow gratification by subterfuge.

[a]Adapted from N. Haan, Coping and Defending. New York: Academic Press, 1977, with permission.

simply enjoying sensual pleasure. A pivotal assumption about human nature underlies this model—people will cope when they can, simply because coping works better, but they will defend if they must in an overpowering situation.

Ego processes are actions that people take at particular times, but people develop preferences, characteristic ways of solving problems that come to be durable aspects of their personality. Thus, people develop preferred strategies. For example, intellectuals often cope cognitively (objectivity, intellectuality, and logical analysis), whereas artists characteristically cope more emotionally (sublimation, substitution, and suppression). Nevertheless, people are intelligently responsive to the character and demands of different situations. They may first attempt to solve a problem with their characteristic methods of coping and defending. If these strategies do not work, they can and will choose other methods. Ego processes describe the way people *interact* with situations, so whatever ego processes they use are determined by both situations and personal preference.

Next, we describe how the students' ego strategies were measured. Then we will consider whether their individual backgrounds related to their characteristic ego processing. Differences among the ego processing of individual students in the same groups are illustrated. Finally, the ego functioning of members of game and discussion groups and of the adolescents and young adults are compared.

Measuring Ego Processing

Two methods were used to measure the ego processing of the young adults. The first, based on a set of 20 experimental ego scales recently developed by Joffe and Naditch (1977), measured the students' preferred, characteristic ego processes. The second method, based on the Q sort of ego processes developed by Haan (1977), measured the students' situational strategies, that is the processes they actually used in the group sessions. The specific items of this Q sort are shown in Appendix B.

The Ego Scales: Measures of Characteristic Ego Functioning

For descriptions of the students' characteristic ego processing, we turned to the work of Joffe and Naditch (1977). Using items from the 480-item California Psychological Inventory (C.P.I.; Gough, 1956), Joffe and Naditch developed one scale for each of the 20 coping and defending processes listed in Table 8.1.

Personality scales do not directly represent ego processing except in one sense: People's ego strategies can be brought into play as they decide to answer "true" or "false" to items on a personality inventory. For example, persons who habitually defend themselves by denial may persistently answer "false" to troubling items, or persons who are very doubting may leave troubling items unanswered. Scores on personality inventories are widely thought and used by psychologists to represent the way people are, no matter what situation they are in; we followed this reasoning in this study. Joffe and Naditch (1977) developed their scales by comparing people's ego strategies in clinical interviews with their responses to items on the C.P.I. As a result these scales indirectly measure ego processes.

The Q Sort: Measures of Situationally Evoked Ego Functioning

After four or more training sessions, graduate students in clinical psychology and psychiatric social work each observed the ego processing of two adolescents or young adults during the group experiences. Immediately following each session, each observer sorted the 60 items of the Q sort of ego processes (Haan, 1977) into ranks of nine steps to describe how the students used each strategy. The highest steps described the student's most characteristic processes; the intermediate steps were for processes ranging from least to most descriptive; the lowest steps described the extreme opposite of the processes that a student used to resolve a problem.

The Q sort provides three items for each of the 20 ego processes. The three items for coping objectivity provide an example: 1. Distinguishes between his/her feelings and the facts of the situation; 2. Views self in an objective light; 3. Evaluates both sides of arguments, including those contrary to his/her own point of view. A student's score for objectivity was the sum of scores for these three items. In this fashion we had scores for ten coping and ten defensive processes.

Because two judges described the young adults' ego strategies, their agreements were checked in two ways. First, the agreement between the two Q sorts were calculated. If agreement was low, a third and sometimes a fourth observer watched the videotape of a session until two observers agreed on their descriptions of the student's ego processing. (A Q correlation of .40 was the cutting point.) By checking each pair of Q sorts and improving their level of agreement, we ensured that all observations would be reliable.

The second check of reliability concerned each ego process for all pairs of observations. For game students, agreement was acceptable for all 20 processes. For discussion students, agreement for coping substitution and defending projection was marginal. The reliability of the judges' averaged evaluations ranged from .57 to .94 with a median of .73. Once these checks were completed, the two judges' scores were averaged for each process. These scores provided the most reliable estimate for each ego process and were used in all analyses. The estimates of agreement for each ego process ranged from .55 to .81 for the game participants with a mean of .71. For the discussion participants, the range was .50 to .81 with a mean of .68.

Comparing Characteristic and
Situationally Evoked Ego Processes

The young adults' scores for characteristic ego functioning were obtained for two reasons. First, the students' scores for characteristic strategies could be used to adjust their scores for their actions in the group situations so that the latter would reflect "pure" action. Second, a question exists as to whether moral action is due entirely to situations or whether moral action simply reflects the "character" of people. The results we will now report need to be treated with some caution since Joffe and Naditch (1977) only recently devised these ego scales. More work by other investigators is needed before the usefulness of the scales can be fully established. Additional studies (Joffe & Bast, 1978; Vickers, Ward, & Hanley, 1980) have suggested that some scales may be more accurate than others. Nevertheless, these 20 ego scales are probably the best now available for assessing ego processing by means of paper-and-pencil tests. If one or all of these scales turns out to be unreliable, then its scores will be random, and associations with the averaged session scores would presumably be zero. With this caution in mind, we correlated the young adults' scale scores (their characteristic strategies) with their Q sort scores (their situational strategies) averaged across all sessions. Averaging the session scores has the effect of "leveling" differences due to particular sessions.

The overall result of correlating these two sets of scores for all students and for the game and discussion groups separately was not overly impressive. Forty-eight percent were statistically significant; correlations ranged from $-.21$ to $.59$ with an average of $.15$. As is often the case when people's test scores are correlated with scores from observations, the students' cognitive functions—both coping and defending—showed the greatest number of significant positive relations, but students' ways of handling their emotions showed the least number. When the positive correlations for the game and discussion students are considered together, seven out of 12 cognitive correlations were significant (the range was $.19$ to $.46$; average $= .31$), but only four out of 11 correlations concerned with the regulation of emotion were significant (the range was $.20$ to $.34$, average $= .26$). These results might be expected. Actions almost always involve feelings, whereas personality tests evoke more cognition than feeling.

Another important trend emerged. When the separate sets of cor-

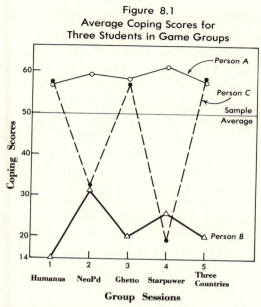

Figure 8.1
Average Coping Scores for
Three Students in Game Groups

relations for the game and discussion students were compared, the number of strong relations between characteristic and situationally evoked ego processing was greater for discussion than game students (eight significant out of 20 compared to five significant for the games students). When risk and stress are low, as they were in the discussions, characteristic and situational strategies are probably more alike.

Individual Differences in Ego Processing in the Same Situation

People act differently in the same situation, and different situations lead the same person to act differently. Still, some kinds of people are less likely to react to changes in situations; they behave the same in different situations. Some situations have such potent effects—degrading and conflicted or joyful and harmonious—that everyone present acts differently than they usually do. These different patterns of interchange between "person" and "situation" are reflected in the strategies people use.

Consistency as well as variability in ego processing can be illustrated with the scores for three young adults. For simplicity's sake, the sum of each student's coping scores was calculated for each session. Figure 8.1 shows the different patterns of coping for three game participants across the five sessions. Participants A and B were members of the *same* friendship group, so the setting for their experiences was the same; individually, however, they coped with the games very differently. Student A's spectacular level of coping in all five situations was 75 percent higher than all other students. Student B's poor coping was 99 percent lower than all other students. Their differences underscore the point that an individual person's strategies can have more potent effects on how they solve problems than situations. Participant C's level of coping illustrated high responsiveness to situational differences in the games. She coped more effectively than 75 percent of the other participants in sessions 1, 3, and 5 but less effectively than 95 percent in sessions 2 and 4! In other words, she was especially reactive and distressed in the stressful situations of NeoPd and Starpower.

The Participants' Background and Their Ego Processing

Objective characteristics of the young adults including their age, the size of their hometowns, their social class, the number of children in their families, and their birth order might have influenced their ego processing during the group sessions. To determine if this was the case, the averaged ego process for all five sessions was again used to represent the students' action-evoked processing (compare Epstein, 1980). A number of correlations were significant, but none was greater than .20, so we do not burden the reader with their detail or consider them in later analyses.

The sex of the young adults did have an influence on their ego processing. Sixty-five percent of the correlations between ego-processing scores and sex were significant. (None was above .37.) The men were significantly more likely to cope by using intellectuality, logical analysis, ego regression (playfulness), and concentration, and to defend by intellectualizing, rationalizing, projecting, and displacing. Women were more empathic and suppressed their feelings more; they also defended more by doubting, regressing, and by becoming rigidly "socialized" (reaction formation).

The adolescents' characteristics of age, socioeconomic status, and sex did not have numerous associations with their ego processes. During the sessions, older adolescents were slightly more tolerant of ambiguity and those of higher socioeconomic status were more coping cognitively. But frequent associations between race and ego processing occurred; 56 percent of the correlations were significant. During the group sessions, the black adolescents coped more and defended less. They coped by using objectivity, intellectuality, logical analysis, tolerance of ambiguity, ego regression, and concentration more than the white adolescents. The white students depended more on defensive isolation, rationalization, denial, and repression. The adolescents' sex was also associated with their ego strategies. The girls were more objective, but also more denying, and likely to isolate feelings and ideas than the boys. In subsequent analyses the sex of both adolescents and young adults was always taken into account as was age, race and socioeconomic status for the adolescents.

The Young Adults' Ego Processing

We expected the students' experiences in gaming or discussing or in led or dominated groups to affect their situationally evoked ego processing, which would then affect their level of moral action. Comparisons among ego scores for all the groups are shown in Figure 8.2 (along with the adolescents' scores). Clearly students in all groups coped more when they faced these moral dilemmas than they defended. Other general features are evident. As is shown by all groups' peaks for coping on logical analysis and concentration, the students generally gave the tasks full attention and tried to solve the problems. Their favored modes for handling emotions were sublimation and substitution; in other words, they transformed hostile or angry feelings into "socialized" forms of expression (substitution) and expressed their emotions in appropriate ways (high scores for sublimation and low for suppression). When defending, the young adults most often expressed their feelings by displacing them from the threatening person onto others who were less threatening. For example, they sometimes directed their frustration at the staff leader or threw empty soft drink cans at a waste basket rather than confront their friends. Another strong defense was their tendency to project their own feelings and ideas onto others.

Differences among groups further illuminate the way students handled the moral problems. The game students displaced their feelings more than the discussion students, probably because their greater stress generated more frustration and anger. The more potent influence was the natural structure of the friendship groups. Members of led groups generally coped more and defended less than did members of dominated groups. The former obtained higher scores for objectivity, logical analysis, and empathy, and lower for defending themselves by isolation and denial. In sum, these differences in ego strategies in favor of the led groups are consistent with the descriptions of group functioning set forth in the last chapter. We learn here that the equality of the members of these groups generally allowed them to cope; the disjointed hierarchical functioning of the dominated groups forced members to use defensive strategies.

Comparing the Adolescents' and Young Adults' Situational Ego Strategies

The differences between the adolescents' and young adults' game groups are developmentally interesting; their similarities highlight the common meaning of their experiences in the two projects.

As was the case with the young adults, the adolescents were not overly taxed by the games, as examination of Figure 8.2 indicates. Their ten scores on coping were all higher than their ten scores on defending and their *pattern* of coping was generally the same as the young adults. Only their score for suppression varied: They were actually significantly more suppressive than the young adults. In addition, the adolescents tried to be logical; they expressed their feelings; and when they were angry, they became self-righteous (reaction formation). But compared to the young adults, the adolescents coped less and defended more. In fact, all but three processes were significantly different. The young adults showed much more of a tendency to be playful (ego regression) and to concentrate and less tendency to isolate feelings from ideas, to become doubtful, and to put themselves in a good light when stressed (reaction formation). The adolescents' relatively young age and greater naïvete about the university and research

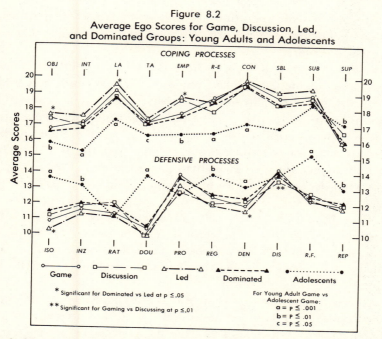

Figure 8.2
Average Ego Scores for Game, Discussion, Led,
and Dominated Groups: Young Adults and Adolescents

probably accounted for their comparative lack of skill in problem solving.

Summary

In this chapter we laid the groundwork for the idea that people solve moral problems by coping and defending. Moral exchange is often trying, but full, accurate, and sincere dialogue about the legitimacy of each discussant's self-interests is expected as well as needed if social harmony is to be restored and enhanced. Therefore people with a moral problem do better when they cope rather than defend.

Several rather modest assumptions underlying the model of coping and defending were discussed. First, the array of ten coping and ten defensive processes are meant to be—however approximately—a complete presentation of the ways that people solve problems. Second, people typically have hierarchies of characteristic ego processes, but they will switch to less-preferred processes when their usual methods do not work. Third, people would rather cope than defend themselves, but they will defend when they are pressed to protect their sense of well-being. For the students in this project, this meant their sense of themselves as moral.

The ways that ego processing were measured, in both its characteristic and situationally evoked version, were described, and information about the reliability of these measurements was presented. The relations between the characteristic and situationally evoked measurements were not particularly high, especially for functions that regulate emotions; however, they were higher for the cognitive functions and generally higher for discussion than game students. Consistency of cognitive processes in the face of changing situations is generally expected in psychological research, but the games evoked more disruption than did the discussions. The discussion students were probably better able to use their characteristic ways of solving problems. In contrast, the game students probably needed to bring seldom-used strategies into play to deal with their unusual and more stressful situations.

The preliminary analyses showed that both adolescents and young adults coped more than they defended. Few differences were found between game and discussion students in ego strategies averaged over all the group sessions. Consistent with the differences in the functioning of led and dominated groups reported in the previous chapter, students in the led groups coped more and defended less. Although clear similarities in the adolescents' and young adults' patterns of situationally evoked ego functioning were found, the teenagers' youth and unfamiliarity with research and the university setting seemed to diminish their ability to cope and increased their defensiveness.

Strategies for coping and defense are the way that individual people try to make sense out of what life demands of them. These processes represent complex interactions between people and situations that can shift, not only between the modes of coping and defending, but also among various processes within each mode. The special contributions of the students' ego strategies to their moral action and development are considered in later chapters.

PART III
STUDIES OF
MORAL ACTION

Chapter 9

IS MORAL ACTION
THE RESULT OF
CHARACTER OR SITUATION?

MIKE: Yeah, it was a matter of trust. I was really surprised you
didn't trust us.
TED: But you screwed us already; it takes time to get over that.
JANICE: We at least had the right to get mad at you! But you
didn't have the right to tell us to forgive you! How can anyone promise not to be mad?
—Three 19-year-olds after the heated game Starpower

Framework of the Studies

IN EVERYDAY LIFE, action—not pious talk, good intention, or
scholarly demonstration of moral knowledge—is the test of a person's moral authenticity. Aware of human fallibility, common sense
construction takes into account people's tendency to be overly impressed with their own moral worth. Consequently, the doing of morality—not its protestation or pretense—is thought to be the critical
test of a person's good faith.

Over the centuries, practical moral transactions have been carried
out without regard for the advice and proclamations of professional
moralists—whether they were theologians, philosophers of the En-
lightenment, or nowadays, social scientists. Moral theories were usually
constructed at some distance from practical moral action. The present,
special task of social scientists is to discover the characteristics of the
particular transactions that people have commonly called "moral." If

social scientists are to contribute significantly to humanity's comprehension of its moral commitment, they must first understand the ordinary conditions under which moral action is taken.

In this chapter, we first discuss the ordinary characteristics of moral action. Then we lay the groundwork for analyzing two contradictory explanations of moral action: Is its quality due to people's moral character? Or is it the result of the nature of the situations in which people find themselves? And we go on to report the research results that focus on these alternatives. (A third explanation, that individual modes of coping and defense interact with contexts, is not considered in this but in the next chapter.)

Ordinary Characteristics of Moral Action

Some psychologists focus not on the processes of moral action but only on people's final decision, called the "judgment" by the cognitive theorists or the "behavioral choice" by the social learning theorists. The study of outcomes has seemed rigorous since these can be clearly seen, even though their meaning may be uncertain. We use the richer word "action" to mean not only the outcome but also to mean people's behavior during decision-making, which includes their understandings of the situation and its options. From the standpoint of the interactional theory, "action" better matches life since different behaviors can fulfill the same judgment, and different judgments can result in the same behavior.

Action of Means and Ends. The morality of procedures and processes that precede the final action are as important as the outcome. Without moral means, the end can be only accidentally moral. Therefore, means are also moral actions that are part of disputes from the very outset. Initial actions often reflect only people's self-interest, tempered by vague, approximate understandings of the other participants' views of their legitimate self-interests. But "feedback loops" invariably operate to correct people's self-preoccupation. Although people initially act only to persuade their protagonists, their intents shift during interim and concluding transactions. This morality of procedures is spelled out in the interactional theory in the three previously mentioned requirements: All participants *should* be able to speak their minds; any participant *should* be able to veto suggested resolutions that are nonequalizing; no participant *should* dominate. These are the normal expectations for a moral dialogue. When these requirements are violated or some participants fail to exercise their procedural rights, chances of constructing a moral balance are obviously lessened. Of course apparent imbalances may actually be authentic balances when they rectify past imbalances or are rectified by future action. Moral dialogues have histories and futures.

Moral Action Is Always Occurring. From the interactional view, moral incidents interrupt normal social discourse and exchange. Minor interruptions are frequent, so moral processing occurs almost incessantly but with varying emotional intensity. A resolution is merely punctuation in social exchange; people's relations with one another are never forever resolved. New competitions and needs for reparation arise. From this view, the final moral "behavior" is a paltry representation of everyday moral action. Even as people make preliminary attempts to persuade one another by talking—by saying that their interests are morally legitimate, or saying that they recognize the other's interest—they are *already* acting.

The Artificial Separation of Thought and Action. Action and thought are separated only in two special circumstances; both need to be investigated. The first occurs when discussants distort their thoughts (though at some level aware of their contradictions). They will then act differently than they would if they did not need to compartmentalize or rationalize their thoughts. For example, the defensive process of isolation ruptures connections between related ideas and between ideas and associated feelings, so the isolating person "cannot see the forest for the trees." Or to use the students' term, such a person "can't get it together." The second separation between thought and action occurs when people deliberately dissemble during the dialogue while secretly intending to freeload.

In situations of good faith, these anomalies do not occur; or, at any rate, common sense says that they *should not* occur. Moral outrage follows inconsistency between means and ends and is evidence, in itself, of the expectation that moral actions should carry out people's promises. When people make an explicit promise, it goes without saying that they implicitly promise to act to the best of their ability (Sesonske, 1957). People of all ages understand these tacit rules so well that when they do default, they rationalize it by claiming extenuating circumstances.

Psychologists have separated moral thought and action probably for the convenience of their research. But unfortunately the division acquires a kind of reality. This tendency is noticeable in both the cognitivists and their critics (see, for instance, Kurtines & Greif, 1974). Both sets of researchers seem to think that pure thought is collected in interviews about hypothetical dilemmas (the method of data collection most often used by the cognitivists). But our view is that people act even when they face a hypothetical moral dilemma because they have a stake in being, or at least seeming to be moral. Those being interviewed know full well that they are exposing their moral adequacy to the interviewer; so they act as best they can to impress the researcher and reassure themselves. Interviews generate intentions and actions, but these are of a different kind from those occurring in direct moral conflicts.

Two results show the kind of action provoked in interviews. Young adults who habitually use the defense of intellectualization attained significantly higher scores for both the interactional and cognitive systems during interviews (for the interactional scores, $p \leq .01$; for the cognitive score, $p \leq .001$). In another study of 108 middle-aged adults (Haan, 1977), significantly higher cognitive interview-based scores ($p \leq .01$) were also produced by those who preferred intellectualization as a defense. This latter finding held even after socioeconomic level, IQ, and level of logical operations were controlled.

The Penetration of Moral Emotion.   There is still another reason why a person's final judgment does not reflect all there is to moral action. Emotion permeates all serious moral negotiation but the emotion that accompanies a morally equalized outcome is particularly the glow of mutual satisfaction and relief. Interim emotions are very different. They inform and direct moral processes and may, in fact, determine the particular moral balance that discussants achieve and accept. At first, only the victim may react emotionally and this is an action as far as other participants are concerned, since it signals the importance and the meaning that the victim attaches to the moral conflict. Emotion is also contagious, a phenomenon regarded by at least one psychologist (Hoffman, 1978) as innate mimicry. Aroused emotion is also a rough index of the problem's importance and level of difficulty.

The importance we attribute to emotions in moral processing does not mean that people resolve moral issues solely by emotions. Perceptual-cognitive grasps of situations occur in milliseconds, and, as Piaget (1950) noted, all thought seems intuitive—or here, emotional—until it is analyzed. Instead, emotions accompany and enrich understandings, and they convey far more authentic information about a person's position in a dispute than any well-articulated thoughts. In ordinary circumstances, emotions instruct and energize action. In situations of great moral costs, emotions can overwhelm and disorganize cognitive evaluations. At that point, understanding of the issue and the quality of moral action deteriorate.

Recognizing another person's emotional state is a reciprocal act, and mutually experienced emotion is a reaction called empathy. Within the interactional system, the process of empathy is assumed always to be a *central* feature within moral action. Empathy may not appear at the beginning of a moral dispute, but, from the interactional view, it evolves in circumstances of good faith, and it must evolve if equalization is to be achieved. The cognitivists regard "role taking" (which is near in meaning to empathy) as a nonmoral, psychological process that lies outside their view of pure moral thought. This separation of the nonmoral from the moral or the psychological from the philosophical (Kohlberg, 1970) may not be a productive strategy for research by social scientists. The holistic reality of practical moral functioning does not respect this division.

Although emotion is a constant companion of all human thought and experience, some moral problems like those involved in the two games NeoPd and Starpower involve greater emotion than others because the violations are actual, not theoretical. Also, different moral problems are likely to "pull" different emotions, for instance, outrage when people themselves are violated or anguish when a bystander recognizes the plight of a victim.

Summary of the Interactional View. Altogether then, it seems that moral action cannot be separated from moral thought for a number of reasons. 1. People act by attempting to persuade others. 2. Their interactive ways of deciding morally are acts in themselves. 3. The powerful common motivation to appear moral turns "pure" thought even in pallid situations into action thoughts, so people act by speaking morally. 4. Moral emotions are acts in themselves that fuse people's cognizance of their own self-interest with both their feelings and their empathy for their protagonist. 5. Finally, moral emotions swiftly communicate the protagonists' positions.

The Cognitive Position on Action.   The interactional theory is different from the cognitive theory in the five ways described above. The cognitive theory views morality as the logical, hypothetical judgment of a single person acting dispassionately. In this view, people think first so that they can rise above the confusing, emotional, and interpersonally corrective detail of their context; they then make a "deontic" choice; later they act if they additionally judge that they are responsible (Kohlberg, Levine, & Hewer, 1983).

Although Kohlberg has not ignored the question of action, he himself has not so far reported on a systematic program of research that seems to elucidate the relationship between action and the cognitive stages of reasoning. Nevertheless other investigators have conducted such studies, either by directly observing action or by comparing persons of contrasting tendencies, like legally identified juvenile delinquents with nondelinquents.* Because investigators with varying interests and research opportunities have conducted these studies, subjects of different ages and of different kinds have been studied. Authentic moral action is difficult to study, so some actions seem not very consequential or clearly moral. Another shortcoming of the research is that more than half of the studies cited in the footnote, which is a reasonably comprehensive listing, did not include female subjects. Given these variations, general conclusions are difficult to draw. However, hostile, aggressive males—like juvenile delinquents, or some small groups of student activists who were personally angry and at odds with their parents, or persons who acted in a gratuitously aggressive fashion when given the opportunity—do often appear to be of lower stage. See Blasi (1980) for an extensive review.

*See the following studies cited in the Bibliography for examples of studies of moral behavior from the cognitive point of view: Anchor and Cross (1976), Campagna and Harter (1975), D'Augelli and Cross (1975), Fodor (1972), Haan (1975, 1977, 1978); Haan, Block, and Smith (1968), Harris, Mussen, and Rutherford (1976), Holstein, Stroud, and Haan (1974), Hudgins and Prentice (1973), Krebs (1967), Krebs and Rosenwald (1977), Rothman (1976), Saltzstein, Diamond, and Belenky (1972), Schwartz, Brown, Feldman, and Weingartner (1969), Staub (1975), Turiel and Rothman (1972).

Conditions of Moral Actions Considered in the Research

Everyday observation shows that people do not always act in morally consistent ways, as expected under the cognitivists' theory of structural stages. Not only do people vary within themselves in the adequacy of their acts, but the level of refinement required for the resolution of different moral issues varies. In everyday life, the complexity of justice is not always needed nor is it always applicable. Carol Gilligan (1982) has highlighted a set of moral problems arising from unplanned pregnancies which she points out are not well handled by the cognitive theory. She suggests that caring and responsibility better describe the morality that is used and needed. In addition, the moral costs of *some* situations for some people are low, whereas the costs of the same situation for other people are high. The assumption that moral character *should* transcend situations may be a corruption of historic judgments based on theology that people should always aspire for moral perfection.

The remainder of this chapter is concerned with the consistency and inconsistency of moral performance in various contexts. So far several explanations have been given for variation among people in the adequacy of their moral actions.

1. *Moral character* or *capacity,* which the cognitivists say is usually represented by the person's stage of moral reasoning about a set of hypothetical dilemmas.

2. Aspects of *situations,* here gaming or discussing. Also influential may be the *content* of the moral issue at stake, represented in this study by the different dilemmas presented to the discussion groups and the different simulations and games presented to the game groups.

3. *Stress* of situations, roughly equivalent to the moral costs that arise not only from threats to self-interest, but also from witnessing or participating in threats to others' self-interests.

4. Nature of *interpersonal situations,* represented here by friendship groups' functioning hierarchically in being dominated by one member, or communally in being led by a member who is seen as fair.

5. Individual persons' *characteristic and situationally chosen modes of adaptation and problem solving.*

The effects of individual person's ego strategies on action are considered in the next chapter. Here we investigate only whether the level of moral action is due to moral character, situation, or interpersonal context.

Results

Action as Actualization of Moral Character

If people's moral character determines the adequacy of their actions in all situations, the research task is straightforward. To predict the quality of a person's moral action, researchers need only to determine his or her stage of development if the cognitive system is being followed, or level if the interactional system is being used. In this explanation, the context of morality is irrelevant because character shapes action, meaning it transcends variations in situations, interpersonal contexts, and the participants' particular needs and emotions. This idea of character has a time-honored grip on Judeo-Christian thought about morality.

Context may not be so easily set aside. Research on moral action has so far failed to demonstrate that people act as consistently as this explanation entails. The eight moral scores, obtained from three interviews and five group sessions and collected on both the adolescents and young adults, made it possible for us to test whether character is a critical determinant of action. If it is, strong correlations should be found among *all* eight moral scores, irrespective of differences among the situations in which the students acted.

Although the young adults' moral scores were reliably assigned (agreements between judges ranged from .80 to .91 with an average of .89, as we reported in Chapter 6), weak, albeit frequently significant correlations were found among the eight scores for both systems. Somewhat higher correlations occurred among the three interview scores. (The correlations among the three cognitive scores for the interviews were .44, .40, and .39, $ps \leq .001$, and for interactional scores, .24, .37, and .30, the first significant at .01 level and the last two at .001.) Notice, however, that the interviews involve virtually identical situations so these comparatively weak associations are not convincing evidence that moral character exists and operates consistently in different situations.

The five different sessions had very low correlations (ranging from −.15 to .23 with an average of .12 for the cognitive scores and from −.07 to .29 for the interactional scores with an average of .14). Finally, the associations between the scores for the interviews and sessions were lowest of all (ranging from about −.25 to .30 with averages of .04 for both systems).

Virtually the same pattern was found among the adolescents' eight moral scores from both systems. Correlations among interviews tended to be significant but low; but correlations among the different kinds of situations—group sessions or between interview and group sessions—were even lower with only an occasional significant result being brought about by chance. *From all these results, based on highly reliable scores, we may conclude that character did not make its distinctive mark of transcending situations.*

Despite these discouraging results, a different set of findings suggests that given certain situational constraints, something like moral character may operate. The same set of correlations were calculated within each of the four kinds of groups: the dominated game, dominated discussion, led game, and led discussion groups. This grouping has the effect of controlling for the effects of membership in led or dominated groups and for whether the experiences were discussing or gaming. The moral scores for the led discussion groups had greater consistency for both the interactional and cognitive systems than any other group. The average correlations for students in the led discussion groups, whether within sessions and interviews or between these situations, were all near .30, compared to averages for the other three groups which ranged from .08 to .15. For the led discussion groups 29 percent of the correlations exceeded .40 for the interactional scores and 36 percent for the cognitive scores compared to 5 percent for the interactional and 7 percent for the cognitive correlations for all other groups combined. These results suggest that some consistency in moral character occurs when situations are similar, dilemmas are hypothetical, and interpersonal relations are equable. Real life seldom provides such a series of bland moral dilemmas.

With these findings in hand, we turn next to the opposite explanation that situations determine levels of moral performance. Did differences between gaming or discussing and/or between membership

ferences between gaming or discussing and/or between membership in a dominated or led friendship group have stronger and more consistent effects on moral action?

Effects of Situation: The Task and the Interpersonal Contexts of Friendship Groups

Social-learning theorists counter the explanation of moral character with the proposal that aspects of the situation itself—its permissions, prohibitions, possible rewards or punishments, and the presence of an authoritative, rewarding person to model—account for both moral action and development. Whether people will behave according to their learning is thought to depend on the incentives—the rewards or punishments in particular situations (Rushton, 1980). Presumably then—to make an overly simplistic statement to underscore the point—people will act morally in the presence of a police officer because they will have incentive to do so.

The impact of situational variations on moral action scores was studied in three different analyses of the young adults' moral scores. Each provides a somewhat different kind of information. Because the adolescent groups played games and could not be typified as led or dominated, we could not conduct similar analyses for them. In this section, the goal is again limited. We want to demonstrate the variation in these moral scores and suggest the influences of contexts.

Comparison among Four Groups. The first analysis compared the moral action scores achieved by the four different kinds of groups: the led game, dominated game, led discussion, and dominated discussion groups. Each group's average cognitive and interactional scores is shown in Figure 9.1 for each session. As readers can see, the four groups were significantly different from one another (all ps ≤ .001) on both kinds of moral scores for sessions 1, 2, and 5 and additionally for session 4 on cognitive morality.

During session 1, both game groups produced high level morality when they dealt with the interesting and easy moral problems posed by Humanus, but they floundered when they faced the difficult and stressful game of NeoPd. Both discussion groups performed well in session 2 when they had the opportunity to discuss three easy moral dilemmas concerning civil rights. The significant differences in the

Figure 9.1
Average Moral Scores for Four Groups:
Led or Dominated Game Groups,
Led or Dominated Discussion Groups

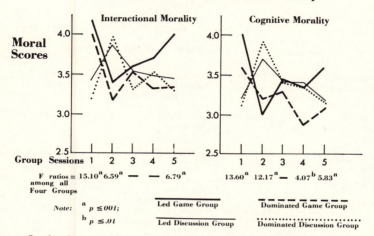

scores for both cognitive and interactional morality in session 5 result from the led game groups' high scores. In addition, the significant difference for cognitive moral scores in session 4 is due to the striking drop ($p \leq .001$) in cognitive moral action for the dominated groups when they played Starpower.

The most general conclusion that can be drawn from these profiles is that dramatic fluctuations occurred for both kinds of moral actions, clearly for the game students as they moved from one situation to another. Readers should notice the erratic course of the scores for the games and the differences between led and dominated groups that favor the former. These fluctuations seem to result from the groups' functioning and the effects of their natural structure already described in Chapter 7. Finally it can be seen that if the scores for session 2 were removed, the profiles for both discussion groups would essentially be flat.

Analyses for the Whole Sample with Statistical Controls. The specific effects of gaming or discussing separated from the effects of dominated versus led groups were not determined in the analyses described above. Consequently a second set of analyses on the moral scores for the entire sample was done. Statistical controls were introduced first,

Table 9.1.

Significant Effects of Experience, Group

Structure, and Sex on Moral Action Levels

(Entire Sample)

	Cognitive Morality	Interactional Morality
Analyses of External Effects with Controls (Entire Sample)		
Effects of situation (sex and structure controlled)	Session 1: game higher[a] 2: discussion higher[a] 4: discussion higher[c]	Session 1: game higher[a] 2: discussion higher[a] 5: game higher[c]
Effects of group structure (sex and situation controlled)	Session 1: led higher[c] 4: led higher[c] 5: led higher[b]	Session 5: led higher[a]
Effects of sex (situation and structure controlled)	No significant effects	Session 5: women higher[b]
Interactions		
Sex by structure	Session 5: dominated males lower than all other groups[c]	No significant interactions
Experience by structure	Session 5: dominated game groups lower than all other groups[c]	

[a] $p < .001$.

[b] $p < .01$.

[c] $p < .05$.

for the effects of group structure while the effects of gaming and discussing were studied, second for the effects of gaming and discussing while the effects of group structure were studied. The students' sex was also examined as a third factor in case women and men varied in their reactions to differences in experiences or group structure.

Overall, the results shown in Table 9.1 are somewhat more numerous for the cognitive scores than the interactional scores. Led students (experience controlled) produced higher cognitive scores than dominated students in sessions 1, 4, and 5. Game students (group structure controlled) produced higher cognitive scores than discussion students during session 1 when they played Humanus, but lower scores during sessions 2 and 4 when the stressful games of NeoPd and Starpower were played. The sex of the students did not directly affect their cognitive moral scores, but two significant interactions indicated that dur-

Table 9.2.

Effects of Sessions, Group Structure and Sex

on Moral-Action Levels within Discussion and Game Groups

	Cognitive Morality	Interactional Morality
	Within Discussion Groups	
Effects of sessions	Overall comparison[a] Session comparisons: Session 2 higher than each other session[a] or b Session 1 versus 3[c], 3 higher Session 1 versus 5[c], 3 higher	Overall comparison[a] Session comparisons: Session 2 higher than each other session[a] or b Session 1 versus 4[c], 4 higher
Effects of group structure	Neither overall nor session comparisons significant	Neither overall nor session comparisons significant
Effects of sex	Neither overall nor session comparisons significant	Overall comparison not significant Session comparisons: Session 2 versus 3, women dropped less than men[c] Session 2 versus 5, women dropped less than men[c] Session 3 versus 4, women dropped and men gained[c]
Interactions: structure with sex	Neither overall nor session comparisons significant	Overall comparison[c] Session comparisons: Sessions 1, 2, 3, 4 versus 5, all[b] Led females always gained; all other groups dropped or held steady
	Within Game Groups	
Effects of sessions	Overall comparison[a] Session comparisons: Nonstressful (sessions 1, 3, 5) versus stressful (2, 4)[a] 1, 3, 5 higher Session 1 versus 3[a], 1 higher Session 1 versus 5[a], 1 higher (3 versus 5 and 2 versus 4 not significant)	Overall comparison[a] Session comparisons: Nonstressful (sessions 1, 3, 5) versus stressful (2, 4)[a]. 1, 3, 5 higher Session 1 versus 3[a], 1 higher Session 1 versus 5[a], 1 higher (3 versus 5 and 2 versus 4 not significant)
Effects of group structure	Overall comparisons[b] Session comparisons: Session 2 versus 4[b], led groups gained, dominated lost	Overall comparison not significant Session comparisons: Session 3 versus 5[b], led groups gained, dominated lost
Effects of sex	Overall comparison not significant Session comparisons: Session 1 versus 5[c], men lost more than women Session 3 versus 5[c], women gained, men lost	Overall comparison not significant Session comparison not significant

Table 9.2 (cont.)

Interactions:	Overall comparison[b]	Overall comparison not significant
	Session comparisons:	Session comparisons not significant
	Session 3 versus 5[b], dominated	
	males lost, all other groups	
	gained or held steady	

[a] $p < .001$.
[b] $p < .01$.
[c] $p < .05$.

ing session 5, males in dominated groups as well as all members of dominated groups had lower cognitive moral scores than students of all other classifications.

Situation and group structure had fewer effects on interactional moral levels, but the pattern is similar. Only session 5 seems to have had a different influence on interactional morality. Students in game groups had significantly higher scores than those in discussion groups, and women performed higher than men.

This pattern of results suggests that the costs of situations affected moral actions, cognitive somewhat more than interactional morality. The minor moral difficulties posed by the game Humanus elevated moral functioning, while the impact of the stressful moral problems posed by NeoPd and Starpower depressed moral functioning. The egalitarian structure of the led groups facilitated cognitive moral action in three sessions, while the atmosphere of the dominated group had a deleterious effect on cognitive moral action that became especially strong for males by the last session. The late appearing results for session 5 need special comment. They may be due to the depressing or stimulating effects of being in moral conflict with one's friends for some 15 hours within the contexts of dominated or led groups.

Comparison among Sessions within Discussion and Game Groups

The third set of analyses separately compared the moral-action scores, first for the discussion and then for the game students. Overall comparisons among all five sessions as well as specific comparisons between pairs of individual sessions were done. The results for the discussion groups, shown in Table 9.2, are considered first.

Comparisons within Discussion Groups. Since the discussion sessions were all alike, we expected that the magnitude of the moral scores also would be the same. This was the case for both moral systems except for session 2. Inadvertently, we chose three dilemmas for session 2 that were very easy for politically conscious and generally liberal Berkeley students: a black man seeks to rent a room from a white, impoverished landlady; a high-school principal breaks his agreement not to censor the school newspaper; and an attendance officer attempts to force a truant back to school although his impoverished family needs the money he earns by working in the fields. When specific sessions were compared with each other, all differences with session 2 were significant in both moral systems; only three other individual contrasts (out of ten) were significant. We conclude, then, that similar situations produce similar levels of moral scores, except when the contents and resolutions of a moral issue are involving and well known.

Whether discussion groups were dominated or led had no effect on either set of moral scores. The groups' natural structures were undoubtedly overridden by the tutorial role of the staff leader. Neither the students' sex nor any combination of sex and group structure had significant effects on the cognitive scores. However, several sex differences occurred between the interactional scores for the various sessions. We will not discuss these in detail but they suggest that the civil rights issues of session 2 gave the men a special opportunity to function at an unusually high interactional level; all their other scores were lower. The contents of a dilemma for session 3 especially motivated the women students—a professor offers a woman student money for her tuition in exchange for a shared vacation—so their scores for all other sessions were lower. Finally, compared to other groups, the women who were members of led groups improved in moral functioning by session 5. This is the only effect of group structure on the discussion groups. Its strength suggests that the women students' level of interactional morality thrived especially in egalitarian atmospheres.

Therefore, the content of the dilemmas seemed to be the critical factor that accounted for moral change from one discussion session to another. This finding is counter to the cognitivists' contention that morality is based on structural stages that function the same, whatever the moral issue's content. Group structure was generally not important, but several differences based on sex occurred for interactional morality that seemed due to the sexes' different responses to the contents of various dilemmas.

Comparisons within Game Groups. Turning to the game groups, whose results are also shown in Table 9.2, we find, not unexpectedly, that the overall difference among these very different sessions was highly significant for both moral systems. Since we held the hypothesis that the quality of moral action varies with the intensity of stress, the moral scores for the two stressful sessions (NeoPd and Starpower) were combined and then compared with the scores for all other sessions. The highly significant results were identical for both moral systems (both $ps \leq .001$) with the scores for the nonstressful sessions being higher. Other comparisons between scores for the two stressful sessions and among the scores for the three nonstressful sessions were generally not significant. *The main finding is that stress, resulting from moral difficulty, lowered the quality of moral action.*

Comparison of the overall effects of group structure on cognitive scores was significant, a finding that again suggests the special responsiveness of cognitive morality to the difference between led and dominated contexts. This trend was most evident in the comparison between the two stressful sessions. Led groups improved their cognitive moral functioning in Starpower in comparison to NeoPd, whereas the dominated groups produced significantly higher scores in NeoPd and lower scores in Starpower. Possibly the dominators organized their groups during NeoPd, while the interpersonally sensitive led groups may have been overwhelmed by the unexpected loss of good faith among friends.

Neither comparison of effects of sex nor sex combined with group structure were significant. Several specific contrasts were significant, but we will not take them up in detail.

Summary. In essence, the third set of analyses showed that in discussion sessions, both kinds of moral action were at the same level except during session 2. This does not mean that individual persons' moral functioning was stable, since the correlations among session scores were low. Instead, this consistency suggests that the costs of the hypothetical issues presented in the five discussion sessions were much the same. Of importance is the indication that the contents of a dilemma give special advantage, in session 2 (civil rights) to the men and in session 3 (sexual exploitation) to the women.

In contrast, the game sessions produced radically different levels of moral action in accordance with the degree of the stress. Cognitive morality was more affected than interactional morality by the groups' organization as led or dominated.

Session Dialogues: Discussion, Simulation, and Game

From the statistical analyses, we determined that the students' approach to the moral dilemmas varied, depending on whether they were discussing hypothetical dilemmas, simulating action in response to hypothetical issues, or actually experiencing moral problems with friends. From the standpoint of the students, these experiences meant participating from the detached position of a third person, or simulating the position of a first person, or acting as a first person for him or herself. The dialogues below are meant to illustrate these differences and give readers a fuller grasp of the different experiences.

Discussion of the Peace Corps Dilemma

In the first session the discussion groups took up the issue as to whether Andrew, an only child, should go overseas on his scheduled tour of duty for the Peace Corps or stay with his widowed mother, who has just developed a serious, chronic illness. The exchange begins a few minutes into the discussion. Readers will want to notice the students' third-person position, their relationship to the staff leader, and the group's continuously sidestepping the necessity of deciding. (These transcripts have been lightly edited for readability; SL will refer to staff leader.)

SARAH: You can care and you can be with them but there is nothing you can do. They are dying and it's a fact.

LUKE: You may feel that way now *(interjections by Ruth)* but I am just trying to put myself in the mother's place. You know maybe I'd want to stay, too.

RUTH: I think the mother would be very concerned about her son's career. It's like—I don't know—it's like his going off to the Peace Corps would make him, you know, so much farther ahead in having—I don't know—a fulfilling life. Although I'd like my son near, I wouldn't feel like I would be doing my duty as a parent in keeping him with me.

JEREMIAH: First I want to say two things. He can go on this Peace
Corps later. In other words, he can enter at any stage in his life.
(Interruption from Sarah.) It is not like he is missing out on a once in
a lifetime . . . *(interruptions)* well, just remember what you were
trying to say, 'cause I just want to say something I've been trying to
say. You can't save their life. But you're talking about while the
person is alive you want to make it as comfortable as possible. You're
talking about—someone you love. It is not a physical thing and it is
so much more important. Like those experiments with apes—they
put an ape in a thing without a mother *(interruption)* and the little
monkey dies because there is not a physical person—there is nothing there. And that is what happens when you put people in these
convalescent homes. They are not getting any love at all. The
whole—they just have no will to live and they die. *(Several voices at
once.)*

RUTH: As a mother I would feel burden knowing. . . . I'd feel the
burden!

SARAH: I don't want to burden my children. *(Many talking at once.)*

RUTH: I wouldn't want my kids around. I would feel bad. *(Many talking at once.)* I would live my life in such a way that I wouldn't need
my son here. I wouldn't. . . . I hope that I live my life independently.

LUKE: Are you sure of that?

MARTHA: *(to the man)* Are you going to expect them to take care of
you? Are you going to expect them to take care of you when you
are old?

LUKE: I think I will want them to strongly. . . . I am sure. I want them
to take care of me . . . you know.

MARTHA: Of course you'll want them to . . . *(interruptions)*. . . . Do you
want them to give up part of their life. Okay, you've just graduated
from college, you're still young. . . .

LUKE: He is an only child, yeah, right.

MARTHA: There is so much opportunity for him. Do you want to
stagnate his life right now at this point in time?

LUKE: I'm pretty much undecided about this whole thing. I still feel
very strongly about the mother thing.

SL: Abe, what do you think?

ABE: I just had the feeling why can't you accomplish something? Why
do you have to go to these foreign countries to accomplish something? There are so many opportunities in the cities and even the
Peace Corps operates in the United States *(interruptions)* a lifetime
goal.

MARTHA: But what he wants to do is go to a foreign country.

RUTH: For someone else it might be to work for IBM and that might be personally fulfilling but for this guy he wants to be. . . .

SARAH: *(interrupts)* But can I just make one point? No matter how much love there is for the mother and how much love there is for the son—in the son's mind he's being kept back. He may never admit it, but there does build up a sense of bitterness. . . . *(Others: Yeah!)* . . . and I don't want that.

SAUL: I think it depends on the individual.

JEREMIAH: It does depend on the individual. I think you're speaking for what you would want. *(Many people speaking at once.)*

SL: Let me interject a question . . . uhm, to those of you who have raised the point that you should do what you need to do. Does it logically follow from what you're saying that as . . . I am really asking this as an open question . . . that as people get older and are widowed and there is no husband or wife in the home and they get ill, are you saying they then should be put into institutions for care . . . I mean, is that the solution to the problem?

LUKE: No. *(Others: No!)*

SL: Then what is the solution then? How is she going to be taken care of and while you're also getting to do what you want to do? The problems are not mutually exclusive. How would you handle both of these situations? You are giving a lot of weight to the need for the individual to be able to go out and to live their life, but you are also concerned about what to do with people who are older and ill. How do you balance those two?

SAUL: First you could try hiring a nurse or someone to stay at home with her . . . that is a lot more personalized. It's not the cold nursing home.

DEBRA: But he might not be able to afford it. Do you know how much a full-time nurse is?

SAUL: Right, right. . . .

DEBRA: I tell you—a lot more than a Peace Corps worker makes. *(Laughter . . . yeahs)*

ABE: I think his dilemma is a secondary part of the question. He should first decide whether he is going to go or whether he is going to stay and then if he is going to go, it is up to his mother to decide. Does she want to go to a convalescent home, does she want to have a nurse hired? If he stays, does she still want to go to a convalescent home? That's what I think. *(Sarah interjects: Yeah.)* I think that would be my solution. But first the question has to be answered by him alone, whether to go or to stay.

SL: How do you think he should answer?

ABE: I think you should stay.

SARAH: What about the bitterness that is going to build up in him?

SAUL: Why would there be bitterness?

ABE: There is not always going to be bitterness. *(Jeremiah: That's true.)* But you have to realize that these people are getting older and they always can't be as they were.

SARAH: And they lived their life and had their chance and it's your turn.

SL: How would you balance out the problem I posed to you a few minutes ago. Is there a balance between what you do with your life and what they want to do?

SARAH: I know I don't want to live to the point where I can't take care of myself. I don't want to see that day—because I don't want to have anyone think they have to take care of me *(interruptions)*.

SL: What I'd like you to do is to generalize beyond this one situation. Is the solution for Andrew and Andrew's mother the one you would recommend for the whole society?

RUTH: I don't think an older or ill person should go to the convalescent home. That should be farther down the line of alternatives. You know, first of all, if you can afford it, hire a nurse. If you couldn't do that, maybe your mother has an older friend and they could live together and look after themselves—I think that would be an ideal situation and maybe it is unfortunate that *he* has no brothers and sisters that they could all help out together. But I don't think you should totally abandon her *(interruption)* altogether. Yeah, yeah. I don't think he should abandon her and stick her in a convalescent home and send her a check every month *(many interject agreement)*.

SARAH: You know, there is like a contract and. . . . *(Ruth interjects: That's right.)*

ABE: There are—has to go with a balance, you know. One grandmother may be perfectly fine in a convalescent home—that may be what she thrives on—interaction with these people of her own age that will replace the friends she is losing but it may not be right for a grandmother who just enjoys spending time with people 20, 30, 40 years younger—it has to do with the situation. The best person to realize that would be the children.

JEREMIAH: But first of all, it depends on whether she's really to the point where she needs a nurse 'cause she may be really ill, then of course if you can't afford a private nurse the only alternative is a convalescent home as the cheapest way to go. It just matters that the son is there and that she is being taken care of and at a different level, more abstract, she knows that she is being loved more than if she just was in a place where they have hard floors.

MARTHA: Do you have any relatives in a convalescent home?

JEREMIAH: I have—and both of them have suffered. We don't have the money to support them. I know my uncle did have money, but he wanted to live his own life so he sent a check and he thought that was love. I think that the whole question here is—what are the morals we're talking about? What is most important in our lives? Is it our work? Or is it our relationships with people—our lives or whatever? *(Many interject.)*

ABE: I think it depends on the individual.

Simulating Survival in Humanus

As the "last group of survivors after a worldwide disaster," the following students, members of a led group, are directed by Humanus, a "computer's voice print-out," to decide how they will regulate their group. They first decide leadership will be rotated and decisions made by vote, but then the problem of tie votes and the minority's rights comes to their minds, and the following debate ensued. Readers will note that in this simulation the discourse is in first person. The activity leader, although present, is not involved, and the group seems to experience some urgency about coming to clear decisions.

PHIL: Then we'll just talk and talk and vote and vote.

HILDA: We'll need a coin, too.

CISSY: Everyone would have to listen and respect each other.

BETTY: What if that doesn't happen?

RAY: The best we can hope for is mutual cooperation, but beyond that, we're just going to have to try.

CHARLES: If we have *any* rule that we'll all accept—without having to evoke it—it is everyone has to accept the right of argument. Every person must be able to talk without their talk being oppressed or interrupted.

ED: We'll have to have every individual evaluate everyone else's ideas.

RAY: But you can't force that on other people! When someone has an opinion just allow him to express it totally.

HILDA: Is your rule that everyone has to cooperate?

PHIL: It's not a rule; it's expected. It is an agreement—that's what we're doing—we're doing a mutual agreement.

RAY: It's a mutual agreement to listen to other people. We've all agreed on a mutual agreement.

BETTY: There is still a problem: What if someone doesn't want to follow the other seven people? Are you going to force him?

CHARLES: I think we all would realize we can't be loners. It's like a dance; I want to count the steps in fourths and the rest of you count in eighths, then I should realize that the dance won't work.

PHIL: We are supposed to have basic life supports in here, so I don't think that a situation where we are *so* desperate that we can't get agreement is going to arise—or should arise. We're just going to have to work things out as they come up.

CHARLES: But you can't ask someone to go against their principles.

CISSY: But maybe we'll change our minds if we listen, respect, and vote, or maybe he'd change his mind; we can listen and vote again.

BETTY: I would still want to act on my principles.

EVE: But, Betty, just try to convince us of them! If you believe something so *strongly*, you could change our minds.

CHARLES: Betty, you're twisting situations. We would probably find out we had the *same* morals if we really talk.

CISSY: It's really hard; there are no clear answers for that, Betty. You just have to see what's going to happen.

BETTY: Would you take action against me if I opened the door [to the outside contamination] and the group didn't want me to?

CHARLES: You'd be acting violently by doing that. You'd not be respecting everybody else. If we forced you to stop, we'd just be saying there has to be fair representation.

The Stressful Game, NeoPd

We enter toward the end of this game in order to witness its resolution within a dominated group. The winning and losing teams are identified to make the action intelligible. Although the winners have about five times more points than the losers, both teams have just agreed to play for moderate and equal points, which can be accomplished if no player turns up blue cards. Breaking this explicit agreement was called "burning" by the students, and this label was taken up by Martin Packer (in press) in his microanalysis of NeoPd. The following comments draw heavily on Packer's analyses. Readers may note that talk *about* morality is now at a minimum; emotion is prevalent in the form of subtly expressed moral superiority. The winners "are willing to give" while the losers don't want to be objects of charity. They want their fair share. The winning team is composed of Bill, Katy, John, and Lisa; the losing team is made up of Jim, Louise, Gary, and Betty, who remains silent.

Immediately following the burning, the Losing Team gave few clues as to their reactions; they seemed controlled and deliberate. They sat, saying little, save for an exclamation from Louise ("That's it!"), and surprisingly they continue to play cooperatively. We begin just as the burning occurs.

(Bill puts down a blue card, a huge grin on his face. Lisa, Katy and John all cover their faces to try, unsuccessfully, to suppress their laughter.)

SL: Choose. One and zero. Five and two points.

LOUISE: *(to Gary)* That's it, that's it! *(The other members of the Losing Team say nothing.)*

JOHN: *(to Lisa and Katy)* If they're gonna go down here see *(pointing to the payoff matrix).*

SL: Winning team has 147 points; losing team has minus 31.

BILL: That was mean! *(Laughs.)*

JOHN: I know! *(Members of the winning team laugh, and talk together in whispers.)*

SL: All right, ready to go another round?

JIM: Yeah, oh yeah *(pleased).*

(Winning team members nod their heads.)

(At the end of this round, Jim, talking for the losing team, is actually eager to continue playing. During the next round both teams play cooperatively. If the losing team feels any impulse to punish the winning team for the burning, it is not evident. However, in the subsequent round it becomes clear that the losing team was playing in an organized way, with motives not immediately apparent on the surface. Midway through the round the winning team burns again, and the losing team this time responds immediately:)

SL: Choose. Zero, zero.

SL: Four and four points.

SL: Choose. *(All four members of the winning team play blue cards, in a manner which is clearly prearranged. They laugh as they do so.)* Four, zero cards.

SL: Eight and minus four point.

SL: Choose. *(The losing team now also plays blue cards.)* Four, four cards.

BILL: *(in a loud voice)* That one hurt!

BILL: Zero, zero points.

(Now that the winning team has burnt a second time, the losing team plays the

competitive four blue cards for the remainder of this round, and the next. Their views became clear in the subsequent negotiation which takes place at their request:)

GARY: Okay, here, we came up with a new option (since) you guys violated the trust. *(Laughter from the other members of both teams.)*

BILL: What's your option? Ah, okay, wait . . . let me, you wanna . . . okay, because you violated our trust on the last option, (but) we're willing to give you this. . . . *(He refers to the losing team's having played four blue cards on the last two rounds.)*

GARY: *(interrupting)* No! We *want*. . . . *(He raises his index finger, to emphasize his point.)*

BILL: You *want*? *(His tone is incredulous. Katy and John laugh.)*

GARY: No, listen. . . .

BILL: *(interrupting)* You're not in much of a position to *demand*. . . .

GARY: *(interrupting)* No, listen, listen. We want four rounds where we get to use four and you guys go zero. That's the first four. And then the fifth one, we'll, we're willing to go zero, zero every time. You guys violated the trust, not us.

BILL: That's pretty stupid.

GARY: Right now we'll just go four, four every time *(picks up his card)*.

KATY: *(calling out)* No!

JOHN: *(calling out)* Hey, no way!

BILL: And *we're* going to end up winning. *(He points to himself.)*

GARY: It's not a contest.

KATY: *(calling out to Bill)* Don't give in.

BILL: We get 50¢ though, each, I mean that's quite a lot.

GARY: Aaaw, alright, fine, you have to remember, you have to remember that . . . what you're doing to get that 50¢.

JOHN: *(calling out)* That's okay!

BILL: Yeah!

GARY: Okay, I mean as long as you guys *realize* what you're doing.

Summary

We again argued that the study of practical moral action is the prime target for social scientific research and then went on to enlarge the usual definition of moral action to include all instances where persons do anything more than privately think *about* a moral dilemma. We justified this expansion. People are centers of activity, and when they confront a practical moral issue, they act. Moral situations vary in cost, and the stresses of appearing moral and disrupting relations with others arouse emotions which can depress or boost the quality of moral action. Although hypothetical dilemmas are generally of low cost, people care about ideas, as the women students most certainly did when their group discussed Academic Weekend. The contents of moral issues were found to be one determinant of moral action in at least two ways: whether they bear on personal experience—like grandparents in a nursing home—or represent issues of general intellectual familiarity—like civil rights and nuclear disaster.

The main analyses focused on two explanations of moral action—the effects of character and the effects of two situational factors of gaming or discussing and group context. First analyzed was the idea of moral character as a development that rises above situation and content to determine the quality of moral action. Weak support was secured for this explanation and then only when the circumstances of context were the least demanding. This occurred when the led discussion groups were dealing as third persons with hypothetical dilemmas. Surely differences in moral performance exist, for instance, across age groups, but whatever level of moral functioning is activated in any one situation seems due to factors other than the sheer possession of moral concern by individual students. This finding, which was replicated with the adolescents' data, strongly questions the validity of the stage explanation of immutable moral character. In their meaning, accepted by the cognitivists (Kohlberg, 1969), stages have the qualities of immutability, durability, and irreversibility. This is a strict view of moral capability, and if stage levels do not become evident in people's action, the worth of the concept is not clear. No important differences between cognitive or interactional functioning were found.

The second main set of results concerned the impact of situations—gaming or discussing—and membership in led or dominated groups. Here our observations showed that the quality of moral action varied in accordance with certain aspects of these experiences: 1. the contents of issues (especially in discussion sessions 2 and 3); 2. the emotional engagement of situations (for instance, playing the interesting game Humanus resulted in high moral levels, and the emotional trauma of NeoPd resulted in low levels); 3. the interpersonal threats in moral situations (for instance, the threat to friendships posed by NeoPd and Starpower and the eroding effects of being a member of a dominated friendship group, or the facilitation of being a woman in a led group).

Again the qualities of cognitive and interactional morality were *both* highly responsive to these situational influences. At this point, then, the two systems seem more alike than they seem different.

The individual student's contributions to his or her own level of moral action were not directly considered in this chapter. In the end, moral action is almost always the choice and act of a person—or so it is ultimately regarded by the legal systems of all cultures. The individual person is held responsible for his or her own actions.

All we have shown in this chapter is that the contexts of moral experience make it easy or difficult for individual persons to act in morally adequate ways. Nonetheless, single persons did act adequately even in the most stressful contexts and others acted poorly in benign contexts, as we bring out in the next chapter.

Chapter 10

STRATEGIES OF COPING
AND DEFENDING
IN MORAL ACTION

Moral theory cannot be rounded off and made complete and tidy, partly because so much that is of value in a human life depends on uncontrollable accident, partly because we still know so little about the determinants of behaviour and about human nature in general, partly because individuals vary so greatly in their dispositions, partly because new ways of life should always be expected. . . . We expect also leaps of imagination . . . will lead to transformations of experience (Stuart Hampshire, 1978, p. 53).

Coping, Defending, and Moral Conflict

WE START with two simple ideas. First, people have preferred ways of solving problems, and when they face a moral problem, they initially rely on these methods. Second, whether people solve problems by defensiveness or by coping—either habitually or just at a particular moment—affects the morality of their action. These two ideas underlie the research described in this chapter. They draw on the more intimate and individuated aspects of people—the processes of personality used to deal with the major and minor problems of living. By moving in this direction we are not disputing our main finding that it is context and not character that affects the quality of moral action. Instead we are building upon it. We suspect that the situational explanation alone is not sufficient. We also suspect that the seemingly consistent and durable quality of "moral character" lies not so much in morality as in the consistent ways that individuals deal with conflict of any kind. In this chapter, we bring all possible influences on moral action together to determine the magnitude of their effects.

There is an essential difference between coping and defending. In natural language and by technical definition, coping means that people *accurately* identify and adhere to the "realities" of their own mind and their situation. Defending means that people twist or negate the realities of their situation and their own feelings when they feel that above all they must protect themselves.

In moral conflict, discussants cope when they accurately and mutually recognize all parties' legitimate self-interests and act together to come to a decision. *Accuracy seems, on logical grounds, to be the precondition of adequate moral action. Being only human, moral actors are often not accurate, but from the standpoint of interactional theory, it would be better if they were. Thus we merge the value grounds of coping and morality in our work.*

This stipulation for ideal moral interchange is fundamental to interactional theory, with its moral ground that human relations should be authentically equalized. The cognitivists assume that the highest level of morality is achieved through rational discourse and detached judgment that does not depend on or utilize intuition or emotion. The interactional theory is based on the assumption that morality is a total experience and that meanings must continuously be generated and regenerated by living people, who rely upon rationality, intuition, and emotion to equalize their relations. As a consequence, their personalities—especially their processes of adaptation—are surely involved. We make, then, two proposals. Moral action can be better understood by studying general methods of problem solving, and the opposite effects of coping and defending on conflict resolution mean that personality needs to be included in the study of moral action.

If this acceptance of personality as critical to morality is carried to its extreme, personality absorbs all there is to morality. And this has the same consequence as the supposition that moral character wholly determines people's moral action, an explanation we have found wanting (see Chapter 9). Both conceptualizations view people as entities unto themselves, as solitary, individualistic actors. Both contain an unexamined assumption about human nature: People are who they are and they scarcely change and adapt. Currently, some psychologists hold the view that morality is only one part of personality (for instance,

Figure 10.1

Possible Pathways to Moral Action

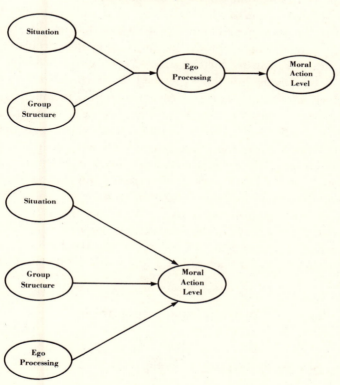

Hogan, Johnson, & Emler, 1978). Within this view, there is no pressing need to identify the distinctive features of morality. Of course,
whether or not morality is nothing more than one aspect of personality
depends on how personality is defined. Does personality encompass
all there is to a person, or does it refer more to the stylistic, socioemotional expressions of people?

In any event coping and defending do not encompass all that there
is to personality nor all there is to morality. But they are relevant to
moral action for several reasons. First, people of different personalities, who are nevertheless equally moral, may use the same processes
when they confront moral issues. Second, to designate one kind of
stylistic personality as *the moral personality* is to abandon all hope of
identifying a common morality. If anything at all distinguishes people

from one another, it is their personality. Third, it is strategically prudent for researchers to separate morality from the larger concept of personality. If different kinds of personalities are moral, then the specific aspects of personality that bear on moral action need to be identified. These may be either the strategies that people characteristically use or inventively deploy whenever they face problems.

Ego strategies can be further divided then into two kinds—those people habitually use and those they evoke for the moment. A person's characteristic strategies are well known by family members, friends, and coworkers; they can usually predict how a person will handle particular conflicts. The young adults' characteristic ego processes were measured before the group experiences were begun, using the ego scales of the California Psychological Inventory. Measurements of situationally evoked strategies were derived from clinicians' observations and Q sorts of both the adolescents' and young adults' problem-solving during the group sessions.

The students' scores for characteristic ego processing were used to "correct" their situationally evoked scores, so the latter would only reflect their coping and defending in the moral action situations.

Preliminary Considerations

Effects of Context on Ego Functioning*

Differences between Groups' Ego Strategies.   First, we briefly consider two secondary matters that could confound the main analyses of moral action. The first concerns whether or not the contexts of gaming or discussing or membership in led or dominated groups wholly shaped the students' ego processing; if they did, then context would still be the primary determinant of moral action, and it would be superfluous to bring individuated ego processes into the account. This line of reasoning is depicted in the top diagram, shown in Figure 10.1. The contrary possibility, shown below it, is that individual's ego processing

*Readers may find it useful at this point to glance at Tables 8.1 and 8.2 which present the various ego processes and the properties of coping and defending.

makes contributions to the quality of their moral actions that are separate and independent of contextual influences. We will show in this chapter that the second explanation turns out to be correct.

At this point we report that analyses produced no differences in ego strategies between games and discussions or between led and dominated atmospheres except for session 1. During that session members of led groups were more coping and less defensive than members of dominated groups when everyone was first experiencing being a research subject. This single result, which suggests ego functioning did depend on context, does not make the lower diagram incorrect. When people are in new situations, they often do not act in individuated ways. The students apparently fell back on standardized resolutions to act in accordance with the way their friendship group usually functioned—either hierarchically dominated or communally led.

The second diagram has two implications. First, context may set outer limits that facilitate or inhibit the quality of moral action rather than directly "cause" moral action. Second, the moral problems just in themselves had forceful meanings. The main evidence supporting these statements is reported in this chapter.

Differences in Ego Strategies within Groups. Another analysis of the individual students' ego strategies—but now within rather than between different groups—is informative. If task-oriented groups are to function well, they benefit from variety in individual members' skills and solutions—for instance, clarification, humor, and initiative. The smooth, efficient operations of the led groups suggest that members' ego strategies would be individuated; thus no significant differences between the leaders and the led were expected. That was the essential result for each session with but minor, marginal exceptions.

Quite the opposite occurred for the dominated groups. Their more stressed and polarizing confrontations produced a substantial difference in ego strategies between the dominators and the dominated in each session (between 25 and 40 percent were significant, $ps \leq .05$ to .001). The nine dominators seemed to enjoy themselves; they were more playfully coping (ego regression) during four sessions, but also defensively displaced their negative, angry emotions onto their friends in all five sessions. Faced with that behavior, the dominated coped in all five sessions by tolerating the ambiguity of their position and by recognizing, but suppressing, their feelings. But in all five sessions they also became defensively self-righteous as is shown by their higher scores for the process of reaction formation. Also they were defensive, doubting in four sessions and regressive in two sessions. Altogether the dominated seemed to have tolerated the dominators' treatment by controlling their feelings and quietly regarding themselves morally superior.

Relations between Characteristic and Situational Ego Strategies

Psychologists sometimes assume that people are highly consistent in their functioning. If this were wholly true, the characteristic and situationally evoked strategies would be identical, and our measures of characteristic and situational functioning would merely duplicate each other; consequently we analyzed relationships between characteristic and situational ego functioning. The 20 C.P.I.-based ego scores were correlated with their 20 situational counterparts, the latter summed for all sessions to represent the students' most general ways of acting, called an aggregation, following Epstein (1980). These correlations were not high. They ranged from .46 to − .24 with an average of .19 (eight significant, or 40 percent, with ps from ≤ .01 to ≤ .001). Correlations were *also* calculated between the characteristic strategies and the strategies for individual sessions. No game or discussion session produced stronger stability. Because these correlations were not high, either the group sessions evoked considerable strategic ingenuity in the students' problem solving, or one or the other set of measures is meaningless. The former is more likely, given the results described below.

Main Results for the Young Adults

The analyses reported in the remainder of this chapter focus on a major expectancy in this research: Moral conflict commonly requires actors to mobilize certain patterns of ego functioning to take simultaneously other people's interests and their own self-interests into consideration. We will show that the simple presence of moral problems was the most important factor in the students' considerations, whatever the nature of their friendship group, whether its task was discussing or gaming. Readers should notice the results for the two moral systems reported in this chapter come from parallel analyses, not from direct comparisons, which are reported in the next chapter. Parallel analyses allow us to observe similarities in the two systems and see how they differ.

Various Influences on Levels of Moral Action: Proportional Contributions

To identify the important influences on moral action and determine the percent of variation in the moral-action scores that each influence explains, we constructed "multiple regression models" for the men, the women, and men and women combined for each session. Readers need not be statisticians to understand the logic of these models. Our purposes were to ascertain whether or not a factor influenced the action scores and then determine what percent of the variation in the moral scores each influence accounted for. These "candidates" for explaining why moral action levels varied were entered into these models one after another in the following order and for the following reasons.

1. For the model representing the entire sample, the variable of sex was first entered because the influences might affect men and women differently. This controlled all subsequent entries for the effects of sex. Therefore the final results for the entire sample represent the most general ways that moral action by people of either sex was influenced. Sex was obviously not entered into men's or women's models. From here on, candidates could enter the models *only* if their contribution would be significant at the probability level of .05 or better.
2. Considering the more impersonal, contextual factors first, situations (game or discussion) and group structure (led or dominated) could enter the models.
3. Next, ego processes, first characteristic and then situational, were allowed to enter the models.
4. Finally, the students' moral scores on their presession inter-

view, which are usually regarded as the "true" indication of moral status, could enter the models.

Comparing the Power of Different Influences

Although detailed results for these models are given in Table 10.1 for social scientists, we draw the general reader's attention to Figure 10.2, where the percents contributed by each influence on the moral scores can be seen. For the moment we do not consider whether the influences encouraged or discouraged moral action.

The overall power of these models in accounting for variation in the moral action scores first needs to be pointed out. Twenty-six of the 30 models (two kinds of moral scores, three samples including men, women, and men and women combined, and five sessions) were highly significant at the .001 level of probability; three were significant at the .01 level and one at the .05 level. By social scientists' usual standards, these results are impressive. There was no consistent difference in significance between cognitive and interactional morality.

Of primary interest is the comparison between the strengths of the contextual and personal influence in accounting for the variation in moral action scores. We consider the totals for all five sessions and for all three models—the entire sample and men and women separately. The total percentages accounted for were very nearly equal for the two moral systems—424 percent for the interactional models and 432 percent for the cognitive models. The order of influences by strength was also identical. Moving from the strongest to the weakest influence, we find situational ego processing, situations of gaming or discussing, characteristic ego structures, and, lagging far behind, the groups' structure. The students' sex never made a significant contribution, and the presession interview scores had only one minor effect on the men's interactional scores in session 3. Situational ego processing accounted for 175 percent of the variation in all interactional scores, but 211 percent for the cognitive scores; gaming or discussing accounted for 130 and 132 percent of the variation in the scores for both systems; characteristic ego processing, 80 percent for interactional and 63 percent for the cognitive scores; group structure, 39 percent for interactional and 26 percent for cognitive scores.

As it turns out, the situational strategies used by individual students were the strongest determinant of their moral actions, even after all the effects of context were controlled. Three specific differences for cognitive and interactional morality are evident. First, situational ego processing made a greater contribution to cognitive than to interactional scores, 211 to

Table 10.1.

Situational and Personal Influences on Levels of Moral Action

(Percent of Variation Explained)

All Participants	Percent Contribution	Women	Percent Contribution	Men	Percent Contribution
Session 1		**Cognitive**			
Sex	1	Game groups higher	22^a	Game groups higher	20^a
Game groups higher	20^a	Session denial	-6^c	Session displacement	-11^a
Led groups higher	3^c			Session regression	-5^c
Session regression	-4^b				
Session displacement	-4^c				
Total	32^a		28^a		36^a
		Interactional			
Sex	0	Game groups higher	32^a	Game groups higher	26^a
Game groups higher	29^a	Session empathy	$+5^c$	Led groups higher	7^c
Led groups higher	3^c			Characteristic projection	$+5^c$
Session empathy	$+4^b$			Session regression	-7^b
Total	36^a		37^a		44^a
Session 2		**Cognitive**			
Sex	-1	Discussion groups higher	19^a	Discussion groups higher	28^a
Discussion groups higher	23^a	Characteristic ego regression	10^b	Session objectivity	$+9^b$
Characteristic ego regression	-3^c	Session intellectuality	$+9^b$		
Session intellectuality	$+9^a$				
Total	36^a		38^a		37^a
		Interactional			
Sex	-0	Discussion groups higher	7^c	Discussion groups higher	20^a
Discussion groups higher	13^a	Session isolation	-15^a	Characteristic doubt	-6^c
Characteristic tolerance of ambiguity	-3^c			Characteristic repression	$+7^c$
Session intellectualizing	-14^a			Session intellectualizing	-14^a
Session intellectuality	$+3^c$				
Total	33^a		22^a		47^a
Session 3		**Cognitive**			
Sex	1	Session denial	-13^b	Session logical analysis	$+15^b$
Characteristic doubt	-4^c	Session tolerance of ambiguity	-10^b	Session reaction formation	$+19^a$
Characteristic substitution	-4^c				

Table 10.1 (cont.)

Session logical analysis	$+7^b$			Session denial	7^b
Session reaction formation	$+6^b$			Session sublimation	$+8^b$
Session sublimation	$+3^c$				
Total	25^a		23^a		49^a

Interactional

Sex	-1	Characteristic intellectuality	$+9^c$	Session displacement	-12^b
Characteristic suppression	$+5^c$	Session intellectuality	$+20^a$	Presession interview scores	$+8^c$
Session intellectuality	$+8^b$	Session tolerance of ambiguity	-5^c		
Session displacement	-6^b				
Session tolerance of ambiguity	-4^c				
Session rationalization	-3^c				
Total	26^a		34^a		20^b

Session 4 — Cognitive

Sex	-0	Characteristic isolation	-20^a	Led groups higher	-7^c
Led groups higher	4^c	Session displacement	$+8^b$	Characteristic denial	$+8^c$
Characteristic isolation	-8^a	Session ego regression	$+5^c$	Session displacement	-10^b
Characteristic concentration	-6^b	Session logical analysis	-5^c	Session doubt	-8^b
Session empathy	$+3^c$			Session reaction formation	$+5^c$
Total	21^a		38^a		38^a

Interactional

Sex	-0	Characteristic isolation	-9^c	Characteristic suppression	$+11^b$
Characteristic suppression	$+7^b$	Session repression	-8^c	Session empathy	$+14^b$
Characteristic isolation	-3^c				
Session empathy	$+10^a$				
Total	20^a		17^b		25^a

Session 5 — Cognitive

Sex	-1	Session regression	-9^c	Led groups higher	15^b
Led groups higher	6^b			Session empathy	$+7^c$
Session isolation	-6^b				
Total	13^a		9^c		22^c

Interactional

Sex	-3	Led groups higher	20^a	Characteristic displacement	-8^c
Led groups higher	9^a	Characteristic isolation	-7^c	Session intellectualizing	-8^c
Game groups higher	3^c	Session regression	-8^b		
Session isolation	-7^b				
Total	22^a		35^a		16^b

$^a p < .001.$
$^b p < .01.$
$^c p < .05.$

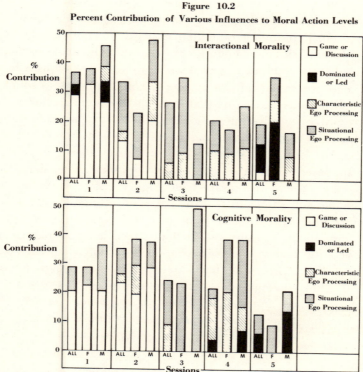

Figure 10.2
Percent Contribution of Various Influences to Moral Action Levels

175 percent. Second, the group's structure had a stronger effect on the interactional scores than it did on the cognitive scores, the ratio being 39 to 26 percent. Third, characteristic ego processing contributed more to the interactional scores than to the cognitive scores (80 to 63 percent). These three results continue the trend we previously noticed. Cognitive morality seems somewhat more responsive to situational influences than interactional morality, so the latter may be the more stable and persistent.

Gaming compared with discussing had its strongest effects on the moral action scores in the first two sessions for both systems, as can be seen in Figure 10.2, undoubtedly because Humanus in session 1 was a very easy game while NeoPd in session 2 was a very difficult game. But thereafter, neither games nor discussions had impressive effects on either set of moral scores. The students' own personal ego functioning, and to a lesser extent, their group's structure as led or dominated became stronger influences, especially in session 5. These delayed effects of group structure probably arose from the students' cumulated moral experience with one another, specifically the erosion or enhancement of their good faith in either dominated or led groups.

The students' situational ego processing generally made significant and sizable contributions to moral scores in all five sessions. Characteristic ego processing influenced interactional morality to some degree in all sessions, indicating that students consistently utilized their usual resources to solve interactional problems, but it made no contribution at all to cognitive moral action in sessions 1 and 5. Sizable contributions from characteristic ego processing to cognitive moral scores appeared when these scores were the lowest, in session 4.

Altogether then, the graphs in Figure 10.2 inform us that 1. situational ego strategies had the strongest effects, 2. situations of gaming or discussing had important effects in early sessions, 3. being in led or dominated groups usually had effects later, 4. characteristic ego processing had stronger effects on interactional morality, while 5. situational ego processing had stronger effects on cognitive morality. Neither the students' sex nor their scores on the presession interview affected their moral action scores. *In sum, both the person and the situation need to be taken into account to understand moral action.*

Direction of Influences on Moral-action Levels

The specific identity and direction of influences that lead to higher or lower moral action scores are shown in Table 10.1. A summary and interpretation that clarify the main meanings follow.

Directionality for Contextual Influences. Although strong effects of gaming or discussing appeared only in the first two sessions, they are probably not due to these activities per se but to the varying difficulty of the moral dilemmas presented by Humanus and NeoPD played by the game students in sessions 1 and 2 and the easy civil rights dilemmas the discussion students considered in session 2. Highly contrasting effects on scores of being in a led or dominated group, always in favor of the led groups, appeared in later sessions. We suggest that the groups' customary way of operating facilitated or frustrated individual members' attempts to reach moral resolution and that these effects became progressively stronger across the sessions.

Directionality for Ego Strategies. In considering the effects of the students' ego processing, we combine characteristic and situationally evoked processes to simplify discussion so the results (shown in Figure 10.3 and drawn from Table 10.1) are for the summed percentages of coping and defending.

A number of questions are of interest. Were we correct in our hypothesis that coping should facilitate and defensiveness hinder levels of moral action? In other words, did the coping processes consistently produce higher moral scores, and did the distortions and negations of defensive processes lower them? Also, did either recourse affect scores in the same way in both moral systems? What were the exceptions to this hypothesis? Were specific ego processes persistently associated with moral functioning? Did the patterns of strategies associated with interactional morality differ from those associated with cognitive morality?

Figure 10.3 shows the contribution of the ego processes for each session. The ego processes are classified as positive or negative coping, as well as positive or negative defense (meaning that coping could make either a positive or negative contribution to higher moral scores as could the defensive processes). Contributions from positive coping and negative defense (avoiding defensiveness) support the main hypothesis, whereas contributions from negative coping (failing to cope) and positive defense do not. Incidences are shown for all students and separately for women and men. The dotted line drawn horizontally across the sessions in Figure 10.3 represents the division point for the main hypothesis. All influences below the line confirm the hypothesis that positive coping and negative defense facilitate moral action and all influences above the line contradict the hypothesis. As can be seen, coping encouraged moral action in both systems and defensiveness discouraged it, *but the hypothesis was more strikingly supported for the interactional system and more frequently violated for the cognitive system.* (The totals summed for all sessions are shown in Table 10.2.) Only 24 percent of the variation in interactional moral levels for all five sessions contradicts the hypothesis, compared to 231 percent in support; a total of 85 percent contradicts the hypothesis for cognitive stages, compared to 189 percent support.

Considering just the two divisions in Figure 10.3 that support the hypothesis, we can see that abstaining from defensiveness (negative defense) made a proportionately larger contribution to moral scores

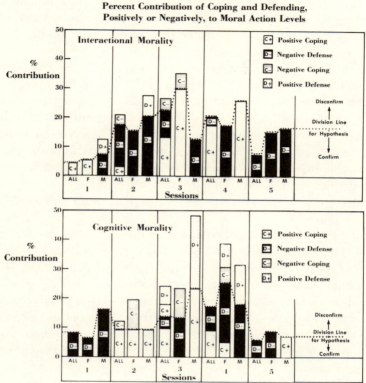

Figure 10.3
Percent Contribution of Coping and Defending,
Positively or Negatively, to Moral Action Levels

for both systems than actively coping (positive coping). For interactional morality the ratio was 96 percent for positive coping to 135 percent for negative defense; for cognitive morality, the ratio was 81 to 108 percent. Within the two divisions that contradict the hypothesis, positive defense made a proportionately larger contribution to cognitive scores than did the failure to cope (53 to 32 percent), whereas these two nonsupportive categories were equally balanced at 12 percent for the interactional scores. Altogether, then, avoidance of defensiveness encouraged performance in both systems, but also, surprisingly, being defensive helped cognitive performance.

Disproportionate contributions of ego processing in various sessions can also be seen in Figure 10.3. The sessions that drew the strongest support were the most stressful, namely, sessions 2, 3, and 4. In contrast, the contextual influences of the situation and/or group structure made their largest contributions to raising scores during sessions 1

Table 10.2.

Total Contribution of Ego Strategies to Moral Action,

Summed across Five Sessions

(Percentages)

	Interactional Morality				Cognitive Morality			
	Contributions Affirming the Hypothesis							
	All	Women	Men	Total	All	Women	Men	Total
Positive coping	37%	34%	25%	96%	28%	14%	39%	81%
Negative defense	33	47	55	135	26	48	34	108
Total	70	81	80	231	54	62	73	189
	Contributions Not Affirming the Hypothesis							
Negative coping	7	5	0	12	7	25	0	32
Positive defense	0	0	12	12	6	8	39	53
Total	7	5	12	24	13	33	39	85
Grand Total	77	86	92	255	67	95	112	274
Percentages support-ing hypothesis	91	94	87	91	81	65	65	69
Percentages viola-ting hypothesis	9	6	13	9	19	35	35	31

and 5. This contrast suggests that these research subjects—and perhaps people in general—more likely mobilize their individuated adaptive resources when the costs are great (but not *too* great). The three stressful sessions also resulted in mixed patterns of coping and defense, especially for cognitive moral action. In other words, to act in morally adequate ways in the stressful situations, the students needed both to defend and to cope.

Altogether, the supposition that coping is an essential feature of adequate moral negotiation applied to both systems but more certainly to interactional morality. Since cognitive moral action also depended on ego strategies, it is a sector of influence that might be considered by the cognitive theorists.

Repetitive Contributions of Certain Ego Processes

Identification of the particular processes that repeatedly made significant contributions to moral scores will refine our understanding of

Table 10.3.

Ego Processes with Repetitive Contributions

to Moral-Action Levels[a]

	Interactional Morality		Cognitive Morality	
	Number and Source Contribution	Total Percent	Number and Source Contribution	Total Percent
Positive Coping				
Intellectuality	1 characteristic 2 situational	40	--	--
Logical analysis	--	--	2 situational	22
Empathy	4 situational	33	--	--
Suppression	3 characteristic	23	--	--
Negative Defense				
Isolation	3 characteristic 2 situational	41	2 characteristic 1 situational	34
Intellectualizing	3 situational	36	--	--
Displacement	1 characteristic 2 situational	26	3 situational	25
Positive Defense				
Reaction formation	--	--	3 situational	30

[a]Criterion includes at least two contributions < 20%.

the requirements of moral action. Only those processes that made significant contributions twice and accounted for at least 20 percent of the variation in the moral scores will be mentioned. Again, the processes can have positive or negative effects on moral scores. These processes are shown in Table 10.3.

Two processes contributed to moral action scores for both systems and both are negative defenses. Avoiding the process of isolation, which defensively separates related ideas and feelings, made strong contributions to both sets of moral action scores (five times to the interactional scores for a total of 41 percent and three times to the cognitive scores for a total of 34 percent). In other words, adequate moral action seems to require the integration of ideas and emotions, or, to use the students' words, "getting it all together."

Negative displacement also contributed five times to the interactional system (41 percent), and three times to the cognitive system

(34 percent). Therefore, when the students took their frustration out on their friends, they did not achieve high-quality moral action. From the cognitive view, displacement would interfere with thought processes. But a different reason applies for the interactional system. If parties to a dispute vent their fury on each other, accurate, sincere dialogue cannot occur, and bad faith will increase.

Aside from isolation and displacement, the processes which make repeated contributions are different for the two systems. For the interactional system, coping intellectuality, which is a strategy of freely ranging over the possibilities in diverse ideas, made four positive contributions for a total of 40 percent. Empathy with friends' feelings and thoughts also resulted in four positive contributions to interactional scores for a total of 33 percent. Coping suppression—a matter of being aware of one's feelings but regulating them—made three contributions for a total of 23 percent. Finally, defensive intellectualizing made three negative contributions for a total of 36 percent. Altogether then, the ego processes that exclusively supported interactional morality are coping empathy, intellectuality, and suppression of emotions, while defensive intellectualizing especially thwarted moral action. The order of contributions to interactional morality, according to the amount of variation accounted for in the moral action scores, was negative isolation (41 percent), positive intellectuality (40 percent), negative intellectualizing (36 percent), positive empathy (33 percent), negative displacement (20 percent), and positive suppression (23 percent).

As mentioned earlier, ego processes accounted overall for a somewhat larger proportion of the variation in cognitive than in interactional moral scores. Nevertheless, only two processes were specific to cognitive moral action and both accounted for only a small amount of variation. Therefore the strategies that facilitated cognitive action were not consistent in nature. Reaction formation, whereby people transform their angry feelings and present themselves as controlled and self-righteous, resulted in three *positive* contributions, for a total of 30 percent. Logical analysis—the coping process that should be the keystone of cognitive morality—brought about two increases in the scores, for a total of 22 percent. The order of ego processes according to the percent of their contribution was negative isolation (34 percent), positive reaction formation (30 percent), negative displacement (25 percent), and positive logical analysis (22 percent).

These repeated ego processes were associated with high-quality moral action in both systems. Clearly both kinds of moral action called for cognitive coping processes, but in interactional morality, it was the freedom of intellectuality, and in cognitive morality, it was the focused method of logical analysis. Abstaining from cognitive defensiveness also helped, that is, isolation in both systems and intellectualizing in interactional morality. Displaced emotion resulted in lower scores in both systems. Interactional morality additionally required that students understand the views of others and take care in regulating their own feelings. Cognitive morality was *facilitated* when the students presented themselves as self-righteous. More will be said about these repetitive processes in the chapter summation.

Main Results for the Adolescents

In this section the concern is whether the adolescents' ego strategies generally replicate those used by the young adults. However, less data were available for understanding the adolescents' moral action. They only played games and no means of identifying led or dominated groups or measures of characteristic ego processing were available. Consequently neither the differential effects of situation or group structure nor the contributions of characteristic ego processing on moral scores could be analyzed.

The group experiences for the adolescents included three games that were also presented to the young adults—Humanus, NeoPd, and Starpower. The order of the games for the adolescents followed the same rationale as that for the young adults: Keeping the participants involved and not continuously stressed. We remind readers that the first game, BaFa, which involved role-playing citizenship in two different cultures, had low moral cost; the second game was NeoPd, as it was for the young adults; the third was Humanus, which the young adults played first; Starpower was the fourth game, as it was for the young adults; Role Play was the fifth game.

Funding limitations prohibited hiring additional persons to rate ego processes. Consequently only single ego Q sorts for each adolescent for each session were done. To achieve reasonable reliability, we reduced the number of Q items by statistical analyses which combined related items. This increases reliability, but sacrifices distinctions among processes. Fourteen groupings—or factors—resulted. Nine represented coping and five defensive strategies. The pattern of Q sort items that typified each factor suggested the following names for the coping factors: *expressive coping, cognitive empathy, emotional empathy, objectivity, cognitive coping, concentration, interpersonal logic, suppression,* and *affectively socialized.* The defensive factors were called *doubting, denial/repression, emotionally unregulated, defensively restricted,* and *displacement.*

Because the adolescents were not a homogeneous sample with respect to age, race, and socioeconomic background, these differences needed to be taken into account. Also only 57 adolescents played games, so analyses with sexes separated were not feasible. In constructing the same kind of multiple regression models to account for variations in moral scores, as for the young adults, we took the differences in the adolescents' background into account. Furthermore, we thought at that time—as did many developmental psychologists doing research on morality—that interviewing people about hypothetical dilemmas produces "true" moral scores. Consequently, the models for each game were constructed by entering moral scores for the first interview and then allowing socioeconomic status, age, sex, and race to enter, followed by any ego factor score if its contribution would be significant at the .05 level of probability. The details of these models can be seen in Table 10.4, while the following discussion summarizes their main implications.

The total variation in moral scores, which included the adolescents' objective characteristics, was greater for cognitive scores, at 198 percent, than for interactional scores at 159 percent. But the students' objective characteristics accounted for 52 percent of the variation in the cognitive scores but only 29 percent in the interactional scores. Being of a higher socioeconomic level gave advantage to the adolescents' achievement of cognitive scores (for a total of 20 percent) but had only a minor effect on their interactional scores (7 percent). Being black was associated with higher interactional scores (14 percent). The students' sex had a small and equal effect on moral scores for each system (about 8 percent). The students' age, which ranged from 13 to 18 years, was associated with higher cognitive scores but not with their interactional scores. This result suggests that the cognitive system has

Table 10.4.

Contributions to Adolescents' Moral-Action Levels

(Contributions include presession interview scores, ego processes,
and demographic variables)

Interactional Morality		Cognitive Morality	
Variable	Percent Con- tribution	Variable	Percent-Con- tribution
First Session: BaFa			
Presession interview scores	+1	Presession interview scores	+22[a]
Affective empathy	+15[a]	Age (years)	+15[a]
Suppression	+11[c]	Affectively unregulated	-11[a]
Interpersonal logic	+7[c]	Suppression	+15[a]
		Being female	+7[c]
		Interpersonal logic	+5[c]
		Cognitive empathy	+3[c]
Total	33[b]		78[a]
Second Session: NeoPd			
Presession interview scores	+4	Presession interview scores	-3
Cognitive coping	+21[a]	Defensive doubting	+21[a]
Interpersonal logic	+7[c]	Interpersonal logic	+18[a]
		Cognitive coping	+17[a]
		Age (years)	+7[c]
		Denial-repression	-3[c]
Total	32[b]		69[a]
Third Session: Humanus			
Presession interview scores	+3[c]	Presession interview scores	+2
Affective empathy	+7[b]	Higher socioeconomic level	+13[c]
Higher socioeconomic level	+7[b]	Age (years)	+9[c]
Being black	14[b]		
Total	31[b]		24[b]
Fourth Session: Starpower			
Presession interview scores	-4	Presession interview scores	1
Affective empathy	+8[b]	Affectively unregulated	+9[c]
Sex	-10[c]		
Total	22[c]		10
Fifth Session: Role Play			
Presession interview scores	-2	Presession interview scores	1
Defensive doubting	+11	Affectively unregulated	-8[c]
Interpersonal logic	+11	Higher socioeconomic level	7
Affective empathy	8[c]		
Concentration	+8		
Total	40[a]		15

[a] p < .001.

[b] p < .01.

[c] p < .05.

a stronger developmental thrust during these years than the interactional. This is consistent with the two theories' views of development which are thoroughly considered in a later chapter.

The moral scores from the presession interview did not generally predict the adolescents' moral action scores. The overall contributions of ego strategies to interactional and cognitive moral action scores are of similar magnitude in all five sessions: 114 percent for interactional scores and 110 percent for cognitive scores. Coping processes resulted in larger contributions to interactional scores than to cognitive scores—95 to 58 percent—as had been the case with the young adults. Avoidance of defensive strategies facilitated cognitive moral action, but coping increased the interactional scores, a trend that is again consistent with the hypothesis that moral action is enhanced by effective and accurate problem solving. Violations of the hypothesis, smaller in magnitude, were observed, and totalled 19 percent for the interactional scores and 30 percent for the cognitive scores. Defensive doubting brought about substantial contributions to cognitive scores when NeoPd was played and to interactional scores during Role Play.

Only two ego factors contributed repeatedly to each system. The first was *interpersonal logic* which resulted in three positive contributions to interactional scores (total of 25 percent) and two contributions to cognitive scores (23 percent). This factor is defined by two Q items, "not having a tentative attitude toward others and their problems" and "giving accurate reasons as to why interpersonal events arose."

The second was affective empathy, which was never associated with higher cognitive scores but made four contributions to interactional scores (a total of 38 percent). This factor is typified by the Q items of "reacting sensitively to others," "trying to understand others' feelings and perceptions," "anticipating others' reactions with accuracy," and "being vigilant in ferreting out others' reactions" (a projective item). These results reflect an essential difference between these two systems in that interactional morality depends on reciprocity among people, whereas cognitive morality is based on the achievement of an independent thinker. Finally, the factor *emotionally unregulated* made negative contributions to cognitive scores (a total of 19 percent). This factor is typified by the Q items of "taking hostile feelings out on others," of "not controlling or suppressing feelings" and "not acting with excessive moderation when feelings are actually warranted."

Summary

1. The Interrelationship of Context, Group Structure and Ego Strategies

Having learned that the students' moral scores were inconsistent in level and from one situation to another, we turned to a different kind of explanation. It seemed that contexts—either objective, like gaming or discussing, or interpersonal, like working in led or dominated groups—only partially explained moral action. Consequently we took into account the students' *personal* ways of adapting to the various kinds of moral conflict. This explanation was substantiated because *ego strategies accounted for the largest portion of variation in both cognitive and interactional morality.*

Our understanding of moral action can be improved by understanding the relations *among* the different influences of context, personal adaptiveness, and action. Since the ego strategies strongly influenced moral action and since they were independent of gaming and discussing, and almost independent of membership in led and dominated groups, we concluded that three separate factors—situation, group structure, and ego strategies—affect the quality of moral actions. The relations, shown in the bottom half of Figure 10.1, now seem to be essentially correct.

Minor exceptions only for the led and dominated groups did show 1. that students in groups used different ego strategies when they first experienced being research subjects, and this variation had a moderate effect on their interactional but not their cognitive scores; 2. that the groups of dominated students used different strategies than their dominators in all five sessions. For the most part, however, context and individual adaptiveness seemed to have separate rather than additive effects on moral action. This is understandable since ego adaptation is always the personal act of an individual person who faces an internally or externally posed question. Situation and group structure are environmental variables, and they seemed not to have always posed the central problem from the students' point of view.

We now suggest how situation, group structure, and ego adaptation synchronized with one another to affect moral action. *Neither group structure nor situation entirely incorporated the overriding, critical feature from the students' point of view—the simple fact that they were consistently having disruptive moral problems with their friends. Instead, the situation and group structure and indeed, even the content of the problems set outside limits on the individual student's self-chosen acts of adaptation.* The differences due to gaming or discussing in the first and second sessions could be attributed to the easy moral problems of Humanus, the difficult moral problems of NeoPd, and the easy civil rights dilemmas posed for discussion during session 2. Still, the results also suggest that membership in led or dominated groups generated secondary moral problems that become more evident in later sessions after the groups had experienced prolonged but mild frustration. In the dominated groups frequent violations of the rules of moral dialogue that all may speak, all may veto, and none can dominate occurred.

Our conclusion that the major influence on action was the students' individuated construction of the moral problems they faced is consistent with the common assumption that morality is an overriding and riveting human concern. It is also consistent with our contention that to, be, or appear moral is a compelling motivation. In the early stages of this research project, we reasoned that the external impacts of gaming and discussing and membership in led or dominated groups should strongly affect moral action. But the results led us to the more articulated formulation, which subordinates these two external factors.

2. Ego Strategies' Influences on Moral Action

The adolescents' and young adults' adaptations of coping and avoiding defensiveness resulted in moral action that was more equalizing for the interactional system and more just for the cognitive system. This was expected since coping is thought to be a more effective and defensiveness a less effective way of dealing with problems. Some psychologists (for example, Lazarus, 1983) do not agree with this definition. They correctly point out that defensiveness reduces people's anxiety. Therefore, defensiveness should improve, not depress, performance. But no person is an island so this argument is incomplete. Anxiety can be reduced by defensiveness *if* its distortions and negations are not exposed by others, but exposure is exactly what a moral protagonist is likely to do. According to the interactional theory, people commonly, but usually implicitly, assume that parties to a moral dispute will be accountable to each other; that is, they will in good faith mutually assess and achieve a practical formulation of the real moral issues involved and then jointly create a plan that will rebalance relations and allow normal interchange to resume. When one discussant distorts or negates the problem, good faith suffers and the other party confronts a second problem of deciding whether to continue the dialogue or not. Moreover, distortion and negation are often met in kind. This moral underpinning of social reality means that defensive reactions almost always cost, no matter what relief they temporarily allow.

Highly individuated reactions were also observed within the same situations. Some students produced their highest scores in the most stressful situation of NeoPd when most others produced their lowest scores. A number of students in dominated groups registered much higher scores than other members of their own group and higher scores than some members of led groups. Again, the most general and important determinant of the level of moral action seems to lie in the interactions of individual students with the particular moral meanings of the problems they faced. These exceptions are fully considered in Chapter 12.

The situationally adaptive ego strategies that individual students immediately brought into play when they were confronted with particular moral problems accounted for a larger amount of variation in both sets of moral scores than did their characteristic strategies. This implies that the students were inventive when they faced situations of unusual moral costs.

3. Differences between the Interactional and Cognitive Definitions of Action

In the next chapter we report the results directly comparing the two systems. Here we comment on their similarities and their differences derived from the parallel analyses reported in this chapter. Several similarities occurred in the influences on interactional and cognitive morality: The ordering of the influences, according to importance, on both sets of moral-action scores was the same, ranging from situational ego strategies to membership in led and dominated groups. Also two ego defenses—isolation and displacement of emotion—depressed both sets of moral-action scores.

On balance, however, cognitive moral action seemed somewhat more responsive to the situational pressures than interactional morality. Characteristic ego processing made a smaller contribution to cognitive scores than it did to interactional scores. Adequate cognitive moral action was more often achieved if certain defensive strategies were brought into play. In addition, moral action, according to the interactional system, was assured if the students coped and avoided defensiveness.

These contrasts in the ways the students had to act to achieve higher cognitive or interactional morality are consistent with a theoretical difference between the two moral systems. Interactional morality regards moral decision making as an inductive, inventive interchange among people who work to create a solution—the moral balance. Coping processes involve this kind of inductive, open-ended, future-oriented, inventive interchange. However, in the cognitive system, moral decision making is a private achievement and an act of logical deduction on the part of separate persons. In order to judge and then later act, they draw on the moral structures that represent their stage of moral development. The integrity of this rational process of logical deduction depends on pure moral thought being separated and protected from emotion and all other "extraneous" activity going on inside the person, in the situation, or with others. The moral reasoner must transcend the situation to find the appropriate moral principle. In this scenario, decisions are not so much created as first "looked up" within the person's repertoire of possibilities and then used. If this thought exercise is to be successful, the entire operation needs to be protected from the details of the situation and personal emotions.

Quality moral action was furthered by coping and avoiding defensiveness. In stressful situations, defensiveness also was sometimes needed, especially for achieving higher cognitive scores. That the defensive process of reaction formation strongly supported cognitive action suggests that self-righteousness works to protect the privacy of cognitive judgment.

The students' characteristic ego processes significantly differentiated among levels of interactional morality more often than among levels of cognitive morality. Consequently the way individual persons *usually* solve problems seems to have especially affected the way they decided if they had to act, and if so, how they solved interactional problems. Interactional morality seems, then, to be the more stable, practical skill. People's tendency to carry over their characteristic ways of solving problems to moral problem solving may explain why common sense puts great stock in the idea that moral character is immutable. Interactional morality seems to be an expression of the way people usually act while cognitive morality seems to be produced more adventitiously.

4. Limitations of the Conclusions

Despite the fact that the results for the 30 regression models shown in Table 10.1 were impressively significant, they do not account for *all* the variation in the moral scores. In fact, the variation accounted for ranged from 9 to 49 percent with an average of about 30 percent for both moral systems. For readers who are unacquainted with the inevitably modest and rough accomplishments of social and psychological research vis-à-vis the inventiveness of humans and the variety of their conditions, these figures may not seem impressive. Understandably they will ask what about the other 70 percent?

The first source of the unaccounted variation in moral scores certainly arises from the approximate nature of the measurements applied to exceedingly complex phenomena—the students' moral processing, their situational and characteristic forms of ego processing, the designations of their groups as led and dominated, and so forth. The second main source was effects that we could not consider and in some instances did not anticipate. From our some 300 hours of direct observations, we can suggest what some of these influences might be. Certainly one is the idiosyncratic nature of each person's previous history with the contents as well as the structure of particular moral problems. For instance, strongly feminist women were especially outraged but also morally energized by the dilemma of Academic Weekend. Students with institutionalized grandparents were especially reactive to the dilemma of whether a young man should go to the Peace Corps or stay with his chronically ill mother.

In addition, individual students assumed or accepted roles within their friendship group that were probably not always apparent to observers. Approximately a year after the data collection was completed, a woman participant dropped by to tell the staff that she and the other women in her group—a dominated group—had given up during the last two sessions because they felt "put down" by the men in the group. Interchange among eight people is exceedingly complex and takes place on a number of preconscious and nonverbal levels, whereas our data collection was necessarily focused on manifest levels. Our attempts to capture the peculiar interactions of single members with their groups were crude, compared, for instance, to the more subtle and detailed understandings psychotherapists achieve.

The group sessions were planned to provoke moral problems among the students so we could observe their interaction. Despite our urging that the students not take their disagreement and anger out of the activity room, many reported that they continued arguments after the sessions.

Other unexpected circumstances developed. Members of one dominated group told us six months later that they were in the process of splitting up when they entered the project. Nevertheless, they decided to keep their previous commitment to participate as a group. We chose to work with friendship groups so the participants would have a stake in their relationships; members of this group obviously did not and their interchange was particularly tumultuous.

Finally, the moral problems varied in the closeness with which they matched real life; for instance, the moral problems of NeoPD and Starpower became real-life situations, since the students themselves generated the moral conflicts. Clearer results would be obtained if all moral problems used in research matched real life and varied only in level of difficulty. Although not all possible influences on moral action were included, we think the most significant were considered in the young adults' project.

Chapter 11

CONTRASTS IN THE
CONDITIONS OF
MORAL ACTION IN
THE TWO SYSTEMS

The contrast can be represented as that between noticing a great number and variety of independently variable features of particular situations on the one hand, and on the other hand bringing a few, wholly explicit principles to bear on situations . . . as in some kind of legal reasoning (Stuart Hampshire, 1978, p. 28, contrasting the moral systems of Kant and Aristotle).

THE TWO theories' different implications for practical moral action are highlighted when the conditions that support each are directly compared. These analyses are the subject of this chapter. The first part will be much like the last; that is, the results of constructing multiple regression models will be reported. The same influences will be analyzed—situation, group structure, and ego strategies—but here influences will be analyzed in terms of whether they "pulled" higher scores on one system as opposed to the other. We will next describe the kind of people who persistently acted at higher moral levels in one system as compared to the other, and finally present the comments of several students who persistently favored interactional or cognitive ways of acting.

Comparison of Influences

The Young Adults

So far, only parallel analyses of cognitive and interactional scores have been described, followed by observations of the similarities and differences between the conditions that fostered moral action in both systems. Direct comparison will make the differences clearer. At the same time, direct comparison does not allow the systems' similarities to appear. To accomplish this end, we subtracted each person's inter-actional score from his or her cognitive score to obtain a difference score for each session. Then we constructed the same kinds of multiple regression models as before. One exceptional procedure was intro-duced because a particular problem arises when difference scores are manipulated. For example, when a score of "4" is subtracted from "5," the difference of "1" is the same as when "1" is subtracted from "2," even though these difference scores of "1" represent shifts within two very different ranges of moral skill. To remedy this problem and make our results clearer, a statistical technique was used to control whatever effects absolutely high or low levels of morality might have on later scores (the sum of each person's cognitive and interactional scores was forced into each model on the first step). Results for these sums will not be discussed because they are simply factors of control, not substance; they reflect the already reported fact that in general interactional scores are absolutely higher than cognitive scores.

As before, sex was next entered into the models for the entire sam-ple so that the most general understanding of the two systems' differ-ences, without a basis in sex, could be obtained. All other elements became part of the models only when their contributions had a prob-ability level of .05 or better. Group structure and/or group experience of gaming or discussing were considered next, followed by character-istic and situational ego processes.

Table 11.1 shows the results for the entire sample and for men and women separately but the discussion is based on a summarization of that table. Because the interactional scores were subtracted from the cognitive scores, a plus sign on an item means that it resulted from higher cognitive scores but lower interactional scores; a minus sign means that the item resulted from higher interactional scores and lower cognitive scores.

The Meanings of the Comparisons

Of the 15 models, two were significant at the .001 level, four at the .01 level, two at the .05 level, and four were not significant. Three of the four nonsignificant models were for women. This difference between the power of the men's and the weakness of the women's models suggests that although the distinction between cognitive and interactional morality was marked and meaningful for the males, it was not for the females. The total variation accounted for by the women's models is only 44 percent compared to 109 percent (summed moral scores not counted) for the men's. (Statistically oriented readers may

Table 11.1.

Differential Influences on Interactional

and Cognitive Moral Action: Direct Comparisons

	Percent Con-tribution		Percent Con-tribution		Percent Con-tribution
All Participants		**Women**		**Men**	
Session 1					
Sex	0	Sum	6[c]	Sum	0
Sum	2			Characteristic projection	-11[b]
Session isolation	+4[c]			Session intellectuality	-13[b]
Session logical analysis	+4[c]		---		---
Total	10[c]		6[c]		24[b]
Session 2					
Sex	-1	Sum	-2	Sum	-15[b]
Sum	-7[c]	Session tolerance of ambiguity	-7[c]	Led-interactional/ dominated-cognitive	9[b]
Led-interactional/ dominated-cognitive	7[c]			Characteristic projection	-5[c]
Game-interactional/ discussion-cognitive	3[c]			Characteristic rationalizing	+5[c]
Objectivity	+5[b]			Session intellectualizing	+7[c]
Session intellectualizing	+7[b]			Session rationalizing	+4[c]
Session ego regression	+4[c]		---		---
Total	33[a]		-9		46[a]

Table 11.1 (cont.)

Session 3

Sex	0	Sum	0	Sum	1
Sum	-5	Session intellectuality	-9^c	Characteristic intellectualizing	$+9^c$
Total	5		9^c		10^c

Session 4

Sex	0	Sum	0	Sum	1
Sum	0	Session concentration	-8^c	Characteristic suppression	-13^b
Game-interactional/ discussion-cognitive	4^c			Characteristic intellectuality	-8^c
Session concentration	-4^c			Characteristic denial	$+8^c$
Total	8^c		8^c		27^b

Session 5

Sex	0	Sum	-20^a	Sum	0
Sum	5^c	Led-interactional/ dominated-cognitive	9^b	Led-cognitive/ dominated-interactional	8^c
Characteristic isolation	$+4^c$			Session regression	-10^b
Total	9^b		29^c		18^b

[a] $p < .001.$
[b] $p < .01.$
[c] $p < .05.$

think that the lack of results for the women might be due to a very narrow range of variation in their difference scores. But this is not the case; in fact, the range for three out of their five scores exceeded the males'.)

This sex-differentiated result bears on a current controversy concerning whether sex differences affect the cognitive moral scores. Kohlberg and Kramer (1969) had earlier stated, "While girls are moving away from high school to college to motherhood, sizeable proportions of them are remaining at Stage 3, while their male age mates are dropping Stage 3 in favor of stages above it. Stage 3 personal concordance morality is a functional morality for housewives and mothers; it is not for businessmen and professionals" (p. 108).

This implication that women are morally less mature disturbed psychologists, the most articulate and thorough objections being raised by Carol Gilligan (1982). Her analyses showed that the morality of caring and responsibility is not encompassed by Kohlberg's system. In two recent reviews Walker (1984) and Lifton (in press) conclude that few studies have actually found sex differences.

Still the present results arise from analyses that are unique, and they address the issue with somewhat different questions: Are people who produce favorable scores in one system as opposed to the other different in their interactions with situations and their group's structure? Are they different in their use of characteristic and situationally evoked ego strategies? The findings here indicate that it is male students (not the women) who are meaningfully differentiated according to their cognitive or interactional skill.

It appears then that women may function equally well under both the cognitive and interactional systems, while some kinds of men may excel in cognitive morality, and others excel in interactional morality. We tested this possible asymmetry by asking what kind of men and what kind of women favor one system of morality over another and what manner of situation and ego strategy induces them to choose one system over the other. The results are reported later in this chapter.

Actually, little can be said about the few contributions to the women's difference scores. Women whose interactional scores were higher than their cognitive were distinctive in coping situationally. Depending on the circumstances, they tolerated ambiguity, concentrated, and freely explored ideas (coping intellectuality). Women members of led groups had higher interactional scores in session 5, while women members of dominated groups had higher cognitive scores.

Men with higher interactional than cognitive scores used the characteristic ego processes of intellectuality and concentration, and during the sessions, they coped intellectually and suppressed their feelings. But they also became defensively regressive and vigilant, even suspiciously involved in interpersonal concerns (projection). Conversely, men whose cognitive scores were higher than their interactional characteristically intellectualized, rationalized, and denied and, during the group sessions, they also rationalized. It seems clear that men of cognitive bent were habitually defensive and not able or willing to cope with the moral problems.

Comparison of the overall portions of contribution to scores achieved in gaming or discussing as against led or dominated groups shows that the group's structure had a more powerful influence on scores; 33 percent of the total variation is due to the group structure compared to 7 percent for the experiences of gaming or discussing. In five significant contributions, higher interactional scores were associated with led and game groups. Conversely, higher cognitive scores were associated with dominated and discussion groups in five contributions. This trend is countered only once for the men in session 5.

Ego processes made 21 significant contributions to these models for a total of 149 percent; 11 processes (61 percent) positively typified higher cognitive scores and 10 (88 percent) positively typified higher interactional scores. The main hypothesis that coping should facilitate and defensiveness should deter higher moral action was again examined. Contributions from scores for positive coping and negative defense enhanced interactional morality for a total of 110 percent, compared to 39 percent for cognitive morality. By the same token, the total contributions from negative coping and positive defense were 39 percent for interactional morality and 110 percent for cognitive morality. Thus coping and avoiding defensiveness were strikingly characteristic of persons with high interactional scores, whereas defensiveness and failure to cope characterized persons with high cognitive scores. The reciprocity of these findings—meaning a positive contribution to interactional scores is necessarily a negative contribution to cognitive scores and vice versa—is shown in Figure 11.1, where the differences in ego strategies associated with each system are very clear.

Characteristic ego strategies made a proportionately larger contribution to the difference scores than did the situational strategies (though none to the women's). Of the men's total contribution of 110 percent, 59 percent is due to characteristic ego strategies, as compared to 34 percent to situational processing. Men who had higher cognitive scores characteristically isolate, intellectualize, rationalize and deny, and men who had higher interactional scores characteristically cope with intellectuality and suppression but defend with projection.

Relaxing the criterion for identifying ego processes that repeatedly made contributions to two or more significant entries (since there are 15 rather than 30 models here), we find that all three cognitive defenses repeatedly were relied upon by students with higher cognitive scores: intellectualization, for a total contribution of 23 percent; rationalization, of 9 percent; isolation, of 8 percent. That all three cognitive defenses typify students with higher cognitive scores affirms the inferential conclusion presented in the last chapter that cognitive moral action of higher stage is brought about by defensive maneuvers. Here,

Figure 11.1

Reciprocal Contributions to Differences in Moral Action Scores

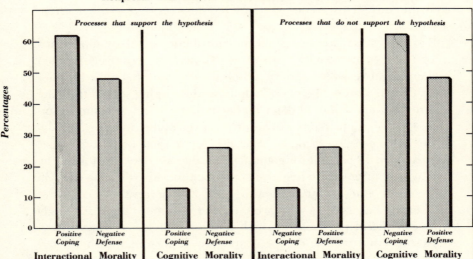

however, we find that intellectual defensiveness is especially needed for cognitive action.

Three processes were typically relied upon by students with higher interactional scores: intellectuality, with a total contribution of 30 percent; concentration, with a total contribution of 17 percent; projection, with a total contribution of 16 percent. This pattern substantiates a previous interpretation that interactional moral processing, although inductive and exploratory, is at the same time closely focused on the details of situations and their interpersonal implications, albeit here by men who were interpersonally vigilant and even suspicious.

Comparisons of the Adolescents' Difference Scores

Difference scores and multiple regression models were also generated for the adolescents. The analyses were more restricted because of the lack of discussion groups, measures of characteristic ego processing and means of designating groups as led or dominated. The smaller number of students also made it impossible to set up analyses for each sex. Variations in the adolescents' age, race, and socioeconomic status were entered first to ascertain whether these objective factors accounted for variations in moral scores. (Also their entry meant that later influences were then controlled for these factors.) The results for each of five sessions were comparatively uninformative. For session 1, when the groups played BaFa, adolescents of higher socioeconomic status had higher cognitive than interactional scores, and they also had higher scores for cognitive empathy and interpersonal logic ($p \le .001$). The model for NeoPd was not significant. For session 3, when Humanus was played, males achieved higher cognitive than interactional scores ($p \le .05$). During Starpower, higher cognitive than interactional scores were obtained by students whose scores for affective socialization were higher ($p \le .01$). Finally, during Role Play, higher cognitive than interactional scores were again obtained by adolescents of higher socioeconomic status, while higher interactional scores were obtained by those who had higher scores for defensive doubting ($p \le .01$). The repeated finding is the tendency for upper-middle-class youngsters to have higher cognitive than interactional scores. We cannot know whether the reduced power of the available data or a simple lack of meaningfulness is responsible for the meagerness of these results.

Comparing Students Who Preferred Cognitive or Interactional Morality

Some students *persistently* achieved either higher cognitive or higher interactional scores in most sessions. The question is: What kinds of people do better in one or the other form of morality? As noted above, Carol Gilligan (1982) suggests that women react morally in terms of caring and responsibility, whereas men are more apt to react in terms of justice, as proposed by Kohlberg. However, two different ideas are involved: simple preference of one form of morality over the other or a higher level of performance in one moral system as compared to the other. It is the latter idea that we can address. We identified 17 young adults whose difference scores in four out of five sessions showed that they produced higher interactional scores and 24 who had higher cognitive scores.

These two groups were compared with respect to sex, group membership, and group experience. The sexes were approximately equally divided within the cognitive group. But more women than men were in the interactional group (11 women and six men), so more women persistently did better in the interactional system, but this difference is not significant. A sizable proportion, 71 percent (17 out of 24), of the cognitive group were from dominated groups while the interactional group was almost evenly split. Nine were from led and eight from dominated groups. This difference between the systems was nearly significant. Students preferring cognitive morality were almost equally split between game and discussion groups, but 94 percent of the interactional group (16 persons out of 17) were members of game groups ($p \leq .05$).

Situational necessity more than personal propensity may determine which moral score is higher since no comparison between these two groups of students was significant on any of the scales of characteristic ego functioning, and only two situational ego processes, averaged for all sessions, were significant (this small number could occur by chance). The interactional group was more tolerant of ambiguity and the cognitive group more rationalizing (both ps $\leq .05$). Neither did the two groups differ in the eyes of their friends, either on the pre-session ratings or after the sessions, when scores represented change from presession levels.

These distinctive differences suggest a conclusion. Whether persistently high interactional or cognitive scores are achieved seemed to be more the function of the students' situation than of their intrinsic qualities. Students who had persistently higher cognitive scores were often members of dominated groups. In other words, the dominated atmosphere may have stimulated them to use this kind of reasoning. Students who had persistently higher interactional scores were often members of game groups. In other words, when action was required interactional morality was used. Cognitive reasoning may be especially useful to people in dominated, stressful contexts as a means of fortifying their own rightness and setting themselves apart. Interactional morality may be more useful when people directly engage issues and protagonists and act from the position of first person.

Descriptions of Four Students
and Their Style of Participation

In this section we describe four game students who had persistently higher interactional or cognitive scores. Giving examples of all possible groupings based on favored morality, sex, and membership in led or dominated groups would be lengthy. We chose two women. One had consistently high interactional scores and belonged to a dominated group. The other achieved persistently high cognitive scores and belonged to a led group. We reversed this pattern for the men. One male had persistently high interactional scores and belonged to a led group. The other had persistently high cognitive scores and belonged to a dominated group. We excluded discussion students for three reasons. Their talk is far more lengthy and less personal; examples of discussion students with high interactional scores were few in number, and the game dialogue is more unusual. We do not include game scores in these examples because they are not meaningfully understood outside of their context. We do not reproduce the entire discourse for these students; also their descriptions are changed, but their statements are only lightly edited for clarity.

The examples highlight several broad differences in the young people's approach to their friends and the moral problems they faced. Maria and Gerald, who persistently had higher interactional scores, are much more oriented to their friends, to the realistic and particular possibilities within the immediate situation, to their own emotions, and to their own fallibilities and uncertainties. Also they are both more critical of their friends. Fallibility was probably easier for Gerald to admit than it was for Maria because he was a member of a led group. In contrast, Babs and Dirk searched for clarity, generality, and "the facts." Babs could probably better afford to make frank statements and pursue an individualistic course since she was a member of a led group. But Dirk, although not the dominator in the estimation of his group, expressed his individualistic certainty by dominating several sessions.

Persistently High Interactional Scores

A Female Member of a Dominated Group. Maria's parents were divorced and she was the older of two children. Her father worked in space sciences, and her mother was a student. Maria indicated that her major was "possibly psychology" and that she planned to do graduate study, but added that she would need to work part time. She had moved many times but most recently lived in a large Midwest city. Her friends from the dormitory gave her moderate marks on most traits, and slightly lower evaluations on leadership, on making clear arguments, and being well liked. Maria was steadily and highly involved in the sessions and willingly assumed the role of participant rather than observer, except for her marked disengagement in NeoPd. She participated especially in the fantasy of Three Countries. Her analysis of her friendship group's functioning was low for NeoPd, but her moral score was as high as it could possibly be. Only in this session did her ego strategies become more defensive than coping. Characteristically she preferred to cope more than defend. With only one mild reversal, Maria's eight interactional scores were higher than her cognitive scores.

While playing Humanus, Maria made the following statements among others: "They don't have to express their opinion if they don't want to. *But* it's not fair to someone if they have an opinion and can't voice it. Everyone should get equal time if they want it." Later on when some members think that rules could reduce emotional isolation, Maria argues, "I don't see the necessity for rules since there are only eight of us. You can't put artificial rules with only eight of us." In regard to the survivor's entering the cell, she laments, "We can't be too idealistic; we should all be compassionate but we've got to be realistic. I value my life." Later she regrets her position on the survivor. "We should have let him in since we all die sometimes. I just feel guilty." With regard to helping a suicidal person in another cell, she says, "We're not infallible; besides there are other possibilities. We should open it up, let other cells try, too. Restrain him; don't let him die."

During NeoPd, Maria becomes highly outraged. "I trusted you!" (she said to the other subgroup who had broken an agreement to equalize points). And to her own subgroup, after they propose that they burn, "Let's not do that. . . . I don't want to! I wasn't raised that way." Later on when her subgroup wants to refuse negotiation, she counters, "Oh, I trust them. I'll negotiate. That's silly not to negotiate." In response to another's comment that negotiation only results in the other group's lying, "That really doesn't matter; it depends on what we do. But let's do it my way because it's random." Later, "I don't want to do winner take all; we worked hard; I want something." When the other subgroup went back on their word, "That made me a bit angry; I don't know. I always respect someone's word." Then, betraying her emotional ambivalence (this was just a "game" but people's acts were unfair), "I wasn't angry. I realized it was a joke, but I thought we were going to play fairly!" In the postgame discussion, Maria asserts with regard to cheating and burns, "I don't think I would have done it. Because we made a rule of the game and I wouldn't have wanted them to be feeling what we felt. I know it wasn't heavy duty, but I haven't done it for any moral—I mean I wouldn't have taken great pleasure in it like they did."

During Ghetto, she observed, in regard to her friend who had the role of police officer, "I don't think it's fun being police; I'd hate being the police." Later she says to the dominator of this group, "What you're saying is a tiny bit ruthless; we've got to band together and oppose the System."

Maria continually expressed dislike and discomfort with Starpower but trades chips "just to keep pace." She sadly notes, "This whole game is mixed emotions." In the postgame discussion, she says to the group dominator, who has many chips, "What if you had been always struggling to get points [as she herself was], do you think you would have been as magnanimous as you were?"

In Three Countries, Maria argues with her fellow citizens, "But they don't have any resources and they really need it." Later in the postgame discussion she says, "Hiding balloons irritated me. If we're all going to be open and equal, why were we hiding our circumstances from each other? This was like the card game [NeoPd] because we came to realize the bad feelings that can get generated."

A Male Member of a Led Group. Gerald's father was a chemical engineer and his mother a secretary. He was the oldest of six children, all boys. His major was prelaw, and he planned to attend law school. His friends gave him high marks for being dominating and a leader and his ability to make clear arguments, but he received rather low marks on understanding others' points of view and on willingness to change his mind. Gerald's involvement was consistently and markedly high throughout the five sessions, as was his willingness to enter the interchange as a participant. During the first two sessions he was only average in analyzing his group's processes, but starting with the third session he became highly analytic about his group's functioning. Gerald consistently coped more than he defended, and his characteristic coping and defending had the same pattern in favor of coping. His interactional moral scores always were higher than his cognitive scores except for a slight reversal in pattern during the first interviews.

While playing Humanus, Gerald urged, during the discussion of group regulation, "You have to compromise; you can try to persuade if there is conflict, but in the end you have to compromise." Concerning the fate of the possibly contaminated survivor, Gerald says heatedly, "What if it was your mom or dad out there? . . . If we were out there, we would have known. . . . If the vote were seven to say okay and one not, we couldn't say yes on crucial life and death decisions." (He changes his position and votes with the group to keep the survivor out.) "It'd be different if we were really there. Here we're safe; we wouldn't be so calm and cool."

Gerald becomes his subgroup's negotiator while playing NeoPd and pushes through an agreement for equalization as well as an agreement for penalties if one subgroup breaks this agreement. After a "burn" nevertheless occurs and heated discussion ensues, Gerald argues, "The rules are: We can make whatever rules we want. We're the negotiators. But the thing I want to tell you is, let's make an agreement." Later, during the discussion, he presses his observation: "I think one issue was group cooperation. I admit I'd launch up there and say I was speaking for the group [as the negotiator], but I noticed Sarah was getting quiet and that kinda made me feel bad. . . . I don't think any of us should have broken an agreement. What's the use of going through the trouble of making an agreement if you're going to back out of it?"

While playing Ghetto, Gerald entertained the idea of revolution but could not convince his friends to follow suit. He says, "I think it's outrageous that she [the System] orders both arrests and interpretations [from the judge]. It's an infringement on my rights. I want to hold a little meeting and discuss revolution." (He laughs.) "I've been reading Marx lately." Gerald manages to shoot his marble so a trouble marble is removed and he says gleefully, "Hey, you guys, do you realize what I did for you?" He pays back a loan to a citizen who is quite well off and then says, "No, keep it. I owe you one. Thanks, but I owe you one." Later on he comments on this incident, pointing out that he needed to keep his sense of independence and pride even though he had accepted charity. His final comment was, "Where do you draw the line in helping yourself and in helping others? I always see myself as part of a family. To me that's a very complex decision. I haven't figured out an answer. How much do you work all together?"

During Starpower, Gerald gives a fellow Square a bonus chip, saying to the group at large, "I gave him the bonus chip because he's poorer; besides, I'll still be ahead anyway." As the ruling Squares contemplate making rules that will sustain their power, Gerald warns, "After this screw job there will be trouble from the others." However, he agrees to the oppressive rules and then later pleads that the Squares should be forgiven: "If we make a deal with you, will it be so the three of us are not blacklisted?" Then he comments to his fellow Squares, "They don't realize that we're being nice. We'll just be unseated and then people will try to unseat the new Squares." During the discussion, he reports, "If we tried to be fair, we'd lose; if we kept in power, the group would have got hostile. Still I wanted a fair chance." Later on: "But what if someone really was the best leader? . . . Everybody refused to be equal with us [a reference to Gerald and his friends' wish that they not be "blacklisted," which the group did not accept]. Was that fairminded of you? . . . You just assumed our new rules wouldn't be fair." Then he comments to his former fellow Squares, "Maybe we should have told them why we did it and that it was all going to come out all right."

While playing Three Countries, he reassures citizens of another country, "We'd offer help but we're at the minimum. It's not that we don't want to help." Later on, with outrage, he shouts, "You lied to us!" When his country is in really bad straits, he urges, "Let's go for it. I can't bear to think of losing eight million [people]. Let's go for it. I'm so pissed." During the discussion he says, "On the next round when you declared war on us to get us, my blood was flowing 'cause I was so pissed. I knew you didn't need the food. It never occurred to me that you were doing it for Turk [another country]."

Persistently High Cognitive Scores

A Female Member of a Led Group. Babs's father was a small businessman in a specialized aspect of building construction; her mother did part-time work for a company in California's Silicon Valley, where Babs grew up. She came from a large family of five children and she was born in the middle. She tentatively planned a law career. She was viewed as one of the more dominating members of her otherwise led group. The members gave her rather low marks on likeability and being able to understand the other's point of view. She was highly

involved throughout the five sessions and willingly became a participant. She was analytic about her group's operations except during
Starpower where her scores dropped. Although she was consistently
more coping than defensive for all five sessions, her characteristic
strategies were more defensive than coping. Seven of Babs's cognitive
scores were higher than her interactional scores; the substantial exception was made during Ghetto.

Examples of her comments while playing Humanus follow. (Early
in the game) "I think we should have someone who we can look up
to and consult." Later she urges, "We have to do things for each other
constantly so we all know we care about each other and can work
together." Still later she grows impatient with her group's meandering
and comments, "Look, this is the same thing; we've already decided
that issue."

Playing NeoPd, she explains her position: "Just because I'm out to
make money doesn't mean I want them to lose money. . . . Look, we
have to decide whether we're working together or competing." During
the postgame discussion she points out, "Some of us thought we were
being judged by whether we wanted money, so we held back a little. . . .
I felt bad putting that card down by accident [which violated a stated
agreement between subgroups]. I said, 'Oh, no, I made a mistake!' I
thought it would mess everything up. I was really dismayed."

During Ghetto, Babs urges initiative. She says, "Can't three or four
of us get together and make a taller structure [to defeat the System]?
I say do it. It's up to us; we don't have anything to lose." When the
System rolls the dice again, which results in fewer jobs, Babs protests:
"That's not fair. I want to take that to court. Look, if there were jobs,
we wouldn't need welfare." Later, "What's the fairness of the quota
system? The law enforcement around here is terrible. If you have to
pay a traffic fine, why should that mean that you can't get welfare? I
just want this kind of reasoning explained." During the postgame
discussion, she observes, "Most of us were against the System and we
appealed when we thought she was unfair. The System is supposed to
work for the people but she didn't give jobs. Her excuse was that she
wouldn't have enough for welfare. But if people had jobs, they
wouldn't need welfare." When a friend points out that they should
have organized against the System, Babs says, "What do you mean,
revolution? We followed the rules because this was a game, so we took

her to court. Did you expect us to change the rules? I, too, was getting mad at the judge because she wasn't being consistent."

While playing Starpower, Babs had chips of high value and made the following comments: "We have to see some productive effort before we'll distribute the wealth. . . . Well, you can help people move up if you want, but it's a simple fact that life is not equal. . . . Morals get lax when people act for power and money. . . . But if you started out equal, it would still end up in a class society, but does that matter if everybody is happy? Look, democracy isn't equality, that's communism."

During Three Countries, Babs matter of factly tells another country, "We're willing to risk one food balloon, but if you guys want to trade, that's up to you." At a later point she speculates about trades between countries and says, "It's still the same amount of people starving whichever way." During the postgame discussion she points out the surplus of resources at the beginning of the game and concludes, "So that's how trust got started. . . . When you think about it, it doesn't matter who risks—it all evens out—it depends on who has responsibility for the people."

A Male Member of a Dominated Group. Dirk's father is a mechanical engineer and his mother, a secretary. He grew up in Los Angeles, the older of two children. His friends gave him rather average marks for most qualities but slightly higher grades on leadership, domination, and his ability to handle himself in a conflict. Dirk's involvement and willingness to commit himself to the experience beyond being a subject were average to high in the first two sessions, very high when he played Ghetto, but dropped to the lowest levels during Starpower and rose moderately when Three Countries was played. His interest in analyzing his group's processes was low except for a moderate increase during Ghetto. Although Dirk's characteristic ego strategies were somewhat more defensive than coping, situationally he consistently coped more than defended except during NeoPd. Five of Dirk's cognitive scores were higher than his interactional scores except for Starpower.

Humanus was much to his liking. He pointed out to his group that they didn't have a choice about whether to be a group or not: "Living in a cell like this, we're going to have to come out of our shells or we will have great difficulties among us." When they discussed letting the possibly contaminated survivor enter the group's cell, Dirk was the only member of this group to argue for the survivor. "I think a human life is worth preserving. . . . It's a question of my conscience, knowing we left somebody out there who could have been perfectly healthy and maybe even added to our group; he could help build us and make us stronger. . . . I agree we do have to think beyond ourselves, but how do we justify keeping him out? . . . It's a question of race preservation versus life preservation; you may be able to do it, but I can't." In the postgame discussion, Dirk stood by his position, perhaps a little self-righteously: "I place a high value on human life, any human life, obviously more than you do because you weren't going to let him in."

During NeoPd, he began assuming direction of his subgroup with plans to "burn" the other group by breaking an agreement for equalization. Faced with the other subgroup's indignation after the burn, he rebuts, "We'll negotiate with you if you have something to negotiate about. . . . Let's say you have to skip a number every other time—word of honor. We just blew it the first time. We went along with you the second time. We kept honorable the second time." But then he returns to his group and quietly instructs them, "We'll make it look like we're doing it random." During the postgame discussion, Dirk described himself: "I was on the winning side so I laughed; I thought it was all right because we all cheated together; it was the way the situation worked."

While playing Ghetto, he comments, "I didn't mind the enforcement of the technical rules, but when I had to scheme against the rest of the group to get my quota, I didn't like that." When Starpower was played, the only session where Dirk's interactional score was markedly higher than his cognitive score, he was not much involved in the game and much more concerned with the reactions of two women in the group. He had little to say. He offers chips to another, saying, "Then we will be fairly equal."

In Three Countries, Dirk became heavily involved but mostly with the strategy of the game, but he points out, "Either way we're playing with odds—what we're doing is playing with people, like Hitler did." Later he says to another member, "The way this game keeps going, each group feels a moral obligation to the other." During the postgame discussion, he says, "There was no way not to be competitive in that game [Ghetto], but this game has two goals: You could stockpile or save lives. . . . After all, we sell grain to Russia so that their people don't starve. . . . It didn't go anywhere because everybody wanted to keep everybody equal."

Summary

Review of Findings

1. Variations in the males' difference scores were explained to a far greater extent than were the women's.

2. The morally relevant contexts of led or dominated groups were important in all these analyses of differences. Higher interactional scores more often typified members of led groups and higher cognitive scores typified members of dominated groups.

3. A central hypothesis of these studies that coping and avoiding defensiveness support moral action of higher quality was strongly supported for interactional activity, but reversed for cognitive morality. Higher cognitive scores were repeatedly supported by all the cognitive defenses of isolation, intellectualization, and rationalization.

4. The men's characteristic ego processes were more important than their situational processes in determining whether they produced higher interactional or cognitive scores.

5. Comparisons of the two small subgroups of persistently high interactional or cognitive reasoners showed that more women and more members of game groups persistently produced higher interactional scores, while more members of dominated groups and fewer members of game groups produced higher cognitive scores. However, these two small subgroups did not importantly differ in ego processing or in their friends' ratings.

Interpretation of the Findings

The two findings that membership in the led game groups and that coping and avoiding defensiveness characterized students with higher interactional but lower cognitive scores lead to an interpretation: *Interactional morality seems to describe the ways these students acted when their circumstances were optimal and when they could cope. Interactional morality may therefore be the way people prefer to deal with moral problems.*

The second interpretation rests on a series of results: Consistent with their nature, a subgroup of men defensively produced higher cognitive scores in stressful conditions. This interpretation is based on their disproportionately greater membership in dominated groups, the frequent positive associations between higher cognitive scores and characteristic defenses, and the negative associations between higher cognitive scores and coping processes. *Although interactional morality may be closer to the morality that people cherish, cognitive morality may be the method some people use when they are personally threatened.*

If the results of these analyses have merit, then the continuing argument among some psychologists over whether or not there are differences in cognitive morality due to sex needs to be reconsidered. *In action situations, the women seemed to use either form of morality, whereas some men who are characteristically defensive, had higher cognitive scores when they were stressed.* This formulation may be a better explanation for differences based on sex reported in some studies than the usual supposition that women are morally immature in cognitive morality. In any event, the latter conclusion has usually been based on interview scores.

Evaluation of the Theories' Description of Moral Action

The ultimate value of these analyses lies in their uncovering the conditions that support one kind of moral action as compared to the other. In other words, identification of these distinguishing conditions gives meaning to the relatively abstract scores of the two systems. Social science researchers may eventually be able to address the question of which moral theory, among all those proposed, most closely fits practical morality in both its idealized and practiced forms. We made some progress toward that goal but many more studies comparing other moral theories are needed. We consider now whether the cognitive or interactional system better matches the moral action of everyday life. (Further, similar evaluation is contained in the summary of Chapter 16, where all results including those for moral development are brought together.)

Certain criteria can be applied to test the adequacy of scientifically based theories of morality, but they will never provide a final answer to the question of which moral ground is "best." This will always remain a matter of value choice. We evaluate the findings for moral action in terms of three interrelated criteria:

1. Given acceptance of our argument that practical morality is the only proper target for social scientific research, how closely does each theory follow the processes of moral action that occur in everyday life?

2. Which theory's description better expresses (or sensibly explains or revises) the suppositions of common sense about the outcomes of quality moral action?

3. Which theory provides the more intuitively convincing account of moral action?

The Match with the Processes of Practical Moral Action. Following common observation, dialogue is taken as the most obvious feature of moral activity in the interactional system. Further, and again following common sense, the participants' ease and freedom of interchange is expected to facilitate quality moral action. In contrast, Kohlberg and his colleagues (Kohlberg et al., 1983) now describe moral action as coming on the private conclusions of moral agents who will act, if they reason according to substage B, if they are of a higher stage, and if they judge that they are responsible. If these conditions are met, their subsequent action will be commensurate with their major stage of reasoning. Whether this sequence of internal events has validity remains to be seen. This explanation has not been extensively tested and was proposed too recently to be examined in these studies.

The findings here, however, seem consistent with the interactional but not the cognitive system's account and prescriptions for quality moral action. Higher interactional scores characterized led and the action-requiring game groups as well as students who used coping strategies and avoided defensive manipulations. The reverse was the case for higher cognitive action scores. Dominated contexts and the use of defensive strategies promoted higher scores. We suggest then that the interactional description may more closely match the moral action in everyday life. Its processes seem consistent with the common wishes of people in moral conflict—that they should be entitled to speak and veto, that they should not be dominated, and that consensus is the ideal goal.

The Match with the Outcomes of Moral Action. Given acceptance of the argument that moral action is likely to be the authentic morality, or in any case that it must be so understood, then the conditions that facilitated each kind of moral action uncovered in these studies, suggest that the interactional system better describes quality moral resolution as it is defined in common sense. Interactional morality was supported by coping while cognitive morality was disproportionately supported by defensiveness.

Natural language and dictionaries define psychological defense as involving self-fortification to the point of distorting or negating reality, and coping as involving open engagement, accuracy and admission of reality. When these definitions are taken seriously, it follows that resolutions can hardly be moral if they are achieved through defensiveness—although factually, false resolutions are not uncommon. Quality moral resolution surely does not arise from self-deception, or the deception of others, whether willed or unwilled, nor can defensive strategies enhance social relations or restore moral harmony. We suggest that cognitive moral reasoning is a specialized form of problem solving, readily available in the culture. The experience of some males may have helped them to learn this process well. Under threat they may use these means to protect their sense of moral well-being since cognitive morality has provisions for conflict to be resolved on an impersonal basis and by rules.

Comparison of the Theories on Intuitive Bases. Being a matter of intuition, this criterion cannot only be evaluated by research findings; nevertheless this intuitive judgment is fundamental and still determinative. We can only present our own convictions and hunches about the two moralities' account of action.

Cognitive morality carries the mark of its elite philosophical ancestors in its orientation to intellectualism and to individualism. But this is not the same as practical morality. As a ground, justice seems most relevant to institutionally related conflict, and seems not to encompass some kinds of moral events, as one example the dilemmas of pregnancy out of wedlock that Gilligan (1982) has discussed. In our view, justice is needed in some societies but it is proliferation of a more general and basic morality that is, very simply, the equalization of relationships among people. If this reasoning has merit, it explains why high-level cognitive reasoners are not found in societies that neither have nor need highly complex bureaucratized institutions and why the cognitive theory is based on the assumption that young children are without moral concern. To understand the impersonality of justice, considerable abstract knowledge and sophistication must be acquired.

We suggest that by equalizing relationships among people, the cherished morality in the interactional system is the far simpler, but more fundamental and general moral impulsion that people understand, endorse, and feel toward one another. Our social difficulties are not due to lack of moral concern, but because of lack of skill in resolving conflict and social circumstances that make quality moral action difficult to enact. Humans come soon and forcefully to understanding the inevitable reciprocity and community of social living. However, the enactment of these concepts is affected by both internal and external circumstances as these studies have shown. In other words, young children, preindustrial peoples, and peoples in times past come easily to high quality moral action in some circumstances and undoubtedly, these views have come to us because of our own practical experience in watching moral actions for many hours.

Chapter 12

AFTERTHOUGHTS ABOUT THE COSTS OF MORAL ACTION

In doll play, a sensitive four-year-old, Gary, faces up to corrupt authority, his friend's mother who unfairly rules Gary's toy belongs to her son. Gary asserts his ownership but then ducks his head and fidgets with his hair. The interviewer follows up:

INTERVIEWER: How come you said that to Jamie's mother?
GARY: I wanted my toy back.
I: Oh. So you decided to say that to his mom. (Pause)
I: How did you feel?
GARY: Happy. I have a magic spell.
I: A magic spell, huh? What would you do with a magic spell?
GARY: I made Jamie's mom nice to me.
I: So your magic spell would make Jamie's mom nice. How come?
GARY: 'Cause in a pretend story you can be a magic kid.
I: Yeah, in a pretend story you can be a magic kid.

The Person-situation Connection in Moral Action

DURING THE early stages of our work we confidently expected that dealing with moral conflict in games would be a more difficult experience for the students than the vicarious experience of discussing hypothetical moral dilemmas. We even thought—as have most investigators—that the students who discussed hypothetical dilemmas would produce the same moral level, whatever the dilemmas they confronted, but that the vivid, direct experience of playing games would have a two-pronged effect: Some games might especially motivate participants, who would then produce high moral scores, while other games might distress participants, so they would produce low moral scores.

Although these ideas were not radically wrong, the results did not take such a clear, simple form. Not only were the correlations among scores for individual discussants low, but the average moral scores for the similar discussion sessions varied in level, especially for discussion session 2 as well as discussion session 1 where the scores were among the lowest. Thus people's moral actions were not consistent even when situations were similar. Still the game scores turned out as expected. They were significantly lower for NeoPd and Starpower and higher for Humanus and Three Countries. And Ghetto turned out to be more stressful than we had anticipated.

After the multiple regression models were constructed to determine the sources of moral variation, we gradually dropped our idea that there is a strong, systematic difference between *talking about* a dilemma and *living out* a dilemma. Significant but by no means overriding differences between gaming and discussing occurred only for the first two sessions. Consequently we began to suspect that the effects for these two sessions were partly due to different contents of moral problems. On hindsight, we finally recognized that gaming and discussing are morally neutral, whereas the dilemmas are not. (We have also seen that experiences in led and dominated groups are morally relevant.)

Why did the scores for the less-stressful sessions vary among themselves? Were the scores for discussion session 2 actually higher because the dilemmas were easier? Gradually we recognized that we were not taking into consideration the fact that people care about the worth of their moral ideas, sometimes as much as they do about their actions. We had intuitions but no hard evidence as to why some hypothetical dilemmas evoked intense reactions while others obviously did not.

We also needed to examine our idea that the structure of friendship groups would affect members' moral scores. Students in led groups were expected to have higher scores because the group's egalitarian functioning would facilitate a thorough and sincere exploration of the circumstances of moral issues. The hierarchical and power-oriented functioning of the dominated groups was expected to thwart moral dialogue. In fact, the group structure did have the expected effect for some sessions: Membership in led groups made a difference in sessions 1 and 5 for interactional moral scores and in sessions 1, 4, and

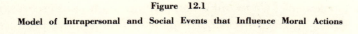

Figure   12.1

Model of Intrapersonal and Social Events that Influence Moral Actions

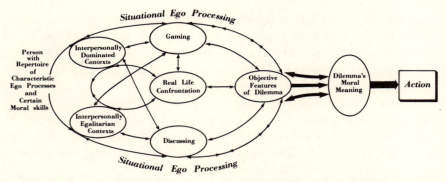

5 for cognitive scores. Nonetheless, our ideas were too simplistic. We had not taken into account the moral reactions of the indignant "whistle blower" in dominated groups. Thus, merely discussing dilemmas or being a member of a dominated group did not automatically lower moral-action levels. Neither situation was consistently influential, and both could result in high or low scores. Thus, in a roundabout way we came to recognize the powerful effect of moral meaning. Neither games or discussions nor even group structure incorporated the most critical, external impact on the students from their own perspective— the meanings of the moral problems.

We presented two possible models of moral action in Figure 10.1 (page 171), based on two different sets of structural relationships, each involving ego processing, experience, and group structure. The model that we now propose may be nearer to matching the reality of students' moral action. It is shown in Figure 12.1.

The model in Figure 12.1 provides a third explanation that is both more simple and more complex. It is simpler because it suggests that the single, overarching effect is the moral meaning that people draw from a dilemma and the immediate interpersonal context. It is more complex because it assumes that moral meanings present varying levels of difficulty and cost to participants in accordance with the following influences:

1. The person's previous experience with each kind of problem and his or her accrued level of moral skill
2. Whether the person's characteristic repertoire of ego pro-

cesses gives priority to the particular coping processes that facilitate moral action or to defensive processes that inhibit moral action

3. Whether the person is able to evoke sequences and patterns of situational ego processing that are sufficiently complex and sensitive to deal with the problem and the situation

4. Whether the person confronts the moral dilemma in an egalitarian or a hierarchical context

5. Whether the moral experience is actual and direct or vicarious (the latter is almost always the case in research projects)

6. Certain objective features of the dilemmas themselves.

Moral Meanings and Costs

The concept of moral meaning clearly needs illumination. Precisely what are the moral meanings that make some situations more costly than others? Moral problems continuously punctuate human interchange in conflictual ways, but plainly some problems wreak more havoc. As we now see it, moral meaning flows from three sources: the objective features of the dilemma, the nature of the interpersonal relationships, and the personal history and strengths and weaknesses of the participants. Each is examined anew in the next three sections.

The general meanings of interpersonal relations have already been made clear and the objective features of moral problems are discussed in detail below. But for the moment we offer an example of the most dramatic feature, whether or not the "victim" in a moral dilemma—actual or hypothetical—is threatened with death. The possibility of someone's death usually resolves an issue forthwith because the ambivalence of all concerned is immediately reduced. Human bonding and our empathy with one another does not allow *unwarranted* and *avoidable* death to occur; life is valued in all moral systems. This is why people usually achieve their highest score for Kohlberg's famous dilemma of Heinz, who must steal a drug to cure his wife who will otherwise die of cancer.

The third source of moral meaning rises from the personal history and characteristics of the individual participants. Because moral conflict is frequent and these students were 19 years old, no dilemma that they encountered in these projects could have been entirely new. Still, each person has a different moral history that builds strengths and vulnerabilities. For example, discussion students whose grandparents were in nursing homes were especially upset with the question of whether or not Andrew should go overseas with the Peace Corps after his widowed mother became chronically ill. Had we been sensitive to these effects we would have asked the students about their past experiences with similar problems. How people's ego processes mesh with the moral problems they confront is yet another way that personal circumstances add moral meaning. To learn about this source of moral meaning we conducted further analyses that are reported below.

How Interpersonal Contexts Affect
Moral Dialogue and Decision

To learn more about the moral meanings of the various dilemmas, we undertook new analyses. The 49 items of the Q sort of group processes for each session were averaged for all ten game groups to achieve a composite description of the way groups *generally* acted when they confronted each game. The same procedure was followed for the five discussion sessions. We thereby obtained summary descriptions of how the groups acted for the five game and five discussion sessions.

The ten descriptions were correlated with each other and then ordered according to their similarity. Table 12.1 shows this ordering. Sessions that are adjacent to each other are similar. The correlations just above the diagonal are the highest (or very nearly the highest) in all cases, and along the rows and columns the magnitude of correlation drops off in an orderly fashion. (Statisticians will recognize this ordering forms almost a perfect Guttmann simplex.) The table shows that, according to the groups' behavior, NeoPd and Starpower were much alike (their correlation is .81), and that, situation by situation, NeoPd and Starpower progressively became less like Ghetto, Three Countries, and Humanus and the various discussion sessions. The middle section of Table 12.1 shows that discussion sessions 5 and 4 were like Humanus and Three Countries. As for the discussions, sessions 2 and 3 seem to form a group and are less like sessions 1, 4, and 5.

We already knew (from the work reported in Chapter 7) that the stress scale, group disintegration/integration, which was also developed from the Q sort of group processes, had its highest scores for

Table 12.1.

Intercorrelations among Group Functioning for Different Sessions[a]

49-item Q Sort of Group Processes

		Game Sessions				Discussion Sessions					
		Neopd	Star-power	Ghetto	3 Countries	Huma-nus	5	4	1	2	3
Neopd	2	--	.81	.22	25	-.05	-.15	.01	.17	.26	.10
Starpower	4		--	.51	.54	.21	.05	.19	.24	.22	.14
Ghetto	3			--	.73	.58	.56	.50	.42	.31	.21
3 Countries	5				--	.69	.59	.55	.51	.38	.26
Humanus	1					--	.76	.74	.64	.52	.45
Discussion	5						--	.88	.74	.71	.66
	4							--	.85	.79	.73
	1								--	.79	.75
	2									--	.82
	3										--

[a]Sessions reordered according to similarities in groups' functioning. Q correlations are based on 49 items, each averaged across all groups experiencing a session.

discussion sessions 2 and 3 and also for the games NeoPd and Starpower. It can be seen, however, that these "stressful" game and discussion sessions are not alike. Therefore, stress seemed to have been handled differently in game than in discussion groups. To understand this difference, we located Q items that had high or low values for NeoPd and Starpower and high or low values for discussion sessions 2 and 3.

The items characterizing the stressful games were: members were pressured to become involved; members took analytic attitudes toward the groups' processes; members became angry; groups optimized their solidarity; and members rejected the game rules presented by the staff leader. In contrast, when the discussion groups were placed under stress, they turned to the staff leader (apparently hoping that she would handle the situation). Their characteristic actions included the following: the staff leader imposed direction on the groups' processes; members oriented themselves to the activity leader; and individual students actively helped the group complete its discussion.

Thus, it seemed likely that the student leaders or dominators could not affect their group's functioning in discussion situations as they could in games. When a group depends on an authority figure for moral resolution, its own natural structure will be superseded.

Figure 12.2 shows relations between the led and dominated groups' averaged moral scores and their averaged scores for integration (the stress scores reversed) for each session; the sessions remain ordered according to their similarity. Four important differences hold for both moral systems. First, a clear order of moral difficulty arising from stress can be seen for the game groups, from NeoPd to Humanus. Second, the led groups were consistently more integrated *and* achieved higher scores for moral action compared to the dominated game groups, who were less integrated and achieved lower scores for moral action in all five sessions. Third, although moral action improved for both systems in concert with the game groups' integration scores, this pattern did not occur for the discussion sessions. Fourth, although the led discussion groups were consistently less stressed than the dominated groups, there was *no* relation between their stress and moral action.

The rank-order correlation between the game sessions' averaged scores for group integration and moral action across led and dominated game groups (making ten groups in five situations) is .88 for both the interactional and cognitive systems, compared to .02 for the discussion groups' interactional scores and − .27 for their cognitive scores.

The dynamic impact on the game groups of being led or dominated was clearly important in affecting their stress and levels of moral action. But the staff leader's control of the discussion groups seemed to have produced a different situation of moral meaning that prevented the group itself from affecting the members' levels of moral action. The most likely influence seemed to be the objective contents and features of the moral dilemmas that they discussed but did not resolve as a group—a procedure that complied with the cognitivists' curricular recommendations.

Objective Contents of Moral Issues

After some 300 hours of observation, we came to believe that the objective contents of different dilemmas affect levels of moral dialogue

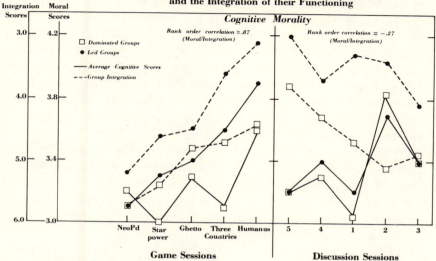

Figure 12.2a

Relationships between Groups' Average Moral Action Scores and the Integration of their Functioning

Cognitive Morality

Note: Sessions reordered according to the similarities in the friendship groups' functioning

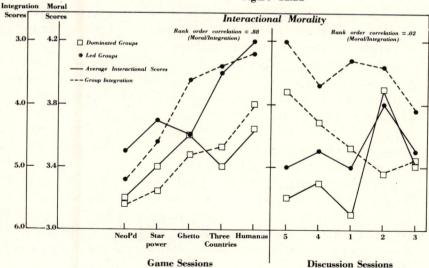

Figure 12.2b

Interactional Morality

Note: Sessions reordered according to the similarities in the friendship groups' functioning

and resolution. This conclusion contradicts the cognitivists' contention that the form of thought transcends contents. It also corrects our initial vague supposition that all moral dilemmas are resolved at the individual's level of moral skill (in the interactional system) or his or her stage of development (in the cognitive system). Thus we moved on to identify the elements of moral issues that make them easy or difficult to resolve. Five features seemed relevant in this particular sample of five games and 15 hypothetical dilemmas presented in the discussion sessions. Another sample of moral dilemmas might reveal more or different features.

Familiarity. The first feature was whether the contents of a dilemma are familiar. We assumed the participants would have already formulated and resolved familiar dilemmas; consequently they would be dealing with issues they had already identified. Their dialogue would be more efficient because they already have opinions as to the relevance and the potential damage involved.

Power of solution. The second feature was whether or not a dilemma's contents were close to the participants' lives and therefore within their power to resolve. The two games of NeoPd and Starpower were actual moral experiences in and of themselves, whereas other games and most hypothetical dilemmas did not involve issues the students could act on (for example, whether or not to risk lives to prevent an accident in a nuclear plant). But in NeoPd, they did have the power to decide how they themselves could and should act.

Vicarious or direct experience. The third feature was whether the dilemmas were experienced vicariously or directly. This does not differentiate the games from the discussions because some games, like Humanus, involved moral problems that could only be vicariously experienced, whereas some discussion stories were concerned with issues that could happen in a young person's life, like being wrongly accused of cheating during an examination.

Subtle or obvious issues. The fourth feature was whether a dilemma involved obvious or subtle moral issues. An example of an obvious issue is whether a man should abandon his post of civilian defense during a fire bombing whereas a subtle issue is whether anger should be expressed over the losers' attitude of moral superiority in NeoPd.

Harm to the "victim." Finally, the severity of harm to the potential "victim" also seems to be a prominent feature. Severe damage, like death, reduces uncertainty, whereas minor cost or postponement of gratification produces ambivalence.

To understand variations in moral scores that might be due to variation in the objective features of the dilemmas, we asked 15 people who were neither professional researchers nor previously associated with our projects to read and rate descriptions of the 20 dilemmas, one for each of the five games and the 15 dilemmas presented in the discussion sessions. Each dilemma was rated on a seven-point scale for these five objective features. Because we argue that the evaluation of practical morality is within every person's purview, we neither trained these people nor directed their evaluations. The modal or most frequent rating was used.

The three dilemmas taken up in each discussion session were assigned ratings on all five dimensions; then these ratings were averaged for all judges. We did not initially think that dilemmas of different kinds varied in difficulty, so we apparently grouped dilemmas according to their relevance to the students' lives. The dilemmas for sessions 1 and 2 were all close to the students' concerns while dilemmas for sessions 4 and 5 were not. The ratings brought out this difference.

Table 12.2 gives the average ratings for the game and discussion sessions on all five variables. As can be seen, low and high scores were given to the dilemmas presented in both game and discussion sessions. Since a rating of "4" was the midpoint on those seven-point scales, we can conclude that our raters thought that the contents of all the moral dilemmas were more commonplace than not. Two games—Humanus and Three Countries—and three discussion sessions—sessions 3, 4, 5—involved issues that our judges thought would be distant from the participants' experience. Three games—NeoPd, Ghetto, and Starpower, along with discussion session 1—were judged to involve direct experience. Only Humanus and NeoPd were judged to involve subtle issues, and only discussion sessions 2 and 3 were thought to involve little damage to the "victims." Altogether the ratings were not influenced by whether the dilemmas were encountered in games or discussions.

To determine whether the objective features of the different dilemmas made it easier or more difficult for the students to deal with them, we calculated rank-order correlations between these ratings and the average moral scores achieved by the four kinds of groups for all sessions combined. Because only five situations are involved for each

Table 12.2.

Average Ratings of Objective Features for Game and Discussion Sessions[a]

	Contents Known/ Unknown 7 = Known	Contents Close Distant 7 = Close	Obvious Subtle Issues 7 = Obvious	Contents Great/Little Damage 7 = Death	Experience Vicarious Direct 7 = Vicarious
			Games		
Humanus	4.1	1.2	2.5	6.3	6.4
NeoPd	5.7	5.7	2.2	4.2	2.0
Ghetto	5.7	4.0	5.5	4.6	2.4
Starpower	6.3	5.4	5.8	4.8	2.6
3 Countries	6.3	2.2	5.6	6.3	5.5
			Discussions		
Session 1	6.3	5.1	5.9	4.4	3.9
Session 2	6.3	5.4	5.4	3.7	5.0
Session 3	5.9	3.6	4.4	3.6	4.8
Session 4	5.6	1.8	4.9	5.9	6.4
Session 5	4.9	2.0	6.1	6.1	6.1

[a]Ratings for sessions that are double underscored are highest; those that are single underscored are lowest.

rating, a correlation must reach .90 to be significant at the .05 level of probability, but all correlations are shown in Table 12.3 to illustrate several suggestive but nonsignificant trends. These correlations cannot be regarded as *results*. There are better ways of investigating these questions that we will suggest below.

A first glance at Table 12.3 suggests that vicarious experience generally allowed higher levels of moral action in both games and discussions. However, the other objective features of dilemmas seemed not to have the same effects on game and discussion scores. We will not comment on differences between led and dominated groups, nor between the two moral systems, given the crudity of these analyses.

Comparatively, discussion students produced higher scores when the issue was familiar but subtle and little damage to the victim was involved. Perhaps these features made it necessary for them to work harder. Game students produced higher scores when the issues were

Table 12.3.

Rank-order Correlations between Objective Features and

Average Moral Scores across Sessions

Objective Features	Discussions				Games			
	Interactional Morality		Cognitive Morality		Interactional Morality		Cognitive Morality	
	Dominated	Led	Dominated	Led	Dominated	Led	Dominated	Led
Known/ unknown	.23	.55	.40	.55[a]	-.42	-.05	-.85	-.25
Close/ distant	.08	.35	.30	.35	-.78	-.95[a]	-.50	-1.00[a]
Vicarious/ direct	.63	.25	.40	25	.78	1.00[a]	.20	.90
Obvious/ subtle	-.28	-.55	-.60	-.55[a]	.08	.30	-.70	.10
Great/little damage	-.08	-.50	-.60	-.50	.66	.88	.08	.88

[a] $p < .05$

less familiar, more distant from their experience, and had the potential to cause great damage to the victim.

Altogether, game groups did poorly when the confrontation among members was close and direct whereas the discussion groups actually did better when the members were more closely and directly involved. This exploratory analysis is by no means definitive, but it does suggest that the contents and features of dilemmas are a potential source of moral meaning that needs further study.

Characteristics of Individual Persons and Moral Meaning

To understand how individual student's personal characteristics can interact with a situation to produce idiosyncratic moral meanings, we compared moral "heroes" and "casualties." A student was designated a "hero," somewhat tongue-in-cheek, for the particular session in which he or she made his or her highest scores—for example, a NeoPd interactional hero or NeoPd cognitive hero. Students whose lowest moral score was achieved during a particular session were designated as "casualties" for that session. We planned to compare heroes and casualties, but this process did not identify a sufficient number of persons (at least eight) for every session, so analysis of differences could not be done. Too few people met the criteria for Humanus and the discussion sessions—Humanus because only two students produced their lowest scores in this session, and the discussion sessions because this subsample was already small. Subsequent analyses addressed the possibility that certain kinds of people may react well or poorly to different kinds of moral dilemmas and contexts.

Heroes and Casualties in NeoPd

For NeoPd, 15 heroes and 24 casualties were identified using the interactional system and 20 heroes and 15 casualties using the cognitive system, the sexes being approximately equally divided between heroes and casualties within each system. But cognitive heroes were significantly more often members of dominated groups ($p \leq .01$). Cognitive heroes and casualties could not be further distinguished.

Although ten interactional heroes were members of led groups compared to five members of dominated groups, this difference was not significant. Being a casualty in NeoPd apparently had an instructive effect because casualties had significantly higher interactional scores than did the heroes in the two immediately subsequent sessions of Ghetto and Starpower (ps are $\leq .05$ and $\leq .001$, respectively).

Interactional heroes and casualties were also strikingly different as people. Comparison of the two groups' characteristic ego processes showed, surprisingly, that the casualties were more coping. They had significantly higher scores (ps range from $\leq .05$ to $\leq .001$) for coping objectivity, intellectuality, logical analysis, tolerance of ambiguity, empathy, and suppression, and they had lower scores for repression.

The casualties' characteristic pattern of greater coping and less defensiveness was further substantiated when the two groups' situational ego scores (averaged across all five sessions) were compared. Again the casualties were significantly (ps range from .05 to .01) more playful (ego regression) and sublimating, but also defensively displacing. Despite their situational and characteristic coping, the casualties in

NeoPd were significantly less objective, less empathic, less tolerant of ambiguity and suppressing. And they were more defensive—intellectualizing, rationalizing, denying and displacing (ps range from $\leq .04$ to $\leq .001$). They less often evoked the defense of reaction formation and defensive doubting. The casualties in the interactional system, except for their behavior in the one game of NeoPd, more persistently coped, both by preference and also in action.

The contrast between the characteristic and situational ego strategies of heroes and casualties suggests that the casualties were especially shocked and hurt by their friends' moral violations in NeoPd. Stated in reverse, although the heroes were characteristically and situationally defensive, they coped during NeoPd. Still, even their pattern of adapting to NeoPd was accomplished with defensive tactics. They were more defensively doubting and evoked the self-righteousness of reaction formation to produce their highest interactional scores in this most stressful of all situations.

Comparison of friends' evaluations showed that before the sessions began, the casualties were judged to be leaders ($p \leq .01$) and able to make clear arguments, but they were also regarded as dominating (both $ps \leq .05$). After the sessions were over, their friends confirmed some judgments but revised others. Compared to the heroes, the casualties were given even higher marks for being leaders ($p \leq .01$), fair, well known, and able to make clear arguments (all $ps \leq .05$).

These characterizations demonstrate that the particular moral costs are experienced differently by persons who are themselves intrinsically different. NeoPd was a situation of high cost, but its cost was particular in that, unthinkingly, the students morally violated their friends. The casualties seemed to be especially gentle, expressive, and cognitively oriented youth, and while playing NeoPd their very openness may have made them especially vulnerable to being violated by their friends. All the while, the "better" defended heroes were true to themselves across the three observations. They were characteristically defensive, and even at the peak of their performance during NeoPd their coping was mixed with defensiveness.

This partial description of the way NeoPd could be approached reveals, among other things, that sometimes "nice guys" morally default. In addition, the solid self-protection that a defensive reaction can provide is demonstrated. The heroes' use of reaction formation did not result in absolutely high-level interactional scores nor did it receive peer approval, but it was a kind of solution, a way to stave off the disintegrative stress that the more sensitive casualties experienced.

Heroes and Casualties for the Other Game Sessions

Small groups of heroes and casualties, numbering from eight to 17, were identified for each system for three other game sessions: Ghetto, Starpower, and Three Countries. Overall, their comparisons did not produce as striking results as occurred in NeoPd. But all results did form a generally consistent and more expected pattern for both moral systems. Heroes generally coped, obtaining higher scores for concentration and logical analysis; casualties were generally defensive and obtained higher scores for isolation, rationalization, and also for tolerance of ambiguity, indicating that moral conflict is not resolved by permissive withdrawal. There was some tendency for interactional heroes to be seen as leaders by their friends, and cognitive heroes to be seen as dominators. Finally, more casualties than heroes tended to be members of dominated groups but these differences were never significant.

Summary

This chapter has related our thoughts and general understandings gained after the fact of our data collection. We have attempted to specify the conditions and nature of moral meaning and confessed our initial naïveté about the impacts of games and discussions and about the varying difficulties of different moral dilemmas. Properly corrected by the results, we came to recognize that people care about the open expression of their moral ideas, even in discussion groups, and especially if the contents of dilemmas are close to their own experience.

We argued that people are not necessarily "immoral" or morally indifferent when they seem to care less about issues that are distant from their lives. Powerlessness to affect moral issues leads to apathy, but this is not the same as indifference. We came to recognize that the differences in moral levels between games and discussions were due more to the varying levels of difficulty in the contents of moral issues, either presented or arising in different sessions.

Moral meaning—which leads to moral costs—was broken down, and three main sectors became evident: the social context in which dilemmas are considered, the objective features of the problems themselves, and personal characteristics of the participants. The last included their previous, idiosyncratic experiences with similar dilemmas, their characteristic ego functioning, and their handling of immediate situations.

The results concerning the objective features of dilemmas themselves are presented as suggestions for future research. They are provocative in suggesting that the type of problems dilemmas present and the way particular people are equipped to handle conflict should not be overlooked.

The analyses of social context, which brought moral action levels in relation with the particular kinds of stress generated by led and dominated groups in game and discussion sessions, also served to probe the conditions of moral actions. Membership in dominated groups constitutes a moral stress in itself, especially when there is no authority that can be counted on to modulate the stress.

Finally, the stress of moral violation was shown to have an invidious effect on persons whose characteristic ego processes resulted in openness, sensitivity, and reactivity. In these circumstances, otherwise coping people morally defaulted.

PART IV

THE COSTS OF
MORAL DEVELOPMENT

Chapter 13

DEVELOPMENTAL OUTCOMES OF MORAL CONFLICT IN FRIENDSHIP GROUPS

The first [self-regulatory rule of development] applies to the . . . mechanisms of coherence that tell the child not to accommodate to novel experimental nourishment, to ignore new facts or to treat them as familiar. . . . The second applies to . . . progressive directionality . . . that tell[s] the child . . . to discover new and anomalous facts and construct new schemes to accommodate them (Jonas Langer, 1969, p. 169).

Two university students evaluating their experiences after five group sessions:

NICK: It made me think about other people a little bit. It makes you feel bad that you did stuff to other people.

PAMELA: It surprised me sometimes. I know people disagree but, on some points, to me it was so clear cut—like even in this homogeneous group, people had their minds working in such different ways. In a lot of these moral issues, I had a chance to vocalize how I felt. It felt good. In the normal course of day you just normally sit around.

Studying Development

THE YOUNG PEOPLE who volunteered to take part in the research projects had the unusual experience of directly dealing with moral problems for some 15 hours. Moral conflict had undoubt-edly occurred within these friendship groups before, but never in such a prolonged, self-conscious way. Although the group sessions provided a setting for studying moral action, they can also be regarded as ed-ucational interventions that foster moral development. The focus of this chapter is on how and why these students developed, if they did.

One way to learn about any phenomenon is to trace how it develops. Psychologists should be especially able to provide understandings of moral development. But there is a difficulty. We do not actually know what practical morality is, so we can hardly be certain about what develops. In the meantime, we must work with provisional definitions. Here we are concerned with *why* and *how* cognitive and interactional development occurs. We take up the question of *what* develops in the next chapter in a study describing the morality of four-year-olds.

Psychologists often study different kinds of development with the same short-term "training" methods we used since it is expensive to study naturally occurring phenomena. Even then important effects on development may not be discerned, or controlled. In conducting "training studies" psychologists must assume that the "microgenesis" of morality is the same as the "macrogenesis" of morality in real life. But whether this miniaturization of life matches the course of normal growth is not certain. For this to be true, the influences that cause progressive growth and regressive change in both natural settings and training sessions would need to be identified and shown to be the same. Psychologists are a long way from knowing whether training studies fulfill these criteria and, we hasten to add, we are not certain that our two studies meet the criteria either. Their main merit lies in the fact that the games provide experiences that are close to everyday life. Moral problems arose as they do in real life; they grew out of the situations and did not result from experimental manipulation.

To date most investigators of moral development have simply re-ported whether or not people changed after undergoing training ex-periences. But intervening transactions need to be understood—in other words, how specific occurrences during training interacted with personal characteristics of participants to produce different outcomes.

In this chapter we will first bring out the differences between the cognitive and interactional views of development. We will then show why the group sessions can be regarded as moral curricula and follow with a discussion of the limitations of these research studies. We start in the results section with a discussion of the presession and the two postsession interviews since they provided the basis for deciding whether individual students developed, stayed the same, or regressed. We will then describe our efforts to determine the characteristics of the students and their experiences that were associated with their different outcomes. Results for the young adults will be described first, and then those for the adolescents.

Development from the Interactional and Cognitive Perspectives

Progressive Development

Simply stated, the central question of moral development is: What develops and how, when, and why? The two moral systems provide different answers. For cognitive theory, moral development is the increasingly comprehensive and differentiated understanding of justice which evolves only as logical reason is acquired. Growth is expected to continue until the individual is an adult. Even then, the highest morally principled stages are achieved only by a few people, only about five percent according to Kohlberg (1981, p. 88). Therefore principled morality, which Kohlberg identifies with the American Constitution, "tends to be expressed or formulated by individuals capable of articulating a more advanced morality than the average man" (Kohlberg, 1967a, p. 173). Several ramifications follow from these views: Children are necessarily morally primitive; development is exceedingly slow and uncertain; the capacity for morally principled reasoning and action—the highest stage—is attained only by the intellectual elite.

Although logical development is the precondition of cognitive development, a secondary condition is the recognition of people of lower stages that their conclusions are not cognitively stabilized. They are thought to recognize their moral limitations when they compare their conclusions with those of their peers and teachers who are at a higher stage (Blatt & Kohlberg, 1975). This seems to provide a self-aware, but gentle motivation for cognitive moral growth.

Altogether, in the cognitive theory, development remedies the infant's initial shortcoming of being self-serving. At first the very young merely respond to the power wishes of adults. Later they become egoistic, but still they are not moral. When they reach stage 3, sometime during late childhood, and stage 4, even later, they are tied to society's standards, so they do not yet exercise a self-chosen way of judging. Independent choice—the hallmark of morality in the view of common sense—is achieved only at stages 5 and 6. As Kohlberg and Turiel (1971) state, "Only at the principled stage . . . are these considerations [justice] treated as principles distinct from the expectations and rules of the child's group" (p. 447).

In the interactional system what develops is increasingly reliable skill in resolving moral conflict, not moral concern in itself. Development is thought to be tied to the child's interdependency with others, which immediately gives rise—even in infants—to all people's needs to make adjustments to one another. In the interactional perspective, children's moral deficiencies are not the result of inherent selfishness. Although very small children are thought to be morally concerned, they are highly vulnerable to stress, so they often default morally. Consequently, we frequently see children acting to serve only themselves. But this is still not evidence that they lack moral concern. We think the very young do have moral concern but that their enactment of it is inconsistent. Some supportive evidence will be presented in Chapter 14.

The course of moral development is marked by gradual improvement in practical reasoning, rational consideration of factual details, and the ability to "read" the emotions aroused during interchanges. These skills are developed over time. Children, and adult caretakers as well, understand that increasing age means increasing responsibility for ascertaining moral truth. Along with this knowledge comes responsibility for acting so as to maintain and enhance social relations. In moral dialogue young people are most vulnerable. They have fewer resources, both material and social, to support their discussing, disagreeing, and agreeing as equals. And often children do not really have the resources for making adequate reparations for unavoidable wronging, which all people do on occasion.

As children experience social disequilibrium and then equalize their relations, they build their moral history. They gradually acquire a repertoire of successful, adaptable ways to solve problems, and in optimal rearing, they learn to expect that others will negotiate in good faith. Nonetheless, another developmental achievement is necessary— learning about the risk and futility of trying to deal with insincere protagonists. Common judgment does not require that we commit ourselves in good faith to dialogue with the insincere, but children are often taken in.

The pervasive motive for moral development is the interest of all people, whatever their age, in maintaining and enhancing social bonds. This motive arises from the dialectic of social living, the nuances of which children increasingly come to understand. People want to protect their own interests, but this need is only legitimated socially, which, in itself, is recognition that other people have a right to protect their legitimate self-interests. The interactional theory takes this dialectic—an immutable feature of social life—as the necessary condition of development. In itself, a claim of justifiable legitimacy assumes the presence of an audience who hears, and then affirms or denies the claim. Apart from social interchange, the concept of moral legitimacy is meaningless (compare Habermas, 1975). With a similar focus on the concept of social validation, Quine (1966) observed that in *no sense* can a private language be said to exist.

Discussants of any age can achieve equalization *if* they make allowance for each others' peculiar needs, contributions, and status. But equalization of relations between persons of unequal power and skill—like parent and young child—is seldom literal. From the interactional perspective, these are allowable and socially necessary imbalances. The person of greater resources makes allowance for the needs of the person of lesser power who in turn understands that he or she must not press all claims, only those relevant to the issue at hand. This sifting of needs, contributions, and resources goes on in all human interchanges, even between child and adult. Even infants press their self-interests, but they soon agree to some limitation on their power.

In fact, the family's dynamics is marked by a series of moral redefinitions, especially during the adolescent's transition to full adulthood. This is a time when the young are expected and expect to give up special privilege in moral negotiation with their parents. It is also a time when parents must give up their moral superiority and benevolence to accept—even require—full reciprocity from offspring as their equals (Haan 1971).

Regressive Developments

Regressive changes pose a different set of considerations. The cognitive theory's stipulations of irreversible structural development mean that it cannot accommodate this phenomenon. Kohlberg (1969) indicated he would not take it into account: "We may simply decide to exclude such regressive processes from our analysis on the grounds that they are outside the psychological system which assumes an intact nervous system and [we] are not required to account for the effects of a blow on the head" (p. 360).

Regressive moves are made often enough that they are social phenomena of great concern. (A distinction needs to be made between temporary regression under stress—discussed at length in the chapters concerned with action—and the more durable, pervasive deterioration in function we consider here.) In the interactional system, pervasive regression can occur when people find themselves inescapably immersed in relationships of bad faith and their attempts to remediate these relationships consistently fail. Even then, people may not totally abandon their moral concern but instead become carefully selective in their commitments to good faith, as the inmates of concentration camps did when they made moral distinctions between their captors and their fellows (Des Pres, 1975).

To be betrayed shakes the ground people stand on. It threatens existence, for people rely on interpersonal accountability as the underpinning of their commerce with others. The threat of personal disintegration can be forestalled by defensive negations and distortions that separate the self and the world, all of which amounts to withdrawal from social accountability. In other words, profoundly betrayed people—like abandoned and abused children—sacrifice social sensibility to protect their private sensibility.

Regressed development can be reversed if old conditions are replaced, but trust is not easily reconstructed. Clinicians who work with juvenile delinquents, criminals, abusing parents, and abused children well know the difficulties. Socially deviant persons are wary about taking the risk that proffered good faith might be authentic. Not only do they require improved social conditions that consistently deliver good faith, but they also need support so they themselves can personally invent new solutions.

Moral Curricula

The study of young adults was designed to provide two different curricula—gaming and discussing. The adolescent project involved only one of these experiences—games—and presumably none for the 17 youngsters who comprised the control group. Strictly speaking, the presumption that no intervention occurred is erroneous. To be interviewed about moral dilemmas may be a weak intervention since it draws people's attention to the idea of "moral excellence."

Playing games with one's friends to solve moral problems is an appropriate intervention from the interactional view. Because friends have a stake in their future relationship, they are especially disturbed when social disequilibrium occurs. This was a serious worry for the game students. They often sought agreement among themselves after the sessions. Of course, we had no way to assess the effects of these interchanges.

The cognitivists propose that discussion of hypothetical dilemmas is an effective moral curriculum for producing cognitive disequilibrium, their proposed vehicle of development (Blatt & Kohlberg, 1975; Hersh et al., 1979). Hypothetical issues—not moral relations among participants—are the focus. The teacher is the central figure, and his or her aim is to induce cognitive conflict and expose students to thinking at stages just above their own. The cognitivists do not suggest that the adult leader has inordinate power, but we think this is inevitable, especially in moral conflict. Children's experience leads them to expect that the mature and "official" adult knows the morally correct answer. And since each person's opinion is to be respected, there is no implication that discussants have a problem among themselves that they are responsible for solving. The curriculum is an effort to develop the individual person's capacities apart from social context.

All groups in our projects had members of different moral stages, according to the presession interview scores. So we met the cognitivists' stipulation that students of lower stages need opportunity to compare their formulations with arguments of those at higher stages. The average range of cognitive stages within the 15 friendship groups was one and a quarter stages. Two groups had a range of two stages, and the most homogeneous group, a range of two-thirds of a stage. The interactional system had a greater spread in scores, so the average range across groups was one and two-thirds levels.

The game sessions were primarily planned to provide experiences of social disequilibrium, but in some degree cognitive and social disequilibrium always accompany each other. Social disequilibrium did occur in some discussion sessions when the dilemmas involved "hot" issues. Therefore the difference between the two interventions is more of degree than in kind. Still, gaming or discussing represent the two systems' different views of the experiences that facilitate development: social conflict for the interactional system versus cognitive conflict for the cognitive. It should then follow that discussing would especially accelerate cognitive development, whereas gaming would especially accelerate interactional development.

Limitations of the Two Studies

A conventional design was used. First, we interviewed the participants to measure their level or stage of morality. Next, they took part in five group experiences; immediately afterwards their levels and stages of morality were again measured in interviews. Four months later individual interviews were again conducted. The differences in scores between the first and the two later interviews provided the bases for determining whether development occurred.

Nevertheless the results of the action studies and our conclusions about moral costs (Chapter 12) give reason to question whether the differences between presession and postsession measures are "true" anchor points for measuring development. The results from our studies of moral action suggest, first, that moral dilemmas, whether actual or hypothetical, do not all have the same level of difficulty; second, the interpersonal context in which moral dilemmas are confronted influences the costs; third, the subject matter of a dilemma affects the quality of moral performance and has private meaning for some but not all participants. All of these effects also apply to the hypothetical dilemmas presented in the interviews.

After data collection was completed, we could do nothing about this variation in the levels of difficulty of the test dilemmas nor the special meanings some dilemmas might have for individual participants. However, the interpersonal contexts of interviewing were always the same except that interviewers were switched (a procedure used to avoid possible biases for or against particular students). But the use of the interview has still other limitations. Although we argue that it is an action situation of one kind, the action evoked cannot be as important, authentic, and clear as it is in moral games or group discussions where opinions are expressed publicly. The interviewer is the only audience. Also interviewers are inevitably in control. They have the power to determine how much time will be allotted for each dilemma. In addition, they cannot avoid subtly "rewarding or punishing" respondents as they accept or reject answers or ask for more information. Siegert (1982) gives an analysis of the control the interviewer possesses. Furthermore, people who favor certain ego strategies, like intellectualizing, have an advantage when hypothetical dilemmas are discussed, but they may be disadvantaged in action situations of greater reality and uncertainty. All in all, interviews are artificial contexts for learning about people's morality.

The ideal design for a study of development would provide for measurements of moral level before and after training with dilemmas that require action. But even now, we know too little about the levels of difficulty of different dilemmas to choose them appropriately. In general, our inability to control level of difficulty should weaken our findings but not result in strong erroneous findings.

Preliminary Results

Conditions That Produced High Scores in Interviews

Since the interview scores provide the means of knowing whether development occurred, we needed to know whether the conditions that influenced these scores were reasonably like those that influenced the action scores. To explain the variation in each of the three scores achieved during the interviews, we constructed multiple regression models for the men, the women, and the entire sample, like those used for studying action. We first entered the students' sex into the model for the entire sample and then allowed the following influences to enter (if they had a probability level of .05 or better): experiences of gaming or discussing, membership in led or dominated groups, scores for characteristic and situational ego processing (averaged across all sessions), and moral scores for the first interview.

The results of these analyses are shown in Table 13.1. We consider only their general import. First, significant higher cognitive scores for the first and third interviews were achieved by the males. This finding is consistent with many reports by researchers—most based on interview scores—that adult men are more "morally mature" than women. Walker (1984) and Lifton (in press). We disagree since we found no sex differences in cognitive moral action scores. Males may have higher cognitive scores in interviews, but not in action situations.

Second, the presession interview scores were associated with scores

Table 13.1.

Conditions Supporting Moral Scores Based on Interviews

All Participants	Percent Contribution	Women	Percent Contribution	Men	Percent Contribution
Presession Interview Scores					
Interactional Morality					
Sex	+2	Dominated groups higher	14[b]	Characteristic repression	-9[c]
Characteristic repression	-7[b]	Characteristic repression	-8[c]	Session tolerance of ambiguity	-9[c]
Session tolerance of ambiguity	-6[b]			Session rationalizing	+9[c]
Session rationalizing	+5[b]				
Total	20[a]		22[a]		26[a]
Cognitive Morality					
Males higher	4[c]	Dominated groups higher	7[c]	Characteristic reaction formation	7[c]
Characteristic intellectualizing	+6[b]	Characteristic intellectuality	+9[c]	Session logical analysis	+11[b]
Session logical analysis	+5[b]	Session ego regression	+8[c]		
Total	15[a]		24[a]		19[b]
First Postsession Interview Scores					
Interactional Morality					
Sex	+2	Game groups higher	14[b]	Characteristic objectivity	+12
Characteristic suppression	+7[b]	Dominated groups higher	6[c]	Session regression	-8
Characteristic intellectuality	+4[c]	Characteristic repression	-6[c]	Session tolerance of ambiguity	-6
		Session intellectualizing	-9[b]	Session sublimation	+7
Total	13[a]		35[a]		32[a]
Cognitive Morality					
Sex	+1	Characteristic repression	-14	Characteristic objectivity	+8[c]
Characteristic objectivity	+9[a]	Session doubt	+7	Presession scores	29[a]
Presession scores	+14[a]				
Total	24[a]		21[a]		38[a]

Table 13.1 (cont.)

Second Postsession Interview Scores

Interactional Morality

Sex	$+0$	Characteristic repression	-21^a	Characteristic intellectuality	10^b
Dominated groups higher	4^c	Session concentration	$+7^c$	Presession scores	10^b
Characteristic repression	-12^a	Session rationalizing	-5^c		
Session concentration	$+8^a$	Session isolation	-5^c		
Session ego repression	$+3^c$	Presession scores	$+5^c$		
Presession scores	$+6^b$				
Total	32^a		44^a		20^b

Cognitive Morality

Males higher	3^c	Characteristic repression	-14^b	Characteristic intellectualizing	$+9^c$
Characteristic repression	-10^a	Presession scores	$+16^a$	Session displacement	$+9^c$
Session displacement	$+4^c$				
Presession scores	$+10^a$				
Total	28^a		29^a		18^b

[a] $p < .001.$
[b] $p < .01.$
[c] $p < .05.$

for the first and second postsession interviews in both systems. This is evidence for consistency among moral scores, but it occurs in situations that are much alike.

Third, both characteristic and situational ego processing made a larger total contribution to interactional scores (183 percent) than to cognitive scores (150 percent). This difference was primarily due to the proportionately smaller contribution of situational ego strategies to the cognitive scores (44 percent for situational to 86 percent for characteristic ego strategies) compared to nearly equal proportions for interactional scores (87 and 96 percent, respectively). Therefore the students' ways of handling moral problems in action and interview situations were more alike for interactional performance. But cognitive performance was due more to the way the students habitually solved problems.

Fourth, the contributions of coping and defense to the interview scores again affirm the hypothesis that coping strategies facilitate and defensive strategies thwart moral functioning, and the hypothesis is again more strongly supported in the interactional than in the cog-

nitive system. For the interactional scores, the ratio is 138 percent in
support for positive coping and negative defense to 45 percent not in
support for negative coping and positive defense. The same ratio for
the cognitive system is 88 percent in support of the hypothesis to
42 percent not in support. Two conclusions are suggested. The difference in the proportions of coping and defending that support
moral functioning in the two systems is again confirmed by results for
the interviews; ego processing is involved in cognitive morality even
in interview situations, so it seems this morality cannot be solely regarded as functionally disembodied acts of moral logic.

Fifth, some consistency in the choice of ego functions is evident.
Characteristically repressed students did not generally achieve high
moral scores in the interviews, especially not high interactional scores
(six negative contributions to the interactional interview scores for a
total of 63 percent and three negative contributions to the cognitive
scores for a total of 38 percent). The only other total contribution
above 20 percent was for situationally evoked tolerance of ambiguity,
which contributed three times to lower interactional scores for a total
of 21 percent. This ego strategy also caused lower interactional session
scores.

Altogether, the conditions that encouraged moral action and performance in interviews were basically similar. Both sets of moral scores
were strongly influenced by ego strategies, but interactional scores
were more enhanced by coping strategies and depressed by defensive
strategies in contrast to the cognitive scores. Dissimilarities included
sex differences, with males achieving better cognitive scores in interviews; strong influences of characteristic and situational strategies on
interactional scores but disproportionately strong influences of characteristic strategies on cognitive scores. But altogether we conclude
that within each system, the interview and action scores were reasonably similar.

The Index of Absolute Development

To understand the effects of the training sessions on development,
two different indices of development were constructed. The first was
based on the simple difference between each student's presession and
his or her postsession scores and provides then a straightforward in-

dication of the direction and amount of absolute change. The scores for the second and third interview were averaged because one score based on two measures after the sessions would provide a more reliable measure. Each person's presession score was subtracted from this postsession average to achieve a single developmental score. Due to a staff mistake, eight students had no scores for the first postsession so their scores for the second postsession were used. Participants were designated as "gainers" when their developmental score was one-half a stage or level above their entry score; and as "losers" when their score was one-half a stage or level below their entry score. They were identified as "stable" when their score was within one-half a stage or level above or below their first score.

The distribution among these three developmental outcomes for each moral system was different. There were more interactional gainers (26 percent) than cognitive (16 percent). More students were stable in the cognitive system (70 percent) than in the interactional (57 percent). The incidence of loss is about the same for both systems (17 percent for the interactional and 14 percent for the cognitive systems). Apparently, then, the group experiences accelerated the students' interactional functioning more than their cognitive functioning, but the difference is not significant. The loss for some participants is considered in a later section after the students' individual characteristics are described.

Analyses were done to compare the effects of gaming or discussing, led or dominated groups, and sex, but no results were significant. Direct analyses of the changes in the absolute scores across all three interviews (not developmental scores) showed that levels of interactional functioning significantly and progressively improved ($p \leq .001$), while levels of cognitive scores did not.

The Refined Index of Relative Development within the Entire Sample

A second, statistically refined developmental index was constructed to use in more complex analyses of the interactions between person and kind of experience. The question was: What kind of people interact with what kind of experience with what developmental result?

These scores were generated according to the following procedures.

1. The effects of the presession scores on the first postsession scores were removed to derive, say, X. 2. The effects of both presession scores and first postsession scores were removed from the second postsession scores, to derive, say, Y. 3. Then X and Y were added to obtain the developmental score. This statistical manipulation controls the level of each participant's scores; in other words, persons who move from Stage 2 to 3 are made mathematically equivalent to persons who move from Stage 4 to 5. However, estimates based on the entire sample must be used to construct these kinds of scores, so this developmental index is meaningful only in relation to this sample.

The cognitive and interactional developmental indices correlate .35 ($p \leq .001$) for the entire sample. Since this low correlation means that only 12 percent of the variation in both sets of developmental scores was shared, the two developmental indices are by no means identical.

Main Results

Analyses of the Relative Developmental Index for the Entire Sample

To ascertain whether certain kinds of students undergoing different kinds of experiences had different outcomes, we turned to other sources of information: 1. the groups' experiences as gaming or discussing; 2. the groups' structure as led or dominated; 3. moral action scores for each group session to ascertain whether levels of moral actions could have predicted developmental outcomes; 4. characteristic ego processing; 5. situational ego processing averaged for five sessions; 6. friends' ratings of one another before and after the sessions.

None of these analyses for the entire sample was informative, although there were two noteworthy results. Within the cognitive system, more game students gained (59 percent) and fewer lost (41 percent), whereas fewer discussion students gained (31 percent) and more lost (69 percent) ($p \leq .01$). Despite the cognitivists' expectations, gaming turns out to be a more effective intervention for cognitive moral learning than discussing hypothetical dilemmas. Analysis of the moral action scores for five sessions resulted in the finding that both the cognitive and interactional scores for session 1 modestly and positively predicted the participants' level of development ($p \leq .05$). These findings suggest that achievement-motivated students did especially well in both the first group session and later interview situations.

Coping with Disequilibrium as a Developmental Experience

The analyses discussed above did not consider whether the groups' functioning caused social or cognitive disequilibrium, the two proposed vehicles of development in the cognitive and interactional systems. Instead, game and discussion as well as led and dominated groups were assumed to represent two different kinds of disequilibrium. Still, neither led nor discussion groups were always inequable nor were all dominated or game groups always turbulent. Furthermore, individual members' level of coping with their group atmosphere—whatever it might be—needed to be taken into account.

With these ideas in mind, we undertook the next set of analyses to test the following possibilities:

1. Individual students will gain in cognitive and interactional morality if their group undergoes social or cognitive disequilibrium *and* either they are the kind of people who characteristically cope or they cope within the group sessions.

2. If a group experiences little disequilibrium, its members' development will not be affected (nor will they need to cope in an energetic or clear way). In general, the led groups probably provide such an example.

3. Individual students will lose developmentally if their group undergoes disequilibrium and either they are the kind of people who characteristically do not cope or they fail to cope within the sessions.

To measure disequilibrium we used two scales derived from the Q sort of group processes which described each friendship group's functioning within each session (see Chapter 7). The first scale, previously called *disintegrative versus integrative processes,* represents social disequilibrium. Its items include members stonewall in conflict, members distrust one another, conflict is a free-for-all, group is in disarray, and members use power to win points. The second scale, previously called *easy versus cautious disagreement,* represents cognitive disequilibrium. Its items include members overtly disagree, members are direct with one another, and members work to sharpen their differences.

These two measures of each group's functioning, for all sessions combined and each session, were multiplied by the appropriate measure of each member's situational coping scores. Furthermore, students' overall score for characteristic coping were also used as measures and multiplied by the measures for all sessions combined and each session. However, the essential meanings of the session-by-session analyses are economically summarized in the results for all sessions combined. These are shown in Table 13.2, and we first note the findings that might be expected but did not appear. First, situational coping interacting with either kind of disequilibrium had *no* systematic effect on development in either moral system. Second, cognitive disequilibrium interacting with either kind of coping had no systematic effect on either kind of development. Third, a clear and systematic result emerged. Characteristic coping interacting with the groups' social disequilibrium generally predicted development in both systems, for the entire sample and dominated groups. Fourth, the complete absence of significant results for the led groups is particularly interesting. Despite the strong results reported in previous chapters that members of led groups had consistently higher levels of moral action, *the equable experience of led groups had no effect on their members' development. The more perturbed and stressed atmosphere characterizing the dominated groups did predict development. In other words, the situational conditions that bring about quality moral action and development are directly opposite from each other.*

Altogether then, social disequilibrium, when handled by students who characteristically coped, predicted both interactional and cognitive development, whereas cognitive disequilibrium did not. Moral opinions, feelings, and even outrage seem to be a necessary condition of development. If conflict is to have developmental force, more is involved—even for cognitive development—than people's recognition that their moral structures are less comprehensive and differentiated than others.

A second important implication concerns the power of characteristic coping (compared to situational coping) interacting with social disequilibrium to predict development. Situational ego strategies, even

Table 13.2.

Relationships between Development and Group Disequilibrium

Interacting with Personal Coping

	Social Disequilibrium		Cognitive Disequilibrium	
	Interactional Morality	Cognitive Morality	Interactional Morality	Cognitive Morality
Coping in Action x Disequilibrium				
All	3.25	1.89	.98	.07
Game	1.07	.21	1.17	1.42
Discussion	1.61	1.39	.09	.00
Dominated	5.06^c	1.74	.14	.02
Led	.62	.88	.28	.68
Women	3.13	.82	.50	1.11
Men	.43	3.43	.69	.57
Characteristic Coping x Disequilibrium				
All	7.14^b	9.97^b	1.57	2.79
Game	2.06	4.62^c	2.23	8.75^b
Discussion	6.10^b	3.31	2.68	.68
Dominated	6.86^b	9.65^b	1.28	3.20
Led	.85	.40	.14	.03
Women	5.43^c	3.12	2.66	.28
Men	1.84	7.55^b	.01	3.29

^{a} $p < .001.$
^{b} $p < .01.$
^{c} $p < .05.$

when they are averaged across situations, are contingent adaptations taken for the moment. These adaptations strongly supported higher levels of action, but they were not important in moral growth. Instead *the critical factor was whether or not the students were already the kind of persons who can make sense out of moral conflict.*

Finally, neither the occurrence of social stress nor intrinsic ability to cope explained development. Instead the interaction of self and situation predicted development. The developmental course seems specific. It was experiencing one's self and one's friends in moral conflict, perceiving the deleterious effects of moral violation on oneself and others, and persistence in working through ways that these difficulties could be handled and resolved.

Comparisons of Three Developmental Groups

Given these results, we explored the possibility that students whose developmental level was not affected might be alike in warding off experience and be different from the students who were affected—whether they lost or gained. The latter might share some characteristics despite their different outcomes. Thus for further study, three developmental groups were formed according to such strict criteria that there could be no mistake that the developmental outcomes of stability, gain, or loss would be exemplified. Cutting points for both systems were established on the distributions of developmental indices. Gainers' scores were at least +1.5 levels or stages above the sample average of 0.0; losers' scores were at least −1.5 below the average; and stable students' scores were between +1.5 and −1.5. In all, 18 gainers, 19 losers, and 82 stable students were found in the cognitive system; 15 gainers, 20 losers, and 84 stable students were found in the interactional system. A total of 72 students were identified as gainers or losers within one or both moral systems; but only 13 students had the same classification as a loser or a gainer in both systems. These developmental groups were then compared on the descriptive data.

Effects of Sex, Experience, and Group Structure. Analyses of the effects of sex, experience, and group structure on membership in the groups were not significant for either moral system. Consequently these variables were not taken into account in subsequent comparisons. However, a trend in both cognitive and interactional development was again discerned: The gainers were more often members of dominated groups than led groups even though the latter had provided an atmosphere that facilitated higher quality action, as the results reported in previous chapters showed.

Moral Action. The developmental groups' levels of moral action were compared in order to determine whether their eventual developmental status was foreshadowed by distinctive profiles of moral ac-

Figure 13.1

Moral Action Scores for Developmental Groups

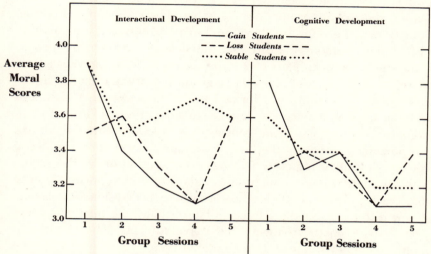

tion scores that might suggest the nature of their learning. The resulting, surprising curves are shown in Figure 13.1.

The stable students' profile for interactional morality was quite level across all sessions, and different from both the loss and gain groups, which were rather alike. Gainers had unusually high scores in session 1, but their scores progressively dropped through sessions 2, 3, and 4 and slightly recovered in session 5. In the first two sessions, the losers produced middle-level action scores, but they also slid during sessions 3 and 4; however, in session 5 they made a strong recovery. Differences among the three groups were significant for sessions 3 ($p \leq .05$) and 4 ($p \leq .001$). Because we already knew that the level of moral action is partly a function of stress, these profiles suggested that both gainers and losers had disequilibrating experiences. The level profile of the stable students suggested for whatever reason, they had not been perturbed.

The differences among the profiles for the cognitive developmental groups were significant only for session 1 ($p \leq 0.5$). The action levels of both the gain and loss groups decreased as the five sessions progressed, reaching the lowest point in session 4. The loss group also made a notable recovery in session 5. In general, the stable group had the curve of least fluctuation.

The Students' Personality Status before the Interventions.   Two sources of information describe the students before the interventions were begun: their scores for characteristic ego functioning and the first evaluations that friends made of one another. The results of comparing developmental groups are shown in Table 13.3. Overall comparisons of differences among the three were first made, followed by specific comparisons between pairs of groups, for example, stable versus loss, as well as stable versus "changers," a group comprised of both gainers and losers. This group was formed to determine whether changers were open to experience while stable students were not. Table 13.2 is organized so that significant contrasts are listed only under the developmental group with the highest average score. Other significant comparisons involving other pairings are still listed under the group with the highest score. Our usual standard of only reporting results that reach at least the .05 level of probability is occasionally relaxed. A few differences at the .10 level of probability are mentioned, especially between the changers and stable students. The results for interactional development are considered first.

The Interactional Groups. The students who were stable in the interactional system were characterized by a mixed pattern of coping and defense. In coping, they were characteristically the most objective and intellectual in their cognitive functioning and most aware but controlling of their emotional reactions (suppression). At the same time, they were the most defensively intellectualizing and characteristically presented themselves as self-righteous (reaction formation). Their friends regarded them as dominating and also as not being straightforward or fair; they judged them as not being able to change their views or understand the views of others, and as less likeable. In sum, students who were unaffected by the experiences were cognitively efficient, albeit somewhat pretentiously, and controlled in handling emotion. Friends saw them as having an ascendant, even arrogant confidence in their own self-rightness. By their nature then, these students seem unlikely to be perturbed by the moral conflict that engrossed their friends. The steady level of the moral scores they achieved during the sessions is consistent with this interpretation.

Students who gained in interactional morality were typified by only one characteristic coping process, tolerance of ambiguity, and their friends gave them the highest marks for being straightforward. Apparently these students handled the ambiguity of the moral conflict

Table 13.3.

Personality Differences among Developmental Groups:

Characteristic Ego Processing and Friends' Initial Evaluations

Interactional Development	Cognitive Development

Characteristic Ego Processing

Stable Group Highest

Objectivity S/L^b, S/C^c, G/L^c — Intellectuality S/L^c, G/L^c

Intellectuality S/L^a, G/L^b — Logical analysis S/L^b, G/L^b, S/C^d

Suppression S/C^c

Intellectualizing S/L^b, G/L^c, S/C^d

Reaction formation S/L^c

Gain Group Highest

Tolerance of ambiguity G/L^b — Objectivity G/L^b, S/L^c

Sublimation G/L^c

Substitution G/S^b, G/L^c

Loss Group Highest

Rationalizing L/G^c, L/S^c — Repression L/G^c

Doubt L/S^c

Repression L/G^a, L/S^c

Change (Loss/Gain) Highest

Ego regression C/S^d

Regression C/S^d, L/S^d

Presession Evaluation by Friends

Stable Group Highest

Dominates S/L^c — Makes clear arguments S/L^c

Dominates S/L^b

Gain Group Highest

Straightforward G/S^b, G/L^c, C/S^d

Loss Group Highest

Changes own views L/S^c, C/S^d

Fair L/S^c

Understands others' views L/S^d

Liked L/S^b, C/S^b

^{a}p < .001.

^{b}p < .01.

^{c}p < .05.

^{d}p < .10.

S is the stable group; G, gain; L, loss; and C, change, that is, gain and loss groups combined.

in a direct way. But the profile of their moral-action scores suggests that even though this involvement facilitated their development, the effectiveness of their moral action was temporarily reduced.

Students who did poorly with interactional morality were characteristically the most defensive. They were significantly more rationalizing, doubting, and repressive. Friends thought they often changed their minds. Nevertheless, the losers were also seen as fair, able to understand others' views, and likeable. These differences only became apparent when their achievement level was compared with that of the stable students. In sum, the losers' defenses are self-effacing, nonaggressive forms of adaptation and they were seen as "nice" rather than as competent. These adaptations depressed their moral performance in the stressful sessions and, later, their moral development.

Compared with the stable students, those in the interactional change group (losers and gainers combined) were more flexible in their adaptive strategies, both in coping and defensiveness; they had higher scores than the stable students for coping ego regression (playfulness) and for its defensive counterpart, regression. They also were less objective, less able to control their feelings, and unlikely to intellectualize. Compared to the stable students, friends gave them higher marks for being straightforward, able to change their minds, and understand others' views, and they were better liked. This overall pattern of characteristics is consistent with the idea that the change group was reactive—either vulnerable or able to build on experience—while the stable students were not reactive to the experience.

Essentially, then, the students' status as persons and friends before the study was begun influenced how they would react to the curricular interventions and whether they would be unaffected, gain, or lose in interactional development: Students who were unaffected by the experiences entered the project with impervious, consolidated structures of ego functioning; their friends regarded them as dominating. Students who gained in interactional morality were able to tolerate conflict. Their friends' affirmative endorsement of them as straightforward also suggests they would not avoid conflict. Students who lost were flexible and vacillating in the eyes of their friends, and well liked. Characteristically they made excuses, were doubtful, and tended to withdraw. Those in the interactional change group seemed highly responsive to experience, whereas stable students protected themselves from experience.

The Cognitive Groups. Turning now to the cognitive developmental groups, we find that before the curricular experiences were begun, stable students had the highest scores for coping intellectuality and logical analysis, the latter being the keystone of effective cognitive-moral functioning and development. But this commitment to logical analysis seems to have resulted in their being unaffected by the interventions. In addition, friends of the stable students gave them the highest scores for making clear arguments and being dominating. They were not distinguished from others by the use of any defensive process. The stable students seemed intellectually competent and the only possible indication of their resistance to the influences of these experiences was, perhaps, their friends' view of them as dominating.

Students who gained in cognitive development had the highest scores for objectivity and for coping with their emotions, either by expressively sublimating or by transforming negative emotions into highly socialized reactions (substitution). Their friends only characterized them as leaders ($p \leq .10$). Thus, emotion is relevant in cognitive moral development. But the question is whether emotion is coping or defending. The students who gained in cognitive morality coped with emotion.

Students who lost were highest for only one characteristic ego process—defensive repression. However, they attained the lowest scores for all the coping processes that were significant, and their friends gave them the lowest marks in categories of making clear arguments and dominating. Comparisons between the cognitive change group and stable students for characteristic ego processing produced only one marginal result: The stable students scored higher in logical analysis. Evaluations by friends were not significantly different. Consequently, being open or closed to experience seems not to be a differentiating factor in cognitive development.

Altogether, cognitively stable students seemed comfortable with their logical stance. Students who gained coped with their emotions. Students who lost were generally repressive and did not cope.

Altogether then, the beginning personality status of these students—according to their friends and their scores for characteristic ego functioning—did not strongly predict their cognitive development. In contrast, the beginning personality status of students with different interactional outcomes was important in predicting their developmental outcomes.

Comparisons of Personality Functioning during and after the Sessions. The interactional groups. Students with different interactional outcomes were not frequently distinguished by their situational ego strategies (see Table 13.4). This is not surprising, given the erratic profiles of the interactional action scores achieved by the loss and gain groups.

In these comparisons, the stable interactional students are the most noteworthy, since they are usually involved in the few significant results. They coped by concentrating and did not depend on the defensive strategies of repressing, intellectualizing, or denying. By the end of the sessions their friends had strengthened their conviction that the stable students were not straightforward.

At the end of the sessions the students who had gained in moral level were regarded as even more straightforward, and they were given higher scores for making clear arguments. Those who lost became only more repressive. Students who changed—either gaining or losing—were low in concentration and they intellectualized and denied. Their friends felt, however, that they were straightforward.

Taken altogether the findings indicate that the stable interactional students avoided becoming defensive; instead they coped by concentrating, a strategy that possibly allowed them to be impervious to their group's disequilibrium. Students that gained or lost became defensive. Friends of those that gained became even more impressed with their straightfowardness and increased their assessment of their ability to make clear arguments. Although students who attained different interactional outcomes were clearly distinctive as people, they did not act in strikingly different ways within the sessions, nor did their friends radically change their evaluations by the end of the sessions. An important implication for theories of moral development (and personality) can be drawn from the conditions supporting these outcomes. Ego strategies invented and applied for the moment are contingent ways of adapting to the immediate situation. But they were essentially unrelated to the longer-term meanings that these young people drew from the curricular interventions. *Interactional development depended more on the nature of the students as they themselves were and the persons their friends believed them to be.*

The Cognitive Groups. In contrast, analyses of the situational adap-

Table 13.4.

Personality Differences among Developmental Groups:

Situational Ego Processing and Friends' Postsession Evaluations

Interactional Development	Cognitive Development
Average Situational Ego Processing	
	Stable Group Highest
Concentration S/L[c], S/C[d]	Empathy S/G[c]
	Doubt S/G[c]
	Reaction formation S/G[c]
	Gain Group Highest
	Concentration G/S[c], C/S[c]
	Intellectualizing G/L[c]
	Rationalizing G/L[b], G/S[c], C/S[d]
	Loss Group Highest
Repression L/S[c]	
	Change (Loss/Gain) Highest
Intellectualizing C/S[d]	
Denial C/S[d]	
After Sessions (Corrected for Initial Scores)	
	Gain Group Highest
Straightforward G/S[a], G/L[c], C/S[d]	Makes clear arguments G/L[c], G/S[c]
Makes clear arguments G/L[d]	Dominates G/L[c], G/S[c], C/S[d]
	Fair G/S[c]
	Straightforward G/S[c], C/S[c]
	Loss Group Highest
	Liked L/S[c], C/S[d]
	Change (Loss/Gain) Highest
	Leader C/S[b], G/S[b], G/L[c]
	Handles self in conflict C/S[c], G/S[c]
	Well-known C/S[c], G/S[c]

[a] p < .001.
[b] p < .01.
[c] p < .05.
[d] p < .10.
S is the stable group; G, gain; L, loss; and C, change, that is, gain and loss groups combined.

tations of the cognitive developmental groups produced numerous results. The stable students reacted with a mixture of coping and defensiveness. They were empathic but defensively doubting and self-righteous (reaction formation); they concentrated and rationalized less than those that gained. Still, by the end of the sessions, friends gave the stable students lower marks for a number of characteristics. They were rated lower than those that gained in the categories of making clear arguments, domination, and being fair and straightforward; lower than those that lost for likeability; and lower than the interactional change group for leadership, being well known, and handling themselves successfully in conflict. Although the stable students had seemed to be characteristically the kind of people who would not be perturbed by moral conflict, their strategies during the sessions suggest that they became hesitant and self-righteous. By the end of the sessions they had suffered in their friends' evaluations.

Cognitive gainers are richly characterized by both their situational strategies and changes in their friends' evaluations. But they, too, present a mixed pattern of coping and defense. Although they concentrated more than stable students, their action strategies were predominantly defensive involving intellectualizing, rationalizing, and displacing. Nevertheless, by the end of the sessions, their friends gave the gainers higher scores for making clear arguments, domination, fairness, and straightforwardness. Students who lost were only characterized as being better liked at the end of the sessions than in the beginning. Changers, compared to stable students, concentrated to a greater extent and also defensively rationalized. They attained higher scores by the end of the sessions for leadership, being able to handle themselves in a conflict, and being well known, as well as for domination, straightforwardness, and being well liked. The "successful" detachment of the stable students clearly was not successful as far as their friends were concerned.

In sum, the cognitively stable students did not become totally involved in the problems their friendship group faced, and for this they acquired a measure of disapproval from their friends. The gainers became fully involved—to their friends' approbation; the losers were better liked at the sessions' end. The change group substantially improved in their standing with their friends.

Summary. A major difference in the conditions that influence development in the two systems was found in these analyses: The three kinds of interactional change were more strongly predicted by the kind of person the students were *before* the group experiences—their characteristic ego processing, and their friends' evaluations. The three kinds of cognitive change were more strongly predicted by what happened *during* the sessions—the students' situational ego processing and the changes in their friends' evaluations. Thus interactional change seems to result from the students' own intrinsic and stable ways of dealing with conflict, whether they ward off, deal with, or capitulate to experience. Cognitive change seems to be the result of more immediate and contingent happenings—how the students handled themselves within the conflict and whether or not friends affirmed their ways of acting.

Although rather similar ego strategies supported gain as well as stability in cognitive and interactional development, the adaptive strategies associated with loss in the two systems were not the same. Losing in interactional development involved personal defensiveness and not especially high regard from friends, whereas cognitive loss involved less defensiveness but high regard from friends. The losses in interactional morality seem authentic since the results are internally consistent. But the losses in cognitive morality are not consistent. We suspect that these losers may have deliberately rejected the demands of the research in favor of keeping the peace with their friends.

A repeated finding from the study of action was that coping facilitates and defensiveness thwarts moral functioning and this typified interactional more than cognitive morality. However, this pattern does not emerge in these analyses of development—either as characterizing one morality more than the other or one kind of developmental outcome over the other. In fact, all developmental outcomes in both systems generally include patterns of mixed coping and defending.

In sum, then, development is not simply a matter of coping with experience. More is involved. From the interactional perspective, people need to experience the fragility of moral dialogues. They need to experience their own and others' moral violations to learn that they, as well as others, can violate, however unthinkingly. To develop, they need to realize that "sinners" are not just strange, foreign, or poor people, and that they themselves can sin. With these understandings, people are likely to negotiate carefully and in good faith.

The Harmful Role of Self-righteousness. By contrast, the defensive process, reaction formation, especially highlights the essence of developmentally meaningful experience. Interactionally stable students were characteristically self-righteous, while cognitively stable students were self-righteous during the sessions. Self-righteousness makes sincere commitment to moral negotiation and resolution unnecessary. Dependence on this strategy was probably a main reason why the stable students were not affected by these experiences.

Tolerance of Ambiguity. Parenthetically, an interesting paradox is suggested by the interactional gainers' characterization as being able to tolerate ambiguity. Readers will recall that tolerance of ambiguity made modest *negative* contributions to interactional scores for group sessions and interviews, but here its contribution to development is positive. Therefore, being tolerant of ambiguity in an actual conflict depresses moral action, but being the sort of person who characteristically tolerates ambiguity facilitates development. It seems, then, that tolerating ambiguity in general allows people to experience, work through, and eventually benefit from conflict. But to tolerate ambiguity in moral conflict with friends, as an immediate, situational tactic, has the quite different meaning of passivity and relativism—or "copping out," to use the students' vernacular.

Descriptions of Students Who Gained in One System and Lost in the Other

To provide readers with direct understandings of the kinds of people and their experience that led to their gain or loss in moral levels, we located extreme cases. They were students who gained in one moral system but lost in the other. Five such students were located; we will describe two of them, starting with Paul, a member of a led game group, who gained in cognitive but lost in interactional morality.

Cognitive Gain and Interactional Loss. Paul's father was a commercial designer and his mother a housewife. He had grown up in the Bay Area as the second oldest in a family of four children. His intended major was physics, but he was uncertain about his plans after graduation. His friends initially gave him considerably above average scores for leadership and likeability. Paul's scores for characteristic coping and defending were about equal and both were about average for the sample.

During the five sessions Paul's involvement and willingness to participate as a research subject were very high, but his analyses of his group's processes were only slightly above average except during NeoPd and Three Countries, when he did become very perceptive of the nature of his group's interchange. During the first interview, Paul's moral scores in both systems were slightly above Level and Stage 3. But he went on to produce scores at various levels during the sessions, although his cognitive scores, from Stage 2 to 5, were consistently higher than his interactional scores. He finally achieved Stage 4 cognitive scores in the last two interviews, while his interactional scores dropped back to Level 3 and below after the sessions.

During the discussion of the ten items that Humanus (the computer's voice printout) will allow the group to have, Paul urges, "It should be something that benefits the whole group." Confronted with the possibly contaminated survivor, Paul imagines, "If we bring in this guy maybe we could clean up the whole environment so maybe we could save anyone who comes to our door. . . . If people come to our door, I think we have an obligation to society. We could work on a solution and if this guy dies before we find a cure, maybe we can save the next one. I'm saying it's not worth dying ourselves when we have a chance to repopulate the world."

During the discussion after the game Paul states his position, "It's a final obligation to me and to society. This has to be more important than my own selfish desires to bring my girl friend into this cell. Look, I think we have an obligation to go out and repopulate the world. We should help people but we can't do any of this if we're dead."

During NeoPd, Paul becomes the negotiator for his subgroup. He gets very involved in the mathematics of various strategies and offers various "deals" to the other subgroup. He states he will negotiate and tells his subgroup that its plan is fair because the other subgroup knows "what our strategy is." Later, when anger grows, he first says he won't talk, but then he does and makes the offer, "We'll go zero everytime as long as you go zero" (a tactic that stalemates the groups). Later he says with hauteur to the other subgroup, "You're *not* in a position to demand anything. You violated our trust twice, but then we violated, too, so now we are even," he adds in an evident attempt to justify his stance. "Look, you guys, through all this *we've* learned to be honest; I don't know about you guys. First we were just out to make money but later it turns out to be a trust thing." Afterwards he justifies his participation in broken agreements, "It wasn't so much *who* broke it as *when*. It turned into a holier-than-thou trip. Besides in game you're taught one group wins and one loses, and we are a game group."

During Ghetto, Paul is again actively involved. He says [his marble hitting a friend's]: "If I hit, how about I take two points and you take one? After all, I'm taking the risk of hitting the trouble marble so I should get more." He points out later in regard to the policeman's reprehensible behavior, "We can take the policeman to court if he shoots at us unjustly, but wait till he shoots." Paul later asks, "Are we pitted against the system or ourselves? The only way to beat the System is for us to go together." He declines an offer from the System and says to the group, "Actually you'd be smarter to leave me out [of the plans] because I don't have very much. I won't hold a grudge. . . . Let's side with the System only when she offers a good deal."

During Starpower, Paul becomes a Square, meaning he is a member of the power group. He soon offers a rule: "No one person can have more than one bonus point, and if there's a tie after points are distributed, then the status quo holds." After a challenge by the Triangles, Paul says, "Okay, okay, let them. We'll make a rule now that all bonus points go to us and they're each worth 100 points." During the post-game discussion, he explains, "It was like them against us, and even if they got someone in our group [the Squares] we'd still have people here. So you'd just have to cooperate. . . . We didn't mind until you tried to conspire to get someone in power—Screw that! . . . You'd have done the same thing if you were in power. It would have been to your benefit to come to us and say let's even out the points—instead of conspiring." "A leader is needed; he should be a regulator," Paul says. "Without a leader, everyone would be talking and all. We just need leaders to keep everything going."

In Three Countries, Paul convinces his group to risk a food unit in cooperation with another country on the behalf of a third country. He says, "We'll loan you food if you will give it back on demand. We're not going to ask for it—let's be clear about that—unless our people are dying. Do you want to make a rule that all decisions will be unanimous?" Later he points out, "You know if we let a million die, it will be easier on the next round."

The second student, Kathy, was a member of a dominated game group and she illustrates the reverse phenomenon—of gaining in interactional morality but losing in cognitive morality. Kathy's father was a faculty member in physical sciences at another university while her mother was employed in biological sciences. Kathy was the older of two children and had grown up in the Bay Area. She proposed majoring in political science or history but indicated that she planned to go on to law school. Friends' evaluations of her were not strikingly distinctive; her marks were slightly above average for making clear arguments, understanding others' views, and being fair and straightforward. Her scores for characteristic coping and defending were about equal and near average.

During the sessions with her dominated friendship group, Kathy seemed to set herself aside. Although she continuously coped far more than she defended, her actual involvement was consistently *very* low except for session 5. Her commitment to being a research subject was average to low, and she did not openly analyze her group's operations. Seven of Kathy's interactional scores were considerably higher than her cognitive scores except during Starpower, where they were equal at Stage and Level 4. Her interactional scores ranged from slightly above Level 3 to 5, while her cognitive range was high Stage 2 to 4.

In Humanus, during the discussion about whether the possibly contaminated survivor would be allowed to enter the group's safe area, Kathy volunteered. "I still feel sorry for him. What if you were out there? My first response is let him in." (But Kathy was outvoted 7 to 1). Later in the postgame discussion, she commented on her own reactions, "That was a totally emotional response, but we did agree that we were going to have a democratic society; we should have let him in." During discussion of whether the group should help a suicidal man who is supposedly a member of another group, Kathy tries to persuade her friends, "We're all in the same boat. It's a commonality. We'd want others to do it for us. We said at the beginning, a big part was to help each other with problems, reach out, and stuff like that." When asked during the discussion following the games why she eventually went along with her group, Kathy explained that she saw a contradiction between her group's wishes and her feelings about the survivor: "I decided I was being subjective, so I decided to be rational, but I couldn't be as barbaric as the rest of you. I really wanted the vote to go seven to one to let him in."

During NeoPd, Kathy was in the losing subgroup which suffered a broken agreement at the hands of the winning group. She exclaimed at first, "No more negotiations! We don't trust them. We won't negotiate; they burned us twice." Later she protests, "They'll just do it again." But that is about all she says until the discussion after the game; then she comments, "Look, it's okay if you're a sucker sometimes, if you're a good human being. . . . I thought they (the winning subgroup) were my friends so I trusted them. . . . I didn't want to be as low as them and do it to them just because they did it to us. I don't care what they're saying. It sounds corny, I know. I'm sorry. But I just *didn't* want to do the same thing."

During Ghetto, Kathy pleads with two fellow citizens, who are whispering to each other, "Be nice neighbors, come on, let us in on it." Soon she explains herself, "I knew what was going on. I'm going to let it go on. I'm going to try to get out [of the Ghetto] and then help as many people out as possible. . . . I just feel like we were all trying to help each other. Whoever gets 20 [the amount needed to buy one's way out of the ghetto] will help the rest. I thought we all understood that."

During Starpower Kathy no longer directly criticizes her friends, but she does give some bonus chips to members of another group that has very few. She urges that John would make good laws if they all got together and helped him become a member of the Squares [the power group]. She reminds another player that he owes her chips. Finally, in exasperation she gives away all her chips. In the discussion following the game, Kathy reports that she told another girl who belonged to the Squares what she felt might be done to resolve the difficulties, but she temporizes, "I just didn't feel very competitive tonight."

During Three Countries, Kathy roused herself and urges her fellow citizens, "We have to build up our surpluses. It isn't for gambling; it's because they'll burn us the next round." When another group criticizes her group's "gambling," Kathy argues, "You criticize us for gambling when our people are starving!" During the discussion afterwards, she turns a criticism aside by saying to another member, "Look, how did you feel when you weren't in power in Starpower? You just have to stockpile to protect your country from burns. . . . It was right to get as much food and resources at the same time that you tried to help others in need." Finally she reconciles herself with her friends by noticing, "It was pretty cool that none of us went to war. We tried."

Both Paul and Kathy seemed seriously involved despite the observers' evaluations that Kathy was detached. Neither Paul nor Kathy are self-serving and both were critical of their friends' shortsightedness and violations. But in these interpersonal-action situations Paul seemed to turn to abstract regulations—obligations to society, persistently to rules and the comparatively impersonal mechanics of situations. In contrast, Kathy, who would be a lawyer, is drawn more to the particular nature of the moral issues involved in the interaction, so she seems more indignant about her friends' violations, and she persistently reminds them, "We're all in the same boat; we said we would help each other out; it's okay to be a sucker if you're a good human; remember in Starpower how you felt?" But at the same time, being a 19-year-old among friends, she seems concerned that this research project not alienate her from her friends—a secondary moral problem of no small concern from her own point of view.

Moral Development in the Adolescents

Study of the adolescents' development had the limitations we mentioned before. There was a smaller number of participants and no discussion groups nor designation of groups as led or dominated. There were no evaluations of the students by their friends or measures of their characteristic ego processing.

Development occurred in both systems (Haan, 1978) since the youngsters had significantly higher cognitive and interactional scores in their interviews after playing the games than in their interviews before the games (both $ps \leq .01$). The "control" group of 17 youngsters—recruited as friends of the game students but only interviewed—did not significantly change. Therefore, the games facilitated gain in both systems.

The second set of results concerns other factors that contributed to the adolescents' development: their sex, race, age, and socioeconomic levels, their moral scores before the sessions, and ego functioning averaged across the group sessions. (Readers will recall that these ego scores are based on a factoring of the ego processes so they have different names.)

The model for explaining variation in the cognitive scores for the interviews following the sessions was significant at .05 level; the scores for the first interview accounted for 12 percent and the coping, cognitive process of objectivity accounted for another 7 percent of the variation. The model for predicting the interactional scores after the sessions was significant at the .001 level of probability and included the following contributions: objectivity (12 percent), lack of suppression (9 percent), interpersonal logic (5 percent), and being black (7 percent). Altogether, then, both sets of findings indicate that moral gain was especially supported by the coping strategy of objectivity, but interactional gain was also supported by being black, control of emotions, and understanding interpersonal reactions.

These findings for the adolescents are not easily related to the young adults' except that gaming did accelerate development in both samples. Adolescents who persistently coped by being objective developed in both systems. The additional contributions to interactional gain—lack of suppression and interpersonal logic—seem consistent with the findings for interactional development in the young adults. Involvement and understanding of the feelings and circumstances of others seem central in the growth of interactional morality.

Summary

Summary of Findings

The main findings concerning development are summarized here.

1. Patterns of Development: Absolute Scores. When indices were based on the absolute difference between the students' scores before and after the interviews, a trend was apparent: Somewhat more students gained in the interactional system and more students were stable in the cognitive. Analysis of interactional scores across the three interviews showed that their interactional gain was highly significant.

2. Patterns of Development: Scores Relative to the Sample as a Whole. Analysis based on development relative to the entire sample—a procedure that controlled for students' entry scores—produced two findings:

> Within the cognitive system, game students gained more often than did discussion students, despite the cognitivists' recommendation that the discussion of a hypothetical dilemma is an effective moral curriculum.
> Students who gained in both moral systems had significantly higher moral-action levels in the first group session.

3. Interview-based Moral Scores. Analyses of the sets of scores obtained in three interviews yielded several findings. Men produced higher cognitive scores than women, a frequently reported result, even though there were no significant differences in levels of moral action based on sex.

Characteristic and situational strategies made almost equal contributions to the interview-based interactional system, but characteristic ego strategies brought about much higher cognitive scores than did situational strategies. Therefore interview and action situations seemed to have divergent effects on cognitive performance. The opportunities for intellectualizing in interviews may account for this divergence.

The major hypothesis tested throughout this investigation that coping strategies should enhance and defensive strategies should impede moral functioning, was again strongly affirmed for interactional morality but less strongly for cognitive morality.

Finally, we concluded that the unusual effects on interviews were essentially controlled in our method of generating the developmental indices, but we observed that development would be better assessed in the future if it were based on action situations.

4. Interaction of Situational Disequilibrium and Personal Coping. The two vehicles of moral development proposed for each system—the groups' cognitive or social disequilibrium—were studied in interactions between individual students' coping. Students' characteristic coping combined with their groups' social disequilibrium strikingly predicted developmental gain in both systems. Development for members of the equable, action-effective led groups was not predicted. Neither situational nor cognitive disequilibrium predicted development. Since neither cognitive disequilibrium nor discussion of hypothetical dilemmas resulted in development, the cognitivists' curricular recommendations (Blatt & Kohlberg, 1975) must be questioned.

5. Comparisons among Stringently Defined Developmental Groups. The contrasting profiles of moral action for students with different developmental outcomes, especially within the interactional system, suggested that developmental gains or losses were preceded by erratic moral functioning, especially during later group sessions.

In general, interactional development was more fully described by the students' status before the sessions while cognitive development was more fully described by the students' behavior during the sessions.

The stable students (in both systems) were rather similar. Their distinctive ego processing involved mixed patterns of coping and defense. Although intellectually efficient and emotionally well regulated, they were self-righteous, and in the eyes of their friends, dominating, inflexible, and not very likeable. These students seemed to protect themselves against the chaos and self-exposure of moral conflict and did not seek mutual resolution of the moral problems they and their friends faced.

Students who gained in both moral systems also acted rather similarly. They were much involved in the moral experiences. At the end of the sessions, friends strengthened their judgments that those who made moral gains were straightforward and able to make clear arguments. Their ego strategies suggested that the interactional gainers characteristically tolerated ambiguity. Cognitive gainers especially coped with their emotions, but during the sessions they became more defensive. Altogether, gainers seemed prepared to risk moral involvement and self-exposure, and, when faced with conflict, they did become involved.

The two groups of students whose moral levels became depressed were not alike. Interactional losers were characteristically defensive and vacillating. Their characteristic self-effacing defenses, of doubt, repression, and rationalization, and their friends' views of them suggested that they relinquished moral authority during the sessions. Cognitive losers also were preferentially repressive, but they seemed intent on avoiding experiences of disequilibrium. These students' loss may only be a temporary phenomenon resulting from a desire to keep peace with their friends rather than a "true" function of the intervention experiences.

The hypothesis that the changers, who either lost or gained, were open and reactive to experience and that stable students were closed to and well-fortified against experience was clearly supported for interactional but not cognitive development.

Implications of These Findings

The understandings gained in the analyses of disequilibria as vehicles of development are of great interest and their implications are clear. *The kind of disequilibrium that made both interactional and cognitive development possible was passionate, stressful debate, not abstracted cognitive disagreement. This disequilibrium was not simply generalized stress but was, more specifically, the stress—even the shock—of discovering that one's friends and even one's self could morally violate, easily and unthinkingly.* As a result, morality comes to be seen as a delicate interchange that requires careful nourishment. And it involves the risk of self-exposing commitment; it means frequently attempting to right wrongs that people inevitably commit and frequently forgiving wrongs done to the self. Members of groups that functioned so smoothly that moral violations seldom occurred did not have these instructive experiences despite the fact that they usually acted effectively. This description of how and why development occurred applied to cognitive morality equally as well as to interactional morality.

The Role of Emotion Needs Focused Attention

In everyday life, moral issues and potential violations—whether of immediate concern to one's self or merely observed—are seldom dispassionately considered. That emotion commonly accompanies practical morality can hardly be denied, but its very vividness seems to have confused moral theorizing. On the one hand, some theorists—both psychologists and philosophers—have thought that emotion is the sole, critical feature of moral functioning. In their view, morality is acting automatically in the thrall of compelling, unanalyzable feelings that signal rightness or wrongness. Consider, for instance, the views of the psychologist, Aronfreed (1968) and the philosopher, Stevenson (1960). On the other hand, some theorists like Immanuel Kant and Lawrence Kohlberg have contended that the essence of morality lies in the person's application of logic to moral problems. In this view, emotion either becomes irrelevant or interferes with effective moral activity. Neither of these positions is consistent with the present findings.

It is easy to see that emotions are aroused by moral issues. But the questions are whether emotion is morality or is emotion an irrelevant accompaniment or even an obstacle to morality? Or does emotion serve to inform and qualify moral functioning? From our view the question for moral investigation is none of these but rather how emotion is handled and with what consequences for moral development. It seems to perform the valuable functions of underscoring the meaning and thus the importance of the issues at hand. Invariably emotion signals a participant's basic position to the protagonist. The students who were the least emotional were unaffected by the game experiences, whereas the more emotional students gained. But when emotion could not be dealt with—but was instead overwhelming, defensiveness became necessary and moral development was regressive, most clearly in interactional development.

From the interactional perspective, coping with moral imbalance and its indignations invariably involves foregoing for a time the claim of self-righteousness. If honest dialogue is to take place, the risks of participation and its consequences have to be accepted. The personal imperviousness of the stable students and the anxious, self-effacing defensiveness of the students who lost in interactional morality, indicated that it was impossible for them to accept and deal with these risks.

In this regard, the two systems diverge on the conceptual level. From the cognitive view, the moral actor's question is: How can *I* draw the morally correct conclusion from the principles I already possess and endorse? This self-contained process moves within a closed system. From the interactional perspective, the moral actor's question becomes: How can *we* discover a solution that will equalize and enhance our relationship and also pass scrutiny from outside neutral observers, real or imagined? The commitment to participate in sincere dialogue is an admission that interdependency is an open system, and its integrity and success depend on self-righteousness being relinquished at the outset.

These studies did not support the cognitive idea that moral growth is fostered by the disorganization and transformation of moral structures that follow on their possessor's recognition that his or her structures are flawed or less comprehensive than are those of higher-stage people (Walker, 1983, p. 108). Flaws in reasoning were continuously pointed out by friends, and all friendship groups contained members at different stages of moral development. Consequently, students had ample opportunity to be exposed to disparities between their own stage of reasoning and that of higher stages. Furthermore, the cognitivists' hypothesis that social comparison facilitates development is based on the assumption that a person's stage is a certainty. After the action studies, we can only ask "What stage? Manifested in what situation?" All in all, the cognitivists' formulation that cognitive disequilibrium is the critical catalyst of development was not affirmed for cognitive (or interactional) development. Retrospectively we can see that cognitive disequilibrium characterizes all moral encounters, but still it is not relevant to development.

Patterns of characteristic coping distinguished those students whose interactional outcomes later turned out to be different. But the ways students acted during the group experiences was not related to outcomes. Patterns of situational coping and changes in friends' evaluations at the conclusion of the moral experiences of each group did distinguish students whose cognitive outcomes were different. These two different descriptions of how moral development is generated reiterate a trend noted in the action studies. Moral-action scores were also supported by this same differentiated pattern—greater contributions from characteristic ego strategies to interactional morality and greater contributions from situationally evoked strategies to cognitive morality. *Altogether then, whether enacted or developed, interactional morality was supported by more durable propensities, whereas cognitive morality depends more on contingent adaptations that resolved the immediate pressures of situations.*

This chapter has considered how and why moral development occurs, but it did not address the questions of what develops and when development occurs. In these latter respects, the proposed formulation of interactional morality takes a radical view. First, very young children already have moral concern which they are not always able to enact—but neither did the adolescents or young adults nor do people in general. Second, what we assume as children's moral development is not of morality *per se;* instead it is deepening sophistication in the use of skills and improvement in real resources that allow young children to enact their moral concerns with greater consistency in a wider range of situations. These ideas are the subject of the next chapter.

Chapter 14

MORAL ACTION OF FOUR-YEAR-OLDS

Martin Packer, Norma Haan, Paola Theodorou and Gary Yabrove

TWO FOUR-YEAR-OLD GIRLS have played the game NeoPd so that each has won an equal number of pennies. The staff leader is not certain that they understand this equalizing solution so she asks:

STAFF LEADER: What would happen if you, Jackie, put down a blue card and Mary put down a red card?
JACKIE: I would get pennies and she wouldn't.
STAFF LEADER: Would that be fair?
JACKIE: Nooooo. Because then I get pennies and she doesn't. (*Pause.*) It gets really kinda unhappy.
STAFF LEADER: Mary, how would you feel if you got some pennies and Jackie didn't?
MARY: (*biting her lip*) Sad.
STAFF LEADER: How come?
MARY: I don't like Jackie getting sad and we're friends and we always do the same thing.
STAFF LEADER: When you both put down red, how does that make you feel?
BOTH GIRLS: Happy!
JACKIE: 'Cause then it's more like it, 'cause we both get something. (*Each will receive one penny.*)

Theories of development try to bridge two points—the beginning and end-points—as conceptions of what humans are born with and what they become at maturity. Here we are interested just in the beginnings of morality; it is a focal conceptualization in all moral theories since it sets the stage for all other stipulations that might be made in a theory and all educational recommendations that might be proposed.

In this chapter we will describe the moral concerns and skills of four-year-olds in the action situation of NeoPd, the most stressful game that the young adults and adolescents experienced. Of course, four-year-olds are not at the very beginning of morality, but they are certainly close to it. After setting down the background of psychologists' thinking and work about the beginnings of morality, we report our observations of 40 children playing a modified version of this game. Our particular focus will be on the character of the children's moral concerns and the ways they resolved the conflicts that NeoPd incites.

Background

The Presumption of Moral Incapacity

The presumption that young children lack moral capacity or are even immoral is common to many accounts of moral development. Freud assumed that very young children are instinctively self-serving, motivated only by the impulse to satisfy their own desires. Social-learning theorists regard preschoolers as lacking internalized systems of control so they must learn "conscience" through reinforcement, or observation and imitation.

Cognitive-developmental theorists also regard young children as being morally deficient. The cognitive approach to the study of children's morality began with Jean Piaget, whose seminal work, *The Moral Judgment of the Child* (1965; first published 1932), was written more than 50 years ago. This was his only investigation of children's morality, and he worked with the same methods be used in analyzing children's logical reasoning about the physical world. That is, through interviewing and questioning children, both in games and with hypothetical stories, Piaget studied their understanding of moral rules.

He proposed that between three and eight years, children's moral reasoning in the hypothetical stories was "heteronomous." In other words, their morality was of constraint, they regarded rules as fixed, even sacred, commandments, and defined "right" as adherence to authorities' dictates.

Piaget proposed a sequence of four developmental stages whereby children came to understand games. He placed children of approximately three to six years old (thus close in age to the children we studied) in the second stage. Piaget contended that although children at this level imitated the behavior prescribed by game rules, they did not understand the rules, since they were unable to coordinate their actions with other children. Their play was essentially individual. He described this intrinsic cognitive inexpertness as "egocentricism," meaning that they could not compare their own point of view with others'.

In an example, Piaget (1965) wrote of "two children from the same class at school, living in the same house, and accustomed to playing with each other." Yet, he writes "how little [they] are able to understand each other at this age. Not only do they tell us totally different rules . . . but when they play together they do not watch each other and do not unify their respective rules even for the duration of the game" (p. 40).

After this one study of moral development, Piaget's attention was more exclusively focused on children's reasoning in the nonsocial areas. Much later Kohlberg continued the cognitive study of moral development. He elaborated upon Piaget's stages to offer a systematic and comprehensive theory of moral reasoning. Like Piaget, Kohlberg thought young children could not consider the interests of others because they cannot coordinate divergent points of view. Unlike Piaget, he contended that young children's judgments are based on the threat of punishment, rather than sacred respect for adult authority and rules. In Kohlberg's view, young children's judgments about the "rightness" of an act are associated with its physical consequences—it is wrong to steal another child's toy because punishment results.

Kohlberg (1969) also criticized Piaget's theory for its focus on the content rather than the underlying structure of children's moral reasoning. He proposed a structural description and went on to adopt the research methodology of interviewing people about hypothetical moral dilemmas, which improves opportunity for identifying structures.

Damon (1977) also applied a cognitivist framework to theorize on the moral and social development in young children. He used stories and situations that were familiar to young children and came to conclude that young children are more active and attuned to the social setting than either Kohlberg or Piaget suggested. After studying children's judgments about fair distribution, Damon formulated a sequence of six levels to characterize development from approximately age four to ten years. While children of six to seven years thought all should share equally, younger children could not understand fair distribution. They were characterized as egocentric, since they confused fairness with their own selfish desires—"I should get it because I want it." In this respect, Damon's account of early moral stages did not markedly differ from Kohlberg's and Piaget's. All three regard the preschool child as morally incapable. (We should point out that egocentrism does not necessarily mean "self-centered" in a moral sense. According to these cognitive theorists, children are egocentric because they simply lack ability to take into account the other person's point of view.)

Research since Piaget

The position of cognitive-developmental theorists has recently been challenged by psychologists who focus on the processing demands of several tasks used in investigating children's reasoning. Anderson (1980) for example (see Anderson, 1980; Anderson & Butzin, 1978; Lane & Anderson, 1976), constructed algebraic models to represent the moral integration of various informational sources. Applying this approach to several problems used by Piaget, Anderson (1978) found, contrary to Piaget's findings, that four-year-olds were able to integrate information and make comparatively complex judgments about equity. He suggested that the kind of methodology Piaget used fails to uncover young children's ability to integrate information.

More recent research focused on Piaget's proposal that when young children judge others' acts, they attend only to the consequences and ignore the underlying intentions. For example, children are asked whether a boy who broke ten glasses when he was angry at his mother is naughtier than a boy who broke 20 glasses when he was trying to help his mother. Grueneich (1982) also identified several methodological problems with earlier studies of children's use of information about intention and consequence. These include the way such information is represented in stories, as well as developmental differences in children's memory, and their comprehension of the information communicated in stories. Trabasso and Nicholas (1980) also argue that developmental differences in the comprehension of story material have distorted observations.

The cognitive developmentalists' conclusions are challenged more indirectly by researchers who have studied children's prosocial behavior. The behavior of preschoolers in natural settings suggests that four-year-olds manifest a variety of prosocial actions. They will assist one another, help or comfort each other in distress, punish the cause of another's distress, and ask an adult to help a peer. After extensive review of the great number of studies now available, Radke-Yarrow, Zahn-Waxler, and Chapman (1983) concluded that preschool children "are not only egocentric, selfish, and aggressive; they are also exquisitely perceptive, have attachments to a wide range of others, and respond prosocially across a broad spectrum of interpersonal events in a wide variety of ways and with various motives" (p. 484).

Reopening the Question of Young Children's Moral Capacity

Given the contradictions between the findings of the cognitive researchers and those who study children's information processing, prosocial behavior, and evaluation of intentions and consequences, the nature of preschool children's moral capacity is an open question. The cognitive-developmental methodology probably relies too heavily on young children's verbal responses, while the observational and experimental work gives little information about the way children act when their self-interests are actually at stake. We suggest that children may only *appear* morally incapable because they are especially vulnerable to stress—they are inexperienced; they are subject to a variety of situational pressures; they lack psychological and material resources and knowledge; and in any case adult authority decides most issues. But none of these factors constitutes evidence of moral deficiency.

A study of young children's actions in situations of actual moral conflict is needed, but more must be at stake for the children than altruism. The conflicts should involve a clash of children's self-interests. To avoid confusion between cognitive deficiency and moral de-

Figure 14.1
NeoPd Board used with Four Year Olds

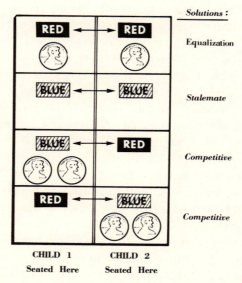

CHILD 1   CHILD 2
Seated Here   Seated Here

ficiency, the moral situations need to be simple. For these reasons we thought NeoPd, which was used with the young adults and adolescents, would provide an appropriate situation of conflict, so we set about reducing its cognitive complexity to make it comprehensible to very young children.

Methods of Study

Preschoolers and Prisoners' Dilemma

NeoPd was changed in several ways. The original version of Prisoners' Dilemma used by most researchers, as well as NeoPd that we used with the students, involves a stalemate (no payoffs), cooperation (moderate payoffs for both), and competitive outcomes (high payoffs for one person, losses for the other). But in our pilot work four-year-olds became *very* upset when they lost pennies. Consequently, we changed the competitive outcome. One child could still get a large payoff but the other child would simply receive no pennies, rather than having to give up any.

The second change was to pay off in pennies immediately after each play, rather than converting points to pennies at the end of the session. The children placed their winnings in small bowls which they kept beside them, so they were able to keep track of what they and their friends had won. A scoreboard was used with the older subjects.

The third change was to use a concrete and colorful board (see Figure 14.1), to show the four possible outcomes. It was placed on a table before the four-year-olds (the young adults had received a printed matrix showing the payoffs). As can be seen in Figure 14.1, blue and red cards and real pennies were glued on the board to illustrate each outcome.

Fourth, we learned in our pilot work that pairs of preschoolers worked better than larger groups; this also made the payoff contingencies simpler.

By preventing four-year-olds from becoming too upset and angry at losing pennies, by providing them immediate and tangential information about the task and its payoffs, and by reducing the number of persons involved, we thought the task would be cognitively within their grasp. *Nonetheless the terms and nature of the moral issues remained basically the same as for the adolescents and young adults.* The main moral questions were still: Do I care about my friend having less? Is it all right to defend my self-interest? Can I trust my friend to keep an agreement?

Participants

The children were from two adjacent nursery schools, 22 children from a university-run center and 18 from a cooperative center. Their families were predominantly of the middle socioeconomic level and represented different ethnic groups. Six children were black, four were Asians and 30 were white. They ranged in age from four years, two months to five years, three months, with an average age of approximately four years, six months at the time NeoPd was played. (It was played second in a series of games in a year-long study on young children's morality.)

The games were played by 18 pairs of the same sex (and in two cases of both sexes) and lasted about 25 minutes. Teachers at the two nursery schools rated the degree of friendship that existed between the pairs of children who played NeoPd. Of the 20 pairs, 40 percent were considered best friends, 50 percent were friends, while 10 percent were considered not friends at all. The children were invited by the staff leaders to come and play a game in a room adjacent to their schoolroom. They were shown the video equipment and told that they could watch themselves on TV after the game. The children were seated side by side, and the staff leader wrote their names on strips of paper which were placed above each child's side of the board. They were told that they could win pennies to keep and take home. Several practice trials without payoff were played. When the children seemed to understand, the real game began and pennies were awarded after each trial.

These four-year-olds were obviously keen to win pennies. The staff leader took a facilitative but nondirective role. Although we wanted to minimize the role of the adult, we were also certain that the children would break off play if the adult was as detached as staff leaders were with the young adults and adolescents. Consequently the staff leaders encouraged the children to confront the issues, express their thoughts and feelings and discuss game strategy with each other. The role of the adult is further evaluated in the summary of this chapter.

Results

Our aims are first, to describe the equalizing nature of the children's interaction as they either directly cooperated or attempted to make reparations for previous imbalances; second, to describe instances of stalemate; and third, to describe instances when children defaulted or betrayed each other by breaking agreements. We did not use the same systems of scoring to rate morality that we applied to the actions of adolescents and young adults, since it was important to stay very close to the way these four-year-olds acted. Instead we focused on five particular kinds of events which are shown in Figure 14.1.

Equalizations: Both children play cooperatively (play their red cards), enabling each to win one penny, or the two children agree that they will take turns. First one will play red (no payoff) the other plays blue to win two pennies; on the next play they will reverse their choices of play.

Reparations: They 'attempt to equalize previous imbalances in total number of pennies won. The winner agrees to play red for no gain so that the loser may play blue and win two pennies.

Stalemate: Both children deliberately play competitively (blue-blue), with the result that neither child obtains pennies.

Default: Competitive play (blue) is continued by the winning child, while the loser continues to play red, apparently attempting to cooperate.

Betrayal: A child breaks a proposed or assumed agreement to play cooperatively.

In 17 of the 20 sessions (85 percent) equalizing solutions were agreed to by both children (either playing red-red, or alternating turns playing blue-red). At some point 12 of the pairs (60 percent) planned to ameliorate earlier inequities in payoffs. In 13 of the groups some occasions of default (65 percent) arose, and in 14 (70 percent) one or more occasions of stalemate occurred. In six pairs (30 percent) one child betrayed the other one or more times. Equalizing solutions were still being adhered to at session's end by 60 percent of the pairs; this incidence compares favorably with the incidence of 80 percent for the young adults.

Equalizing Solutions

When people equalize payoffs, they coordinate their efforts so both benefit. This is the only possible moral solution to the contingencies set up in NeoPd, since competitive play harms one player and either one can retaliate on the next play with stalemate which benefits neither player.

Nevertheless, cooperation has a certain moral ambiguity, for it is always possible for people to cooperate for selfish reasons. For example, in NeoPd the only way to break stalemated play is to equalize, and this choice can be construed as self-serving, or at the very least, prudent or strategic. This ambiguity in NeoPd has been noted by other researchers such as Cook & Stingle (1974) and Sampson & Kardush (1965). But of course all morality can be seen this way. That is, life is usually better for the person who acts morally, and this could be self-serving. Attributing covert self-servingness to moral acts is a hypothesis about a hidden motive that can neither be proved or disproved. In any case, to impute this kind of convoluted reasoning to very young children is to give them even more credit for social cleverness than past theorists thought possible. Consequently, we proceed with the more obvious supposition that equalization in NeoPd is moral.

Careful distinctions also need to be made between two different reasons why some children may *not* adopt an equalizing solution. First, despite the training session and the staff leaders' judgments, some children may still have had trouble understanding the game, so they may not have recognized the cooperative solution. Second, children may recognize the consequences of playing red-red, but they may not consider it seriously. A winning child may continue to compete simply because he or she thinks this is an ordinary game, although most four-year-olds have had very little experience in competitive games. But in part, the burden is on the losing child to bring the inequality to the attention of his or her partner, and not all the children were able to protect their self-interest. But some children did do this by stalemating the play, making verbal complaints, and/or nonverbally, by sighs, facial expressions, body set, and so forth.

The first moral problem of NeoPd comes to the children's attention when they realize rewards are not equal. One child wins pennies but the other doesn't. This is a serious problem for the young children. While adults might think that rewards could be balanced over the course of the game, the four-year-olds seemed not to look far beyond their practical involvement at the moment, so the inequalities of a single trial were very significant.

Of the 17 pairs of children who agreed to a cooperative solution, some hit upon it immediately. In the following excerpt, two girls started to equalize even before the practice trials were finished, and they continued to cooperate for the remainder of the session (staff leader is indicated by "SL"):

SUZY: Yeah. But I'm . . . (*she turns toward Kathy*) but, Kathy, this is red and red. (*Smiles.*)
KATHY: Okay! (*She looks at the board and smiles.*)
SL: You want to play the game for real? (*Suzy nods yes with a smile*)

KATHY: Yeah. (*Smiling at Suzy.*)

SL: Okay. All right. So this time I'll be giving you pennies. And these pennies you can put in these bowls. Okay? So what was your idea? (*Suzy points to the two reds on the board.*) What do you think of that idea, Kathy?

KATHY: Okay (*Both girls play red. Both smile and giggle when they see what the other put down.*)

SL: Red. What happens?

KATHY: (*With a big smile as Suzy points to the board.*) We both get one.

In the practice trials, the girls had each won two pennies as a consequence of competing, by playing blue. It is unlikely, then, that they played red-red accidentally. If either wanted to maximize her own winnings, competing would make more sense. The cooperative solution seems genuinely motivated by a concern that "we *both* get one," and at the same time.

In the next example two boys come up with a cooperative solution. At Tim's suggestion they have just played blue-blue, apparently not anticipating the outcome of the stalemate.

TIM: We both didn't get any.

SL: Well, let's . . . let's try it again.

JEFF: (*interrupting*) Why doesn't it, why don't we ever get, um, one penny? (*To SL.*)

SL: What do you have to do to get one penny?

TIM: Put down, we both put down red.

SL: Uh huh.

JEFF: (*looking at Tim*) Want to do that?

TIM: Yeah. (*Both boys have slightly tentative smiles. They both play red.*)

SL: So what happens?

BOTH: We both get one. (*They smile broadly.*)

The staff leader then asks, "What if you had a plan that you both were going to put down red, but let's say the other person changed his mind and put down blue. Do you think that would be fair?"

JEFF: (*shakes his head*) No.

SL: How come?

TIM: I'm never going to change my mind on the secrets from Jeff.

SL: Oh. What would you think if someone did that?

TIM: (*after a pause*) Dumb. That would be dumb.

SL: How come?

TIM: Because that wouldn't be nice.

SL: How come?

TIM: Because if they do something or change their mind, it wouldn't be fair.

Here Tim underscores his moral alliance with his friend Jeff; Tim will not go back on his word.

The next excerpt involves another pair of girls. In this session we find Ellen ingenuously playing in a way that prevents cooperation, caught up in her own pleasure at winning two pennies each time. She has just played blue, while Sue has played red:

SL: What happens when Ellen puts a blue down and Sue puts a red down? (*Pause.*) You guys know what happens?

ELLEN: She would get none pennies and I would get two pennies.

SL: And you would get two pennies. So here you go. (*SL hands Ellen her pennies.*) Ellen, how come you put down a blue?

ELLEN: (*with enthusiasm*) 'Cause I like pennies!

SL: You like pennies. You wanted two. And how come you put down a red, Sue? How come?

SUE: (*sullenly*) I wanted to.

Notice Sue does nothing to communicate her dissatisfaction and even asserts that her plight is of her own choosing. Consequently, it is not surprising that Ellen does not see that any harm has been done.

We follow these two girls to examine negotiations that eventually result in their agreement to equalize. Ellen continues to be captivated by the pleasure of winning pennies, but Sue begins to express her dissatisfactions with this way of playing. Sue had just played red, Ellen has played blue, to win two more pennies. She now has a total of six; her friend has none:

SL: How many pennies did you want when you put red down?

SUE: (*Mumbles.*)

SL: So you have a lot of pennies, huh Ellen? (*Ellen nods.*) And you (*to Sue*) don't have any. You guys think that's fair? You like that idea? (*Sue shakes her head.*)

ELLEN: I like that idea.

SL: You like the idea? How come you like the idea?

ELLEN: 'Cause I can get more pennies than her.
SL: I see. How does that make you feel, Sue, when Ellen has more
    pennies than you?
SUE: *(grumbles)* It's not very nice.
SL: How does that make you feel, Ellen, when you have more pennies
    than Sue?
ELLEN: Good. *(Smiles with satisfaction.)*

Ellen is still either ignoring her friend's growing distress or ignorant
of it. On the next trial Sue stalemates her friend by playing her own
blue card. As the negotiation begins, Ellen seems happy to continue
playing blue despite Sue's judgment that "it's not very nice":

SL: Ellen, you keep putting down blues. How come you keep putting
    down blues?
ELLEN: *(smiling)* 'Cause.
SL: You want pennies. But when you both put down blues, no pennies.
ELLEN: No pennies.
SL: So what are we going to do?
ELLEN: *(stated matter-of-factly)* Play.
SUE: I have a thousand million and zillion pennies at home. *(She has
    other riches.)*
ELLEN: You must feel good about that. *(Ellen is happy to hear that Sue
    has compensations.)*
SL: You feel good about that? *(Sue shakes her head.)* No.
ELLEN: *(laughing)* She doesn't. She must.
SL: What would be the fairest way to play this game?
SUE: If she put down a red and I put down a red.
SL: How come you think that's the fairest?
SUE: Because I would get one penny and she would get one penny.
    (They play again, this time red-red.)
SUE: We both get a penny.

Like the other children we have discussed, Sue's focus is on the fact
that *both* children would benefit from the proposed solution.

SL: Okay.
ELLEN: *(now with a smile of pleasure and apparent relief)* You're starting
    to get more pennies.
SL: Yeah.
SUE: One penny, but . . .

SL: So how come you both wanted to put down reds?

ELLEN: (*confidently*) Because we got an idea.

SL: Is that fair? (*Sue nods.*) How come that's fair?

SUE: 'Cause I get one and she gets one. (*She says this with satisfaction.*)

Once Ellen agrees to Sue's proposed way of playing, she shows pleasure and perhaps relief. When asked why her solution is "fair," Sue gives the same account that others gave: "'cause you both get one penny."

Another form of cooperation is an agreement between two children that they will take turns. One child will play red while the other will play the blue card to win two pennies. In this next example Lori and Mark, members of a mixed-sex pair, have secretly devised a plan of alternation which they will not reveal to the staff leader.

MARK: Come on, Lori, let's do it a different way.

LORI: No! You said, you said.

MARK: Oh, yeah, then I get to, then you get to put red down, right, yeah?

SL: What are you going to do?

MARK: We made a plan.

SL: What's your plan?

MARK: We can't tell it.

SL: Okay, but do you know what the plan is between yourselves?

LORI: Yeah.

MARK: Yeah.

SL: Ready: one, two, three. Choose. (*Both children quickly glance at each other and without hesitation put down their cards. Lori plays blue while Mark, already two pennies ahead in totals, plays red.*)

Excited by their success, Lori and Mark are eager to implement the second part of their plan:

MARK: And there's another plan.

LORI: Yeah.

SL: Oh, we'll see what happens then.

LORI: Now this time I get to put down a . . .

MARK: (*interrupting*) Red.

SL: Is that what the plan was?

BOTH: Yeah!

SL: Okay, here we go. Ready, one, two, three, choose. (*This time Mark immediately puts down a blue and Lori, in keeping with the agreement, plays her red card.*)

SL: So, Mark, you get two, and Lori doesn't get any. So does that seem fair?

LORI: (*quickly*) Yeah.

SL: Why?

LORI: 'Cause the other time I got pennies.

SL: I see. Since you got two pennies last time it's fair because . . .

MARK: (*interrupting*) And we're going to keep doing that over and over until we stop.

In comparison with the equalizing solution of playing red-red, the alternate playing of red-blue is more complex and risky. The children must sustain their commitment to each other. Not only must they be willing to sacrifice immediate gains on a particular trial, but they must also trust their partners to uphold their end of the bargain and play a red card when it is their turn.

When the children acted in a cooperative manner, it was apparently out of concern for each other's well-being, but at the same time they were also acting to protect their own legitimate self-interest. The two solutions—red-red and alternating red-blue, blue-red—which give equal pennies to the two children, satisfactorily resolve both these concerns, and the children seemed relieved and satisfied when they reached this mutual solution. They were not always able, however, to articulate accurately or fully what motivated them. But whatever they said or did not say, their actions spoke louder than their words.

Seventy-three percent of the children used moral ideas. For example, "We chose red because we each get the same amounts." Or they used moral phrases. For example, "This game is not fair, you're winning too many pennies." Of the 73 percent, 16 percent spontaneously used these ideas before the staff leader did, while 57 percent used them usually immediately after the staff leader asked about fairness. Twenty-seven percent of the children never articulated these ideas.

Reparations

A second more complex moral solution lay in attempts to equalize the total number of pennies each partner was to receive after inequalities had developed. The winners were not always happy about equalizing; nevertheless 60 percent of the pairs did. Each child had a bowl for pennies, and each could see how many they and their friend had won. Frequently a child leaned over to examine both bowls, or paused to count the contents.

In the next example two children work to repair an inequality. (Mimi has two pennies, while Jane has six.) Mimi, the loser, proposes that they play so she can win pennies, while Jane will get none. Jane agrees, although she has reservations:

MIMI: Now this time you put down a red and I'll put down a blue. (*She turns to Jane as she speaks, gesturing with her finger in a forceful manner.*)

JANE: Yeah. (*Mimi smiles.*)

SL: You what, Jane?

JANE: If we both have to take a red. (*More decisively*) Okay, if we both do blue and red. (*She nods her head at this decision, smiles, and points to the cards on the board.*)

SL: Mimi, why don't you tell Jane your idea?

MIMI: I want you to put down a *red,* Jane.

SL: What do you think of that idea Jane?

JANE: Fine. She wants to put down *blue.* Let's do that.

SL: Okay, Ready? One, two, three, choose. Okay, Mimi, you put down a blue; Jane, you put down a red, what happens?

MIMI: I get two and she gets none. (*She has a big grin on her face, and giggles as she speaks. Jane is staring expressionless at the table, sucking on her hair.*)

SL: Okay, here you go. (*SL hands two pennies to Mimi.*) So how many pennies do you have now, Mimi?

MIMI: Four.

SL: And how many do you have?

JANE: Seven. I mean six.

SL: So this time, Jane, you put a red down but didn't win any pennies. How come you did that?

JANE: 'Cause Mimi told me.

SL: 'Cause Mimi told you to?

JANE: I didn't mind (*She begins picking her nose.*)

Notice Jane is aware of what Mimi wants to play; as she puts it, "She wants to put down *blue.* Let's do that." Mimi states the outcome, saying, "I get two and she gets none," with a laugh. Jane is prepared to play as Mimi asks or demands (Mimi is markedly forceful when she proposes this solution). But Jane seems to have some doubts at first, saying, "If we both have to take a red," as if considering her options. Then she seems to make up her mind. Later, she seems downcast, in marked contrast to her smiles when the girls had been playing cooperatively. Her self-interest runs counter to her friend's, but she is prepared to do what is asked.

In the following example, the staff leader questions Brad and Jenny, members of the other mixed-sex pair, about the inequality in their penny totals. Just prior to this episode, Jenny had played competitively for two consecutive trials and won pennies. Now, however, she hears Brad's displeasure at the outcome and, when confronted with the question of fairness, suggests that both she and Brad should have the same number of pennies. She then spontaneously proposes that Brad win pennies on the next trial and she win none:

SL: How many pennies have you got, Jenny?
JENNY: I've got six. (*Brad looks over at Jenny's bowl.*)
SL: And you, Brad?
BRAD: Two.
SL: Is that fair? (*Brad shakes his head no.*) How come?
BRAD: I don't think it is.
SL: You don't think it's fair that what—that you have less pennies than Jenny? (*Brad nods his head yes.*) Well, what would be the fairest way to play the game?
JENNY: We both have six (*smiles*).
SL: You both have six, how come that would be the fairest?
JENNY: Because he would have some more.
SL: So what do you think we should do now?
BRAD: Play again. (*Reaches for cards in excitement.*)
SL: What do you think Jenny?
JENNY: Get some blue.
SL: Are you saying that Brad should put a blue down?
JENNY: Yeah, and I'll put a red down.
SL: You'll put a red down?
JENNY: Yeah.
SL: Would that be fair?
JENNY: Yeah, he'd get one. (*Both smile broadly. As planned, Jenny plays the red card and Brad the blue.*)

Interestingly enough, it is the winner, Jenny, who seeks out immediate reparations in attempt to restore the moral balance. Her notions of fairness are based on a concern for equality that "We [should] both have six." Her further justification that "he would have some more" indicates that she thinks Brad is entitled to the same benefits as she is. Brad, anticipating her intention of equalizing their winnings, is eager to play again even before a concrete plan has been proposed.

The next excerpt immediately follows.

SL: What happened, Brad?

BRAD: (*with a big grin on his face*) I get two. (*Jenny looks over to his bowl*).

SL: Jenny, how come you put a red down, you didn't get any pennies that time?

JENNY: Yeah, because I got more and he gets more, too. And if he gets another blue he'll have two pennies like . . . like . . . and he'll have the same in there. (*Points to her own bowl with a smile.*)

SL: Did you hear what Jenny had to say, Brad? (*Brad nods his head yes.*) What do you think of her idea? (*Brad nods and smiles.*)

JENNY: (*faces Brad*) Are you gonna do it?

(*Brad nods head yes. They play again according to the proposed plan.*)

Again, Jenny acts in a manner contrary to her own self-interest and without pressure from Brad. Having noticed that there is still a discrepancy in the number of pennies each has won, she suggests Brad win two more pennies so they both will have six. Her concern for her partner's well-being seems to underlie her motivation to achieve equitable outcomes. During the entire interchange, Brad, while not verbally expressive, seems delighted with the turn of events. Jenny, too, having acted with a good conscience, seems happy to continue playing.

Stalemate

The third kind of event, stalemate, occurred when both children played competitively, so that neither won pennies. They chose to stalemate for various reasons, and we illustrate two. The first stalemate was brought about early when the children were eager to win pennies; both played blue cards. They did not yet see the need to coordinate their actions and perhaps did not fully understand the payoff contingencies. In this next excerpt, Kate and Sally, who have previously won two pennies apiece, stalemate each other with the two blues for the first time.

SALLY: Uh oh! (*Laughs.*)
SL: No pennies?
SALLY: No pennies.
KATE: I should have putted down a red. (*Sally looks at her.*)
SL: Why should you have put down a red?
KATE: 'Cause I wanted to.
SL: What would happen if you put down a red?
KATE: (*with a shrug*) I don't know.

Kate, even before she fully understands the payoff contingencies, seems to be confronting the problem that a stalemate creates. Still, on the next trial, the girls again play blue-blue.

SL: Two blues. No pennies again.
SALLY: Uh oh (*loudly*) Hey, what's the matter with us? (*Turns to look at Kate.*)
SL: You're not winning any pennies. You guys want to talk about this?
SALLY: Heeeeey. (*Looks at SL with her nose crinkled up.*) What's the matter with this game?
KATE: (*turns towards Sally and points to the board*) And how come you're not winning any pennies when you get two blues?

The two girls, again thwarted in their attempt to win pennies, begin to consider the reasons why they are not. Sally briefly addresses the problem as lying between the two of them: "What's the matter with us?" The two seem to conclude, however, that the game is unfair and that the staff leader who allows such conditions to exist is inept.

On the next trial the girls stalemate once again.

SL: No pennies.
SALLY: Do this, this. Oh, nooo. This is what we win. (*Points to the place where there are two blues.*)
SL: Sally, why did you put down a blue that time? How many pennies did you want to get?
SALLY: Eeeper eeep! (*Looks over at Kate.*) Why didn't we put down two reds?

Continued stalemate frustrated the children but also motivated them to discuss other alternatives. After this trial Kate and Sally agreed to change their play and to cooperate. Much later Sally defaulted.

The second kind of stalemate occurred when children were "forced" to stalemate their partners to protect their self-interest. In the following session, John quickly switches his card from red to blue—achieving a stalemate—to prevent his friend Rich from winning pennies. The score thereby remains at three apiece.

SL: Ready? One, two, three, choose. (*John plays first, putting down a red card. Rich plays a blue. John quickly and unobtrusively switches his blue for the red card.*)

SL: You switched, John. (*John looks up and laughs.*) Why'd you do that?

JOHN: Because. (*He smiles, fidgeting in his seat.*)

RICH: (*in a loud and somewhat angry voice*) He didn't want me to get a penny.

SL: So what happens when you put down blue: no pennies. You guys want to talk about this? (*Rich has turned to confront John, who points quickly at the game board.*)

JOHN: Yeah.

SL: What do you think. . . . (*Interrupted by Rich.*)

RICH: No, put down a red. (*He says this in a loud voice, then reaches over and puts down John's red card.*)

JOHN: No, put down my blue. (*He takes back his red card, and puts down the blue in its place.*)

Rich's remark "He didn't want me to get a penny" shows that he understood John's intention in switching the card and the way their actions impinged upon each other.

Stalemates occurred either because each child played blue wanting to increase his or her own winnings or, more deliberately, to prevent the other player from winning more pennies. The experience of stalemate, however, was productive since it frustrated children and prompted them to create new and often mutually rewarding strategies.

Default

The fourth kind of event occurred when one child defaulted by systematically playing competitively while the other child attempted to play cooperatively. Some occasion of default occurred in 65 percent of the sessions. Sometimes children's self-interest outweighed concern for their friend. Children who were on the receiving end of default frequently expressed anger.

In this example, Sam defaulted by playing blue on every trial except the very first. Consequently, he gave his fellow player, Daniel, no chance to win pennies. At best Daniel could only stalemate; at worst he would lose pennies if he played cooperatively. Sam seemed to think that responsibility for ameliorating the unfairness was not his but rather the adult researcher's. (Several children seemed incredulous that the adult was so lacking in foresight that they faced this contretemps.) Towards the end of the session the following exchange takes place:

SL: What do you think about that, Daniel, that you didn't get any?
DANIEL: Because that's fair.
SL: You think that's fair that you didn't get any? (*There is a long pause. Daniel is looking down. Sam wriggles in his chair.*) Do you think that's fair, Daniel, that you didn't get any?
DANIEL: My mom will ask you to give me pennies.
SL: I see. But for right now, for right now. How does that make you feel when, when Sam gets four and you don't get any?
DANIEL: (*with a smile*) I don't know.
SL: No. Do you think that's fair, Sam, when you have more than Daniel?
SAM: No!
SL: You don't think that's fair?
SAM: (*with an angry shake of his head*) No.
SL: What do you think we should do about that?
SAM: I think we should give Daniel some pennies. (*He pauses, and then gives a little shake of his head.*) Not some of mine!

Sam may have continued to default because Daniel did not communicate his dismay. Daniel first simply denies the inequity ("Because that's fair"), but he then brings up his mother to remedy it. Despite his defaulting, Sam is upset and seemingly angry about the way the session has ended. But he projects responsibility. Thus, the researcher should give Daniel pennies. Daniel listens in silence, but when the researcher is putting Sam's pennies in an envelope for him to take home, Daniel says plaintively, "You guys forgot to give me some pennies."

In the next excerpt Mike, who has predominantly played blue throughout the game, is fully aware of the inequity in outcome. He continues to play blue despite his partner's requests.

BOBBY: Can you put down red, Mike?
MIKE: No, I'm going to put down blue.
BOBBY: Well, you're supposed to put down red.
SL: Mike, why do you keep putting down blue?
MIKE: Because I want to.
SL: How many pennies do you want to win?
MIKE: (*with great emphasis*) A lot.
SL: Do you think that's a fair way to play the game?
MIKE: Yep.
SL: What do you think is the fairest way to play the game?
MIKE: Me get some and he get some.
SL: Is that what's happening now?
MIKE: (*Shakes his head no.*) I get some. Let's do it again.

Mike is intent on maximizing his own winnings and he maintains his intransigence, refusing to play cooperatively. As the dialogue progresses, Bobby continues to complain, but becomes increasingly despondent at the no-win situation he is in.

BOBBY: Why can't I get red and you get red, so next time I get red and you get red so we both get red.
SL: Mike, what do you think of his idea? Bobby says why don't you both put down red.
BOBBY: And then I get as many as you do.
MIKE: I want to put down blue and he put down red.
SL: What happens then?
MIKE: I get some.
SL: And he doesn't get any.
BOBBY: Can I put down red and you put down red?
MIKE: (*with determination*) That I won't.
BOBBY: Well, I feel like it.
SL: What can we do? Can we figure a way to work this out?
BOBBY: I don't know. I can skip playing if I can't get any.
SL: Mike, what do you think of Bobby's idea?
MIKE: I want to get some and he gets none.

SL: Well, should we keep playing the game?
BOBBY: I want to go 'cause he'll get some and I won't.

At first Bobby only threatens to quit playing, but he then exercises his right when he is forced to protect his self-interest as Mike continues to default. Bobby quits and the game comes to an end.

Default can reflect insensitivity to the friend's feelings and wishes, or a strong desire to pursue one's own interests. Mike actively disregards Bobby's suggestions to play cooperatively, though he acknowledges that the fairest way to play the game would be for both to share pennies. In contrast, Sam appeared more sympathetic to Daniel's plight and was aware of the unfair way the game worked out, but he, too, does not act to change the outcome.

Betrayal

The second form of self-centered action is "betrayal." That is, one child breaks an explicit or a tacit agreement. An example was given by Kate and Sally, whom we earlier described in a stalemate. Kate is losing by four pennies to Sally, who has eight. Kate finally expresses her frustration at the inequality in strong moral terms. Then Sally proposes that they cooperate, and Kate readily agrees, but she apparently has no intention of acting on her agreement. We enter at the beginning of this interchange:

KATE: Sally, this game is just not fair!
SALLY: No it isn't! It isn't fair! (*She says this with a big smile, punctuating her words with nods.*)
KATE: 'Cause I'm not getting so many pennies. (*She bangs her fists on the table to emphasize her words.*)
SL: Well, what could you do?
KATE: (*Banging her fists again.*) I don't know!
SL: Do you have any idea you can tell Sally?
SALLY: (*suddenly coming to life*) I know! (*She cocks her head; Kate looks at her quizzically.*)
SL: What?
SALLY: If we put down (*she points to the board*) both red, we'll get one, two, three, four, five, six, seven, eight, and one more (*pointing to the board*) make nine.

SL: Kate, what do you think about that? Do you think it would be fair?

Kate nods her head. The girls play, but Kate puts down a blue card instead of the agreed-upon red.

Sally: Put down red! Uh oh. Put down red. (*She touches Kate's card.*)
Kate: (*She glances briefly at Sally.*) No. I don't want to.

The staff leader asks Kate why she played her blue card. She replies:

Kate: 'Cause I wanted to.
SL: You think that's fair?
Kate: (*looking at Sally*) Yes.
SL: How come?
Sally: (*She looks at Kate, and then turns to SL with a pout.*) No, I don't.
SL: Wait. Kate, how come you think that's fair?
Kate: (*looking down at her hands*) 'Cause, Sally won so many but I didn't, so I tried to win.

Kate justifies her betrayal: she was already unfairly far behind in her winnings.

We learn two things from the betrayals. First, ostensibly selfish behavior may be motivated by a moral sense of fairness. As Kate claimed, an inequity can balance a previous inequity, a result the children consider fair (though two wrongs make a right for many adults also). Second, the children on the receiving end of betrayals or defaults strongly voice their outrage at being wronged. Far from being unaware of another child's selfish behavior, as Piaget claimed, they are acutely sensitive to it. Most often they demand cooperation from rather than punishment for the wrongdoer.

Summary

The main implication of our observations is that the *four-year-olds did not consistently act as one would expect if they were either cognitively egocentric or morally selfish. Of course, they were not always morally concerned nor were all the children equally concerned. But any respectable evidence of concern for others challenges the supposition that small children do not have the capacity to be morally concerned.* They were able to adjust their conduct and comments so as to accommodate the wishes and needs of the other child, and they showed an incidence of moral concern that was not radically different from that of the university students.

The Nature of the Situation

We used the game of NeoPd to learn about the way children spontaneously act when their self-interests are exposed as self-serving or when their legitimate self-interests are threatened. There is no question but that these four-year-olds were highly motivated—they wanted the pennies. *Defaults occurred for at least one or two reasons. The defaulter was selfish and victims failed to make their interests known.* Not all children acted to protect their self-interests. Although NeoPd "engineers" the moral dilemma, once the issue is joined, it is real and not unlike the problems of reconciliation between self and other interests that all age groups face in everyday life.

Our cognitive simplification of NeoPd seemed to overcome preschoolers' difficulties in comprehending and recalling the structure of the task, obstacles that plague investigators who interview young children about hypothetical dilemmas. Also NeoPd has certain advantages over observing naturally occurring moral incidents. The four-year-olds were embroiled in a conflict of self-interests; the moral problems were more difficult than simply helping or giving to another at little or no cost to self and the staff leader helped the children stay with the task.

But at the same time NeoPd has a disadvantage that may have affected actions. The children may have acted out of compliance to the adult. Although the staff leaders accepted all solutions, they had to encourage the children to keep focused on the dilemma. If they had not, play would have been disrupted by early leavetaking, distracting maneuvers, or tears. In another part of this study we used wireless microphones to tape record the playground conflicts of preschoolers when they were some distance from adults. Our preliminary impression is that the children were still sensitive to the interests and needs of one another, but these spontaneous interchanges will undoubtedly differ in some ways from those in NeoPd.

Children's Moral Concerns

The children's articulation of the reasons for their own actions was not always clear. While analysis of their actions in terms of the immediate circumstances and apparent motivations led us to our conclusions, the children themselves only said, on occasion, "I wanted to."

Moral concerns were also not always explicit in the talk between children, or between child and staff leader. For example, a boy warrants his proposal of cooperative play simply as "the nicest way to play," and adds, "I like it that way." He may have been either unable or unwilling to articulate his moral grounds for this explanation. Although not skilled in articulation, they did often act to equalize when confronted with the other child's moral indignation and needs.

We draw these two major findings. First, preschoolers are more sophisticated in their actions than people in general think or the cognitive theories propose, and second, their articulation is not highly differentiated. This pattern may explain why the cognitive and more behaviorally oriented researchers have had such contrasting views of young children. Piaget, Kohlberg, and Damon focus on what children think *about* their own actions, but more often on what they think *about* a hypothetical dilemma. The behavioral researchers focus on children's actions in either experimental or naturalistic settings and do not depend on what they say about what they have done. The latter research, as we noted earlier, has detected a greater degree of moral sensitivity than the former. This contradiction in findings becomes understandable if children's actions are motivated by moral concerns which they do not articulate. Indeed, four-year-olds' articulations did sometimes seem amoral and based on personal preference.

Similarities and Differences between Preschoolers and Adults

In many ways the four-year-olds acted and reacted in NeoPd like the adolescents and young adults. The similarities are at the level of action, brought about by the kinds of problems experienced, the kinds of solutions developed, and the emotions and moods that develop as the problem is being resolved. Like their older counterparts, the preschoolers coordinated benefits, stalemated each other, made reparations for disproportionate totals, defaulted, and betrayed each other by breaking agreements. They became emotional in the same ways. That is, they became frustrated during stalemates, angry during defaults and betrayals, and happy when they arrived at a mutual solution. Their glow of shared good conscience was palpable when they equalized. Like the subgroups of young adults and adolescents, they at first, heedlessly worked only for their self-interests but changed their course of action when their partners made their indignation known.

Both children and the older students employed defensive maneuvers to rationalize their defaults and mute their anxiety. Preschoolers sometimes sucked their fingers or hair, picked their noses, wiggled in their chairs, and stared expressionless at the table; university and high school students became immobilized and repressive or cocky and belligerent. When they realized their wrong-doing, the four-year-olds pleaded ignorance: "We don't know the colors." In contrast, the students more often justified themselves by pointing out they had haplessly thought it was "just a game." (They had volunteered and signed contracts to take part in a study of morality.) The four-year-olds projected responsibility for the inequities on the staff leader's poor anticipation of their needs and implied their mothers would have done better, while the university students accused the project staff of being cheap about pay-offs.

These similarities suggest that the moral experience of four-year-olds was not basically different from that of the adolescents and young adults. Therefore, the preschoolers must have understood the moral issues. If this is true, it is not possible to contend that preschoolers are either morally oblivious or morally oblivious because they are cognitively inept.

There were also differences between the children and the older students—in their anticipations of the future, articulation of their action, and protection of their self-interest. When they played NeoPd, the students quickly read the matrix and saw the possibility of an equalizing solution, but often they did not act accordingly. They mistrusted one another, hoped for bigger payoffs and were sometimes reluctant to equalize because they knew it left them vulnerable to being betrayed. The young children showed little mistrust, perhaps because they did not anticipate that cooperation left them vulnerable to betrayal. But these four-year-olds' interactions with the moral world are well protected by their parents and teachers, so their experience gives them little reason to anticipate that they could be betrayed.

Children of this age find themselves constantly reminded of their relative lack of power and resources, and some of these preschoolers were unable to protect themselves and work for even their legitimate self-interests. But others had ways of dealing with their misfortune that still served to protect their fragile sense of self-agency. Children who played red, trying to equalize, but who nevertheless fell victim to their friends' defaulting seemed chagrined (they justified their choice of red by insisting "I wanted to"). They seemed to cover up their disappointment and confusion about being wronged by insisting that they had made the choice. They were active agents in the vicissitudes of a confusing world. One important moral skill, and one which takes years to acquire, is knowing when it is foolish to trust and wise to be defensive. In sum, compared to the older students, the preschoolers did not plan far ahead. They did not skillfully articulate their self-interests, nor skillfully protect them.

Speculations about Development

Given the exploratory nature of this single study, we can only speculate about what really develops in moral development. *Our study suggests that the moral concerns of preschoolers and adults are basically the same but that children gradually develop skills that enable them to act in a wider range of complex situations.* Our simplified version of NeoPd set up conflict that was cognitively and informationally within the grasp of these young children; they had all the power they needed to resolve it. The staff leader's constant support and encouragement helped them to cope rather than disintegrate. In many other situations these children would likely default, or being very young, capitulate.

To be concise, we suggest that young children's moral concern is much the same as that of adults, but the young lack knowledge, cognitive skills, objective power, responsibility, and material resources to empower their negotiations so they are readily stressed and moral violations only intensify their feelings of helplessness. There is already much in the world that they do not understand or cannot do—like staying upright on a two-wheeler—and moral indignation only adds to the insult.

Another improvement in moral functioning undoubtedly occurs when children become more sophisticated in talking about moral action. There is no doubt but that articulation of a difficulty often serves to clarify its nature. The staff leader helped the children articulate what they were doing and why. Only 16 percent of the children spontaneously used moral words or offered moral explanations, while 57 percent may have picked up on the staff leader's words; 27 percent never openly articulated such ideas. The adolescents and young adults called each other to account for what they were doing and then articulated their disagreements (Packer, in press). But some were so caught up in the conflict that they were unable to pause and take stock. This particularly occurred in the dominated groups during the emotionally heated sessions of NeoPd.

In an action situation, articulating what one is doing when others call one to account is a moral communication if it takes into account the position of both parties and the need of both parties to strike a moral balance. It is not the more-individualistic skill of giving reasons and principles to justify one's judgment, which is the interest of the cognitivists.

The same kind of moral sensitivity we observed in very young children was also described by Robert Coles (1980) after his work with the embattled Protestant and Catholic children in North Ireland:

And what strikes me is not only their seriousness (I suppose you psychiatrist chaps may find that worrisome!) but their consideration for others. These are thoughtful children: they have seen people struggling and dying for something they very much believe in (p. 38) . . .

These can be pensive lads and lasses, even the wee ones of five and six. They ask me tough questions for which I'm not sure Socrates would have easy replies (p. 38) . . .

Many of us psychoanalytically trained psychiatrists emphasize in our discussions of children the relentlessly punitive, demanding side of the superego, and certain cognitive psychologists hand out questionnaires or make experiments in offices or laboratories, and then talk of a "preconventional" or "conventional" stage in children, wherein they do what serves their ("hedonistic") purposes, or what will obviate punishment, or gain the sanctioning nod of a mother, a father. Those same theorists, however, deny to children the more subtle, compassionate, ethically reflective "stages" of moral development—indeed, deny such personal, ethical, psychological, and intellectual progress to many adults as well. Only a handful, we have been told, an ethical elite (Herbert Marcuse's "advancing edge of history," for example) can free itself of the individual (emotional) and the socially or culturally enforced constraints that blind a truly 'mature' ethical awareness. . . . In any event, as we wait for that millennium to arrive, boys and girls the world over may not be fashioning psychological concepts, but they are, it seems, struggling hard and long to construct a moral life for themselves (p. 40).

We too are struck by the seriousness of our four-year-olds and their moral concern for their partners' plight when no authority was telling them what they should do. Whether these children "read" more than each other's words—perhaps like the emotions on their partner's face and the posture and set of their body—we are not certain. But it is clear from their actions and from what they said that most of these children cared.

Chapter 15

FAMILIAL PAST AND
PRESENT HISTORY

The family [as a unit] evaluates experience initiated by the individual member and evokes from him modes of responsiveness to his own behavior and the behavior of others. A prominent element of this dimension is the tendency towards moral evaluation of experience (Robert Hess and Gerald Handel, 1959, p.15).

A N ASSESSMENT of how the young adults' familial experiences might have influenced their moral functioning during the project is presented in this chapter. The family's role in children's moral development is seen differently in the cognitive and interactional theories, so we first discuss these different views and then report results.

Cognitive and Interactional Perspectives on Families

The cognitivists have not been much concerned with parents' influences on children's moral development. This is not out of neglect but logically follows from the view that moral development is the individual's progressive acquisition of more complex and differentiated structures. Family members may have no greater impact on this course of development than other people. Indeed Kohlberg (1969, p. 399) has written that "family participation is not unique or critically necessary for moral development." Older people presumably promote a child's moral development when they use cognitive-moral arguments that are one stage above the child's. The stage of the adult's argument must be close to the child's if the youngster is to understand it and adopt it as a better way of reasoning. But the difference between the adult's and the child's moral stage is usually too great to have this effect. As a result, peers are regarded as more effective agents of change. Since the moral stages of one's peers are likely to be close, children of lower stages are more likely to be affected by the reasoning of higher stage peers.

This line of reasoning leads the cognitivists to think that if children are normally intelligent and have normal experiences of social living, they will eventually reach moral stages appropriate for their age and particular sociocultural environment. Thus the family has no special influence on the child's moral development. The few studies that do consider the family, for example, those by Holstein (1968), Haan, Langer, and Kohlberg (1976), and Hudgins and Prentice (1973) have primarily focused on the relationship between the moral stages of parent and child rather than on the quality of interaction in families.

The following questions concerning family interaction and the roles of other family members are not considered: What is the nature and extent of dialogue within the family? Does the family regard itself as an entity? How is the common interest viewed and defined in relationship to individual interest? How do other members react to parent-child interchanges? Do they support the parent or the child? Do they ignore the problem that has arisen? Do members take advantage of others' difficulties to secure benefits for themselves?

From all standpoints children's moral development should be affected by inconsistencies between the family members' verbalization of moral guidelines and their everyday actions. Inconsistencies can only demoralize children. This and other problems of deviance have not generally been addressed by the cognitivists.

The interactional system involves a different view of the family's role in children's moral development. Its emphasis on social interaction and the contexts in which moral problems occur means that the family has a unique and important role in children's moral development. It is the first and most enduring group to which people belong. Children's experiences with moral negotiation in their families build expectations about others' good faith and understandings about the ways moral disputes are negotiated, conducted, and concluded.

Children's dependency on families as well as their social inexperience should intensify the impact of the familial group. Parents indirectly communicate a system of values to their children as they impose rules and exercise discipline. More important, their ways of dealing with each other and their children establish the specific obligations and rights of each member as a separate moral being.

Moral dialogues within families usually involve several members. But even when only two carry on a discussion, the others are much in mind. For example, if mother and son are concerned with a moral issue in the father's absence, their positions will be colored by their assumptions about the father's view. If the mother is sympathetic but expects that the father will oppose the son's view, she may underscore the good and bad features of each position. She thereby builds an objective basis for further family discussions. If the mother is more committed to her own interests than to her family's, she may subtly reinforce an alliance with her son by supporting his point of view. Morally corrupt interactions within families are generated in this way.

Differences in age and responsibility have consequences for moral decisions so exact moral balances within families are not always achieved. The shorter-term views of young members do not always carry equal merit. Parents must sometimes take responsibility and impose imbalances that are justified by their more comprehensive moral understanding and their responsibility to rear and protect their children. Consequently, family interaction often results in legitimated imbalances.

Unique to the parent-child relation is the fact that children do not initially choose to enter the relationship—they do not ask to be born. Unlike adults interacting with other adults, children usually cannot terminate their filial relationships when these are harmful or stifling. At the same time, most parents initiate the relationship by choosing to have children. Commonly entailed in this commitment are intentions to protect and enhance their children's well-being and stimulate their development. The bond thereby created persists throughout the lives of the parents and children, but children do not often fully reciprocate their parents' concern and responsibility. Justice is done, as Rawls (1971) points out, when children, in turn, take disproportionately greater moral responsibility for their own offspring.

As more or less conscious moral educators, parents usually try to get their children to consider situations more exhaustively and resolve them more sensitively than the children would do on their own. If discussions are to work, however, the parents need to suggest options for children that are within their understanding and power to enact. The parents' problem is different; they need to work for solutions without settling for ideas of lesser moral worth or suppressing their legitimate self-interests. Parents' efforts are not motivated only by their concern for their children's development, but also by their interest in maintaining the family's stability.

The family is critical in the interactional perspective, because it continuously and intensely involves children in moral problems, dialogues, and arguments, and also because this involvement provides the first and most persistent experience that children have in learning that their self-interests cannot always be completely fulfilled. Whether children find this experience basically sensible, thereby becoming convinced that self-interest and common interests are invariably and ultimately linked, depends in large part on the characteristics of their family as a group. Parent-child relations—the main focus of most child-development research—are not carried out in a social vacuum. The ways that family members relate to one another are influenced by the whole group's network of relationships and the expectations that members have of one another, all of which are developed and redefined over time. Therefore, from the interactional perspective, research must give as much attention to the familial group as to the one-to-one relations between parent and child.

A study of the characteristics of the students' families seemed warranted, especially since the friendship group is another kind of small, intimate group in which members have stakes in both the group and in their individual relations. We felt the kinds of experiences the students had had in dealing with family conflict and moral negotiation might affect the way that they would deal with problems in their friendship groups.

Family Interactions of the Adolescents

Information on the family background of the adolescents was collected by Johnson (1980, 1981) as a personal project. The families of 15 males and 16 females of the 57 adolescents were interviewed; all were white and either middle or working class. Both parents and their adolescent child were asked about interactions in the family and the control strategies that the parents used. It was found that the ways in which parents interacted with their adolescent children were related to the adolescents' cognitive stages and interactional levels obtained from the interviews and the games the adolescents played. Results showed that family variables were more closely associated with interactional levels than with cognitive stages. Parents' and adolescents' reports of their involvement in family discussions—how much they talked to one another—were positively associated with the adolescents' interactional moral scores but not with their cognitive scores. Moreover, emotionality in the family—whether family members admitted anger and whether they reported feeling upset when there was disagreement—was also more closely and positively related to interactional than to cognitive morality. The findings thus generally confirm the importance of familial experiences in children's interactional moral development, especially the importance of all family members directly dealing with their mutual problems. Talking and frank expression of feelings within the family supported these adolescents' interactional functioning.

Family Interactions of the Young Adults

Most groups grow out of people's commitment to one another, but the commitments of family members to one another are usually deeper and more encompassing. The commitment of a man and a woman to each other first forms a family group. Their mutual commitment is then extended to the children and provides emotional sustenance and the basis for all family members' identities. As intimate and enduring groups, families have a particularly profound effect on their members' emotional and material well-being. Therefore, the private actions and decisions of individual members—children as well as parents—have consequences for all other members and the family as a whole.

The moral question faced in all families—indeed in all groups—is to weigh individual members' interests against the common interest and vice versa. To function for individual good and group survival, a family needs members who are committed to the common interest to the extent that they will on occasion forego their personal interests. But people only make sustained and full contributions to the common good when they are also able to develop their unique potentialities and abilities as persons. If the family's needs persistently take priority, individual members are denied opportunities to develop their own identities and become persons in their own right. If individual needs and rights invariably take priority, the family has difficulty fulfilling its group functions and surviving as a unit. Thus, the powerful may thrive while the weaker members will fail to secure the support essential to their welfare.

Families throughout the ages have had to solve the fundamental moral issue of community. They must define and then redefine the priorities between group and individual interest, balancing what each member gives to and takes from the community and from other members. These priorities are unobtrusively established by members' daily interactions, but at times more directly in family discussions. But whether unobtrusively defined or formally addressed, these issues always have a moral dimension. They involve the welfare and rights of human beings who have unequal power and unequal levels of dependency on the community and on one another.

The view of the family as a moral entity (Aerts, 1979) is congruent with the interactional system's view that morality arises and develops in human interaction. Because children learn about moral reciprocity within their family, the kind of family they grow up in becomes an important consideration in studies of moral development. Without trying, families transmit moral understandings and expectancies to their young members. Beyond what parents actually say when moral problems arise, their practical ways of dealing with each other and their children provide living examples of how moral issues are defined, negotiated, and concluded. In sum, the family has a unique impact on children's developing moral understanding because it is the group in which children first, intimately, and continuously experience the complex interaction between self-interests and common interests.

The concept that families are groups, characterized by organizational and interpersonal patterns that promote both group and individual growth is compatible with the contextualized views of the interactional system. In a previous study of family life, Aerts (1979) found important variations among 100 middle-class families with adolescent children—in the ways families defined issues of parental authority, in the priorities they set among members' needs, and in the requirements set for members' participation in decision making.

In some families children were all treated alike regardless of their special needs and interests. In other families chores and privileges were balanced in ways that took account of each child's abilities and preferences. The extent of interpersonal openness among members also varied. In some families, members talked a great deal about their personal feelings and opinions, whereas in others, members were re-served and avoided discussions that might reveal private thoughts. Finally, families varied in the standards they set for themselves and their children and in the rules they followed to regulate family life. Some families had flexible rules and standards that were attuned to members' different and changing needs, abilities, and potentials. Oth-ers adhered to conventional social standards which define appropriate conduct for a mother, a father, and a child of a given age and sex. In these families, rules were enforced regardless of members' specific strengths and weaknesses. Although this conceptualization of families as groups was developed without direct attention to moral interaction, these qualities seem relevant to a discussion of moral interchange within the family.

A direct investigation of the young adults' families was not possible. Most families did not live in the San Francisco Bay Area and funding was limited. Consequently, information about family life was obtained from a questionnaire that the students filled out during the second interview. Thirteen items described families as groups, and students were asked to check on a five-point scale whether their families were more like one or the other extreme of two alternative descriptions. One hundred and fifteen of the 119 young adults filled out this ques-tionnaire. (Examples of these items can be seen in the next several pages.)

Preliminary Results

Families as Groups

We first analyzed the 13 items that describe families as groups to determine whether there were subgroups of highly associated items. This analysis yielded four separate groups.

The definitions of each group are given below along with interpre-tations of their meanings. The individual items are listed according to the degree of their association with each dimension (which can vary from −1.00 to +1.00). Slashes separate the two ends of the scaled items because each dimension's name takes both ends into account.

I. Interpersonal Openness/Reserve   Weights

    1. Members are very affectionate with each other/   .79
Members are rather undemonstrative with each other.

    2. The family deals openly and directly with prob-   .72
lems even if it creates bad feelings/The family does not bring up problems in order to avoid bad feelings.

    3. There are a lot of family discussions about opin-   .72
ions and ideas/The family does not discuss opinions and ideas as a group.

    4. Members talk to each other about personal mat-   .69
ters/Members keep personal matters to themselves.

    5. Members do a lot of things together as a group/   .68
Members do not do many things together; each goes his/her separate way.

All these items describe the degree to which family members openly and affectionately share their lives, discuss ideas and tackle problems, even when it is painful. In other words, interpersonal openness/reserve indicates whether a family is an intimate group whose members share personal concerns or whether it is an aggregation of separate individuals held together by their formal membership in a family unit.

II. Autonomy/Conformity   Weights

    1. The children are encouraged to decide for   .80
themselves and do their own thing/The children are encouraged to follow their parents' advice and ideas of what is best.

    2. Members respect each other's privacy/Members   .78
tend to interfere with each other's lives.

    3. Differences of opinion are accepted and easily   .58
managed/Differences of opinion are not easily tolerated and create stress.

This dimension shows whether families permit and support individual growth among members or, conversely, whether members' lives are expected to conform to preset conceptions. Families scoring high on this dimension would regard each member as a unique individual who has interests, opinions, skills, and potentialities that differ from those of other members. In families that value conformity, the group's cohesion would take priority over members as individuals.

III. Internally/Externally Regulated   Weights
1. The family prefers taking advantage of unexpected occasions to have fun/The family prefers to follow plans and be well organized.   .73
2. Religious values and concerns are not important/Religious values and concerns are important.   .71
3. Members are appreciated for doing what they want in the best way they can/Members are appreciated for reaching high standards and following rules.   .50

These items connote families' sensitivity to emerging opportunities and individual talents versus following preestablished rules, standards, and conventional norms. Families scoring high should be more flexible or, perhaps, more loosely organized and creative. Families scoring low should be well organized and conventional.

IV. Cooperation/Competition   Weights
1. Members are cooperative and supportive with one another/Members are competitive with one another.   .73
2. Members do not openly express how angry they feel sometimes about one another/Members openly express how angry they feel sometimes about one another.   .58

In high-scoring families, members are cooperative and sensitive to each other's feelings, whereas in low-scoring families, interpersonal competition and hurtful exchanges are probably more frequent.

Types of Family Groups

The students' descriptions resulted in scores for their families on the four dimensions discussed above, but it seemed that the combination of these dimensions would better portray the complexity of family life. Therefore, further analyses were done to place families together according to their similarity on all four scores. We first worked with a statistical solution that produced five types. However, two groups were very similar except on one dimension that reflected differences in the way daughters and sons were treated. So these two groups were combined to form one type, the reserved families. The final four family types are described below. The dimension most characteristic of each type provides its name.

Open Families (Internal).   The dimensions characterizing open families are, first, openness among family members and, second, the family's reliance on internally defined standards to regulate its life. In these families members were affectionate with one another, participated in family activities, talked about personal matters, discussed opinions and feelings, and brought problems into the open. Fun was more valued than adhering to plans; religious concerns were not important; and members were appreciated for doing what they wanted rather than for following rules and reaching high standards. These families probably gave their younger members an understanding of the complexity of intimate group life and of the differences in individual members' feelings and attitudes. At the same time they provided examples of how a group can be integrated. This kind of family was described by the largest group of students; 32 or almost 30 percent of the sample and included 18 women and 14 men.

Cooperative Families (External).   These families were strongly cooperative, but they relied on externally defined rules and standards to regulate family and individual members' lives. In these families, priority was given to plans and rules rather than having fun, and appreciation was shown for members' achieving high standards rather than for fulfilling personal interests. Family cooperation seemed to require rigid adherence to rules and standards that were not closely related to members' personal interests and abilities.

The combination of cooperation and adherence to conventional standards as guides for family organization and individual conduct suggests that cooperative families were purposeful and highly organized. Little room seemed to be left for ambiguity and uncertainty or acceptance of human frailties. Family life may have been so smoothly organized and buttressed by unequivocal answers that children may not have had opportunities to acquire a sense of human and moral dilemma and the skill to deal with either. Twenty-eight students, 16 women and 12 men, described their families in these terms.

Competitive Families (External). The third type of family showed intense competition among members and relied on external rules and standards. Family members were described as competitive rather than cooperative and as openly expressive of their anger. These families emphasized planning and organization rather than fun in their recreational activities; religious values and concerns were important, and members were appreciated for reaching high standards and following rules. Emphasis on competition and conventionalized success probably thwarted intimacy and prevented interpersonal negotiations that build collective understanding. Pursuit of individual success probably superseded a sense of collective aims and group achievement. Twenty-one students described their families in this way. Of these, nine were women, and 12 were men.

Reserved Families. These families were strongly characterized by members' reserve in their relations to one another. Problems were not brought into the open, members did not talk about personal matters nor discuss opinions and feelings; they seldom joined in group activity. Since members were not emotionally involved in each others' lives, and they restrained expression of personal feelings; these families seem more like corporate entities than intimate groups. This atmosphere probably impaired the development of younger members' interpersonal skill since opinions were not discussed, problems were not brought out into the open, and members did not express their feelings. The sexes disagreed on the question of members' freedom. Women said their families were strict and required conformity to preestablished rules and standards, while men described their families as granting autonomy to members. Reserved family relations were described by 31 students. Eighteen were men and 13 women.

The four family types were compared with regard to their objective characteristics. They did not significantly differ in socioeconomic status, family size, or size of the towns in which they were located. Students coming from families of one type did not differ in birth rank from students whose families fit other types.

Main Results

Two things should be kept in mind in considering the results we gained from our study. First, students were no longer living with their families at the time they answered the questionnaire, although most had very recently left home. Second, the information these students provided is their *personal* view of their families, not necessarily an objective description. These may have affected the results. These students' parents or siblings might have answered the questionnaire differently.

Within these limits, we addressed two main questions: Do students from different types of families handle moral conflict differently? Are higher levels of cognitive and interactional morality associated more with some kinds of family background than with others? Because the analyses of moral action and development described in previous chapters showed occasional effects of the influences of sex, situation, and group structure, we first controlled for these effects in all analyses so we could ask whether family experiences still added significant information about why individual students acted differently or attained different moral levels. These are extensive and complicated analyses; a summary table is included in the discussion section of this chapter.

Friendship Groups and Friends' First Evaluations

The first question arising from the study is whether the students of different family backgrounds were equally distributed between game and discussion groups as well as between led and dominated groups. The answer is that they were distributed in the same proportions as the entire sample in game and discussion groups and in led and dominated groups. The students' family background did have some relation to their friends' designations of them as dominators of their groups. Of the nine students who were identified as dominators, four were from open, three from reserved, two from competitive families, and none from a cooperative family. The six leaders were more evenly distributed among all four kinds of families.

Friends' first evaluations of one another were further differentiated according to family background. We report these results in detail and follow with a summary at the end of this section. Family type itself significantly affected friends' perception of how easily students changed their minds ($p \leq .10$). Students from the two externally regulated families were significantly different. Those from competitive families were seen as the least likely, while those from cooperative families were the most likely, to change their minds.

Family type and the sex of the student also contributed to differences. Women from open and reserved families had the highest scores for knowing right from wrong, while men from these same kinds of families had the lowest scores ($p \leq .10$). Women from reserved and cooperative families, but men from open and competitive families were better known by their friends ($p \leq .05$).

A combination of family background and the natural structure of the friendship groups was also related to friends' perceptions. When students from competitive and reserved families were members of dominated groups, they were seen as more dominating; by contrast, when they were members of led groups, they were well liked. When students from open and cooperative families were members of led groups, they were seen as more dominating ($p \leq .05$); when they were members of dominated groups, they were well liked ($p \leq .10$). This set of results indicates that, even though students with different family backgrounds did not become members of led or dominated groups disproportionately to their numbers in the sample, once they were in these different situations, they were perceived differently by their friends.

The ways that group context and family background interacted to affect peers' evaluations with regard to being well liked and dominating are the most interesting aspects of these analyses because they suggest that students from the four kinds of families were perceived differently in dominated and led groups. Students from competitive and reserved families were rated similarly. When they were members of dominated groups, they were not especially liked and were regarded as dominating. Perhaps old ways of handling conflict were triggered because their groups solved problems impersonally, as they reported their families did. But when these students were members of led groups, they were regarded as likeable and not dominating.

A contrasting pattern was observed for students from open and cooperative families. When they were members of the led groups—which probably provided conditions for dealing with conflict similar to those in their own families—they were seen as dominating and not especially likeable, but when they were members of dominated groups, they were well liked and, in this dominated atmosphere, not dominating. This set of evaluations suggests that when group and family atmosphere were consonant, students took the initiative and were aggressive in ways that were not appreciated by their friends. When group and family demands were dissonant, the students were evidently more cautious in asserting themselves, an approach their friends approved.

Ego Strategies

Characteristic Ego Strategies. Family experience was associated with the students' characteristic strategies of coping and defending, but the significant differences were primarily seen in the contrasts between students from cooperative and open families. Students from cooperative families were unable to cope with their emotions either by expressiveness (sublimation) ($p \leqslant .05$) or by expressing emotions in highly civilized forms (substitution) ($p \leqslant .10$). They were characteristically doubting ($p \leqslant .05$). Students from open families were characteristically the most sublimating and the least doubting. All other differences in characteristic ego strategies were essentially due to the contrasts between students from cooperative and reserved families.

Family type and sex together contributed to variations in the students' scores for coping playfulness ($p \leqslant .10$). Women from both cooperative and reserved families had higher scores than the men from these same kinds of families.

When analyses combined family type and the structure of the friendship groups, significant results were found for concentration ($p \leqslant .001$), doubting ($p \leqslant .10$), and reaction formation ($p \leqslant .05$). First, students from reserved families who belonged to dominated groups attained the highest scores for concentration but not for doubting. Second, students from cooperative families who belonged to led groups were characteristically self-righteous (reaction formation). Evidently the inner directedness of these groups could be tolerated by members of cooperative families only if they had a strong sense of their self-righteousness.

Altogether then, students from cooperative and reserved families were especially distinctive in their characteristic ego functions. Students from cooperative families characteristically coped less with their feelings and were more doubting; the women were playful while the men were not. When they were members of led groups, they were also self-righteous. When students from reserved families were members of dominated groups, they characteristically depended on coping concentration. That is, they were task oriented, and they did not rely on defensive doubting.

Situational Ego Strategies. Family type significantly differentiated among the strategies that the students generally used in all five sessions (summed for all sessions), specifically coping tolerance of ambiguity ($p \leq .05$), suppression ($p \leq .05$), defending intellectualization ($p \leq .05$), and rationalization ($p \leq .05$). Students from cooperative families coped in the sessions and attained the highest scores for tolerance of ambiguity and suppression of feelings. They avoided defensive intellectualizing and rationalization. (Recall that these students were characteristically defensive.) During the sessions, students from open families revealed the opposite pattern. They coped the least, having the lowest ratings in tolerance of ambiguity and suppression of feelings; they were also the most defensive, depending heavily on intellectualizing and rationalizing.

Family type and the sex of the student significantly contributed to differences in the students' intellectuality ($p \leq .05$), tolerance of ambiguity ($p \leq .10$), coping playfulness ($p \leq .05$), and rationalization ($p \leq .05$). Men from all family types generally rationalized more than women but also were more likely to rely on coping intellectually and playfulness. The combination of family type and structure of the friendship groups did not differentiate students' ego strategies during the sessions.

Several observations emerge from the analyses of ego strategies. First, students from cooperative families reacted to the stress of the sessions by recognizing but suppressing their feelings and accepting difficulties rather than trying to resolve them. These are essentially nonconfrontational, perhaps even passive adaptations. Students from open families reacted in exactly opposite ways. They were intolerant, cognitively defensive, and emotional. Second, family background combined with the variable of sex produced important differences which were strongest for students from open and competitive families.

Moral Functioning

Interview-based Scores. The students' family background did not significantly affect either the cognitive or interactional scores achieved in the three interviews. Being interviewed about hypothetical moral dilemmas is a situation quite different from solving moral conflict with friends and also differs from past familial experiences.

Moral Action. After the effects of sex, situation, and group structure were controlled, family background still contributed significantly to the moral scores but only for the last two sessions. Perhaps past familial experiences could emerge as a significant influence on moral action only after the students had become accustomed to the research situation and the ritual of the sessions. Figure 15.1 shows that moral scores for all family groups were very close during the first two sessions but increasingly diverged thereafter. In session 4, family background resulted in a significant difference in cognitive moral scores, with students from reserved families having the highest scores and students from cooperative families the lowest scores ($p \leq .05$). This contrast was duplicated exactly in session 5 for the interactional scores, when students from reserved families again had the highest and those from cooperative families the lowest scores ($p \leq .10$).

During the last session, then, contrasting effects occurred for the students from reserved and cooperative family backgrounds. Those from cooperative families had the lowest levels of moral action. The interpersonal exchanges of the cooperative families were described as smooth, but directed by conventional standards, so these students may have been ill-prepared to deal with the disorderly, sometimes self-serving interactions of their friends. By contrast, students from reserved families, who were likely the least experienced in open moral exchange, had the highest levels of moral action. These students may have been the most naïve when they began the group experiences. However, by later sessions, these unfamiliar situations of open moral conflicts seem to have evoked high levels of moral creativity from these students.

Moral Development. The proportions of gainers and losers in cognitive as well as interactional moral levels (identified by the stringent criterion of shifts one and a half stages or levels up or down) are about equal for all family types. When each family type was compared with

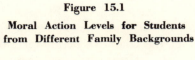

Figure 15.1

Moral Action Levels for Students
from Different Family Backgrounds

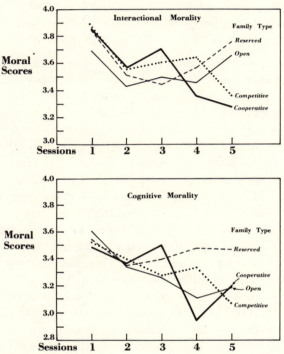

the remainder of the sample, differences were significant in two instances: Under the interactional system, students from competitive backgrounds were more often unaffected than all other students ($p \le .05$), and under the cognitive system, students from reserved families more frequently gained in moral level than all other students ($p \le .05$).

The moral stability of students from competitive families and moral gain of students from reserved families seem congruent with the interactional conceptualization of moral development. Social disequilibrium—seen here as the disparity between the social processes that the students experienced in their families and in their friendship groups—favors development. By reason of their familial experiences, students from reserved families, who gained developmentally, were undoubtedly the least accustomed to open exchange of opinions and feelings and to working out collective solutions. In contrast, members of competitive families, who were developmentally unaffected, were probably the most accustomed to tension and competition in intimate relations; therefore they were the least perturbed by the sessions and continued to think and solve problems as they always had.

Students' Actions during the Sessions

Group Behavior. After the immediate effects of situation, group structure, and sex were controlled, family background still contributed to the students' involvement and ability to suspend disbelief (see Figure 15.2). The students' family background contributed significantly to the degree of involvement each displayed in sessions 1 and 2, to their total involvement during all five group sessions, and their suspension of disbelief in session 2. (*p*s ranged from .01 to .05.) In all instances students from open families were the most involved and most likely to suspend disbelief, and those from cooperative families were the least involved and least likely to suspend disbelief. Students from open families were the most accustomed to discussing differences of opinions in intimate groups, and these experiences probably contributed to their ease in the beginning sessions. Students from cooperative families were probably the most distressed when ordered group cooperation was disturbed. As a result, they may not have focused on the moral issues but tried to accommodate themselves to the moods and opinions of their friends. (This interpretation is confirmed by their friends' evaluations at the conclusion of the sessions.)

The combination of family type and sex was related to students' involvement in all sessions combined and in sessions 1 and 3 and also related to suspension of disbelief for all sessions combined and for sessions 1 and 4 (*p*s ranged from .01 to .10). Men from open and competitive families were generally more involved and better able to suspend disbelief than the women from the same family types.

In Chapter 12 we described individual students who were either heroes or casualties in the stressful game of NeoPd. The question

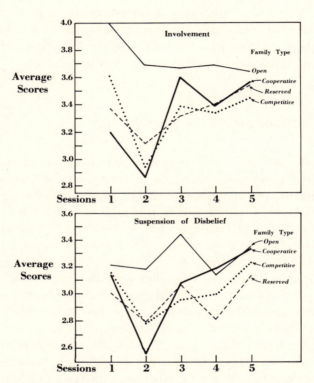

Figure 15.2
Group Behavior of Students
from Different Family Backgrounds

here concerns their family background. Only heroes in cognitive moral action were differentiated. Out of the 19 cognitive heroes, six (32 percent) were from open families and seven (37 percent) were from competitive families. More than one-half of the students from competitive families were heroes, a difference that was significant when compared to the whole sample ($p \leq .05$). No particular familial trends were found for the casualties.

Because students from competitive families clearly contributed more heroes than their numbers warranted, it again seems that family experience especially prepared these young people to deal with strife and hostility. They were probably less upset by their friends' behavior, and therefore less stressed by the entire situation. As a result they produced higher levels of cognitive morality in this stressful situation.

Students' Evaluations after the Group Sessions

Students' opinions of their friends were probably both confirmed and modified by the end of the 15 hours they spent together dealing with moral issues. Consequently the final question is how students with different family background changed in the eyes of their friends after their common experiences. Family backgrounds made a difference in friends' evaluation for five out of the eleven qualities that were assessed: is fair, understands others, changes own views, handles self in conflict, and is well-liked (ps ranged from $\leq .001$ to $\leq .10$). On all five qualities, students from cooperative families significantly gained in the eyes of their friends while those from competitive families lost. The status of students from reserved and open families was either unchanged or changed very little.

Family type and sex of the student combined contributed to change in the evaluation of friends' dominance. For all students except those from cooperative families, men gained in attributed dominance while women lost ($ps \leq .05$). In cooperative families, both men and women came to be seen as less dominating.

After the sessions, men and women from competitive families were the least liked by their friends. The men were also the least liked before the sessions began. Obviously competitive families suggested ways to handle moral conflict that were not appreciated by their off-springs' friends. By contrast, students from cooperative families were the most liked and viewed as most moral, fair and understanding of others, by their friends. But their involvement was low as were their moral scores.

Overall Review of Family Influence

Limitations of This Study

These results suggest, rather than confirm, the implications of family group functioning for their offspring's moral functioning. Several characteristics of these data limited the investigation. First, the descriptions of families were reported by the students themselves, a procedure which is always susceptible to distortion. A nonparticipant observer or another member of these families might have described family processes and interpersonal characteristics differently. Furthermore, these first-year university students were in a period of transition, especially with respect to their relations with their families. At a time like this perceptions of family relationships may be more analytic but also more biased.

Second, students were asked to provide overall judgments of their families rather than describe specific qualities which might have produced more certain but perhaps less-interesting reports.

Third, the methods of data analysis were constructed to control for the immediate effects of situation, group structure, and sex before the more distant influences of family life could be considered. But consistent and sensible effects of past family experiences could still be discerned.

Fourth, the results were based on a relatively homogeneous sample of accomplished, well-functioning young people who, we assume, were members of reasonable families. This means that results were more difficult to obtain than if the sample had been heterogeneous with marked differences in both families and offspring.

Résumé for Each Family Type

A recapitulation of the major findings for each type of family experience provides an overview of the background influences on these young adults' methods of handling conflict and their moral functioning. Table 15.1 provides a summary of the most important results. To simplify the presentation, differences due to a combination of family background and sex are not included in this table but are discussed within each résumé.

Open Families. Students from open families were not distinctive in their moral functioning; their moral-action levels were never highest or lowest, and the group's developmental pattern was not distinctive. But during the game and discussion sessions, they were consistently the most involved and most able to suspend disbelief. More of their members were initially regarded by their friends as dominating, especially when they were members of led groups. When they were members of dominated groups, they were regarded as likable. Therefore, friends of students from open families saw them as taking group roles that were the opposite of those that prevailed in their friendship group. When the group sessions were over, these friends did not markedly change their evaluations. Distinctive and characteristic ego processes of members of open families were coping—emotionally expressive and not doubting. Nevertheless, they generally became defensive during the action sessions. Here they did not tolerate ambiguity or suppress their emotions but tended to rationalize and intellectualize. None of these processes is especially intrusive socially.

A major characteristic of open families was their differential effects on sons and daughters. Sons were outstandingly active, characteristically coping intellectually; during the sessions they were playful but at the same time intolerant of ambiguity. These men were rated by friends and observers as being dominant and leaders, and they came to be seen as even more dominant by the sessions' end. Daughters were generally either average or low on all these same qualities. These students actually dealt with their peer experiences in the same ways that their families handled problems of group unity and conflict—or so they reported. They addressed the tasks with vigor, albeit with defensive adaptations that were uncharacteristic of them, but perhaps understandable, given the group conflict and their highest levels of involvement. Nevertheless, they did not jeopardize their relations with their friends. The group experiences probably did not cause these students stress, and they did not develop morally. From their familial experiences they were accustomed to open discussion of feelings and opinions and dealing with problems of groups.

Cooperative Families. During the last two sessions, the levels of cognitive and interactional morality reached by the students from cooperative families dropped significantly. During all sessions they were the least involved and least able to suspend disbelief. Initially friends thought that these students frequently changed their minds. When they were members of led groups, they were also seen as dominating, but, in dominated atmospheres, they were regarded as likable. Therefore, their friends saw them as taking roles different from the prevailing roles in their group. However, no student from a cooperative family was ever designated as a group dominator by his friends. By the time of the second peer evaluations, students in this group had strikingly improved their standing with their friends. Their ratings

Table 15.1.

Summary of Differences among Students of Different Family Backgrounds[a]

	Moral Functioning	Ego Strategies	Group Behavior	Friends' Evaluation
Open family		**Characteristic:** Sublimating Not doubting **Situational:** Not tolerating ambiguity Not suppressing Intellectualizing Rationalizing	Most involved, most able to suspend disbelief Often cognitive heroes during NeoPd	**First evaluation:** Often group dominators seen as dominating in led contexts, but likeable in dominated contexts **Second evaluation:** No change
Cooperative family	Session 4: lowest cognitive scores Session 5: lowest inter-actional scores	**Characteristic:** Not sublimating Not substituting Doubting Self-righteous in dominated contexts **Situational:** Tolerating ambiguity Suppressing Not intellectualizing Not rationalizing	Least involved, least able to suspend disbelief	No group dominators **First evaluation:** Easily changes mind Seen as dominating in led contexts but likeable in dominated contexts **Second evaluation:** Fair, understands others Changes views, handles self in conflict, well liked

Competitive family	Developmentally unaffected in both systems	**Characteristic:** Substituting	Often cognitive heroes during NeoPd	**First evaluation** Does not change mind Seen as dominating in dominated contexts but likeable in led contexts **Second evaluation:** Decrease in fairness, understanding others, changing views, handling self in conflict, and being well liked
Reserved family	Session 4: highest cognitive scores Session 5: highest interactional scores Developmentally gained in both systems	**Characteristic:** Concentrating, but not doubting in dominated groups	Sometimes cognitive casualties during NeoPd	**First evaluation:** Seen as dominating in dominated contexts but likeable in led contexts **Second evaluation:** Essentially unchanged

[a] Interactions of sex and family types are not included.

had gained significantly for being fair, understanding others, changing their own minds, being able to handle themselves in conflicts, and likability. The ego strategies of these students were characteristically defensive. They were not emotionally expressive, nor did they have socialized control of their emotions; instead they were doubting, and those who had joined dominated groups were also characteristically self-righteous (reaction formation). Nevertheless, in the action situations, their ego adaptations were changed to coping. They tolerated ambiguity, suppressed their feelings, and neither defensively intellectualized nor rationalized. The men and women were much alike, but when differences did occur, the women were more active and involved in coping—playful and intellectual.

The students from cooperative families described their family experiences as highly cooperative but still rigidly controlled. They did not seem prepared for dealing with moral conflict with their peers. In fact, their marked drop in moral levels during the last two sessions suggests that the experiences of peer conflict may have progressively eroded their moral functioning. Nonetheless their friends increased their approval. Although they characteristically did not cope and were defensive, they coped during the sessions but not with confrontational, assertive strategies. From the standpoint of their own possibilities and resources, they seemed to make a necessary adjustment that was consonant with their families' highly interpersonal but also highly controlled orientation. They avoided conflict and appeased anger, but they did this at the cost of dealing with the moral issues.

Competitive Families. The students from competitive families were morally distinctive in two ways. They were the least affected developmentally by the group experiences, and they supplied more cognitive heroes than their number in the sample would warrant. But these students were not distinctive in their group behavior, nor were their characteristic or situational strategies distinctive. Their friends initially saw them as not changing their mind; if they were members of dominated groups, they were seen as dominating, but as somewhat likable if they were members of led groups. Therefore, students from competitive families *followed* rather than countered the prevailing trend of their group. They did not fare well in their friends' eyes. When the sessions were over, their friends significantly lowered their ratings in such matters as being fair, understanding others, changing views, handling self in conflicts, and likability. Competitive families had different effects on sons and daughters. The men were rated as more dominating and generally more active and involved in the group experiences than the women. Although these students were the least liked, the women were liked even less than the men.

Altogether the young adults from competitive families seemed both morally and interpersonally impervious to the group experiences. But rather than being positively uninvolved or passive in the face of moral issues, they seemed to have "stonewalled" both their friends' expectations and the issues. As a result they lost their friends' approval. They were the most stable in their level of moral functioning. These students apparently handled the group experiences in self-protective ways, perhaps in the same way that they had learned to protect themselves when conflicts arose in their families, which they had described as competitive, angry, and requiring high achievement.

Reserved Families. Students from reserved families achieved the highest levels of moral action for cognitive morality in session 4 and for interactional morality in session 5; they registered the strongest developmental gains in both moral systems. Their group behavior was not distinctive, nor were they distinctive in either the first or last set of their friends' evaluations, except for being initially regarded as dominating in dominated contexts and likable in led contexts. This seems to indicate the students from reserved families reflected their group's character. Neither their characteristic nor situational ego strategies were distinctive; those who had joined dominated groups were characteristically concentrating and not doubting. Furthermore the men and women did not behave differently to a great extent. When differences occurred, daughters rather than sons were the more actively involved as well as characteristically more copingly playful.

Reserved families probably provided their offspring with the least experience in direct, sensitive moral negotiation. These students had described their families as undemonstrative, reluctant to deal openly with personal problems and tending not to engage in group activity. Therefore family and peer group experience were dissonant. We give below a possible reason for this group's moral distinctiveness.

Summary for Family Types. The expressive, confident, vigorous students from open families addressed peer conflict in ways that did not put their friendships in jeopardy, but as a group, their moral functioning was not distinctive. From the descriptions of their families' operations, family and peer conflict seem to be similar for these students, and they seemed to act according to their families' ways of adapting.

The students from cooperative families, who characteristically had difficulty coping with their emotions and who were characteristically indecisive, began to cope unobtrusively during the action sessions, undoubtedly because they adapted by refusing to get involved in conflict with their peers. They seemed to make a tradeoff between harmony and moral choice. Although their interpersonal orientation was consistent with that of their families, they seemed to adopt an emergency strategy that was interpersonally efficacious, but morally ineffective. These students had described their families as extremely regulated, so the absence of a strong authority, especially in the game sessions, may have been especially upsetting to them.

The students from competitive families also used a strategy that may have worked for them in their families, whom they had described as angry, competitive, and strict. Faced with the anger and stress of their friends and the demands of the moral tasks, these students seemed to have reacted by thwarting the demand put on them by both their friends and the research. Consequently they lost their friends' approval and they were developmentally unaffected by the curricular experiences.

Students from reserved families attained the highest moral levels in the last two sessions and they gained morally. They had described members of their families as reserved with each other and tending to lead individual rather than shared lives. Consequently, these young 19-year-olds, who were away from home for the first time and who were experiencing the enforced intimacy of dormitory life may have faced a greater social disequilibrium due to the disparity between their families' and friendship groups' interaction. If so, they may have been especially ready to change morally.

Summary

The results of our study of families and their interpretation are focused on how family living builds members' expectations about group interaction which may then affect their actions in other intimate groups. This approach is not consistent with the idea that past family experience has a direct, unilateral influence on offspring's later moral functioning and behavior in groups. Instead the effects of family experience seemed to suggest a general mode of accommodation that was applied by the students to three immediate issues that these young people seemed to regard as critical: keeping and perhaps even improving their standing with their friends, handling and resolving the moral issues that the research situations presented, and preserving a sense of their own integrity in the midst of these conflicting demands.

Offspring of these four family backgrounds addressed and resolved personal and collective issues differently.

1. Students from open families seemed to accommodate straightforwardly as they evidently did in their families; they addressed the moral issues, kept their friends, and became only mildly defensive during the sessions.

2. Students from cooperative families seemed to accommodate by using strategies they may have used within their families. These may have been evoked by the absence of a strong central authority, at least in the game sessions. They did not involve themselves in the moral tasks, but they did cope and actually improved their interpersonal relations with their friends, but at the cost of their own moral choice.

3. Students from competitive families seemed threatened by the conflict with their friends, so they accommodated by stonewalling the demands placed on them both by their friends and the research, a form of self-defense that may have worked well in their angry, competitive families.

4. The students from reserved families seemed to have accommodated to moral conflict with their peers, and they went on to assimilate the moral experiences as opportunities for growth.

There were no differences due to family background in the interview-based moral scores of either system. Therefore *previous family experiences apparently did not provide these intellectually capable young people with any particular formulation of how they should act and what they might say when dealing with hypothetical dilemmas. Instead, family experience seemed to provide these young people with formulations of how they could act when faced with actual moral conflict in group situations.*

We conclude from this exploratory study that the view of the family as a moral entity that works to sustain its common interest at the same time that it works to give opportunity for individual members to fulfill their self-interests provides a promising approach for studying moral action and development. By these young people's own report, and later their actions, only the open families seem to have achieved a balance between the family's common interest and its individual members' interests. The cooperative families apparently placed family interest, harmony, and clarity above individual interest and their offspring did not protect their individual moral interests. The competitive families did not seem to be intimate groups and they did exact a toll on individual members, not for family sustenance but for family pride. They thwarted their young members' ability to be flexible in handling interpersonal and moral conflict. The reserved families seem not to have had a strong interpersonal core—or so their offspring thought at this point in their lives—but at the same time they allowed their sons and daughters to draw full benefit from the friendship of group experiences.

PART V
SUMMARY

Chapter 16

MAJOR FINDINGS, EVALUATIONS, AND CONCLUSIONS

T HE FIVE MAIN concerns of this volume—moral action, development, the beginnings of morality, family interaction in relation
to offspring's moral functioning, and comparisons between the interactional and cognitive theories—are taken up in this chapter. Within
each section, we locate our work with respect to other formulations
that currently guide psychologists' research into morality. The major
findings from our study that were similar for the interactional and
cognitive theories, as well as findings that were different are summarized and evaluated. Within each section we finally suggest how
moral action and development, young children's morality, the effects
of family background, and the relationship between two moral theories might now be seen in light of this work.

Moral Action in Both Systems

Reasons for Our Choice of Research Designs

Moral action was the main concern of this work. We wanted to learn
if moral actions vary in quality and if so, learn about the conditions
associated with the variation. We argued that social scientists should
give highest priority to the study of moral action. It is the morality of
use; it is of greatest social concern because it affects people's lives;

and we cannot know how morality develops before we know what morality is. If social scientists are to help illuminate the moral basis of life, the study of action must surely be their starting point. On all counts it is the authentic expression of practical morality.

Psychologists can be roughly divided according to the way they approach the study of action. On one side are the cognitivists. Their theory is primarily a description and explanation of the development of "pure" moral thought. Its proponents have given little attention to action. When they have (Kohlberg, et al., 1983), they elaborated the moral cognitions that they had already proposed. It remains to be seen if this strategy is productive.

On the opposite side is social-learning theory with its focus on behavior to the exclusion of thought and moral meaning. To achieve the methodological certainty and precision that these learning theorists demand of themselves, they restrict their research to observing behavior; but the moral behaviors that can be instigated in laboratories are usually artificial, trivial, or merely compliant. As we see it, difficulties for the cognitivists lie in the limitations of their theory, whereas difficulties for the social-learning theorists lie in the methodological strictures they place on themselves.

We tried to design our projects—as well as structure the interactional theory—to avoid the cognitive theorists' difficulty in accounting for action and the social-learning theorists' impoverished and fragmented view of moral meaning. At the same time, we tried to build on the strengths of both approaches. The interactional theory makes common cause with the cognitivists in arguing that people's minds are involved in their moral functioning. But this is not a testament that the interactional theory is exclusively cognitivist since practical rationality, not logic, is its essence. The interactional theory also makes common cause with the social-learning theorists in believing that behavior—or action, as we prefer to say—is the essence of morality.

Interactional morality was designed to represent practical moral meanings and actions, so it is focused on the interactions among people involved in moral conflict. We designed the projects hoping to observe moral interaction in situations that were *close* to the moral action of everyday life. Our commitment to studying action does not mean that we endorse the methodological strictures of the social-learning theorists. But our membership in the psychological community requires that we justify the unusual methods we did use.

Several reasons lay behind the construction of our designs. First, moral thoughts are actions in the sense they are always powered by emotion. Even when moral thoughts are not expressed as acts of persuasion, argumentation, or negotiation, or acted out in behavior, they are still acts—internal imaginary dialogues that people enact with other people and, of course, with themselves as they consider first one possibility and then another. The social-dialectical quality of moral exchange enlivens minds, so thought becomes action. This is succinctly communicated in John Dewey's comment that "mind is a verb" (1934, p. 263). The Cartesian separation of mind from body clearly misleads when applied to morality.

In addition, situations of seemingly pure action cannot be sharply separated from situations that elicit seemingly pure, abstract thought undertaken from the position of the third person (say by a student in a moral philosophy class or from people confronted with hypothetical, distant dilemmas during interviews). When it comes to morality, people do not seem to *think* about morality. They seem almost always to *do* morality. *All* moral situations have costs that arise from three human interests: people's hope that their world is just (Lerner, 1980) and their wish to regard themselves and to be regarded as moral. These interests motivate people when they confront moral conflict.

We analyzed action in a general way by determining how links between moral-action thoughts and superficially nonmoral influences affect action. But microanalysis of the sequential and evolutionary details of these dialogues and how they are concluded or broken off is an important step for researchers to take. Martin Packer (in press) has taken just such a step in analyzing the game NeoPd as it was negotiated by these young adults.

Second, the research was designed so that the young people's moral experiences would vary from being close to real life to being at some distance from life. We needed to observe what they did in both situations. These design features were not incorporated simply to determine the difference between talking about morality and doing morality. Instead it was also to determine the differences between situations that allow morality to be professed and situations that require commitment to action.

By studying a variety of situations, we hoped to correct the social-learning theorists' view that moral behavior occurs without modification from strategic considerations. We also wanted to learn how the cognitivists' and the philosophers' views of moral discourse as an abstract activity relate to practical moral action. For contrasting action requirements, some friendship groups were to play games while others discussed hypothetical dilemmas. When the students themselves generated the moral issues by their own actions, usually in games (but sometimes during discussion sessions), we were close to observing real life.

Nonetheless, no research situation is identical to everyday life. Observers are omnipresent; their judgmental role and effect on the observed cannot be denied. But also interviewers and even hypothetical third-party observers of all moral enactments affect the persons observed in a similar way. The imagined presence of observers raises questions in all actors' minds, "What would others think?" and "What would God say about the way I am conducting myself?" Nevertheless, we tried to help the students cope with the fact that we were observing them by being frank about our purposes and continually recognizing their difficult position, for instance, by saying to them at the end of a session, "I know you guys are in a tough spot but you're being really good sports." (When the students were in intense conflicts with their friends they seemed to care very little about being observed.)

To understand the effects of situations on action, we needed to determine the status of individual participants *before, during,* and *after* the group experiences. That is, we needed not only to know the levels of their moral functioning but also their usual and contingently evoked ways of solving problems. In addition, we needed to know the way social situations put pressure on the individual—in our study how the groups affected behavior—because we thought this was critical to individual moral action. Consequently, the friendship groups' usual ways of operating and each member's status within the group were important to learn. All these observations were made because we reasoned that practical morality cannot be understood unless both processes (the means) and conclusions (the ends) are understood. Moral action, according to the interactional perspective, is not only an end product, it is also a procedure; furthermore it is also oriented towards the future, since people are always concerned about the short- and long-term consequences of their actions.

Third, recognition that moral action is always future oriented gave rise to another line of reasoning which we followed, hoping to investigate authentic action rather than posturing. We recruited friendship groups because friends, more than strangers or research subjects observed singly, have a stake in maintaining relationships, and when these bonds are stressed, a full range of problem-solving strategies should become evident. Friends can also discern and often correct one another's falsifications. As Hampshire (1978) observes, disloyalty to friends is "very generally, almost universally, forbidden and forbidden absolutely . . . as being intrinsically disgraceful and unworthy" (p. 9). Of course, by reason of their solidarity, friendship groups can also sabotage the expected impacts of research designs, which is exactly what some of our groups occasionally did.

Finally, in both our theory and methodology we assumed that some moral actions are more adequate than others and that judgments about the quality of different moral actions can be made with consensus and "truth." This assumption answers the question of how moral value—or the moral ground—can and should be handled in scientific research. Both theories we evaluated are openly based on moral grounds, which are evident in the meaning of the cognitive theory's developmental sequence and in the interactional theory's sequential levels of quality. Kohlberg (1970) seems, however, to muddy the value issue when he argues that value in his system is empirically *demonstrated* by findings that show which stages of moral reasoning are "more mature." This reasoning becomes empirically suspect when mature people act poorly and if very young children have sensitive moral concern, which we found to be the case. (Also see Haan (1982) for an extended argument that this question of moral grounds must be squarely addressed and that research can still be "scientific" even when the pretense of value neutrality is foregone.) However, the cognitivists do not seem altogether certain that actions can be evaluated for their effectiveness (Candee & Kohlberg, 1982).

Researchers who believe that psychology is a value-neutral science will probably take little comfort in the precision with which we evaluated the meanings of the students' moral actions.

First, we observed complex situations, and some researchers would surely raise questions about how accurate we were in locating the critical stimuli and the relevant responses. (Incidentally, the results for these two projects could have been simplified if we had had prior knowledge about the array of moral meanings that situations and groups present.)

Second, our evaluation of the adequacy of action was based on a series of judgments (not simply the presence or absence of behavioral act). These judgments were guided by the two scoring systems for interactional and cognitive morality and their five levels or stages, but finally they were based on how judges interpreted the scoring manuals and how the judges interpreted the meaning of each student's arguments. Thus, we reconstructed the students' constructions of moral meaning. This procedure will likely not be endorsed by some of our more "scientistic" colleagues (see criticisms of scientism by Habermas (1975) and Bernstein (1976)). In fact it brings before us a perennial controversy about the procedures and the breadth of variables that best serve psychological research. And this issue is especially crucial in moral research. *We argue that most human activity is so complex that only the complexity of another human's mind has a chance of encompassing and fathoming the critical meanings.*

We understand morality to be a system of common meanings, but individual people function within particular situations that have particular meanings. People in conflict use these common meanings, as do outside, third-party observers who can and do make judgments about the moral adequacy of the dialogues and resolutions they witness. From this standpoint, the meanings of situations, acts, and resolutions are exactly what researchers should observe and assess. This is a different strategy from the social-learning theorists, who assess surface behavior that can be clearly seen and then counted—for instance, the child's choice as to whether or not to give candies and in what quantity to a fictitious needy child.

Our assessment strategy is not identical to the cognitivists' either, despite agreement between the two theories that people's minds are involved in morality. Assessment of the quality of cognitive morality as outlined in the recent manual (Colby, et al. in press) is tied to three hypothetical dilemmas each for forms A, B, and C of the judgment interview. The specific issues to be scored for each dilemma are predetermined. The manual also contains specific statements representing each stage. The respondent's statements must be matched to the statements in the manual. More weight is given to the first response. Thus scoring is done more by reference to specific issues. To score cognitive morality in the action situations, we had to extend the conceptual moral meanings of each stage; eventually we achieved good agreement. To assess interactional morality the scorer must understand first, the conceptualizations underlying each level and second, the central meaning of the respondent's most determinative and frequently stated position. Scores are to be based on the respondent's most vigorously stated position, not on specific words or ideas. The procedures for scoring cognitive morality probably optimize agreement between scorers, whereas the procedures for interactional morality probably result in more penetrating views of respondents' moral positions.

Determination of moral meanings cannot be done by counts of specific behaviors because *this procedure does not permit us to fathom the past and future meaning of a behavior.* Furthermore, different people may speak and act similarly, but for quite different reasons; other people may have the same feelings but act differently (Frenkel-Brunswik, 1942). Admittedly, it is easier to know that a behavior occurred than to show that it is morally meaningful. Nevertheless, we choose to accept the complexity of human moral experience and work from the same, infrequently admitted basis for "truth" and knowledge that ultimately underlies social-psychological knowledge. Since no principles of morality exist in the world apart from human agreement, a rough truth is obtained only from people's mutual experience and agreements with one another—here among our observers and judges. This is the same truth that underlies common sense and natural language, although neither is always logically consistent, comprehensive in coverage, or permanently correct. In taking this stance, we accept the limitations—the uncertainty of most social-psychological truth.

Major Findings for Moral Action that Held for Both Moral Systems

The major findings with respect to action for both cognitive and interactional morality can be simply stated:

1. Durable moral character—a viable explanation only if there is evidence that individuals' moral levels are consistent in diverse situations—did not account for students' moral action (except slightly when hypothetical dilemmas were presented by a staff leader who directed discussion and modulated disagreements in friendship groups that were already structured by the equable situation of being led and not dominated by one of their members).

2. Moral situations of different costs had strikingly different effects on the levels of moral action. The individual participant's level of moral action in one situation did not predict how he or she would act in another, even when the situations were similar. However situations entailing apparently similar costs led to similar *average* levels of moral actions for groups. Stressful games, in which students generated moral difficulties of their own making, resulted in lower moral action levels; nonstressful games resulted in the highest moral levels. Although discussion sessions produced similar levels of morality, higher levels occurred when the contents of a hypothetical dilemma were close to the students' experience and involved issues that they might face and could resolve in their real life. The prime example here is the often mentioned dilemma Academic Weekend.

3. Situations were further analyzed to take the group's level of stress into account. Almost without exception the equable, moral processes of the led groups resulted in higher levels of moral action than the morally violating processes of the dominated groups.

4. Enough evidence was generated to suggest that the objective contents of moral dilemmas affect moral action. In other words, *moral structure did not transcend content.* After the data were collected, the 20 dilemmas presented in group sessions were broken down into various objective features. The results are tentative since the analyses were crude. However, in discussion sessions, higher average moral levels were observed when the contents of dilemmas were well known, were subtle, involved little damage to victims, and were close to the students' experience. These results suggested that these staff-directed groups needed to be motivated—perhaps stressed—by real-life issues to take effective moral action. In contrast, the self-directed game groups were more effective when the contents of the issues were unfamiliar, were distant, and involved great damage to the imagined victims. Thus the objective contents of dilemmas had opposite effects on gaming and discussing. Playing games that involved hypothetical issues energized moral action, but when the issues arose from the students' own actions, moral action suffered. Abstract dilemmas did not energize the discussion students; their levels of action rose only when issues were real.

5. The individual students' personal ways of handling and solving problems had the most important effect on moral-action levels, whether these were characteristic or less-preferred strategies

applied to immediately pressing problems. These personal adaptations were essentially independent of the contextual variations in experiences—gaming or discussing—and most always independent of their group's being dominated or led.

Ego adaptations were strongly associated with the students' moral levels, having more influence on moral action in stressful than in nonstressful situations and less definitive influence when the students were adjusting to the novelty of becoming research subjects. At that time, group structure and experience had more influence. This finding suggests that social-psychological research should collect measurements on several occasions. When people first become research subjects, they may react to different cues than they do after they become accustomed to being subjects.

Effective moral action was almost always facilitated by coping strategies and thwarted by defensive adaptations, thereby affirming an important proposition of the interactional theory that effective moral means and ends depend not just on the level of moral skill or development but on personal, interpersonal, and social honesty—in other words, a mutually satisfactory discovery of "moral truth."

The students' contingently evoked ego strategies influenced their levels of moral action to a greater extent than their characteristic strategies by a ratio of about three to one for both moral systems. Also, certain ego processes repetitively influenced action in each system, but only two were common to both systems. Both were defensive and both made negative contributions. The first was isolation, which prevents related ideas from being integrated and ideas from being associated with the appropriate feelings. Effective moral action seems, then, to require integration and synthesis of both affective and ideational aspects of situations. The second process was displacement, which allows people to negate their own frustration by taking it out on others. Truth-identifying dialogue requires that disputants consider the possibility that their self-interest may not have priority; displacing prevents this consideration.

6. Sometimes a situation had special meaning for students with particular vulnerabilities or strengths; the influences of this interworking on moral action was clearly observed only once, for the heroes and casualties in NeoPd. Here, levels of moral action deteriorated for students whose characteristic coping style was interpersonally sensitive and cognitively focused. They seemed especially distressed by the moral violations of their friends,

whom they seemed to have trusted without question. In the meantime, the heroes, whose particular defensive adaptations were
self-righteous and emotionally detached, produced their highest
level of moral action. This phenomenon probably occurs more
frequently in everyday life than our sample of students and situations suggests.

Evaluation

Several recommendations for improving action research can be
made. In Chapter 12, a crude analysis was made of several objective
features of the dilemmas, namely, whether dilemmas were close to
experience, involved well-known and obvious or subtle issues, vicarious or direct experience, and great or little damage to "victims." Undoubtedly this listing is incomplete and incorrect in some ways.
Nevertheless, this preliminary work underscores the need to break
down the objective features of moral dilemmas, whether they are hypothetical problems or real-life problems that require action. When
we recognized this need, we came to understand why the cognitivists'
famous dilemma concerning Heinz, who must steal a drug to save his
dying wife (a victim who will suffer irreparable damage), is commonly
known to produce higher levels of reasoning than other hypothetical
dilemmas researchers use. The possibility of a death usually resolves
ambiguity.

Another clear need is to analyze the interpersonal aspects of situations in which dilemmas occur. We initially approached this problem
in a relatively superficial way, thinking, for instance, only of the difference between gaming or discussing. As we came to fuller understandings about the interpersonal contexts, we saw that the discussion
students did not need to contend with the question of responsibility.
They could depend on the power figure to keep a modicum of peace,
and they did not need to resolve any problems. Although this resulted
in less strain, by the end of the sessions the discussion students seemed
irritated with each other.

In the games, the students had to depend on themselves. We
thought that those game situations would be more stressful since problems developed among the participants themselves. This assumption
turned out to be sensible. But still other aspects of situations affect

moral processing. The stress of surprise is surely one. Students were surprised and stressed in NeoPd when they discovered that they themselves and their trusted friends could unthinkingly break explicitly stated agreements.

Another aspect of context we thought might affect the quality of moral decision was the natural structure of friendship groups. However, the presence of the staff leader in the discussion groups seemed to override the natural structure of these groups. Finally, members of led and dominated game groups did behave differently, but groups are led or dominated in different ways. Led groups did not always act in an egalitarian fashion, nor were dominated groups always power-conscious and driven. The members of at least one led group seemed not so much to encourage individual expression and creative differences of opinion as subtly to coerce placid groupthink among its members. Furthermore, the dominators of several groups seemed to be not so much authoritarian as vigorous young people filled with great energy and good ideas. In retrospect, we think that we needed a presession measurement of the groups' histories and capabilities of tolerating conflict. The research was made complex by all these effects; some we had not anticipated.

A Formulation of Moral Action

Morality Is Action. Some investigators reason that a theory of action must be formulated separately from a theory of morality. In contrast, we argue that morality is action—more precisely it is interaction—and that it is meaningless to consider disembodied, abstract moral thought as a set of rules that are strictly applied, irrespective of context. The separation of abstract moral thought from experience is an artifact of academic scholarship. The importance of morality in practical life means people seldom just *think* about morality. Instead, their emotionality concerning morality seems always to lead to their *doing* morality.

We also argue that moral action involves more than carrying out conclusions; the morality of the processes that lead to a conclusion are equally important. All parties' needs and contributions must be actively considered, and the practical opportunities and limits of the situation must be taken into account. When all moral consideration is regarded as action, qualitative differences between action-interview situations and game-action situations vanish and become differences in the degree of vividness, in realistic pressure for conclusion, and so forth. Actual moral encounters are likely to be more vivid and real. The interviewer is a different kind of audience from one's moral protagonist.

Research on moral action needs to identify what elements of moral situations have a critical effect on moral action. At present, we provide only general suggestions about what affects action: the objective features of dilemmas, the demands of situations, the structure of the interpersonal context, and the moral agent's characteristic and situationally evoked ego strategies. So-called measures of moral capacities taken in interviews did not predict action levels in our studies, so researchers might do better with samples of a considerable age range, say from childhood through adulthood. *But given optimal circumstances, children can produce high-quality morality; given deleterious circumstances, adults can produce poor-quality morality.*

We propose, then, that there are two major parts to moral action— the processes of deliberation before a conclusion is reached (the means) and the enactment of the conclusion (the end). Anticipation of consequences also brings the future into people's consideration. The end action does not always require further enactment. A conclusion may simply involve, first an agreement that one party is right— a simple way many wrongs are righted; or that both parties are right but in different ways; or that a newly and mutually created balance is right. Thus our view of action is, at one and the same time, a process of deciding on moral action and a concluding action.

Moral Motivation.   Moral action requires motivation to act sincerely (by entering, remaining in, and concluding dialogue), instead of defaulting (by stonewalling, deserting, or refusing to give up any part of one's self-interest). Moral motivation has both a negative and positive thrust; the human network of interdependency makes it so. Its negative push is the threat of disrupted relationships; its positive pull is toward enhanced relationships.

Diverging from traditional views, we argue that moral motivation is omnipresent and compelling, that moral default is due to lack of skill in dialogues, and that some social conditions can make effective dialogue difficult or impossible. Sincere enactment of morality during a dialogue is expected by all participants. When dialogue is insincere, relationships sour and are finally broken off, so no one benefits. Sincere enactment of an agreement, once one is reached, is also expected. When people explicitly agree, it goes without their saying that they are also agreeing to carry out their part of the agreement to the best of their ability (Sesonske, 1957). If they fail to carry out the agreement or fulfill it in slipshod fashion, good faith wanes.

Acting during dialogues and acting to reach agreement enhance human relations and the group's effectiveness. Everyone then has a "good conscience" when a dialogue is successfully concluded, and the group builds a sense of its own good faith, which in turn increases its potential for later accomplishment. When groups and societies are morally sensible, people are reassured. People of "good conscience" and morally functional groups feel good about themselves and lead tactically less complicated and distressed lives. Poor faith and free-loading compel people and groups to engage in convoluted, dissembling manipulations simply to survive as social beings and entities.

People commit themselves to this moral interdependency for more private motivations. They have compelling needs to regard themselves as moral; they need to participate in order to protect their legitimate self-interests; and they want to live in a morally predictable world. But the very expression of these needs entails the recognition that other people also wish to regard themselves as moral, that they too need to protect their legitimate self-interests, and that they also wish to live in a morally predictable world. Thus the interdependency of social living gives birth to moral action and continuously requires moral action on one's own and the other's behalf.

Moral Emotion. Because people's moral motivations are strong, they become emotional when possibilities arise that they will be found out not to be moral, or that they will be victimized ("screwed," to use the students' word), or be excluded from a dialogue that involves their self-interest. The words for the reactions that follow the obstruction of moral motivations are all emotion words: outrage, indignation, disgrace, shame, umbrage, taken-in, cheated, belittled, ripped-off, and so forth. And they follow not just the obstruction of moral motivation; even the threat of obstruction is sufficient. On the other side of the coin, consummation of people's moral motivations produces the glow of the good conscience and in groups, a sense of well-being and camaraderie that their moral viability is affirmed. Thus, it seems moral action must be explained in terms of emotion as well as cognition.

Still, acts of moral violation abound, so a theory of moral action cannot represent life unless it accounts for both effective and ineffective acts. Theories cannot simply say that people act—as the cognitivists now do (Kohlberg, Levine, & Hewer, 1983)—only if their moral stage is of a particular kind (substage-B) or only when they make a judgment that they are responsible. When confronted with a moral problem, people act even if their choice is not to act. There is no denying that common sense judges the worth of moral acts and does not evaluate all acts as being equally meritorious. During dialogues, ineffective moral action occurs when people violate the stipulations that all can speak, none must dominate, and all may veto. Also ineffective action occurs when people proclaim their intentions of carrying out an agreement and then do not, or do so only half-heartedly. When discussants deliberately dissemble or, less consciously, deceive both themselves and others with superficially compliant but defensive maneuvers, then their action is ineffective whatever their level or stage of moral skill. In either event, ineffective balances are the end result. Morally adequate processes tend to insure morally adequate conclusions; the latter can only be accidentally attained when processes are inadequate.

In these studies, effective action was supported by the students' coping in the following specific ways: sincere and accurate consideration of the issues, sensitivity to the needs and contributions of the participants, consideration of whether certain ways of deliberating were good ways to arrive at solutions, and consideration of whether possible resolutions were practical and good, and whether all concerned agreed to proposed resolutions.

Ineffective action was not due to a lower stage development or lower levels of skill. Instead it resulted from incomplete or warped consideration of the issues, failure to consider all participants' needs and contributions, obliviousness to the group's processes, fantastic formulations and resolutions, impractical solutions, and false balances that swept disagreement under the rug. For researchers to distinguish between effective and ineffective action, they logically need to base their measures of morality on value. There is no way to escape value commitment in investigations of morality.

Moral Development in Both Systems

Background Purposes

Moral development is not a central issue for the social-learning theorists, who believe that the laws of growth in general apply equally well to morality, the only difference being changes in content. Development, however, is the primary organizational force for cognitive theorists since this morality is known by its central proposition that moral cognitions become more comprehensive and differentiated with each stage of development. In the interactional theory moral development is also thought to be different from other kinds of growth. However, the cognitive theorists propose that moral concern is developed in a sequence of qualitatively different stages. According to interactional theory, moral concern is present early in life, and development gradually proceeds as people acquire more sensitive and complete skills for resolving moral conflict. Consequently the five levels of interactional theory are only arbitrarily imposed divisions of a continuum of increasing moral quality.

Our investigations of moral development were more limited than our investigations of moral action. We did not attempt to test whether morality develops gradually or by separate stages. Instead, we focused on *why* development occurs. The questions addressed were: What kind of experiences lead to development? What kind of people are likely to develop as a result of these experiences?

We considered two opposing explanations of development set down in each theory—cognitive disequilibrium in the cognitive theory and social disequilibrium in the interactional theory. Our task was to discern the developmental consequences of each. In real moral situations, these two kinds of disequilibrium cannot be separated from each other; nevertheless, they are clearly different views of how morality develops. Notice that different curricular intervention would be needed if one but not the other explanation were "true"—the training of individual children's thought for the cognitive theory or experience of socioemotional moral conflict for the interactional theory. To contrapose these experiences, insofar as is possible, we set up discussions of hypothetical dilemmas by some friendship groups and experiences of moral gaming by others. Discussion experiences should especially give rise to cognitive disequilibrium (Blatt & Kohlberg, 1975) while gaming should instigate social disequilibrium.

Major Developmental Findings that Held for Both Theories

Before we list the major findings, two limitations must be reiterated. The research design included measures made before, during, immediately after, and three months after the educational interventions. This conventional design for studying development presents a question of whether the discrepancy between these early and late interview measures accurately reflects developmental change. Given the present elementary state of knowledge about the nature of the true morality, this problem is irresolvable. But better criteria for measuring the effects of a curricular intervention would be early and later measures for action situations of equal difficulty. The second set of limitations is the same one that plagues all short-term training studies: These situations may not match the situations that promote natural development. Also, participants know that they are being retested and by the same interested researchers, so even three to four months' delay gives no assurance that effects are durable. Instead motivational differences may account for different outcomes.

With these qualifications stated, we turn to the major developmental results that held for both moral systems.

First, the amount of absolute change found within either moral system after the curricular interventions was not great. When one-half of a stage or level was taken as a criterion of change, gain was achieved by 26 percent of the sample for interactional morality and 16 percent for cognitive morality, stability for 57 and 70 percent, respectively, and loss for 17 and 14 percent, respectively. Amounts of gain for the adolescents were comparable, but they also made significant gains in cognitive development.

Second, after gaining and losing were more stringently defined (as shifts of approximately one-and-one-half stages or levels up or down from the students' entry level), we were able to form clear descriptions of the three outcomes of gaining, being unaffected or losing. Students who gained or remained stable, cognitively or interactionally, were rather similar, but students who lost according to each system were very different. (These differences are discussed in the next section, where findings for the two systems are compared.)

Stable students, who were unaffected by the interventions, were identified by their ego strategies and their friends as persons who took intellectual, ascendant, even self-righteous stances; during conflicts they remained essentially uninvolved. Their moral action scores were comparatively level during the five sessions. In other words, by reason of their personal adaptations, the stable students avoided the intrinsic risks of moral dialogue: self-exposure, possible personal loss, and betrayal.

Students who gained were identified by their ego strategies and their friends as persons who exposed themselves to conflict in ways that seemed sincere and straightforward to their friends. Their moral-action levels suggested that they were especially stressed in the later sessions. The students who gained apparently took the risks of dialogue, so their disturbing experiences were useful.

Finally, developmental gain was substantially predicted by the students' characteristic tendencies to cope in interacting with their friendship groups' social stress. This interaction also predicted the students' interactional and cognitive development, except within the subsample of led groups whose lesser degree of disturbance did not benefit members' development. Cognitive disequilibrium did not predict development.

Evaluation

The study of moral development had neither the scope nor depth of our investigations of moral action since the phenomenon of development itself is harder to study. For instance, it is reasonable to assume that the moral games represented fairly realistic opportunities for action, but whether these same five group experiences realistically represented the natural conditions of development is less certain. Whether a 15-hour experience in a research study can result in actual development is also not certain. Longitudinal study is a better way to proceed, but over long periods of time, influences other than those included in the research design impinge on development. Consequently the critically potentiating factors may still not be known. Furthermore, our studies focused only on the causes, not the form, of development. Because of these limitations, we do not now offer as comprehensive a formulation of how development occurs as we did for moral action.

Proposed Formulation

Developmental gain followed vivid, morally troubling experiences; it was not achieved if either the group and/or the individual failed to deal straightforwardly with the moral conflict. Two main strategies were used by students who did not benefit from the experiences. Either they became self-righteous, which separated them from their friends' difficulties and allowed them to avoid the risks of dialogue, or else they self-protectively and ingratiatingly submitted to group-think.

These two methods of evading moral conflict are certainly not uncommon. They imply that moral development cannot be generally facilitated by ordinary school instruction, like having a teacher direct a discussion of hypothetical dilemmas. Not only is the discussion of hypothetical dilemmas colorless and abstract, it is also a superficial experience. And the power allocations in authority-directed sessions relieve participants of real responsibility, and leave resolution to the achievement-oriented, verbally fluent, and aggressive members of the group.

We think, but cannot fully substantiate with present results, that social disequilibrium can be further analyzed. It is not simply generalized, undifferentiated stress. Moral stress has a specific pattern. 1. At the onset of a moral violation there is surprise, shock, and outrage, followed by mutual recrimination (see Packer, in press). 2. After some time, participants force one another to recognize that they themselves, as well as their well-liked and trusted friends, have not only violated morally, but their violations occurred all too easily and unthinkingly. 3. They are then in a state to learn that moral dialogue is a delicate exchange that requires care and sustenance if it is to be successful. Furthermore, they might then see that it is not just "morally weak" or immature people—criminals, the Nazis, strangers or the impoverished—who violate morally.

We suggest that the characteristic defenses of some people make it difficult for them to recognize moral problems as moral. Others recognize moral problems but then minimize their importance. Some groups, like the dominated groups, positively require and encourage these kinds of self-protections. Continuous experience with violations also desensitizes, as in the case of the so-called "good Germans" during the Nazi era who pleaded afterwards that they did not know what was happening and in any case, they were powerless to affect the course of events. In some ways their plea was correct. In this regard, our findings reiterate Hannah Arendt's (1977) analysis of the "banality of evil": It is not just crazy, different, or foreign people who can become morally oblivious and inured. Very bright, accomplished, well-functioning 19-year-old American university students sometimes evoked the same kinds of self-protections with similar but of course not frightening results. The "debriefing" discussion at the end of each session, which served to forgive the "sinners," helped participants recognize and accept their obliviousness and deceptions. We trust that the regressive effects of these experiences were either temporary or they resulted from diminished motivation. In any case, *the two critical conditions of development seem to be a person who can deal with conflict and group functioning that allows conflict to be directly and honestly addressed.*

Comparison of the Interactional and Cognitive Theories

Conceptual Similarities

Before comparing the cognitive and interactional theories, we need to reiterate one point. With the age groups studied, we never expected large, dramatic differences in the conditions that support moral action and development as these are defined in each theory. The larger differences between the systems should appear in samples of children. The two theories have five similarities:

1. Both are consistent with people's common assumption that all people make conscious, deliberate choices about how to resolve moral problems.
2. In consequence, both are consistent with people's common assumptions that all people are responsible for their moral choices and actions; that is, morality is based on willed consideration.

3. Both are consistent with people's common assumptions that their choices are guided by certain principles for the cognitive theory, or understandings that are shared with other people for the interactional theory.

4. Both are consistent with the common assumption that some moral choices are better than others and that decisions can be made that are good, better, best—and worse.

5. Both are consistent with common assumptions that children become increasingly able to make moral decisions as they grow older and that older people make better moral decisions than young children. (They are in clear disagreement about what develops and why older people's moral functioning is generally better.)

The levels of interactional morality also have some similarity to several stages in the older cognitive theory. However, the meanings of the interactional levels are redrawn to make them transactions, rather than capacities. And, of course, the continuum of interactional levels represent increasing quality rather than an invariant and irreversible sequence of stages.

Conceptual Differences

Beyond the five similarities, the two systems are unalike. The basis of the cognitive system's ancestry in certain very old value systems promulgated as ways humankind should live seems responsible for its having violated common sense in four fundamental ways. The interactional theory is an attempt to adhere to common sense in these same four aspects.

First, in the cognitive theory, emotion is thought to be irrelevant or sometimes a clear interference to making an effective moral choice. Common sense expects important moral choices to be accompanied by emotion. When people are not emotional about a moral issue, observers and protagonists often conclude the moral agent does not care how the issue is addressed or resolved.

Second, cognitive moral agents are expected to rise above the particularities of a situation to extract its similarities to universal situations so that the overriding principle, which will absolutely and logically resolve the dilemma, can be applied. In contrast, common sense is struck by the importance of particular extenuating circumstances that allow violators to be forgiven or to make reparations. Instead of rising above situations to discover the overriding rule, common sense seems bent on going deeper to discover the particular meanings and the costs of immediate situations. Transcendental moral abstractions seem rather to be the stock-in-trade of the elite—religious authorities, politicians, and scholars—and people generally endorse these abstractions since they provide reassurance that the basis of community life is moral.

Third, cognitive theory is so structured that adequate and self-chosen moral action and development (and therefore full responsibility) characterize only a handful of the elite who must first achieve the stage of formal logical operations to achieve then the principled morality of stages 5 and 6. People below these stages are thought to suffer the disability of incompleted capacity. But in accord with common sense, we expect that all adults make independent choices. Children are also thought to make choices, although they are more frequently forgiven for their mistakes. But as time goes on, they are increasingly held responsible. Moreover, informed by history and immediate experience, common sense often makes us suspicious of the elite's moral authenticity. Even wise leaders, like Ghandi and Martin Luther King, who spoke nonrhetorical, practical moral truths, come under our close and anxious scrutiny. We worry that they will turn out not to be what they publicly allowed themselves to seem to be.

Finally, higher stages of cognitive morality result from social (more accurately, economic) evolution. Thus the cognitivists expect to find very few morally principled people, nor have they found principled citizens in preindustrial societies. General opposition of anthropologists to the cognitive theory arises from this feature. Their observations of the morally sensitive interactions of some preindustrial peoples (Feurer-Haimendorf, 1967; Schweder, 1982) do not square with the cognitivists' conclusion.

Empirical Findings

Comparisons between the Effects of the Scoring Systems. When the distributions of the cognitive and interactional scores for the young adults and adolescents were compared, the interactional scores were generally higher and of greater range. Agreement was strongest within the range of lower scores but weakest for higher scores. Forty-eight percent of the young adults' interactional scores were one interval higher, compared to 11 percent for the cognitive scores (Chapter 6).

The two differences in the array of scores reflect a basic difference in the theories. According to the interactional theory, ordinary people are often morally effective (higher scores), and moral effectiveness varies in complex interaction between person and situation (greater range); in contrast, the cognitive theory assumes that only a few people are morally effective and that moral effectiveness remains at the same level across situations.

Second, some similarity between the two scoring systems was suggested by correlations between pairs of scores of .51 for interviews and .66 for session scores (Chapter 6).

Differences with Respect to Action.   When the effects of the two external factors of gaming versus discussing and led versus dominated contexts were analyzed alone, cognitive moral action seemed somewhat more responsive to situational factors (Chapter 9).

When characteristic and situationally evoked strategies were brought into parallel models for each system, four major differences were obtained (Chapter 10). (These were not due to unequal amounts of total explained variation, which were approximately the same for both systems.)

First, the main hypothesis that effective moral action is facilitated by coping and avoidance of defensiveness was more strongly affirmed for the interactional theory compared to the cognitive theory.

Second, the two ego processes that ran counter to the hypothesis—failure to cope and the use of defensiveness—contributed weakly and equally to higher scores in the interactional system. The disconfirming contributions to higher cognitive action scores were stronger and disproportionately weighted more toward the positive use of defensive strategies than the failure to cope.

Third, characteristic ego strategies explained more variation in interactional than in cognitive scores. This pattern was reversed for situationally contingent strategies. Variation in cognitive action scores was explained by a greater proportion of contingently evoked strategies than was the case for the interactional system.

Fourth, although the sessions varied in content, make-up and difficulty, certain ego strategies were used repeatedly, which suggested these processes were specific to moral problem solving. The pattern was stronger and clearer for interactional morality, and characteristic ego processes were more frequently involved for interactional morality. The six processes that fostered interactional morality were the coping strategies of intellectuality, empathy, and suppression and the avoidance of defensive isolation, intellectualizing, and displacement. Four such processes supported cognitive moral action: the coping strategy of logical analysis, the avoidance of both defensive displacement and isolation, but the positive use of the defensive strategy of reaction formation.

Finally, when the conditions that supported higher moral action scores in one system but lower scores in the other were directly compared, six additional findings were obtained (Chapter 11).

First, differences in performance between the two systems were not well explained for the women. Such differences as occurred were situational coping strategies which characterized women who had higher interactional scores. The reasons for the women's varying performance are not clear. (The distributions of difference scores for the two sexes were similar.) The implication seems to be that the women readily moved from one form of morality to the other. The men's differences were mostly for characteristic strategies, which implied that their high performance in one system, but not the other, was based on the kind of person they were in themselves.

Second, the hypothesis that coping and avoidance of defensiveness should facilitate quality moral action was strongly supported for interactional morality in contrast to cognitive morality (110 percent typifying higher interactional scores to 39 percent for higher cognitive scores).

Third, higher interactional scores were attained by members of led groups in five out of six significant contributions and, of course, the reverse held as well; higher cognitive scores were produced by members of dominated groups.

Fourth, the pattern of coping and avoiding defensiveness that fostered moral action strongly held for students whose interactional scores were higher than their cognitive scores.

Fifth, the processes that were repeatedly used by students with higher interactional scores included coping intellectuality, concentration, and defensive projection. Processes that were repeatedly used by students with higher cognitive scores were defensive intellectualizing, rationalization, and isolation; all of these are cognitive defenses.

Sixth, almost all the persistent interactional reasoners (who achieved higher interactional than cognitive scores in at least four sessions) were members of game groups, but persistent cognitive reasoners were about equally divided between game and discussion groups. *Therefore effective interactional functioning occurred more in the context of actual than hypothetical moral problems.* Persistent cognitive reasoners were more often members of dominated groups, while persistent interactional reasoners were almost equally divided between led and dominated groups, suggesting that higher cognitive functioning may have been an effective strategy in these stressed, hierarchical atmospheres.

In sum, although moral action in both systems is supported by essentially equal amounts of variation from nonmoral influences, certain qualitative and quantitative differences are clear. Effective moral action from the standpoint of the interactional system was more a function of the following. 1. a pattern of coping instead of defending; 2. characteristic ego processing; 3. membership in led groups and game groups; 4. a particular set of coping processes that involved free exploration of ideas (intellectuality), concern for others' positions and feelings (empathy), and awareness but careful regulation of feelings (suppression). Effective action from the interactional perspective was especially thwarted by compartmentalizing ideas and feelings (isolation), cognitive pretentiousness (intellectualizing), and taking anger and frustration out on others (displacement). When the systems were directly compared, several additional processes repeatedly resulted in higher interactional moral scores: coping concentration, intellectuality, and the positive use of defensive projection, the latter on the part of males.

Effective cognitive action was more a function of: 1. a lesser degree of coping adaptation and avoidance of defensive strategies; 2. contingently evoked ego processes; 3. membership in dominated groups; 4. a weaker and less clearly defined set of repeated ego processes that involved logical analysis, the defensive use of self-righteousness, and not taking anger and frustration out on others. In addition, when the systems were directly compared, all three cognitive defenses—intellectualizing, isolation, and rationalization—typified students with higher cognitive than interactional scores.

These differences imply that there are three conditions for effective moral action (from the interactional view). The interpersonal situation needs to be egalitarian. The moral problems need to be real rather than hypothetical. Finally, participants' ego processes need to include a liberated intellectuality, concern for others, and experienced but modulated feeling. Effective action was prevented by misplaced feelings and attempts to mute moral concern by distancing and intellectualized formulations.

In contrast, the conditions for effective cognitive moral action involved a dominated interpersonal situation, self-protection, distortion of cognitive process, and presentation of the self as morally right. When cognitive morality is applied in action situations, it seems to be in protection of one's moral being rather than a commitment to solve practical problems mutually.

Differences with Respect to Developmental Outcomes. Five major differences between the two systems' description of development were found.

1. More students gained in the interactional system than in the cognitive system, but more students remained stable in the cognitive system. Analysis of the young adults' absolute scores showed that the extent of gain from beginning to end was significant only for interactional morality.

2. When the students' developmental scores were constructed, relative to the entire sample, experiences of gaming resulted in more cognitive gain than did experiences of discussing. No comparable differences occurred for interactional morality.

3. Students with different interactional outcomes were primarily distinguished from one another by the kind of person they were in themselves—that is, by their characteristic ego strategies and their friends' evaluations before the sessions were begun. The opposite pattern held for students with different cognitive outcomes; their situationally contingent strategies and the changes in their friends' evaluations after the group experiences were more differentiating.

4. Students who changed (gained or lost) in the interactional system seemed to be open to experience. Students who were unaffected seemed closed. Being open or closed to experience did not clearly distinguish between students of different cognitive developmental outcomes.

5. The reasons for students' loss in moral level in the two systems seem quite different, although both groups of students were

characteristically repressive. Losers under the interactional system were characteristically defensive in self-effacing ways (doubting, denying, and repressing), but they were initially well liked. Their moral level dramatically dropped in sessions 3 and 4 when they were especially stressed. But at the last session they made a re-markable gain; possibly they were relieved that the experiences were almost over. Their loss seems due to their characteristic vac-illation and minimization of conflict.

Although repression was also a characteristic ego strategy for the losers under the cognitive system, they functioned comfortably and increased solidarity with their group but at the expense of accomplish-ing the tasks the staff had set before them. By the end of the inter-ventions, these losers had improved their standing with their friends.

Differences with Respect to Interview-based Scores. Finally, we take up the differences between the interview scores achieved under the two systems, which provided the bases for the developmental indices (Chapter 13).

1. Male students had higher cognitive scores than women on the first and third interviews; no sex differences were found for the interactional scores. Because no sex differences were found for any of the action scores, this finding suggests men are espe-cially advantaged in cognitive performance during interviews.

2. The main hypothesis that coping and avoiding defensiveness should support higher moral scores was again more strongly sup-ported for the interactional system than for the cognitive.

Conclusions. The conditions for interactional and cognitive devel-opment were more similar than the conditions supporting action, but there were important differences. Gain was more frequent under the interactional system and stability under the cognitive system. This pat-tern is consistent with the interactional system's greater degree of vari-ability. Here developmental gain is a difference in scores between points in time. Furthermore, cognitive gain needed stronger support from vivid, pressing experience, more so than interactional develop-ment, since experiences of gaming, but not discussing, facilitated cog-nitive development. Interactional development occurred irrespective of experience.

This conclusion gathered support in additional analyses. Students who achieved different cognitive outcomes differed in their strategies *during* the curricular interventions. In contrast, students with different interactional outcomes were more strongly distinguished one from another *before* the interventions were begun, which indicates that their development depended on the sort of persons they intrinsically were and whether they were open and responsive to experience or closed and unresponsive. Readiness or resistance to development did not clearly distinguish among students with different cognitive outcomes.

The Basic Relationship between the Two Theories

In this last evaluative consideration of the cognitive and interactional theories, four substantive points are taken up: moral and nonmoral influences on moral functioning, the problem of situational variability, morality as truth, and the causes of development in both theories.

Moral and Nonmoral Influences on Moral Functioning. The cognitivists' discourse about morality and the nonmoral often turns on a separation between psychology and philosophy (Kohlberg, 1970). Academicians' knowledge and labor are thereby divided: Philosophy defines what is moral, and psychology is to provide the hard evidence. The interactional formulation takes the more radical position that the division between psychology and philosophy is a false convention that arises from a latter-day Cartesian separation of thought and experience. Practical moral experience gives no heed to this convention: *When social-psychological knowledge is recognized as an invention of human beings, it becomes clear that neither psychology nor philosophy has privileged or special information. Problems of understanding the common basis of moral life are the same for both disciplines, so disciplinary boundaries are an impediment and they need to be disregarded.*

If this argument has worth, it fits our findings. Nonmoral influences were as important for understanding cognitive functioning as they were for understanding interactional. The regression models accounted for as much variation in cognitive as in the interactional scores. This could not be expected as an outcome from the cognitive position since its advocates assume that morality can be defined as pure thought. Clearly the cognitivists underestimate the necessity of taking the supposedly nonmoral aspects of people and situations into account if social scientists are to contribute understandings about the moral basis of life.

Kohlberg (1969, 1971) has written about "psychological" influences, but recognizing them is not the same as formally incorporating psychological effects into the theory proper, which would surely lead to refining or revising its basic propositions. No systematic research has been undertaken to ascertain how the so-called morally neutral influences affect moral activity. Instead, the nonmoral elements that are expected to relate to cognitive functioning have proliferated as various stage developments: role taking (Selman & Damon, 1975), social conventional (Turiel, 1983), personal (Nucci, 1977), epistemological (Broughton, 1978); sometimes Loevinger's (1976) stages of ego development are also mentioned in this regard. A human being may not be as divided into stages as these proposals imply. In any case, the interactional moral theory is a different proposal since it assumes that unitary experience, not cognition, is the meaningful feature of people's moral functioning. The interactional theory proposes explicit linkages and interactions between the explicitly moral and presumably nonmoral. Our findings strongly suggest that neither cognitive nor interactional moral functioning can be well described or explained unless nonmoral functioning is brought into the account.

Nevertheless, there can be no question the cognitive theory's advocacy of pure moral thought reflects one kind of moral truth. Its immediate acceptance by large numbers of developmental psychologists and laypersons means the formulation strikes a responsive chord; it is convincing. And Lawrence Kohlberg's contribution is to have shown how psychology can serve philosophy. But the still-debated question is: What special kind of contribution can social science make? See Haan (1982) for one point of view and rebuttals from Eichorn (1983), Leary (1983), Houts & Krasner (1983), and Waterman (1983), and Haan's 1983 reply.

At the same time, the cognitive theory has not been universally accepted, either by laypersons or academicians. Most criticisms concern the theory's narrow focus on the development of moral cognitive structures; people seem to have the idea that morality is more than just that. Academicians who have found the theory wanting have especially included anthropologists, for example, Schweder (1982), who questions the supposition that preindustrial peoples are morally primitive. Some sociologists and social psychologists, for example, Feldman (1980), cannot accept the neglect of social influences. Some philosophers find the stages simplistic and logically inconsistent, such as Locke (1980). Laypersons often disagree with the theory because it does not account for emotions, motivation, variability in action, and so forth. Since psychologists are more interested in the capacities of individual persons, they have, understandably, been more hospitable to this formulation.

Still, a sizable body of findings in support of the cognitive theory has been published in the literature of developmental psychology. Consequently, the question is, How can this array of results be accounted for? We suggest two reasons. First, it does reflect the conventional official rhetoric of morality; it certainly represents one way of thinking that is available in the culture, having long been proposed by the intellectually elite. Second, a clear gap seems to exist between the cognitive theory and its realization in the successive versions of its scoring system. Haan, Weiss, and Johnson (1982) made this observation:

> To construct a means of measuring morality that depends on classic, formal logic [here on unadulterated moral cognition] so it can seem morally plausible to subjects and colleagues is undoubtedly a very difficult task. Examination of past Kohlberg scoring systems, as well as the most recent one, does not clearly indicate just how logical deduction penetrates the moral scores. Everyday moral decisions . . . are seldom made according to the rules of bivalent, classical logic, that is, being wholly true or wholly false (p. 255).

The point is that the superstructure theory does not seem to appear in the practical infrastructure of the scoring system. Indeed, the latter better matches practical morality.

If the so-called nonmoral variables had not been available for analyses, we would not have learned much about either cognitive or interactional morality. The separation of moral and nonmoral influences does not, then, provide any concrete research advantage. People do not function in morally immaculate ways. Separating these influences may be an advantage in thinking conceptually about morality, but the hazard for scholars—as the current philosophical impasse well illustrates—is entrapment in one's own conveniences and denial of mind as action.

The Phenomenon of Variability in Moral Effectiveness. The interactional system handles another feature of everyday life, variations in people's moral effectiveness. From the interactional perspective, people achieve a modal level of moral skill, but function within a lower and upper limit. Variation is explained as a result of the interaction of situational and personal effects. According to past descriptions and recent elaborations (Kohlberg, et al., 1983), the cognitive theorists count more on consistency than variability, except for the qualification that higher-stage as well as B-substage people who decide that they are responsible are thought to be more consistent than their opposite counterparts.

Several specific propositions in the interactional system account for variation. First, different moral dilemmas call forth different levels of effective response. High-level morality may not be needed in simple moral situations that can be almost automatically resolved, nor is high-level morality necessarily activated when problems are not real or people lack the power of resolution—as we saw in the moderate levels achieved in most discussion sessions.

Second, the way people are in themselves affects their moral variability. When they are under stress, they may take one of two courses, depending on the situation, the intensity of their stress, and their particular characteristic ego resources. They may use their stress and moral outrage to do far better than they usually do; alternatively, when they are overwhelmed with stress, they may resort to defensive negation and distortion, and then do far worse than they usually do. These divergent adaptations are not simply expressions of individual levels of moral skill or development. As we saw, the shock in NeoPd of discovering that one's own self and one's friends were untrustworthy was painful for most students. But some became "heroes" by producing their highest moral scores in this same situation. In contrast, most students found the more intellectualized stress of Humanus an opportunity for doing better than they did on any other occasion. They were energized by its mild stress and the intellectual opportunities of working with their friends to construct a new society and grapple with the problems of surviving. This kind of variability is expected only in the interactional theory, but we suggest it frequently occurs in real life.

Actually cognitive performance was subject to situational variability. A persistent, but never spectacular, difference between the two systems was found throughout the action and developmental analyses: Cognitive functioning was more affected by situational contingencies—and this, despite the cognitivists' view that morality transcends circumstantial distraction. This trend was first noticed when the effects of gaming or discussing and membership in dominated or led groups were analyzed alone. Further evidence of this trend was provided by the different ratios of characteristic to situationally evoked ego strategies that were found for each system. A larger portion of contingently evoked ego strategies supported higher cognitive action scores while a greater portion of characteristic strategies supported higher interactional scores. Differences in the ego processes that repeatedly supported moral action in each system were also consistent with this conclusion. The strategies typifying interactional morality were coping and they generally made large contributions. The strategies typifying cognitive morality were more often defenses; these were fewer in number and weaker in contribution. Altogether these differences imply that enactment of cognitive morality is less predictable, since any ego strategy that seemed likely to handle the immediate situation was often brought into play.

Finally, when the cognitive-interactional difference scores were analyzed, all three defenses that are themselves cognitive in nature—isolation, intellectualizing, and rationalizing—were repeatedly used by students with higher cognitive than interactional scores. According to the model of ego functioning we use (Haan, 1977), people prefer to cope when they can; consequently defensiveness in well-functioning people—as these students were—can be regarded as an emergency reaction evoked in stressful circumstances. Also, members of dominated groups achieved higher cognitive scores, whereas members of led groups had higher interactional scores. Since independent evidence indicated that dominated environments were more demanding, hostile, and competitive, members of these groups may have needed to use the rhetoric of cognitive morality to protect their rectitude. Defensiveness is always evoked more adventitiously than coping.

All in all, cognitive moral activity was frequently associated with situational defensiveness, so this way of thinking seems not to be a practical, sincere way of acting morally. It seems, instead, to represent a special, self-righteous, sophisticated form of solving moral problems that reflects the intellectual rhetoric and received wisdom of Western culture. Kohlberg himself (1982) identifies this kind of reasoning with Western democracies, and people are thought to need a fair amount of education to move to higher stages (Rest, 1969). Fur-

thermore the cognitive thinker needs to protect the privacy of his or her own thought and judgment. But when people resort to privacy during a moral conflict, they are likely to be understood as avoiding commitment and even asserting moral superiority. The private thinker does not agree to being a negotiator among other negotiators.

Morality as Truth. Unlike several other theories proposed by psychologists, both the cognitive and interactional theories are openly based on grounds of moral value. In the cognitive system, justice is thought to be better achieved—more fully, differentiatedly, and integratively—by persons of high moral stage. In the interactional system, equalization of human relations is thought to be better achieved— more particularly, sensitively, and comprehensively—by persons whose circumstances and problem-solving skills allow them to attain high levels. Therefore it was hypothesized that moral functioning in *both* systems should be enhanced when people accurately perceive all relevant features of the problem, construct adaptations that accurately match the problem and its possibilities for resolutions, or even better, create resolutions with others that enhance people's relations. Although this hypothesis was drawn from the interactional view, it surely must also apply to cognitive moral functioning, since no one would argue that justice can be achieved on false bases. In fact, moral functioning in both systems was supported by the strategies of coping and avoiding defensiveness.

But a difference between the ego strategies that supported effective morality in each system became clear. For the moral action scores, the ratio of support to nonsupport for this hypothesis in the interactional system was almost ten to one, but in the cognitive system a little better than three to one. For the interview scores, the ratios were about three to one for the interactional scores and two to one for the cognitive scores. When the cognitive-interactional difference scores were analyzed, the ratio was about three to one in favor of students whose interactional scores were higher.

The strategic advantage of coping is that it offers possibilities to reconstruct and reorganize features of self and the situation. Its features of leading out and reaching out mesh with the requirements of successful interactional moral dialogue as well as with its future-oriented considerations that are also part of a moral balance. The reaching back and dependence on existing moral capacity to direct judgment, which is the cognitivists' vision of the moral agent's task, does not require social problem solving. The facts of moral issues are assumed, and moral agents must insulate themselves from the distractions of others' thoughts and feelings and even protect themselves from their own emotions. They must decide, individualistically, for themselves.

This consistent set of findings, which show that interactional functioning resulted in success by means of positive coping and negative defense more often than cognitive functioning did, is in agreement with each theory's basic position. And the results provide a basic distinction between the two theories' views of moral processing. From our point of view the interactional description better matches the cherished ideals that people commonly seem to hold about how morality should *function* in their lives.

Causes of Development. Cognitive disequilibrium did not predict development in either system, whereas the heated emotionality and stress of social disequilibrium did in both systems. Interactional development was more affected by the group sessions, whether gaming or discussing, but cognitive development was affected more by gaming than by discussing. The adolescents' development in both systems was facilitated by gaming. Thus, despite the two systems' differences, similar conditions for development were found. The potential for development seems to lie then more in openness to vivid moral experience than in a specific stage of logical competency and comparison with other people's reasoning of a higher stage.

A major difference between the systems' description of development was nevertheless found. At the outset of the curricular experiences, students who turned out to achieve the different interactional outcomes of gaining, losing, or being unaffected were distinctive as persons, whereas the students with different cognitive outcomes were not. During the sessions students with different cognitive outcomes acted markedly differently from one another, whereas the students of different interactional outcomes did not. Changes in cognitive morality may have represented temporary shifts in motivation due to participation in the project rather than development. Nevertheless, this pattern repeats a consistently found difference: the interactional system's affinity with the way people are in themselves and the cognitive system's affinity with the way people contingently act.

Moral Beginnings

Background Purposes

The exploration of the moral actions of very young children seemed necessary, given the following.

1. Our finding considerable variability in the qualities of the adolescents' and young adults' moral functioning, which immediately suggests that moral quality is not tightly linked with age.
2. The lack of evidence that logical development (Haan, et al., 1982) is a necessary precondition of moral development.
3. The positive evidence that social, not cognitive, disequilibrium fosters moral development.
4. The growing number of research reports that suggest very young children are more morally sensitive than previously thought.

Taken together these observations suggested to us that cognitive sophistication may not be a critical requirement for moral understanding. Instead, basic social interchange—with all the practical and emotional understandings this implies—seemed to be the necessary precondition for the development of moral concern.

Young children seem to have moral concerns and understandings that are reasonably equivalent to those of adolescents and adults. But they may frequently fail to demonstrate their understandings because they are easily stressed and can depend on adults to rule on rightness or wrongness. *If these statements are true, many theories would have to be revised since most assume that the core moral problem for society is how to overcome endemic selfishness. Instead, the core problem would become how social conditions and personal resources can be facilitated so people can enact the moral concerns that they already have.*

Major Findings

First, in the game NeoPd, equalizing solutions occurred in 75 percent of the four-year-old pairs, reparations in 60 percent of the pairs, but defaults in 65 percent and betrayal in 30 percent of the sessions. At the termination of the sessions, 60 percent of the four-year-old partners were still managing to cooperate with each other, compared to 80 percent of the members of the young adult friendship groups.

Second, in many ways the four-year-olds acted and reacted the same way as the adolescents and young adults; in other words, they had essentially *the same moral experience.* They coordinated benefits, stalemated, made reparations, defaulted, and betrayed. They became angry or sullen during stalemates, defaults, and betrayals. They palpably experienced the glow of good conscience when they achieved mutually acceptable solutions. (Some well-functioning members of led groups of young adults said they were "proud" of themselves during the post-game discussions.) They worked for their self-interests but changed course when they became aware of their partners' plight. But some children were also very inept—as were some university students and adolescents—in protecting even their legitimate self-interests. All age groups evoked defensive maneuvers to manage their anxiety and minimize defaults. When the four-year-olds confronted their dilemmas, they could not always articulate their moral positions with clarity or skill, but then neither did the students before their subgroups entered into formal negotiations in which they *talked about* what was happening rather than directly acting. The children kept close track of their partners' pennies, and the students kept close track of the other subgroup's points.

Third, differences between the four-year-olds and the other participants were also apparent. Obviously, the vocabulary of moral words the children possessed was less sophisticated; sometimes they acted morally—that is, fairly—but still commented on their actions in words that are moral only by inference, like "it's nice" or "it's not nice." At the same time, they freely used the word "fair," which in itself encompasses all manner of adult moral words like justice, equity, equality, and reciprocity. Also, the children's plans for future action usually took only the next trial into account although some children envisioned the riches both could receive, for instance, up to "nine pennies more" so they devised plans for how to play "'til we stop." The older participants sometimes calculated the considerable number of trials that would be needed for losers to catch up. These differences are in degree rather than in kind.

The preschoolers were more obviously different in their trustfulness and willingness to put up with being violated. However, the adult staff leaders' active involvement, compared to their detachment with the older game groups, may have led the children to the false assumption that the adult would set matters to rights in the end. After all, that is the usual role of pleasant adults when preschoolers are in moral conflict. In any event, the older participants were more overtly distrustful and usually more obviously angry about being violated.

Finally, we are aware that there were individual differences among these preschoolers in the level of their moral concern and especially in their ability to protect their legitimate self-interests. To determine if the possible influences were due to the child with whom each was paired or whether these are differences in character will take more time.

Evaluation

We must emphasize that only one situation and 40 children were the subject of our analysis. Nevertheless this situation was an excellent test since it was essentially the same one that the young adults and adolescents faced. Our simplification of the cognitive requirements for playing NeoPd avoided difficulties of some previous research, but more important, it also served to purify the task and make it more purely moral in nature.

The staff leaders' encouragement and subtle maneuvers to keep the partners working on their mutual problems, instead of emotionally or physically distancing themselves from the problem, were uncertain influences on the children's moral functioning. We think they served to reduce stress and buttress the children's own coping efforts without providing the children with proper answers.

Reformulation

If the results are affirmed by others and by our own future studies, they raise questions about what develops in moral development. It seems it is *not* basic moral concern since the four-year-olds *already* seemed to have basic understandings that they and others have legitimate self-interests, that all participants have the need and right to defend their interests, and that the obvious solution in social interaction is to equalize, if one is better off, or demand equal consideration if one is worse off. If these results are "true," then it seems that the moral impulse is learned, understood, and accepted very early in life. Development, more specifically, would seem then to occur in building a storehouse of past successful adaptations, greater real power in negotiation, and certainly sheer factual information about the way the world—its people, groups, and institutions—operate.

Family Background

Background Purposes

Our study as has been indicated elsewhere, explored the ways offsprings' moral activity might be affected by their families when families are regarded as morally functional entities. The moral dialectic within families—between the self and another and between the self and the family's common interest—was thought to be basically the same as the moral dialectic in all groups. From their intimate and prolonged experience with their families' methods of resolving moral conflicts, children must develop expectations about how moral problems can and should be addressed. We presumed, then, the young adults would bring these ideas into play when their friendship groups were in conflict. Still, these 19-year-olds were away from home for the first time and in a markedly different interpersonal situation, so they would need to establish new kinds of intimate relations and new ways to deal with conflict. Nevertheless, when peer conflict became intense and prolonged, we thought these young people might revert—as people often do—to old, familiar strategies. This contextualized view of the family's implications for offsprings' morality is consistent with the interactional theory, but not the cognitive theory since the latter system regards morality as a function of individual children's development of moral cognitive capacities, apart from context.

Major Findings

First, the four types of family background affected moral action levels in both systems but only in later sessions, presumably after the students were accustomed to being research subjects and after they abandoned their newly invented ways of acting with new friends. Students from cooperative families became the most ineffective in action and those from reserved families the most effective.

Second, students from competitive families were the least affected developmentally by the curricular experiences in both moral systems, while students from reserved families more often gained developmentally than all other students.

Third, the clearest differences associated with family background were in the ways that the students reacted to moral conflict, as shown in analyses of their ego strategies, group behavior, and friends' evaluations. The students from open families, who were characteristically coping, became defensive during the sessions as they most vigorously addressed the moral conflict. But their moral functioning and the evaluations of them by friends were essentially not affected by the group experiences. Students from cooperative families, who were characteristically defensive, became more coping during the sessions apparently choosing not to become involved with the moral issues or help their friends address the issues. Their gain was to improve their standing with friends. Students from competitive families were not distinctive in ego processing or in group behavior. They were morally impervious to the curricular experiences and were initially seen by their friends as inflexible. By the end of the sessions they had lost even more ground with their friends. The students from reserved families were not distinctive in their methods of conflict resolution; instead they were distinctive for their effectiveness in moral action and moral gain.

Evaluation

The young people of different backgrounds seem to have adapted to the moral experiences with their friends by four different accommodations. They acted as they had in familial conflict (open families). They worked to maintain interpersonal harmony at the expense of their moral effectiveness (cooperative families). They stonewalled both their peers and the moral tasks presented in the research design (competitive families). They used the experiences to grow morally without jeopardizing their relations with their peers (reserved families).

Despite its modest scope, this exploratory study produced a set of interesting results. The conceptualization of families as morally interacting groups seems promising. But to strengthen the design, all family members' views would have to be solicited. Direct assessments of how families solve conflict should be collected, and families with less-adequate functioning than was likely the case with the families studied here would have to be included.

Reformulation

Because the core idea that families interact as moral groups produced interesting information about their young members' moral functioning and ways of handling conflict, we continue to be interested in this approach. Morally effective action and growth appear to depend on the general ways that people approach and handle conflict in itself. The influence of family seems to be that it provides its members with a background formulation about the meaning of conflict, how it can and should be resolved, and how group life can be regulated and enhanced. Young people from different family backgrounds either addressed, diverted, stonewalled, or capitalized on conflict. This more comprehensive view of the conditions for moral functioning is consistent with the findings presented in other chapters concerned with moral action and development.

A second consideration, also drawn from the results, concerns the basic dialectic between self-interests of the child and other family members and with the family's common interest. Our data collection indirectly touched on this interchange, but the results suggest that careful, direct study would be worthwhile. The preservation of personal integrity was a fundamental and continuous interest to the students—as it is for all people—but for some young people it meant foregoing individual moral choices to preserve the group's interest; for others, preservation of self-interest took priority over concern for the friendship group's interest. The more-satisfactory solution would be coordination of these two demands. Direct and detailed study of these kinds of interactions seems promising.

Chapter 17

PRACTICAL MORALITY FOR PUBLIC POLICY, EDUCATION, AND MENTAL HEALTH

> We as scientists cannot reject a true formulation for its dis-
> tasteful political and moral implications. But before we accept
> it we are obliged to be certain that it is true (Norma Haan,
> Richard Weiss, & Vicky Johnson, 1982).

Cautions about Application

ALL SCIENTIFIC THEORIES about humans and their affairs start from practical understandings; but once constructed, they lead back again to provide practical recommendations about how life should be lived. Making recommendations seems especially attractive to moral theorists. Perhaps we have an irresistible urge to tell others how to live. Nonetheless, the current controversies among researchers surely imply that application of moral recommendations is premature. Analysis of different theories' implications for public policies is not. In fact, this can be an informative exercise, corrective for theorists and cautionary for citizens who are often unknowingly impressed with "scientifically based" claims. As we mentioned before, *Newsweek* (Woodward & Lord, 1976) reported more than 5000 school districts in this country were using moral curricula and materials based on Kohlberg's theory yet many disagree with this formulation.

In this chapter we will describe the policy implications of various moral theories and then suggest, more specifically, the practical ap-plications that these theories have for education and mental health. A good moral theory should uncover, describe, and explain the conditions of the practical morality that people *commonly use* and *endorse as ideal* at some level of their consciousness. The task of finding such a theory has only begun. Although there may be some debate about our analysis in this chapter, it is always instructive for both scientists and citizens to consider the real life implications of a theory, especially a moral theory.

Throughout this chapter, readers will want to keep in mind that our conclusions are based on *our* conceptualization and on only the three research projects. In this chapter we are entirely partisan in arguing for the interactional proposal. Although the interactional theory and our results have immediately apparent social implications, the designs of these projects are very different from those used by others so we cannot point to independently secured results that refute or replicate our own.

Difficulties of Discerning Covert Valuing

Social scientists have only recently acquired sufficient methodological expertise for their work to be of interest to policy makers. This interest has given social scientists opportunities to make recommendations that influence public life. But as social scientists ply their trade, moral value almost always underlies their work. When they make recommendations, unrecognized values, rather than research facts, can define public policy. Furthermore, the power of policy makers to compromise scientists by selectively granting funds, large consultancy fees, and so forth may be even more worrisome. We cite an example of how social scientists "influenced" decisions during the Vietnam war. Thus, Stuart Hampshire (1978, p. 5), an Oxford philosopher, wrote about the United States involvement in the Vietnam war:

An illusory image of rationality distorted the moral judgment of the American policy-makers. They thought that their opponents in the U.S.A. were sentimental and guided only by their unreflective emotions, while they, the policy-makers, were computing consequences with precision and objectivity, using quasi-quantitative methods. They ignored, and remained insensitive to, the full nature and quality of their acts in waging the war, and of the shame and odium attached to some particular acts. . . . Under the influence of bad social science, and the bad moral philosophy that goes with it, they over-simplified the moral issues and provided an example of false rationality.

It is repetitive to point out again that the concept of value is of consequence in most social science research, and more obviously in all investigations of practical morality. See chapters that bring out the implicit moral commitments underlying work in anthropology, economics, history, psychology, political science and sociology in Haan, Bellah, Rabinov, and Sullivan (1983). However, we press it here, first, to emphasize that moral evaluations unremittingly intrude on our ideas and activities, for we are evaluating creatures, without interruption. Also, we want to point out that social scientists frequently are not aware of their underlying moral assumptions, so they are free in recommending practical policies because they often think their work is morally neutral. But many of their practical recommendations are fundamentally moral by nature—for instance, how children should be educated to become effective citizens or how delinquents and criminals should be treated. Nevertheless, scientists are no more clear about their assumptions than are citizens at large.

As we have seen from our three projects, it is difficult for people to talk directly and explicitly about moral problems even when they know each other, and moral issues seldom draw careful, sincere public discussion; instead public and private moral injunctions are more often offered in condemnatory, dogmatic, or provincial ways.

For instance, the Moral Majority advertises the rightness of its brand of morality while other citizens' bumper-strips counter, "The Moral Majority is Neither." These kinds of moral meanings are not the sort that social scientists either can or should use in their investigations. Bronowski (1965) has said, "Truth is the drive at the center of science; it [science] must have the habit of truth, not as a dogma but as a process" (p. 60). He refers to the scientific ethic which enjoins scientists to evenhanded evaluation of all evidence, meaning here that social scientists must search for the morality that is *both* fair and endorsed by all sectors of society. Needless to say, the identity of this morality is not now known—if, in fact, such a morality actually exists. But social scientists' task is to discover if it does. To state a truism, moralities based on parochial or idiosyncratic moral choices will not be endorsed by all people, since such choices would give the prime advantage of moral superiority to certain groups of people over others. This is one reason why some people have rejected the cognitive theory. Research findings based on this theory often give the advantage of moral superiority to the well educated, to men, and to citizens of industrialized societies. Yet many well-educated male citizens of industrialized societies do not find the cognitivists' results convincing.

We fantasize an impossible shortcut to discovering what if any common moral understanding exists. If all persons could be engaged in a thoughtful, sincere, exhaustive discussion to uncover the moral understandings that they think ideally should direct all moral actions, the nature of practical morality could be found out. Social scientists could then move on to discover the conditions that support or thwart this morality. Since a universal discussion is wildly impractical, we can only attempt to discover the approximate nature of this morality by observation, taking one step at a time. Quine (1969) credits Otto Neurath with having observed that our only course is to rebuild our raft, plank by plank, while we are still at sea.

Furthermore, people are generally not very articulate about the morality that they cherish (but do not consistently enact). This may be due to habit, doubt about the critical facts and features that constitute a moral issue, or anxiety about the worth of their own self-interest. Psychologically, practical moral functioning is more an embedded emotional experience than an abstraction that can be objectively inspected. Nevertheless, across the centuries, authoritative post-Socratic philosophers and Judeo-Christian scholars have led humanity to expect that moral truths are revealed rather than achieved and reachieved by living people. Theologians have interpreted biblical meanings so as to provide the "official," received moralities, as did most post-Socratic philosophers; meanwhile ordinary people went on generating morality within the contexts of their everyday lives. Across the centuries, tension and unbearable contradictions between official and practical moralities have occurred and resulted in social and civil disturbance, sometimes in revolution and social change.

In recent years, however, there has been increasing awareness of the gulf between official and practical moralities. Moral philosophers focus more and more on psychology which studies people the way people are, as Hampshire (1978) and Anscombe (1969) suggest. At the same time, contemporary liberation theologians naturalize morality in their reinterpretations of the Bible. Gutierrez (1973, p. 18), a liberation theologian, has written, "Knowledge is not the conformity

of the mind to the given, but an immersion in the process of transformation and construction of a new world." See, also, Segundo
(1976). Still, this morality we construct to live by is not easily articulated, and furthermore, tradition and habit have behooved us to wait
to hear what intellectually and theologically wise people have to say.
The difficulty is that these official spokesmen have generally been
intent on protecting "morality from the uncertainties of context and
history" (Shields, 1983).

We reiterated the two points that the nature of common morality
is not yet now identified and that moral choice underlies almost all
social-psychological knowledge. (We stressed the latter so as to encourage readers to take a critical attitude toward the recommendations
of social scientists.) But we want to expand those two points: Although
proposals for society's improvement are commonly assumed to be matters of political or ideological preference, *at root* all such programs rest
on particular and often local moral choices. For a political scientist's,
historian's, and sociologist's view on this point, see Narr (1983),
de Certeau (1983), and Flacks (1983). Ideologies are the outgrowth
of people's assessments of society, but ideologies also reflect moral
presuppositions about how societies *should* live.

In practical life, moral assumptions are usually assumed and enacted, but unexamined. They operate outside of awareness and are
therefore above criticism. Consequently, moral choice, disguised as
fact, easily enters theories. As a result, politicians, rather properly,
and scholars, improperly, make recommendations for public policy
from their own constituencies' point of view. Politicians' constituencies
are reasonably confined, but the scientific ethic requires that all humanity must be the scholars' constituency. But for those social scientists who propose an explicit moral theory this requirement has double
force. First, their moral proposal must be fair to all humanity. Second,
they must deal with the root problem of all social science—what value
or values *should* be the ground of the moral theory. Social scientists
have yet to address this problem in any concerted or systematic way,
so they sometimes make recommendations that they surely do not and
would not follow in their own personal lives or, applying the ultimate
test of acceptability to humans, want their children to experience.

A real difficulty for scholars who construct a theory is that the work
in itself is beguiling. Since theories are stated in depersonalized language, their authors' tie to the correction of common sense is easily

cut. The compartmentalization of personal understanding and abstraction—with the result called "vicious abstractionism" by John Dewey (1948)—is an occupational hazard of academics. But it comes from a very old, honest lineage, dating from scholars' constructions after the convergence of the Judeo-Christian and Platonic traditions that discredited the earlier "naturalistic" philosophers of morality. See Havelock (1957) and Segundo (1976). Historically, this abstractionism worked to establish hierarchies of presumed moral capacity, the moral elite being people who talked in abstractions and the moral populace being people who talked in practicalities. This hierarchy of moral worthiness exists even today. The burden for individual and social improvement in morality is still placed on persons who are regarded as morally weak, however debilitating their social circumstances. This is evident in the disproportionately greater penalties for blue collar compared to white collar crime. Of course, the social circumstances of the scholars are almost always better. The academic exercise of promulgating abstract moralisms makes it difficult to recognize the practical moral commitments that occur in everyday life, so official policies are usually constructed from the elite's abstractions. For example, a court may order treatment to improve a ghetto-delinquent's morality. Havelock (1957) notes a consequence: "From these semantic manipulations, there derived in long descent, our later notions of virtuous charity [from the advantaged] and its proper reward of humble gratitude [from the populace]" (p. 399). Plainly the disadvantaged have much to gain from moral improvement, while the advantaged always stand to lose.

The Practical Program of the Cognitive Theory

Some moral theories—like the cognitive—were formulated within this tradition of abstractionism, since they focus almost solely on the logical-moral capacities of the individual. Not surprisingly, the moral character of the adult populace turns out, on empirical investigation, not to be morally principled but rather to depend on convention. This absorption in the different moral capacities of individual persons logically leads to only one program for improving society's moral level: Develop the moral character of ordinary citizens, one at a time. Now it is true that Kohlberg has written about contexts; he has made known his allegiance to just schools and prisons and the U.S. Constitution. But it is important to realize that these contextual considerations are outside the theory proper which is aimed exclusively at the improvement of the individual citizen. It was, accordingly, the basis of Kohlberg's prison program (Kohlberg, Hickey, & Scharf, 1972) which was planned to improve the moral reasoning of women prisoners—mostly black prostitutes—and thereby prevent their recidivism. Since this program threatened no societal arrangements that make prostitution an all but necessary recourse for some women in dire and impossible social circumstances, it probably disturbed neither politicians nor prison officials. The authorities apparently regarded the research as a harmless form of controlling and diverting the prisoners (Feldman, 1980).

Since moral weakness is manifested in an individual by low stage of development, and specific programs are recommended to strengthen individual character, the theory's recommendations for society are clear. It is an optimistic plan for improving society that reflects confidence that industrialized democracies, notably America, are basically sound in their moral operation, and only benevolent, supportive measures need to be undertaken. In his paper, "The Future of Liberalism as the Dominant Ideology of the West," Kohlberg (1980) stated, "The American constitutional system is a Stage 5 social system" (p. 64). However, he noted that the majority of Americans themselves, and sometimes their leaders, are only morally conventional. It will be recalled that only about 5 percent of the population reach Stage 5 (Kohlberg, 1981, p. 88). Specific, minor faults can be admitted (schools should be run more democratically), but the machinery itself is assumed to be right and needs only to be reformed into "the more morally principled terms of Stage 6" (p. 66). Less sophisticated people at a lower moral stage are not expected to understand formulations that are made at a higher stage. Kohlberg states if a child's society "is the only one he knows, there is no basis in experience for post conventional or principled thinking" (p. 61). Therefore the worldly must provide the direction as well as benevolence, as the ideology of the welfare state has dictated.

But people want honest participation in the moral exchanges of their society; they want what is legitimately theirs—for example, real jobs, not charity. From the interactional perspective, altruistic gifts set up a dynamic of obligation and degradation for receivers and enhanced moral superiority for those sufficiently advantaged to give.

The cognitivists write that the working class's lower stage of moral development reflects "differential participation in and identification with the society and its secondary institutions" (Colby et al., in press, p. 70). Since no greater sociological concern enriches their account, this conclusion has the effect—even though it was probably not its proponents' conscious intent—of contending that competent, energetic working-class persons could—if they only would—participate and identify with society.

These kinds of social recommendation fail to question whether in reality the poor *can* participate, given available means and the reality of their existing conditions, or even more important, whether they *would want* to participate and identify with those who already exclude them. Overlooked are the intelligent evaluations that the poor make of their own situation and whether or not they feel obligated to commit themselves to a dialogue in good faith with those who have already shown they will not reciprocate. The disadvantaged are widely and vaguely thought to be naïvely nonselective and eager to enter the same society, unaltered in form, that has already regarded them as nonpersons, that is, essentially excommunicated them as moral beings. These criticisms aside, the cognitivists directly offer a seemingly solid reason for why it is futile for the disadvantaged to participate. Since the poor are at lower stages of moral reasoning, they are not fully developed and are therefore thought *not* able to understand morally principled reasoning, even if they should hear such reasoning (Turiel, 1966)—although they may like the way such reasoning sounds.

Our research results raise serious questions about the match of the cognitive theory to human functioning and possibility. We found that people's moral effectiveness fluctuates with the stress of immediate social contexts. The idea of unchanging moral character that is revealed at the same stage in all situations was not supported.

The Practical Program of the Social-Learning Theory

An opposite set of recommendations logically follows from the social-learning theory. Here all responsibility for moral improvement would depend on the consistency and clarity of the moral-learning experiences that adults offer to children, and societies offer to citizens. Since these theorists attempt to remain neutral concerning values, they are not inclined to propose criteria for effective morality, either for individual persons or for societies. Although this reluctance is under-standable from their scientific stance, the theory logically, but very likely inadvertently, leads to the conclusion that citizens and children should be socialized to adjust to the status quo. Only clarity and con-sistency in learning experiences can be recommended—whether these lessons are presented by an authentically moral or immoral society. Like the cognitivists then—but for a very different reason—the pro-gram that follows from the social-learning theory would not signifi-cantly remediate, reform, or topple *existing* social immoralities.

Two practical social problems are raised by the social-learning the-ory. The first came to the fore in the writings of B. F. Skinner, who departed from the position of value neutrality in his books, *Walden II* (1948) and *Beyond Freedom and Dignity* (1971). Using his scientific the-ory as a guide, Skinner describes the ideal society. However, we hasten to point out that an ideal society cannot be described without moral suppositions. If all social behavior—morality included—is learned control and nothing more, an uncertainty arises as to who directs the learning that is to result in control. As Paul Meehl (1975) observed, the behavior modifiers have yet to address the fundamental question of the Skinnerian system: Who controls the behavior controllers? When the social learning is applied to society, any answer to this ques-tion concerns which morality should be the guide.

The second problem concerns changes in morality from one gen-eration to another. Maccoby (1968) observed that "the social-learning theorists have tended to think of the socialization process as one of moral replacement—a process in which each new generation must acquire the values and conform to the behavioral standards laid down by the preceding generation" (p. 263). Moral replacement between generations can only result in affirmation of the status quo. Since this theory is also concerned only with the learning of moral content, it is not clear how new generations are to solve moral problems new in history.

The Practical Program of the Interactional Theory

The interactional theory's emphasis on context and action imme-diately leads to social programs. Enacted moral effectiveness does not depend solely on people's skill in resolving conflict; the nature of situations in which people find themselves is equally influential. People may attempt to change their contexts, but they cannot always be successful. Alternatively they may redefine the meaning of their context. A prime example is the concentration camp inmates' redefinition of their moral commitments. Although Bettelheim and Janowitz (1964) and Frankl (1962) first described widespread moral regression among Holocaust victims, later evidence suggests that these men unwittingly framed their observations and conclusions to accord with the predictions of psychoanalysis. More recent and well-documented eye-witness accounts (Des Pres, 1975) suggest the contrary. After recovering from their initial shock, the inmates set up sensitive moral systems among themselves, but their commitments to good faith intelligently did not include their captors. People are not required to commit themselves to the risks of moral dialogue with protagonists who persistently demonstrate that they have no intention of sincerely entering dialogue.

According to the interactional theory, recommendations for improving citizens' moral effectiveness cannot be separated from recommendations for improving society's moral effectiveness. Three features of the interactional theory make this linkage necessary: its contextualization of morality, its use of dialogue as the means to achieve resolution, and its identification of morally effective procedures for equalizing relationships. First, contexts work to support (or thwart) dialogue; second, dialogues can only be fully moral if all participants are able to speak their minds, if none dominates, and each can veto. Third, moral balances are achieved only when the relevant needs and contributions of all participants are taken into account and considered in relation to immediate social circumstances.

Since this theory is an attempt to model social-psychological life—and not conventional or historical truths—it avoids some of the "vicious" results of moral abstractionism. For instance, *perfect* solutions derived from absolute guidelines or certain grounds, provided by biology, logic, or biblical injunction, are not necessarily the ideal end point. Extenuating detail and human feeling must be taken into account so balances are regarded as reasonable when they are compromises or become equalized over time when one partner later rectifies his or her earlier advantage.

Effects of Social Contexts

Certain kinds of social circumstances facilitate self-exposing dialogue. Our results showed that equable contexts, represented by the led game groups who usually followed the rules of moral processing, *consistently* fostered more effective moral action than did the dominated groups who usually violated these rules. Furthermore, when differences between cognitive and interactional scores were compared, led groups usually achieved higher interactional than cognitive scores, while dominated groups achieved higher cognitive scores. In real life, these ideal moral processes are frequently deformed so fully moral outcomes are not then realized. Consequently, the theory leads to the recommendation that public policy makers need to be continuously sensitive to the conditions that thwart effective moral action and be ready to take positive action to ensure conditions that facilitate dialogue. In this regard, interactional theory is a radical departure from almost all older moral theories, whether these are based on psychology, philosophy, or theology.

In the interactional theory, moral default, miscarriage of justice, or sin are not fundamentally due to an innate human selfishness. Since morality is a human construction, the very young can hardly be born either naturally moral or immoral; instead, they must be seen as born ignorant of morality. Nor does our study of four-year-olds suggest that the very young are without moral concern due to cognitive limitation (unless one thinks morality is only, or primarily, cognition). Nor is the theory based on the assumption that moral worth typifies only the elite who have proposed the conventions that have been used to define morality throughout Western history.

Legitimacy of Self-interest

Control of selfishness is the obsessive concern of most theorists, otherwise as disparate as social-learning theorists, who view society's moral task as civilizing the self-serving child, or John Rawls, who makes elaborate provisions for preventing people from knowing how they might gain future advantage, or Lawrence Kohlberg who supposes that children are initially egoistic.

According to the interactional perspective, society's need to control selfishness is matched by its need to facilitate and tolerate citizens' pursuit of their legitimate self-interests. In fact, on logical grounds, the theory would fail as a description and explanation of morality if pursuit of self-interest were not allowed. Dialogues would not work and equalized balances could not be achieved. Its very sensibility and workability depend on whether people, by their very nature, are willing and able to pursue their self-interests. (Their social experiences account for their willingness to submit their self-interests to dialogues that will determine the legitimacy or illegitimacy of their claims.)

Of course in real life, some people are unwilling or unable to pursue their self interest (like the interactional losers). But according to the theory, it would be better if they did. When they do not, it makes for short- and long-term trouble in psychological-moral life. But these are adjustments that disadvantaged people sometimes have to make for emotional and economic reasons and not the adjustments that they believe are right and moral. Philosophers have argued over the problem of the "happy slave," the person who willingly takes less (or it could be the masochist in partnership with the sadist). From the psychologist's perspective this is no problem; clinicians are well acquainted with people who candidly settle for less in their lifetime. Their views of the ideal moral life become clear in their hopes for their children. We need only to remember the incredible courage and stark poverty of first-generation immigrants to the United States who lived as they did for the sake of their children's future, or the older slaves who felt that they could not leave the plantations after the Emancipation for economic reasons but made every sacrifice so their children could strike out on their own.

Moral theorists have generally been preoccupied with sin—backlighted by the illusion of moral perfection, and the implicit supposition that the well educated have privileged information about rightness. As a result the power of personal amity and social enhancement in moral life has been underestimated. Segundo (1976), a contemporary liberation theologist, makes the point that the tendency of the theologians to attribute to the Divine all efficacious movement toward perfecting society denies humanity its motivation and its possibilities for doing good. This argument is not new in Christian theology, but contemporary liberation theologians make it a central concern. Similarly, we argue that few people are morally weak by nature and that people's wish to be moral is compelling and omnipresent.

Understanding Moral Violation

From the interactional perspective, moral violation is more frequently due, first, to social arrangements that prevent people from engaging in equalizing dialogue, and second to people's guilt about protecting even the most legitimate of their self-interests. Psychologically, the historic attitude that people are sinners or saints may in itself diminish moral skill. People are anxious about their classification and therefore tentative and guilty about pressing even their legitimate interests to the point of being unable to insist that their societies be morally rearranged. This is undoubtedly the basis of self-hatred in disadvantaged groups. See Havelock (1957) for a similar view and also Segundo (1976) with regard to liberation theology.

Moral violation is an empirical fact of life and always will be, given the inevitable dialectic between one's own and the other's interests, and the self's and the common interest. But even if the moral linchpin for public policy is not to be the curtailment of individual selfishness, moral violation must still be understood and recommendations made for its alleviation. Moral violation occurs mainly for two reasons: Either truth-seeking dialogues do not take place or they are aborted in anger. Otherwise, dialogues occur but agreements are falsely compromised by knowing or unknowing deception.

We consider the absence or abortion of dialogue first. This description of a common occurrence in a Chicago black ghetto was told by a person who had grown up there. A coal train ran through the ghetto and the teenage boys' task was to board the train and throw off coal; younger boys ran behind and put the coal in gunny sacks. When the boys took the coal to their homes, it was divided up among their families' bins. Understandably the ghetto residents did not believe that removing the coal from the train was stealing. The bitterly cold Chicago winters left them with no alternative, so their moral choice for their families was clear. But for a neighbor to take the coal after it was in the bins did constitute stealing. Clearly moral conflicts have different moral meanings to the involved parties—here to the ghetto residents and to the train and coal operators and advantaged society in general. Protagonists have varying amounts and kinds of information as well as different practical options. The advantaged almost always have less information about the disadvantaged's situation than the disadvantaged have about the advantaged's. The impoverished closely study their "betters." The powerful often take the same morally oblivious attitude, as Marie Antoinette supposedly did when she commented, "Let them eat cake."

People like to regard themselves as moral, but sometimes social conditions make less than ideal decisions necessary for both the advantaged and the disadvantaged. Whatever the case, the actual occurrence of moral violation does not necessarily lead to the conclusion that the advantaged or the disadvantaged are always or wholly weak morally. We may think in this categorical way because our moral history leads us only to make condemnatory judgments.

Citizens who betray have usually been betrayed themselves, so they are typically selective in their moral commitments. As Moshe Blatt (1970), a former student and later colleague of Kohlberg's, reported in his dissertation, black ghetto boys produced higher stages of cognitive morality for interpersonal dilemmas than they did for dilemmas that concerned social institutions. Blatt's subjects probably had very few experiences that convinced them that moral commitment to social institutions was intelligent, so understandably they were intelligently selective in their moral commitments.

The Moral Power of the Powerless

Some people, for instance classical Marxists, will contend that parties who hold all the power and who betray in their own way—like the coal company owners, society's officials, and advantaged citizens—will never relinquish their advantage, even if they should enter moral dialogue and acquire complete and convincing information about the disadvantaged's situation. In other words, it's the same old argument, but now made against the advantaged. People are innately selfish and power driven, and it is naïve to think that people give up advantage without being coerced. See Miller (1975) for an argument along this line. History, nevertheless, reveals that the advantaged can relinquish power but hold it tightly as well. Social circumstances and the roles that protagonists take determine outcomes, not the innate characteristics of people.

Whatever the case, although powerless people obviously lack power, they do have a moral advantage in dialogue that they can lose if they themselves resort to gross violation rather than persuasion. But for any moral claim to be considered, it must be known. Powerful people often lack not just factual information but, more important, emotionally convincing information about the situation of the disadvantaged. Emotionally convincing testimony that retains moral power underlies nonviolent strategies as practiced for instance, by Ghandi and Martin Luther King.

The advantaged have historically been provided with a justification for avoiding dialogue with the poor. Since the powerless have continuously been classified as morally weak, dialogue with them is thought to be neither required nor worthwhile. So the advantaged typically alleviate their guilt by benevolence, but this strategy has three results. First, the disadvantaged are maneuvered into the role of recipient instead of participant. Second, the advantaged hold themselves at a distance, thereby assuaging their malaise with rightness of their gifts. Third, they are relieved from the risks and self-exposure of authentic dialogue. Since the elite's moral answers are already at hand, they have no need to become one participant among others.

The tendency for advantaged people to distance themselves from the disadvantaged and regard themselves as "right" was seen in the adolescent project during the simulations of Humanus. When the question arose as to whether to let a possibly contaminated survivor enter the friendship group's safe area (presumably after a nuclear disaster), all white friendship groups decided to keep the survivor out, while all black groups decided to let him in. The bases for their different decisions were clear. The black adolescents correctly observed that no information had been given as to whether or not they themselves were contaminated. Because both they and the survivor were alive, they had to let him enter. They observed that one has to take risks, and life is always a risk. In contrast, the white adolescents maintained distance between themselves and the survivor. They talked abstractly about their responsibility to "continue the human race" and deduced that if they let the survivor enter their safe area, they would surely become contaminated and thus unable to fulfill their responsibility. This reference to their necessity to reproduce often resulted in good-natured teasing and embarrassment in these mixed-sex groups, but the basis for their sense of responsibility to the abstract idea of the human race was not clear. They never considered the possibility that they were contaminated as the black adolescents had. (We must add that most white adolescents agonized about their decision.)

Knowing Deception

We turn now to the second psychological cause for moral violation, deception in dialogue. Although interactional morality makes social conditions critical, people are, nevertheless, active agents who can choose their commitments and actions, and they can deceive others and themselves both knowingly and unknowingly.

In philosophers' terms, knowing deceivers are "freeloaders." Similarly, psychologists label those who knowingly deceive by a term of bad mental health: "psychopath." This easy relegation of people to categories does not increase our understanding of morality or moral violation. The philosophers' closure on the question of violation probably follows from their interest in constructing moral theories that solve moral problems comprehensively and logically. Consequently, persons who do otherwise are exceptions. Psychologists' classification of knowing violators is equally simplistic, yet they are in a better position to understand selective moral commitment. Honor among thieves and juvenile delinquents is well known.

From the interactional perspective, no one is totally uncommitted to moral interdependency, so the selectivity of "freeloaders" and "psychopaths" should also be understood, not simply condemned. Most knowing deceivers justify their acts. When they do not, they frequently yearn to prove their morality, backhandedly, by pleading for punishment, even execution, as Gary Gilmore did in the Utah State Prison. Before Gilmore was finally executed in 1977 for homicide, he answered a letter from an eleven-year-old girl who asked why he wanted to die: "I'm not a nice person. I don't want to cause any more harm. I've harmed too many people." (*Time,* 1977 January 31, p. 48.)

Unconscious deception and the moral issues it raises are at the center of the current debate as to where the line should be drawn between responsibility for a violation and the legal defense of not guilty by reason of insanity. Because human minds are convoluted and inventive, a clear distinction probably cannot be made between conscious and unconscious intent—except in extreme cases. Thus, in our studies we observed many instances of defensive problem solving that probably included both willed and unwitting deception of both self and others. But from the interactional perspective, either self-deception or the deception of others is not always the hallmark of poor mental health or even freeloading. It is a frequent and needed refuge for otherwise well-functioning people who face moral crisis.

Nevertheless, deception in moral dialogue may be more common than is thought because conventional pressures, based on the polarization of saint and sinner, make admission of guilt intolerable. In fact, people's estimations of others' strength and respectibility are frequently diminished when mistakes are too readily admitted. Jimmy Carter's not infrequent admissions of wronging even on the level of fantasy seemed to upset the media and public alike—for instance, when he acknowledged that he had "lusted," but only in his heart. Conventional education and developmental theorists place a heavy burden on growing children always to be right, so admission of wrongdoing is difficult and therefore the righting of wrongs impossible. More detailed analyses of these processes are given in the last section of this chapter which concerns mental health.

Conclusions

Interactional morality defines the conditions that foster society's and individual persons' moral effectiveness. On occasion all people violate. Moral default does not always occur by reason of inner weakness, nor does it result from society's inconsistent or uncertain socialization. Some kinds of social conditions make citizens' moral violation highly likely. In fact, some conditions give citizens no other alternative.

At the same time, we need a program of participation (not charity or welfare) based on the admission that societies are less than morally effective and that societies need fundamental social and moral reorganization. From the standpoint of interactional theory, the society in which participation and dialogue is possible is the epitome of moral social conditions. This is not the society of just conditions, benevolently provided or inherited. The means of participation are as critical as the ends in equalizing relationship, so each generation must engage in dialogue to work out its own conclusions.

Research-based programs for improving social morality need careful consideration by scientists and citizens alike. A moral theory can hardly be valid—that is, represent the common morality that is fair to all—if it places the onus of moral inferiority on some segments of the population and awards the rank of moral superiority to others. If social scientists are to make any recommendations for public policy, they already have the skills to begin considering not just ideology but the morality of social conditions, and not just the morality of individual people, but the social conditions that thwart or support individual moral action and growth.

Implications for the Education of the Young

If the results of our studies eventually are duplicated and so confirmed, they will suggest that moral development is best facilitated by children's having real, emotional experiences in solving the moral problems that they actually have the power and responsibility to resolve. Full moral engagement cannot occur when adults take all responsibility and confront the young only with hypothetical moral problems. Children care about violation but their powerlessness puts them in the same position as adults who care about moral violations in all parts of the world but who can do little. For humans to become fully engaged they need some assurance that they can affect outcomes. So intelligent selectivity is necessary; if selectivity in moral caringness is condemned the absurd result, as Baier (1958) commented, is that we would all be guilty whenever we relax. Misreading moral requirements, some student activists worked day and night during the 1960s for their cause to the point of mental and physical exhaustion. They suffered, their cause suffered, and their fellow activists had to care for them.

This dynamic of unequal power is inherent in parent-child relations. In our research it appeared in the teacher-directed discussions and was sometimes hinted at by the four-year olds. The discussion students simply did not need to take the kind of responsibility that might have stimulated their moral growth and understandably some four-year-olds with similar intent wished their mothers were present to take over responsibility. After all, it is sensible and efficient to relinquish responsibility to authorities who will in the end rule on rightness or wrongness.

If children are to grow morally, they need especially to take the possibility of moral violation back into themselves. This means tolerating their own guilt without evoking defensive strategies. When people must defend themselves against the possibility that they have violated, they often project and conclude that the other fellow was responsible. The results showed that the students who were developmentally unaffected by the curricular experiences typically assumed a stance of self-righteousness; either they did not enter dialogue, or if they did, did not continue even though they were physically present. The students who regressed as a result of the group experiences were also defensive but in self-effacing, uncertain and vulnerable ways suggesting their anxiety was so great that they surrendered their right to moral choice.

We have argued repeatedly that real moral problems are always stressful to some degree. Our results consistently suggested that children and people need both personal strategies and social support for dealing with conflict and stress in order to address, rather than avoid and negate, moral issues. Emotional, conflictual, and stressful moral encounters fostered development, but *only* when the group and student were able to cope with these difficulties.

As pointed out earlier, another main reason why people default morally is that historically all protection of self-interests, however legitimate they might be, has been surrounded with guilt. Considerable research effort is currently concerned with the development of children's prosocial and altruistic behavior; its ultimate educational goal is to determine how children can be helped to think of others. But little attention is given to how children can learn to protect their legitimate self-interests. An interesting exception is the recent endeavor to provide small children with the moral basis for fending off sexual abuse. "It's your body and it's not fair for a grown-up to touch it if you don't want them to." Or, "If you feel it's wrong, you're right."

An insight of modern psychiatry and clinical psychology is that people have difficulty giving to others unless others give to them. Consequently, when people are pressured only to think of others, they must of necessity bootleg their self-interests. Of course, parents have the same problem with their own self-interests because they especially are enjoined to be selfless. Covert moral agenda make for convoluted family dialogues that are frequently the point of ironic Jewish humor. A mama asks her small son to take the garbage out and the boy sullenly says, "No." Papa roars, "How dare you disobey your mother? Are you any better than your father?" (adapted from Spalding, 1976, p. 391.)

The interactional proposal leads then to practical proposals for the education of children. The findings of our studies suggest the following guidelines for moral development:

1. *Children need to argue with one another without adult control but with responsibility for the outcomes and with occasional adult guidance. Children, especially small children, need adult guidance because they are easily stressed and typically abandon dialogue and conflict by leaving the field.*

2. *Children need to learn, without undue anxiety, that on occasion they themselves and all others including their parents and teachers morally violate but that reparations can be made, and when they are, relations improve.*

3. *Children need to feel that the protection of their self-interests is legitimate, within the context of their recognizing and reciprocating the self-interest of others.*

4. *Parents and teachers need to recognize that although their power is awesome compared to the child's, the process of proper moral negotiation is always among equals. Nevertheless, between the young and adults, imbalance in conclusions is sometimes necessary and legitimate, given the young's shortsightedness and their comparative inexperience. But as the father of a four-year-old girl said, "We have to come down on her sometimes, but the important thing is that she's got to walk away with her moral honor intact."*

5. *Children need to understand that moral conflict is a necessary and inevitable part of life.*

Implications for Mental Health

Morality permeates mental health professionals' activities of diagnosis, treatment, and prevention in two major ways: how they themselves act and how moral confusion affects clients. These considerations cannot be discussed separately, since the professional and client are involved in a profound moral interaction with each other. Just how morality is involved in the origin of psychopathology has been of long-term interest. Ideas about the prohibitions of society and religion against human self-servingness were represented in Freud's early formulation of the neurotic's guilt-producing, harsh superego. The logical implications of these ideas were followed out in later psychoanalytic formulations by August Aichorn (1925) and others who speculated that delinquent and adult character disorders were the result of gaps in conscience, or "superego lacunae." For the most part, the role of morality in the genesis and diagnosis of psychopathology has been and still remains a question as to whether troubled people have too much or not enough in the way of conscience.

This view of morality as superego readily led to the idea that when troubled people are treated, professionals should become the emotional equivalents of good parents. They should give severe superegos permission to relax in order to relieve guilt, and they should take responsibility for the moral learning of social deviants. Aichorn felt, for instance, that delinquents could only be cured by first becoming neurotic—that is, guilty—so that their guilt could then be tempered and reeducated.

Treatment itself involves a host of moral problems that have been amply and formally addressed as ethical: clients' rights, therapists' professional behavior, the nature of contracts between therapist and client, both parties' relationship to the legal system, and so forth. Ethics are a formalization of moral rules, and their codification makes them into conventions. We do not take up these codifications here, although the concerted attention to them in recent years is obviously salutary. More to the point of the present context are the less formal and nonlegal moral meanings that arise in exchanges between client and mental health professional. These concern the moral spirit of diagnosis and the therapeutic dialogue which result in moral experience for both client and therapist.

The interactional theory has relevance for both psychodiagnosis and therapy. The proposals discussed below are couched in the language of moral meanings but they rest on widely accepted clinical practices and conclusions. Like social science's attempts to achieve value neutrality, mental health professionals have also attempted to persuade themselves of their neutrality. But the accuracy of their protestations has been repeatedly challenged and forceful recommendations continuously made about the moral position that therapists should take. One of the earliest was Mowrer's (1961) idea that therapists *should* take a clear moral position—rather than a covert one—by "rediscovering" their responsibility. Thomas Szasz (1961) questioned the morality of mental health practices and argued that decisions about diagnosis and therapy are usually made in terms of conventional cultural standards that work to ostracize people who do not fit in society. The behavioral modifiers have taken yet another tack. Criticizing the so-called insight therapists for their moral fuzziness (London, 1964), they make a point of their own moral clarity declaring that they only attempt to cure what the client wants cured.

From the interactional perspective the following moral meanings seem embedded in the relationships betwen clients and mental health professionals.

First, the reason why psychotherapy helps people—when it is successful—is that it can be defined as a joint search by the therapist and client for the truth of the client's status and situation and the meanings of the client-therapist relationship. See Habermas (1971) for a similar view. These truths include moral issues, for example, how clients use other people as a means to gain an end and how clients are used by others as the means to an end. But given the overweening need of all persons to regard themselves as moral, clients usually first choose to examine how others use them. This is clearly less guilt provoking.

The lives of most people who select psychotherapy—and many more who do not—typically involve convoluted, morally corrupt relationships, marked by unconscious, confused and guilty tradeoffs with members of their families, friends, and others. Troubled people are never troubled just within themselves; their relationships with others are also always troubled. At one and the same time, they take too much and give too much and neither the receiving or giving is satisfying. Like moral education, the processes of psychotherapy can be viewed as learning how to negotiate morally with others. A successful relationship with the therapist can be a first, safe setting for this learning.

Second, therapists are known to burn out with some frequency. One reason the occupation of psychotherapy is hazardous is that clients usually attempt to involve therapists in the same morally corrupt interchanges they have with other people. The training of therapists helps them to avoid such interchanges, since clinical prudence indicates it is bad for the relationship. But morality is involved and moral dialogues are delicate, stressful, and fraught with surplus meaning, and agreements are fragile. Conventional instruction in psychotherapy could be helped if the moral components of the clients' invitations to corruption were understood and the therapists' moral options examined.

Third, on its surface, the psychotherapeutic relationship seems in-balanced since therapists appear to give more than the client when they put themselves and their trained honesty at the client's disposal. Clients are encouraged to say whatever they are inclined to say, even when their impulses are harsh and personally hostile to the therapist. This freedom to transgress is a special and pivotal feature of the therapeutic relationship and it is like no other. This imbalance is temporarily necessary since the truth of the client's feelings needs to be discovered by both client and therapist so they can then jointly consider its meanings and implications for the client's options. Nonetheless, there are restrictions. Although clients are urged to voice all possible demands on the therapist, some may be refused if their fulfillment would violate the therapist's moral role or the therapist as a moral being. For instance, clients can ask for extra appointments. The therapist as therapist is ordinarily required to fulfill this demand but need not if requests are excessive, since excessive giving may unbalance the therapeutic relationship.

In fact, the therapeutic relationship is actually a legitimated balance since therapists are compensated, either directly by the client or by society. If therapists work altruistically, the relationship is known to be easily compromised. A more subtle compensation for therapists is the client's improvement. But the therapist morally violates if he or she uses the client as a means to personally validate his or her skill and defines the client's improvement in this way. Although troubled people understandably want all possible benefits, they, like all other people, need and are helped the most by receiving only what is legitimately theirs. Gifts tip the balance of the relationship, obligate clients, increase their guilt and give the therapist moral superiority. The useful moral relationship—useful for both client and therapist—is a fully legitimated balance, but this is only achieved during the terminal phases of successful therapy.

Finally, consistent and prolonged moral betrayal is a profound and enduring outrage that restrain people's willingness to commit themselves in good faith to dialogue. Persistently betrayed people betray; they even anxiously provoke betrayal to secure immediate confirmation of what they await. Also, they need to justify their own betrayals. In other words, they have little or no trust. By analyzing the moral meanings of trust and distrust, we have proposed an explanation for the inconsistency between troubled people's moral commitments and their actions. In some degree this explanation eases the moral onus on people called psychopaths or considered to have character disorders. It also provides a moral understanding of why some psychiatric clients have difficulty committing themselves to the therapeutic exchange. Continuous and vigilant poor faith is often the *only intelligent strategy* for survival that persistently betrayed children and people believe they can use.

Our research results support several well-known points that affect diagnosis and therapy.

1. When the students were stressed, like other poeple, they were morally inefficient, but there was no support for the explanation that they were characteristically immoral or amoral. For example, students whose levels of moral action were lowest in the interpersonally violating situation of NeoPd were otherwise especially sensitive and well functioning.

2. Students who could address and tolerate conflict grew morally. The circumambient and morally corrupt interpersonal relations of troubled people usually involve incessant and unresolvable moral conflict, so they yearn for peace and harmony and are quite unable to undertake the work of dialogue and resolution. Students who avoided or negated moral conflict either regressed or were unaffected by the moral experiences.

3. Self-righteousness in moral negotiation and therapy is a specific and special defense against guilt. It is a way of remaining aloof from conflict so as to be untouched by moral conflict and uncommitted to its resolution. Tolerance for violations committed by oneself or others and learning how to make reparations for one's inevitable violations were preconditions of moral growth.

4. The multiple, moral feedback from a group, as occurs in group and family therapy, helps people see that all people violate morally on occasion.

Summary

The fundamental justification for social science's existence as a discipline lies in its possibilities for elucidating the nature and reasons for human activity. When social scientists do not interact with life, the knowledge they provide can be warped, erroneous, or meaningless. We leaped ahead in this chapter to talk about the broader implications of our findings. We feel these anticipations and imaginations are necessary to bring the public's attention and valuations to bear on the academic theories of morality. These theories need the corrections and suggestions offered by real-life implications. We have also acted, by writing this chapter, to say that morality is not only a problem of individual persons' morality, it is also a problem of how societies practice morality. A correct moral theory—correct because it illuminates the moral basis of real life—will embrace the morality of collectivities *and* individual human beings.

HYPOTHETICAL MORAL DILEMMAS

Dilemmas for Group Sessions

Session 1

A. THE SCIENCE EXAM

Gary is taking an important exam in science. Gary has studied for weeks and he feels confident that he will be able to make a good grade. As Gary's teaching assistant passes out the test, he says that if he sees anyone talking, that person will fail the test. When Gary receives his test he gets right to work. The girl next to him asks for help on a question. He motions her that she is not to talk, and that he will not help her out. His science teaching assistant sees him and tears up his test. Gary feels terrible, even close to tears. The girl explains to the science teaching assistant that she was asking for his help. The science teaching assistant says he did not see her talking. The girl tears up her paper, saying she was the one at fault. She demands that she receive a failure for her test. The science teaching assistant refuses. Everyone in the class thinks the teaching assistant was unfair, although throughout the quarter, he had been supportive and helpful to all the students.

B. PEACE CORPS CANDIDATE

Andrew is a recent college graduate who has been offered a job with the Peace Corps. He has always wanted to help less fortunate people in other countries, and he enjoys traveling. However, his mother has a severe chronic illness and must stay home most of the time. He is her only child.

C. A Visit from the F.B.I.

One afternoon Bill is working alone in his office at the university. A stranger knocks at the door and asks Bill if he may talk with him for a few minutes. He identifies himself as an F.B.I. agent and explains that he is making a routine investigation of a person who has applied for a Federal job and is being seriously considered for the position. The person is Dave Harrison, Bill's roommate during his junior year at the college where Bill did his undergraduate work. Bill has not been in touch with Dave since they both graduated in the previous spring, but he knew that Dave has taken several Civil Service exams and had hoped to find a job in Washington with the Federal government. The questions from the F.B.I. man do not present any problem for Bill until the interview seems to be about over. The agent asks, "Do you have any reason to believe that Mr. Harrison has been at any time a regular user of illegal drugs, or has been involved in the purchase or sale of illegal drugs?" As a matter of fact, Bill remembers very well one evening in which Dave came in quite late and excited. He told Bill he had just made $500 for four hours of work. He had picked up a quantity of heroin at one address, delivered it to another and had been paid immediately in cash. Bill warned Dave he could get into really big trouble through this activity, and Dave said, "Don't worry. You can count on me to be careful." Dave had never mentioned the subject again. Bill would prefer not to mention this incident to the F.B.I. man, because he knows it might get Dave into trouble. He does not know quite what to do.

Session 2

A. Mrs. Webster's Rooming House

When her husband died five years earlier, Mrs. Webster converted her house into a rooming house which would hold seven roomers.

The rent from the rooming house provided her with just enough money to make ends meet.

All of her roomers were white and Mrs. Webster knew them very well. They had told her that if she ever rented to a Negro they would move out. If this happened she would receive much less money than the small amount she now received. But she also knew that if she refused a Negro a room she could get into trouble because the state open housing law made it illegal for her to refuse to rent a room to a person because of his color.

A young black man, Mr. Johnson, had just received a job in town. He had looked around town all day without success and toward evening noticed the sign, "Room for Rent," in front of Mrs. Webster's house. When he asked Mrs. Webster about the room, she told him that she had just rented the room and that there were no more left. In fact, there were two vacant rooms in her house at the time.

B. School and Migrant Work

Juan is a 13-year-old in eighth grade in public school. He and his family are migrant laborers and each year his father takes him out of school for about four months to work in the fields. This is necessary for the family to have enough to live on. Juan is a very bright student and likes school. Until sixth grade he could keep up his work enough to pass each year. His schoolwork is getting more difficult and he failed last year. Juan's teacher is concerned about him and the cycle of poverty that passes from generation to generation. She has to decide whether or not to report his parents to the authorities and force them to leave him in school for the full year.

C. School Newspaper

Fred Berger, a senior at Kitsap High School, near Seattle, thought of putting out a newspaper for students which would express many of his strong feelings. In particular, he wanted to voice his opposition to the war in Viet Nam and to many of the school's regulations, like the one forbidding boys to wear long hair. Fred was a consistently high honor student and one of the three chosen by the faculty as "outstanding students." He was also a student-council representative and a regional winner of a "What Democracy Means to Me" contest, which was sponsored by a national patriotic group.

Before publishing his newspaper, Fred asked his principal for permission. The principal agreed on the condition that Fred submit all his articles to him for approval. Fred agreed and began to submit his articles. The principal approved all of them and Fred published two issues of the paper in the next two weeks.

But the principal did not think about the great attention that Fred's paper would receive. Students read the paper eagerly and began to organize against the hair regulation and other school rules; rallies were held before and after school. Many class hours were spent talking about the paper. Furthermore, many parents who favored the Viet Nam war phoned the principal and angrily told him that the newspaper was unpatriotic and should not be published.

As a result of the commotion, the principal ordered Fred to stop publishing the newspaper. He gave as a reason that Fred's activities were disruptive to the operation of the school.

Session 3

A. STRIKE

Mary was one of 15 teachers in a junior high school for children in a very small poor community. She was one of the few really good teachers there. Some of the parents were very dissatisfied with the school. Their children were supposed to get medical and dental care as well as a hot lunch as part of a special government project. The doctors and dentists almost never came, and the lunches were often cold and small. The parents complained to the principal, and when that did not work, they wrote to their congressman and to officials in Washington. Still nothing happened. Then about half of the parents got very angry and decided to strike the school by keeping their children home. The children of the other half still went to school. The principal and the Washington officials ordered the teachers to go to work and said they would be fired if they didn't work. Most of the teachers decided to go to work, but Mary was having a hard time making up her mind because she knew the parents had tried very hard to get some attention paid to the problems.

B. ACADEMIC WEEKEND

Susan needs money badly to go to college. A college education is her ambition, and her parents' ambition for her. They would like to help her, but they do not earn enough money. She receives an offer from her professor to spend Thanksgiving vacation with him in the Bahamas in exchange for next quarter's tuition.

C. TV NEWS

Students at the university are demonstrating in a march on campus against the university's investments in South Africa. The president threatens to declare the march on campus illegal and to call in the police. The local TV news station is in support of the demonstration and wants to highlight the issue on television. When they hear the president has threatened to declare the march illegal, the students discuss the possibility of a sit-in in the president's office. Mary, a reporter for the news station, arrives on the scene and has to decide whether or not to encourage the students to sit-in, knowing it will make the coverage more exciting and help her get a promotion. Moreover, Mary does have deep concern about this issue and wants to develop support for the students' position.

Session 4

A. REELECTION CAMPAIGN

A black politician, Adam Marshall, is campaigning for reelection. His record indicates that he has introduced significant legislation on behalf of his constituency. However, he has just gone through a scandalous divorce. His opponent has capitalized on this issue. This election is the closest race of Adam's career, and Adam has been invited to share a political ticket with two candidates whose reputations are doubtful. They are backed by a powerful political organization able to almost guarantee his reelection.

B. Nuclear Accident

An accident has occurred at a nuclear-power plant which has the potential of exploding the plant. It may only be a matter of minutes before a hard decision must be made. If the situation worsens, everyone working at the plant will have time to get to safety if one man stays back to control the core reactor. There is about a one to four chance that the man who stays back will be killed. The plant manager must decide who will stay back to do the job. The manager would do the job but he is the one who knows about what happened and is able to theorize on what circumstances led to this accident. He must get this information out to prevent further accidents. He asks for volunteers but no one will volunteer to stay back in the core reactor. He must decide whether to stay himself or designate someone else.

C. Civilian Defense

Everyone in the Bay Area heard that bombs were being dropped on Honolulu and they realized that bombs might be dropped on them in a short time. Some ignored the threat but others prepared for the attack.

The air raid sirens began to sound. Everyone realized that a hydrogen bomb was going to be dropped on the city by the enemy, and that the only way to survive was to be in a bomb shelter. Not everyone had bomb shelters, but those who did ran quickly to them. Since Mr. and Mrs. Edwards had built a shelter, they immediately went to it, where they had enough air space inside to last them for exactly five days. They knew that after five days the fallout would have diminished to the point where they could safely leave the shelter. If they left before that, they would die. There was enough air for the Edwards only. Their next door neighbors had not built a shelter and were trying to get in. The Edwards knew that they would not have enough air if they let the neighbors in, and that they would all die if they came inside. So they refused to let them in. So now the neighbors were trying to break the door down in order to get in. Mr. Edwards took his gun and told them to go away or else he would shoot. They would not go away. So now he either had to shoot them or let them in.

Session 5

A. CITY BOMBING

During the war in Europe, a city was often bombed by the enemy. Each man in the city was given a post he was to go to right after the bombing to help put out the fires the bombs started and to rescue people in the burning buildings. A man named Diesing was made the chief in charge of one fire-engine post. The post was near his place of work, so he could get there quickly during the day, but it was a long way from his home. One day there was a very heavy bombing and Diesing left the shelter in the place he worked and went toward his fire station, but when he saw how much of the city was burning, he got worried about his family. He decided, therefore, that he had to go home first to see if his family was safe, even though his home was a long way off and the station was nearby.

B. HOUSING

Bruce needs a job to support himself, his wife, and two children, but he only has a high-school education and little training. He is offered a job with a public agency that supplies housing for poor people. The director offers him a job despite his lack of qualifications because he feels Bruce is "right" for the job. After Bruce accepts the job, he finds out that the director, who decides which people get housing, is pressuring the applicants to make a contribution to a political party before he gives them an apartment to rent.

C. MARRIAGE

Jim and Leona were married soon after they graduated from high school and soon Jim had a good job, they had two little children, and life was great. But then Jim was called to go to Viet Nam because he was in the Army Reserve. Three months later he was reported missing in action. Leona was very depressed and sad for a long time. Finally the Defense Department declared that he was dead. After a time Bob, an old friend of Leona and Jim's, began taking her out and soon said that he wanted to marry her. Finally they were married. When the war was over, Jim was returned as a prisoner of war. He came back and was deeply depressed and upset about Leona's new marriage, as were Bob and Leona and all their friends. Leona goes to her friends to talk it over. . . . Jim goes to his friends to talk it over. . . .

Dilemmas for Individual Interviews

Pre-Session Interviews

I. Cognitive Dilemmas

A. HEINZ

In Europe, a woman was near death from a rare kind of cancer. There was one drug that the doctors thought might save her. It was a compound of radium that a druggist in the same town had recently discovered. The drug was expensive to make, and the druggist was charging ten times what the drug cost him to make. He paid $200 for the radium and charged $2000 for a small dose of the drug. The sick woman's husband, Heinz, went to everyone he knew to borrow the money, but he could only get together about $1000, which is half of what the drug cost. He told the druggist that his wife was dying and asked him to sell it cheaper or let him pay later. But the druggist said, "No, I discovered the drug and I'm going to make money from it." Heinz became desperate and considered breaking into the man's store to steal the drug for his wife.

B. OFFICER BROWN

Heinz did break into the store. He stole the drug and gave it to his wife. In the newspapers the next day, there was an account of the robbery. Mr. Brown, a police officer who knew Heinz, read the account. He remembered seeing Heinz running away from the store and realized that it was Heinz who stole the drug. Mr. Brown wonders whether he should report that Heinz was the robber.

II. Interactional Dilemmas

A. BICYCLE

Ella is a student in an elementary school where a lot of kids were "borrowing" each others' bikes, but some kids and parents got bothered about it, and the principal and some of the teachers got very angry. The principal called in the juvenile authorities who said they are going to put a stop to this. One day after school Ella was leaving late because she had been helping her teacher, and she saw Mike, a boy in her class, admiring a bike that was not his. Then Mike got on it and rode off. The next morning the owner of the bike found it on the edge of the playground, but the principal and juvenile authorities began to question the students. The juvenile authority asked Ella if she had seen anybody on the playground take the bike. What do you think Ella should do?

B. DESERT STORY

Omar was travelling through a lonely desert by foot; he had been to a city 30 miles away attempting to find help for his people who were starving, since they were without food or money. He came across a man who was clearly very near death, likely of a heart attack. In the man's last moments, he gave Omar some bags of gold and made Omar promise to give them to his wealthy cousin. The wealthy cousin had helped the dying man during his lifetime, and he said his cousin would give Omar a reward. Then the man died. Omar thought about taking it to his people, rather than to the wealthy cousin.

Post-Session—Interview 1

I. Cognitive Dilemmas

A. JOE TO CAMP

Joe is a 14-year-old boy who wanted to go to camp very much. His father promised him he could go if he saved up the money for it himself. So Joe worked hard at his paper route and saved up the $40 it cost to go to camp and a little more besides. But just before camp was going to start, his father changed his mind. Some of his friends decided to go on a special fishing trip, and Joe's father was short of the money it would cost. So he told Joe to give him the money he had saved from the paper route. Joe did not want to give up going to camp, so he thought of refusing to give his father the money.

B. DR. JEFFERSON

There was a woman who had very bad cancer, for which there was no known treatment that would save her. Her doctor, Dr. Jefferson, knew that she had only about six months to live. She was in terrible pain, but she was so weak that a good dose of a pain killer like ether or morphine would make her die sooner. She was delirious and almost crazy with pain, and in her calm periods she would ask Dr. Jefferson to give her enough ether to kill her. She said she could not stand the pain and she was going to die in a few months anyway. Although he knows that mercy killing is against the law, the doctor thinks about granting her request.

II. Interactional Dilemmas

A. SMALL BOY

Dick was on his way home from high school one day when he saw Tom, a boy from his school, hitting and taking money away from a smaller boy. There was no one else around. Tom told Dick to get lost or he would take care of him next. Dick knew that he could not talk Tom out of keeping the money and that he was the same size and strength as Tom. Dick thought there was not enough time to get back to the school people or call the cops.

B. AFFAIR

John was an important official with a company where he had worked for many years. A new secretary, Evelyn, came to work in the company; she was 18 years old, but John was 50 years old. After a while she realized she had fallen in love with John and he realized the same. They began to have lunch together and then see each other alone after work, but John always had to get home to his wife and children. Evelyn told John she loved him, and John told her he loved her as he had never loved anyone before. But John said he could not promise anything more than just seeing her for a very short time, since he could never leave his wife and children. She asked if his wife knew and he just said no, that it would just her hurt her feelings.

Post-Session—Interview 2

I. Cognitive Dilemmas

A. HEINZ

Story repeated from Cognitive, Pre-session Interview. See above.

B. ROCK CONCERT

Judy was a 12-year-old girl. Her mother promised her that she could go to a special rock concert coming to their town if she saved baby-sitting and lunch money for a long time so she would have enough money to buy a ticket to the concert. She managed to save up the $15 the ticket cost plus another $5. But then her mother changed her mind and told Judy that she had to spend the money on new clothes for school. Judy was disappointed and decided to go to the concert any-way. She bought a ticket and told her mother that she had only been able to save $5. That Saturday she went to the performance and told her mother that she was spending the day with a friend. A week passed without her mother finding out. Judy then told her older sister, Louise, that she had gone out to the performance and had lied to her mother about it. Louise wonders whether to tell their mother about it. Louise wonders whether to tell their mother what Judy did.

II. Interactional Dilemmas

A. JOHN AND CHARLES

John and Charles are friends. John has no driver's license. One evening he "borrows" his father's car and goes for a short ride with Charles. In the darkness he does not notice a poorly lit motorcycle and hits it. The motorcycle rider falls but does not seem to be badly injured.

B. DESERT STORY

Story repeated from interactional dilemmas, Presession interviews. See above.

Q SORT OF EGO PROCESSES: COPING AND DEFENDING

Item Listing

Cognitive Functions

Discrimination

Objectivity: Coping

1. Distinguishes between his own feelings and the facts of situations
2. Views self in an objective light
3. Evaluates both sides of arguments, including those contrary to his own point of view

Isolation: Defense

4. Fails to see connections between related ideas
5. Compartmentalizes his feelings
6. Misses connections between feelings and ideas

Detachment

Intellectuality: Coping

7. Lets mind roam freely to consider possibilities (low, if restricted in range)

8. Applies abstract, formal ideas in solving problems (low, if thinks concretely)
9. Attempts to get at the "truth," even if it is against own self-interest

Intellectualization: Defense

10. Produces intellectualizations rather than cogent solutions
11. Applies abstract ideas and terms to situations to avoid feelings
12. Produces intellectualizations which seem self-serving

Means-end Symbolization

Logical Analysis: Coping

13. Deduces seemingly accurate consequences of an event (place low if either not interested or inaccurate)
14. "Backtracks" to reconstruct a plausible chain of events (low if does not use past to understand present)
15. Gives seemingly inaccurate reasons as to why interpersonal events arose (low, if not interested, or inaccurate)

Rationalization: Defense

16. Deduces unlikely and possibly self-serving consequences of events (low if rational)
17. Offers unlikely reasons for his past actions (low if not interested or accurate)
18. Reconstructs implausible chain of events (low if not interested or accurate)

Intraceptive Functions

Delayed Response

Tolerance of Ambiguity: Coping

19. Can defer decisions in complicated situations (low, if unable to make decisions *or* acts on spur of moment)
20. Tolerates uncertainty in the structure and rules of situations (low, if needs certainty)

21. Able to wait for other people to make up their minds in complicated situations; tolerates indecision or slowness in others

Doubt and Indecision: Defense

22. Unable to commit self to personal courses of action even when possible to do so (low, if action oriented)
23. Rethinks what he or she has already decided (low, if decisive)
24. Has a tentative attitude toward problems and human relations

Sensitivity

Empathy: Coping

25. Tries to understand others' feelings and perceptions (low, if oblivious to others' feelings)
26. Reacts sensitively to others' feelings
27. Anticipates others' reactions to situations with accuracy, that is, can put himself in other fellow's boots

Projection: Defense

28. Preoccupied with the possibility that other people will act badly
29. Feels accused and criticized by others
30. Vigilant in "ferreting" out others' reactions

Time Reversion

Regression in Service of Ego (Playfulness): Coping

31. Enjoys surprising aspects of situations, for example, situational humor, or sudden insights
32. Plays with ideas, and feelings without being constrained by situational demands (low, if constrained by situations)
33. Integrates past memories with present to *enhance* his understandings

Regression: Defense

34. Seems to expect that he will be cared for in difficult situations
35. Acts non-age-appropriate in some situations or in important relationships (low if in charge of self and situation)

36. Views self as not being responsible in difficult situations; rejecting responsibility

Attention-focusing Functions

Selective Awareness

Concentration: Coping

37. Focuses attention and effort on most relevant problems of situations
38. Completes tasks even if he must set aside interesting distractions (low, if acts on whims)
39. Organizes self to complete tasks according to work plans

Denial: Defense

40. Oblivious to complex, problematic nuances of situations
41. Ignores aspects of situations that are potentially threatening
42. Focuses attention on the pleasant aspects of problems and ignores others, for example, "Every cloud has a silver lining"

Affective Diversion

Sublimation: Coping

43. Can express aggressive, even angry feelings when the situation needs and warrants it
44. Expresses warm feelings toward a variety of activities and people
45. Expresses feelings in a variety of satisfying, socially tolerated ways

Displacement: Defense

46. Displaces feelings in form (for example, has a stomach ache instead of temper tantrum) or to an object (kicks dog instead of boss)
47. Misdirects positive, warm feelings from original aims or object (such as, dogs are better than people)
48. Expresses aggressive, even hostile feelings in nonrelevant contexts and objects (irrelevant irritability)

Affective Transformation

Substitution: Coping

49. Acts fairly, even in trying circumstances
50. Acts civilly even in trying circumstances
51. Regulates expression of feelings proportionate to the situation

Reaction Formation: Defense

52. Acts with conformity in most circumstances
53. Acts with such fairness that legitimate self-interest seems negated (for example, masochistic)
54. Acts with excessive moderation in circumstances that seem to warrant expression of feeling

Affective Restraint

Suppression: Coping

55. Suppresses, but is aware of own feelings and thoughts in most circumstances (low, if expresses or unaware of feelings)
56. Controls expression of affective reactions when not appropriate to express them, for example, older person not hurting children even when provoked
57. Inhibits reactions for the time being when appropriate

Repression: Defense

58. Constricts and inhibits cognitive associations
59. Forgets aspects of trying circumstances
60. Unable to recall painful experiences

Glossary

Behaviorism was an early main form of scientific psychology. It was less a theory and more a method which required that psychologists study only observable stimulus and response; all mental events were to be excluded from consideration.

Categorical imperative is a term used by Immanuel Kant to mean moral mandates that people are naturally required to follow irrespective of the circumstances and what individual humans might want; an example is "Thou shalt not kill."

Ego is the psychoanalytic term for that part of the personality which allows people to deal with reality, demands of conscience, and internal impulses; thus, it represents people's reasoning, perceiving, and problem solving.

Ego ideal is a psychoanalytic term that refers to a person's ideal of what they should be morally, represented in their minds by some person or persons with whom they identify.

Empirical fallacy is a term used by Rudner (1966) to point out a basic error of behaviorism, that is, all that one can see is not the whole of truth since people also follow their internal more subtle meanings.

Existentialism is a philosophical-psychological view that takes humans' need to be true to themselves, understand themselves, and actualize these truths in their lives as the focal problem of existence.

Factor analysis is a statistical method of reducing associations among a large number of variables to a smaller number of factors that represent the main general groupings of the original variables.

Id is the psychoanalytic term for the basic instinctual, even biological, drives that supply all energy for human functioning; the id is regarded as primitive and always egocentric.

Induction is a matter of reasoning from the specific to the general; it is applied in this book to the interactional system's view that the course of people's moral dialogue is an open-ended mutual search, at first, for the source of their conflict and then later—in optimal circumstances—a search for a generalized moral balance that will be acceptable to all involved parties.

Logical positivism was set forth in the 1920s and 1930s by a group of Viennese philosophers who were concerned with empiricism and the application of logical and mathematical propositions to empirical observations. Since neither logical nor mathematical propositions are necessarily related to things in the real world, this approach excluded consideration of historical and psychologically meaningful phenomena.

Moral actor and *moral agent* are terms used in this volume, especially in the studies of action, to underscore the point that people almost always take an active, problem-solving approach to moral problems they experience or even witness.

Multiple regression models result from a statistical procedure that allows the amounts of various influences on a variable of interest—in this volume often the level of people's moral action scores—to be estimated. Stepwise multiple regression is used to determine the effects on moral-action scores of situations, structure of friendship groups, and then the students' personal strategies of adapting to moral conflicts. In this special case of multiple regression, different effects are successively removed one by one. After each step, the question is whether there is any remaining influence left, say, for personal strategies, after the effects of situation and friendship group structure have been removed (or controlled, which amounts to removal).

Naturalistic fallacy is a philosophical term and argument that the ideas expressed by what "is" in the world are of a different class than ideas about what "ought" to occur in the world. Given this distinction, philosophers have gone on to argue that an "ought" cannot be logically derived from an "is" in the world, since an "ought" statement requires that someone approve of some factual state of affairs.

Neobehaviorism (*see Behaviorism*) is a recent psychological approach that focuses on stimulus and response but accepts the importance of some general internal events like the person's formulation of a whole from its parts or formulation of a general meaning from discrete stimuli.

Nihilism means the total rejection of the idea that values and morals should and do underlie human choice.

Oedipus complex is a psychoanalytic term that refers to the erotic feelings that children are thought to have toward their parent of the opposite sex; Freud believed that the oedipal experience was universal and only became the basis for a neurosis if it was not adequately resolved. He thought its resolution laid the groundwork for the development of conscience since after the oedipal resolution children came to identify with the conscience of their parent of the opposite sex.

Operant conditioning refers to a particular kind of learning that takes place after a desirable behavior is rewarded or an undesirable behavior is punished and no longer used.

Q sort is a method of assigning values, usually to various elements of people's personalities. Cards with statements representing an element or trait are placed in piles that represent steps from least characteristic to most characteristic; the number of each pile is then assigned to the cards placed in that pile.

Reinforcement refers either to the rewards or punishments that follow a response and serve to strengthen possibilities that the response will be repeated, if rewarded, and it will not if punished.

Social-learning theory assumes that learning is mostly or entirely due to social influences that result in a person's imitating or emulating another person; thus learning is determined by external stimuli and reinforcement (see above) as well as by the person's thinking and judgment about these environmental influences.

Superego is the psychoanalytic term for conscience which is thought to be composed of society's standards as well as persons' aspirations about how they should act.

Trans-situational personal functioning is used in this volume to represent the idea that people may act the same in different situations or they may act differently in different situations or even act differently in the same situation that recurs at points in time.

Utilitarianism is a very early but still prestigious philosophical theory which first held that right actions can be chosen on the basis of which one or ones will produce the greatest happiness (pleasure or absence of pain). Different variants have been proposed, but almost all focus, as did the original proposal, on the social consequences of acts.

Value relativism maintains that there are no universal standards of right or wrong or good and bad.

References

Aerts, E. *Organizational and interpersonal patterns in whole families.* Unpublished doctoral dissertation. University of California, Berkeley, 1979.

Aichorn, A. *Wayward youth.* New York: Noonday, 1955.

Anchor, K. N., & H. J. Cross. Maladaptive aggression, moral perspective, and the socialization process. *Journal of Personality and Social Psychology,* 1974, *30,* 163–168.

Anderson, N. H. Progress in cognitive algebra. In L. Berkowitz (ed.), *Cognitive theories in social psychology.* New York: Academic, 1978.

Anderson, N. H. Information integration theory in developmental psychology. In F. Wilkening, J. Becker and T. Trebasso (eds.). *Information integration by children.* Hillsdale, N.J.: Lawrence Erlbaum Associates, 1980.

Anderson, N., & C. Butzin. Integration theory applied to children's judgments of equity. *Developmental Psychology,* 1978, *14,* 593–606.

Anscombe, G. E. M. Modern moral philosophy. In W. D. Hudson (ed.). *The is-ought question.* London: Macmillan, 1969.

Arendt, H. *Eichmann in Jerusalem: A report of the banality of evil.* New York: Penguin, 1977.

Aronfreed, J. *Conduct and conscience: The socialization of internalized control over behavior.* New York: Academic, 1968.

Baier, K. *The moral point of view.* Ithaca, N.Y.: Cornell University Press, 1958.

Berkowitz, L. *The development of motives and values in a child.* New York: Basic Books, 1964.

Bernstein, R. *The restructuring of social and political theory.* New York: Harcourt, Brace, Jovanovich, 1976.

Bettelheim, B., & M. B. Janowitz. *Social change and prejudice.* New York: Free Press, 1964.

Blasi, A. Bridging moral cognition and moral action: a critical review of the literature. *Psychological Bulletin,* 1980, *88,* 1–45.

Blatt, M., & L. Kohlberg. The effects of classroom moral discussion upon children's level of moral judgment. *Journal of Moral Education,* 1975, *4,* 129–161.

Blatt, M. *The effects of classroom discussion upon children's moral judgment.* Unpublished doctoral dissertation. University of Chicago, 1970.

Bronowski, J. *Science and human values.* New York: Harper & Row, 1965.

Broughton, J. Development of concepts of self, mind, reality, and knowledge. In W. Damon (ed.). *New directions for child development.* San Francisco: Jossey-Bass, 1978, vol. 1.

Brunswick, E. The conceptual focus of some psychological systems. *Journal for a Unified Science,* 1939, *8,* 36–49.

Brunswick, E. In defense of probabilistic functionalism: A reply. *Psychological Review,* 1955, *62,* 236–242.

Candee, D., & L. Kohlberg. The relationship of moral judgment to moral action. Paper presented at the American Psychological Association Annual Meetings, Washington, D.C., August, 1982.

Campagna, A. F., & S. Harter. Moral judgment in sociopathic and normal children. *Journal of Personality and Social Psychology,* 1975, *31,* 199–205.

Colby, A., L. Kohlberg, J. Gibbs, B. Speicher-Dubin, & D. Candee. *The measurement of moral judgment: Standard issue manual.* Cambridge, Mass.: Center for Moral Education, Harvard University (in press).

Colby, A., L. Kohlberg, J. Gibbs, & M. Lieberman. A longitudinal study of moral judgment. *Monographs of the Society for Research in Child Development,* 1983, *48* (1–2), 1–124.

Coles, R. Ulster's children: Waiting for the Prince of Peace. *Atlantic,* 1980, *246,* 33–34.

Cook, H. & S. Stingle. Cooperative behavior in children. *Psychological Bulletin,* 1974, *81,* 918–933.

Damon, W. *The social world of the child.* San Francisco: Jossey-Bass, 1977.

Darley, J. M., E. C. Klossen, & M. P. Zanna. Intentions and their contexts in the moral judgments of children and adults. *Child Development,* 1978, *49,* 66–74.

D'Augelli, J. F., & H. J. Cross. Relationship of sex guilt and moral reasoning to premarital sex in college women and in couples. *Journal of Consulting and Clinical Psychology,* 1975, *43,* 40–47.

Dawkins, R. *The selfish gene.* London: Oxford University Press, 1976.

de Certeau, M. History: Ethics, science and fiction. In N. Haan, R. Bellah, P. Rabinow, & W. Sullivan (eds.). *Social science as moral inquiry.* New York: Columbia University Press, 1983.

Des Pres, T. *The survivors.* New York: Oxford University Press, 1975.

Dewey, J. *Art as experience.* New York: Hinton, Balch, 1934.

Dewey, J. *Reconstruction in philosophy.* Boston: Beacon Press, 1948.

Einhorn, J. An unequivocable "yes" for morality study. *American Psychologist,* 1983, *38,* 1255–1256.

Epstein, S. The stability of behavior: II. Implications for psychological research. *American Psychologist,* 1980, *35,* 790–806.

Feldman, R. E. The promotion of moral development in prisons and schools. In R. Wilson & G. J. Schochet (eds.). *Moral development in politics.* New York: Praeger, 1980, pp. 286–328.

Flacks, R. Moral commitment, privatism and activism: Notes on a research program. In N. Haan, R. Bellah, P. Rabinow, & W. Sullivan (eds.). *Social science as moral inquiry.* New York: Columbia University Press, 1983.

Fodor, E. M. Resistance to temptation, moral development and perceptions of parental behavior among adolescent boys. *Journal of Social Psychology,* 1972, *88,* 155–156.

Frankl, V. *From death camp to existentialism.* Boston: Beacon Press, 1962.

Frenkel-Brunswick, E. Motivation and behavior. *Genetic Psychology Monographs,* 1942, *26,* 121–265.

Freud, A. *The ego and the mechanisms of defense.* London: Hogarth, 1937.

Freud, S. *The ego and the id.* New York: Norton, 1923.

Furer-Haimendorf, C. *Morals and merit: A study of values and social controls in South Asian societies.* Chicago: University of Chicago Press, 1967.

Garfinkel, H. *Studies in ethno-methodology.* Englewood Cliffs, N.J.: Prentice-Hall, 1967.

Gilligan, C. In a different voice: Women's conceptions of self and of morality. *Harvard Educational Review,* 1978, Reprint No. 13, 52–88.

Gilligan, C. Woman's place in man's life cycle. *Harvard Educational Review,* Summer 1979.

Gilligan, C. *In a different voice.* Cambridge, Mass.: Harvard University Press, 1982.

Goldiamond, I. Moral behavior and functional analysis. *Readings in psychology today.* Del Mar, Calif.: CRM Books, 1967, pp. 165–169.

Gough, H. G. *California psychological inventory.* Palo Alto, Calif.: Consulting Psychologists' Press, 1956.

Grueneich, R. Issues in the developmental study of how children use intention and consequence information to make moral evaluations. *Child Development,* 1982, *53,* 29–43.

Gutierrez, J. *The theology of liberation.* Maryknoll,, N.Y.: Orbis Books, 1973.

Haan, N. Proposed model of ego functiong: Coping and defense mechanisms in relationship to IQ change. *Psychological Monographs,* 1963, 77 (8).

Haan, N. Moral redefinition in the family as the fundamental aspect of the generation gap. *Youth and Society,* 1971, *2,* 259–284.

Haan, N. Preference for reasoning of various stages. Unpublished manuscript. Institute of Human Development, University of California, Berkeley.

Haan, N. Hypothetical and actual moral reasoning in a situation of civil disobedience. *Journal of Personality and Society Psychology,* 1975, *32,* 255–270.

Haan, N. *Coping and defending: Processes of self-environment organization.* New York: Academic, 1977.

Haan, N. Two moralities in action contexts. *Journal of Personality and Social Psychology,* 1978, *36,* 286–305.

Haan, N. Adolescents and young adults as producers of their own development. In R. M. Lerner (ed.). *Individuals as producers of their own development.* New York: Academic, 1981.

Haan, N. Can research on morality be "Scientific"? *American Psychologist,* 1982, *37* (1), 1096–1104.

Haan, N. Replies to David Leary, Arthur Houts and Leonard Krasner, Alan Waterman, and Jane Einhorn. *American Psychologist,* 1983, *38,* 1256–1257.

Haan, N. Systematic variability in the quality of moral action, as defined by two formulations. *Journal of Personality and Social Psychology* (in press a).

Haan, N. Cognitive or social disequilibrium as vehicles of moral development and who develops. *Developmental Psychology* (in press b).

Haan, N., R. Bellah, P. Rabinow, & W. Sullivan (eds.). *Social science as moral inquiry.* New York: Columbia University Press, 1983.

Haan, N., J. Block, & M. B. Smith. Moral reasoning of young adults: Political-social behavior, family background, and personality correlates. *Journal of Personality and Social Psychology,* 1968, *10,* 184–201.

Haan, N., J. Langer, & L. Kohlberg. Family patterns of moral reasoning. *Child Development,* 1976, *47,* 1204–1206.

Haan, N., R. Weiss, & V. Johnson. The role of logic in moral reasoning and development. *Developmental Psychology,* 1982, *18,* 245–256.

Habermas, J. *Knowledge and human interests.* Translated by J. J. Shapiro. Boston: Beacon, 1971.

Habermas, J. *Legitimation crisis.* Translated by Thomas McCarthy. Boston: Beacon, 1975.

Hampshire, S. Morality and pessimism. In S. Hampshire (ed.). *Public and private morality.* Cambridge: Cambridge University Press, 1978.

Hare, R. M. *The language of morals.* New York: Oxford University Press, 1964.

Hare, R. M. *Freedom and reason.* New York: Oxford University Press, 1965.

Harré, R., & P. F. Secord. *The explanation of social behavior.* Totowa, N.J.: Rowan and Littlefield, 1973.

Harris, S., P. Mussen, & E. Rutherford. Some cognitive, behavioral, and personality correlates of maturity of moral judgment. *Journal of Genetic Psychology,* 1976, *128,* 123–135.

Hartmann, H., E. Kris, & R. Loewenstein. *Papers on psychoanalysis.* New York: International Press. *Psychological Issues,* Vol. 4 (No. 2), Monograph 14, 1964.

Havelock, E. *The liberal temper in Greek politics.* London: Camelot, 1957.

Hersh, R. H., D. P. Paolitto, J. Reimer. *Promoting moral growth.* New York: Longman, 1979.

Hess, R. & G. Handel. *Family worlds.* Chicago: University of Chicago Press, 1959.

Hoffman, M. L. Toward a theory of emphatic arousal. In M. Lewis & L. Rosenbaum (eds.). *The development of affect.* New York: Plenum, 1978.

Hoffman, M. L. Moral development. In P. Mussen (ed.). *Carmichael's manual of child psychology,* 3rd ed. New York: Wiley, 1970, Vol. 2, pp. 261–360.

Hogan, R., J. Johnson, & N. Emler. A socioanalytic theory of moral development. *New Directions for Child Development,* 1978, *2,* 1–18.

Holstein, C. *Parental determinants of the development of moral judgment.* Unpublished doctoral dissertation. University of California, Berkeley, 1968.

Holstein, C. Irreversible, stepwise sequence in the development of moral judgment: A longitudinal study of males and females. *Child Development,* 1976, *47,* 51–61.

Holstein, C., J. Stroud, & N. Haan. Alienated and non-alienated youth: Perceptions of parents, self-evaluations and moral reasoning of hippies and college youth. *Youth and Society,* 1974, *5,* 279–302.

Houts, A. C., & L. Krasner. Values in science: Comments on Haan. *American Psychologist,* 1983, *38,* 1253–1254.

Hudgins, W., & N. Prentice. Moral judgment in delinquent and non-deliquent adolescents and their mothers. *Journal of Abnormal Psychology,* 1973, *82,* 145–152.

Hudson, W. D. (ed.). *The is-ought question.* London: Macmillan, 1969.

Joffe, P., & B. A. Bast. Coping and defense in relation to accommodation among a sample of blind men. *Journal of Nervous and Mental Disease,* 1978, *166,* 537–552.

Joffe, P., & M. P. Naditch. Paper and pencil measures of coping and defense processes. In N. Haan (ed.). *Coping and defending: Processes of self-environment organization.* New York: Academic, 1977.

Johnson, V. A. *Family interaction and adolescent moral reasoning.* Unpublished doctoral dissertation. University of California, Berkeley, 1980.

Johnson, V. A. Family interaction and adolescent moral reasoning. Paper presented at the Meetings of the American Educational Research Association, Los Angeles, April, 1981.

Karniol, R. Children's use of intention cues in evaluating behavior. *Psychological Bulletin,* 1978, *85,* 76–86.

Kobasa, S. Stressful life events, personality and health: An inquiry into hardiness. *Journal of Personality and Social Psychology,* 1979, *37,* 1–11.

Kohlberg, L. Moral and religious education and the public schools: A developmental view. In T. Sizer (ed.). *Religion and public education.* Boston: Houghton-Mifflin, 1967a.

Kohlberg, L. The child as moral philosopher. In *Readings in psychology today.* Del Mar, Calif.: CRM Books, 1967b, pp. 180–186.

Kohlberg, L. Stage and sequence: The cognitive-developmental approach to socialization. In D. Goslin (ed.). *Handbook of socialization theory and research.* Chicago: Rand McNally, 1969, pp. 347–480.

Kohlberg, L. Education for justice: A modern statement of the Platonic view. In *Moral education: Five lectures.* Cambridge, Mass.: Harvard University Press, 1970.

Kohlberg, L. From is to ought: How to commit the naturalistic fallacy and get away with it in the study of moral development. In T. Mischel (ed.). *Cognitive development and epistemology.* New York: Academic, 1971, pp. 151–284.

Kohlberg, L. Moral stages and moralization: The cognitive-developmental approach. In T. Lickona (ed.). *Moral development and behavior.* New York: Holt, Rinehart, & Winston, 1976.

Kohlberg, L. Preface. In R. Hersh, D. Paolitto, & J. Reimer (eds.). *Promoting moral growth.* New York: Longman, 1979.

Kohlberg, L. The future of liberalism as the dominant ideology of the West. In R. Wilson & G. Schochet (eds.). *Moral development and politics.* New York: Praeger, 1980, pp. 55–68.

Kohlberg, L. *Essays on moral development.* Vol. 1. *The philosophy of moral development.* San Francisco: Harper & Row, 1981.

Kohlberg, L., J. Hickey, & P. Scharf. The justice structure of the prison: A theory and intervention. *Prison Journal,* 1972, *51,* 3–14.

Kohlberg, L., & R. Kramer. Continuities and discontinuities in children and adult moral development. *Human Development,* 1969, *12,* 93–120.

Kohlberg, L., C. Levine, & A. Hewer. *Moral stages: A current formulation and a response to critics.* New York: Karger, 1983.

Kohlberg, L., & E. Turiel. Moral development and moral education. In G. Lesser (ed.). *Social influence and educational practice.* Glenview, Ill.: Scott, Foresman, 1971.

Krebs, D., & A. Rosenwald. Moral reasoning and moral behavior in conventional adults. *Merrill-Palmer Quarterly,* 1977, *23,* 77–87.

Krebs, R. L. *Some relationships between moral judgment, attention and resistance to temptation.* Unpublished doctoral dissertation. University of Chicago, 1967.

Kroeber, T. C. The coping functions of the ego mechanisms. In R. White (ed.). *The study of lives.* New York: Atherton, 1963.

Kurtines, W., & E. Greif. The development of moral thought: A review and evaluation of Kohlberg's approach. *Psychological Bulletin,* 1974, *81,* 453–469.

Ladd, J. *The structure of a moral code: A philosophical analysis of ethical discourse applied to the ethics of the Navaho Indian.* Cambridge, Mass.: Harvard University Press, 1957.

Ladd, J. *Ethical relativism.* Belmont, Calif.: Wadsworth, 1973.

Lane, J. & N. H. Anderson. Integration of intention and outcome in moral judgment. *Memory and Cognition,* 1976, *4,* 1–5.

Langer, J. *Theories of development.* New York: Holt, Rinehart & Winston, 1969.

Lazarus, R. S. The cost and benefits of denial. In S. Breznitz (ed.). *Denial of stress.* New York: International Universities Press, 1983.

Lazarus, R. S. Thoughts on the relations between emotions and cognitions. *American Psychologist,* 1982, *37,* 1019–1024.

Leary, D. E. On scientific morality. *American Psychologist,* 1983, *38,* 1253.

Lerner, M. *The belief in a just world.* New York: Academic, 1980.

Lifton, P. Gender difference and moral development: Fact or fiction. *Journal of Personality* (in press).

Locke, D. Cognitive stages or developmental phases? A critique of Kohlberg's stage-structural theory of moral reasoning. *Journal of Moral Education,* 1979, *8,* 168–181.

Locke, D. The illusion of stage six. *Journal of Moral Education,* 1980, *9,* 103–109.

Loevinger, J. *Ego development.* San Francisco: Jossey-Bass, 1976.

London, P. *The modes and morals of psychotherapy.* New York: Holt, Rinehart & Winston, 1964.

Maccoby, E. The development of moral values and behavior in childhood. In J. Clausen (ed.). *Socialization and Society.* Boston: Little Brown, 1968, pp. 227–269.

Meehl, P. Control and counter control: A panel discussion. In T. Thompson & W. S. Dockers III (eds.). *Applications of behavior modification.* New York: Academic, 1975.

Milgram, S. *Obedience to authority.* New York: Harper & Row, 1974.

Miller, R. Rawls and Marxism. In N. Daniels (ed.). *Reading Rawls: Critical study of a theory of justice.* Oxford: Blackwell, 1975.

Mischel, W., & H. Mischel. A cognitive social learning approach to morality and self-regulation. In T. Lickona (ed.). *Morality: A handbook of moral behavior.* New York: Holt, Rinehart & Winston, 1976.

Moore, G. E. *Principia ethica.* Cambridge: The University Press, 1903.

Mowrer, O. H. *The crisis in psychiatry and religion.* New York: Van Nostrand, 1961.

Murphy, J. M., & C. Gilligan. Moral development in late adolescence and adulthood: A critique and reconstruction of Kohlberg's theory. *Human Development,* 1980, *23,* 77–104.

Nagel, T. *The possibility of altruism.* Oxford: Clarendon, 1970.

Narr, W-D. Reflections on the form and content of social science: Toward a consciously political and moral science. In N. Haan, R. Bellah, P. Rabinow, & W. Sullivan (eds.). *Social science as moral inquiry.* New York: Columbia University Press, 1983.

Nucci, L. P. *Social development: Personal, conventional and moral concepts.* Unpublished doctoral dissertation. University of California, Santa Cruz, 1977.

Packer, M. *The structure of moral action: A hermeneutic study of moral conflict.* Basel: Karger, 1985.

Phillips, D. C.,& J. Nicolayev. Kohlbergian moral development, a progressing or degenerating research program? *Educational Theory,* 1978, *28,* 286–301.

Piaget, J. *The psychology of intelligence.* London: Routledge & Kegan Paul, 1950.

Piaget, J. *The moral judgment of the child.* New York: Free Press, 1965.

Piaget, J. *Structuralism.* New York: Basic Books, 1970.

Quine, W. V. *The ways of paradox.* New York: Random House, 1966.

Quine, W. V. *Ontological relativity and other essays.* New York: Columbia University Press, 1969.

Radke-Yarrow, M., C. Zahn-Waxler, & M. Chapman. Children's prosocial dispositions and behavior. In P. H. Mussen (ed.). *Handbook of child psychology.* Vol. IV. *Socialization, personality, and social development,* 4th ed. New York: Wiley, 1983.

Rawls, J. *The theory of justice.* Cambridge, Mass.: Harvard University Press, 1971.

Rest, J. R., E. Turiel, & L. Kohlberg. Level of moral development as a determinant of preference and comprehension of moral judgment made by others. *Journal of Personality,* 1969, *37,* 225–252.

Rheingold, H., & D. Hay. Prosocial behavior of the very young. In

G. Stent (ed.). *Morality as a biological phenomenon.* Berkeley, Calif.:
University of California Press, 1980.

Rieff, P. *Freud: The mind of the moralist.* New York: Viking, 1959.

Rothman, G. The influence of moral reasoning on behavioral choices.
Child Development, 1976, *47,* 397–406.

Rudner, R. S. *Philosophy of social science.* Englewood Cliffs, N.J.: Prentice-Hall, 1966.

Rushton, J. P. *Altruism, socialization and society.* Englewood Cliffs, N.J.:
Prentice-Hall, 1980.

Saltzstein, H., R. M. Diamond, & M. F. Belenky. Moral judgment level
and conformity behavior. *Developmental Psychology,* 1972, *7,* 327–
336.

Sampson, E. E., & M. Kardush. Age, sex, class, and race differences
in response to a two-person non-zero sum game. *Journal of Conflict
Resolution,* 1965, *9,* 212–220.

San Francisco Chronicle, April 19, 1976.

Schwartz, S., H. Brown, K. Feldman, & A. Heingartner. Some personality correlates of conduct in two situations of moral conflict.
Journal of Personality, 1969, *37,* 41–57.

Segundo, J. L. *The liberation of theology.* Maryknoll, N.Y.: Orbis Books,
1976.

Seligman, M. E. P. *Helplessness.* San Francisco: Freeman, 1975.

Selman, R., & W. Damon. The necessity (but insufficiency) of social
perspective taking for conceptions of justice at three early levels.
In D. J. DePalma & J. M. Foley (eds.). *Moral development: Current
theory and research.* New York: Wiley, 1975, pp. 83–118.

Sesonske, A. *Value and obligation: The foundation of an empiricist ethical
theory.* Berkeley, Calif.: University of California Press, 1957.

Shields, D. *Resolving hierarchical dualism: Toward an interactional model
of religious education.* Unpublished doctoral dissertation. Graduate
Theological Union, Berkeley, 1983.

Shweder, R. Liberalism as destiny. A review of L. Kohlberg: *Essays on
moral development,* Vol. 1. *Philosophy of moral development. Contemporary Psychology,* 1982, *27,* 421–424.

Siegert, M. T. Adult elicited child behavior: The paradox of measuring social competence through interviewing. Max Planck Institute
for Human Development and Education. (Paper presented at the
10th World Congress of Sociology, Mexico City, 1982.)

Simpson, L. Moral development research. *Human Development,* 1974, *17*, 81–106.

Skinner, B. F. *Walden II.* New York: Macmillan, 1948.

Skinner, B. F. *Beyond freedom and dignity.* New York: Knopf, 1971.

Spalding, H. D. *Encyclopedia of Jewish humor.* New York: Jonathan David, 1976.

Staub, E. To rear a prosocial child: Reasoning, learning by doing, and learning by teaching others. In D. De Palma & J. Foley (eds.). *Moral development.* Hillsdale, N.J.: Erlbaum Associates, 1975, pp. 113–136.

Stent, G. *Morality as a biological phenomenon.* Berkeley, Calif.: University of California Press, 1980.

Stevenson, C. L. *Ethics and language.* New Haven: Yale University Press, 1960.

Szasz, T. *The myth of mental illness.* New York: Harper & Row, 1961.

Teague-Ashton, P. Cross-cultural Piagetian research: An experimental perspective. *Harvard Educational Review,* 1978, Reprint #13, 1–32.

Time. The idyll of Gary and Amber Jim. January 31, 1977, 48–49.

Trabasso, T. & D. W. Nicholas. Memory and inferences in the comprehension of narratives. In F. Wilkening, J. Becker, & T. Trabasso (eds.). *Information integration by children.* Hillsdale, N.J.: Erlbaum Associates, 1980.

Trainer, F. E. A critical analysis of Kohlberg's contributions to the study of moral thought. *Journal for the Theory of Social Behavior,* 1977, *7*, 41–63.

Turiel, E. An experimental test of the sequentiality of developmental stages in the child's moral judgments. *Journal of Personality and Social Psychology,* 1966, *3*, 611–618.

Turiel, E. Conflict and transition in adolescent moral development. *Child Development,* 1974, *45*, 14–29.

Turiel, E. Conflict and transition in adolescent development. II. The resolution of disequilibrium through structural reorganization. *Child Development,* 1977, *48*, 634–637.

Turiel, E. *Development of social knowledge.* New York: Cambridge University Press, 1983.

Turiel, E., & G. R. Rothman. The influence of reasoning on behaviorial choices at different stages of moral development. *Child Development,* 1972, *43*, 741–756.

Vickers, R. R., Jr., H. W. Ward, & M. I. Hanley. *A comparison of three psychological defense questionnaires as predictors of clinical ratings of defenses*. San Diego: Naval Health Research Center, 1980.

Walker, L. Sources of cognitive conflict for stage transition in moral development. *Developmental Psychology*, 1983, *19*, 103–110.

Walker, L. Sex differences in the development of moral reasoning: A critical review. *Child Development*, 1984, *55*, 677–691.

Waterman, A. S. On the possible contributions of psychology to knowing what is moral. *American Psychologist*, 1983, *38*, 1254–1255.

Weiss, R. J. Understanding moral thought: Effects on moral reasoning and decision making. *Developmental Psychology*, 1982, *18*, 852–861.

Wilson, E. O. *Sociobiology*. Cambridge, Mass.: Harvard University Press, 1975.

Woodward, K. L., & M. Lord. Moral education. *Newsweek*, March 1, 1976, 74–75.

Zajonc. R. B. On the primacy of affect. *American Psychologist*, 1984, *39*, 117–123.

Index